Strategies for Teaching in a Diverse Society
Instructional Models

Strategies for Teaching in a Diverse Society
Instructional Models

Thomas J. Lasley II
University of Dayton

Thomas J. Matczynski
University of Dayton

Wadsworth Publishing Company

I(T)P® An International Thomson Publishing Company

Belmont, CA • Albany, NY • Bonn • Boston • Cincinnati • Detroit • Johannesburg • London • Madrid •
Melbourne • Mexico City • New York • Paris • Singapore • Tokyo • Toronto • Washington

Education Editor: Sabra Horne
Assistant Editor: Claire Masson
Editorial Assistant: Kate Barrett
Marketing Manager: Jay Hu
Senior Project Editor: Debby Kramer
Production: Vicki Moran/Publishing Support Services
Print Buyer: Karen Hunt
Permissions Editor: Jeanne Bosschart
Designer: Cloyce J. Wall
Copy Editor: Adrienne Armstrong
Cover: Jeanne Calabrese
Cover Photo: © Deborah Gilbert/Image Bank
Compositor: Publishing Support Services
Printer: Quebecor Printing/Fairfield

Printed in the United States of America
1 2 3 4 5 6 7 8 9 10

For more information, contact Wadsworth Publishing Company, 10 Davis Drive, Belmont, CA 94002, or electronically
at http://www.thomson.com/wadsworth.html

International Thomson Publishing Europe
Berkshire House 168-173
High Holborn
London, WC1V 7AA, England

International Thomson Editores
Campos Eliseos 385, Piso 7
Col. Polanco
11560 México D.F., México

Thomas Nelson Australia
102 Dodds Street
South Melbourne 3205
Victoria, Australia

International Thomson Publishing Asia
221 Henderson Road
#05-10 Henderson Building
Singapore 0315

Nelson Canada
1120 Birchmount Road
Scarborough, Ontario
Canada M1K 5G4

International Thomson Publishing Japan
Hirakawacho Kyowa Building, 3F
2-2-1 Hirakawacho
Chiyoda-ku, Tokyo 102, Japan

International Thomson Publishing GmbH
Königswinterer Strasse 418
53227 Bonn, Germany

International Thomson Publishing Southern Africa
Building 18, Constantia Park
240 Old Pretoria Road
Halfway House 1685, South Africa

Library of Congress Cataloging-in-Publication Data
Lasley, Thomas J.
    Strategies for teaching in a diverse society : instructional
models / Thomas J. Lasley II, Thomas J. Matczynski.
         p.   cm.
    Includes bibliographical references and index.
    ISBN 0-534-51645-9
    1. Teaching—United States. 2. Multicultural education—United
States. 3. Instructional systems—United States—Design.
4. Minorities—Education—United States. 5. Educational change—
United States. I. Matczynski, Thomas J. II. Title.
LB1025.3.L37 1997
371.1'02—dc20   96-41180

This book is printed on
acid-free recycled paper.

There is no need to add to the criticism
of our public schools. The critique is extensive
and can hardly be improved on.
The processes of learning and teaching,
too, have been exhaustively studied.
One thinks of the books of...Jonathan Kozol,
Herbert Kohl.... The question now is what to do.

GEORGE DENNISON

Brief Contents

Contents

ⓈECTION B: EFFECTING INSTRUCTIONAL MODEL USAGE

UNIT 1: MODELS THAT FOSTER REASONING SKILLS

UNIT 4: MODELS THAT FOSTER RELATING SKILLS

Chapter 10
Cooperative Learning   *270*

SECTION C: REFLECTING ON INSTRUCTIONAL MODEL USAGE

Preface

Teachers often bemoan their teacher-preparation experiences with horror stories concerning the lack of involvement with the "real world of teaching," instructors who were not aware of the technological advances available to teachers and students, programs and instruction that did not expose preservice teachers to the numerous culturally diverse groups in our society, programs where courses and experiences were fragmented and splintered, and a curriculum that rarely focused on the repertoire of instructional models and the corresponding academic and social skills needed by tomorrow's citizens. In most instances, we have no significant disagreement with these criticisms—though positive changes are occurring at selected teacher-preparation institutions (Tyson, 1994). Although many teacher education programs have begun to address selected structural and curricular problems, the profession must do something about the current teacher workforce in terms of valid criticisms about teacher instructional intransigence. Far too many teachers teach just as they were taught. This text is a partial response to this circumstance. It provides a means to identify, describe, apply, and explore various instructional models and their subset of pedagogical skills.

Strategies for Teaching in a Diverse Society: Instructional Models is designed for either undergraduate or graduate students of any subject area who are interested in exploring more fully the instructional options that students in America's classrooms need in order to achieve learning goals. The culturally diverse context of this text is limited to an examination of how the cognitive processing skills of learners, based upon gender and racial characteristics, can be enhanced or diminished by the instructional models used by teachers.

When I heard a schoolteacher warn the other night about the invasion of the American educational system by foreign curriculums, I wanted to yell at the television set, "Lady, they're already here." It has already begun because the world is here. The world has been arriving at these shores for at least ten thousand years from Europe, Africa, and Asia.

Ishmail Reed

The intended audience is preservice and inservice teachers who are in the process of expanding their repertoire of instructional models and teaching skills, and who have not been exposed, in a practical way, to the expanding body of research findings concerning the teaching–learning process. Teachers play a central role in defining the teaching–learning process; they are the central players in reforming education; and, they must acquire a repertoire of teaching abilities and skills and the knowledge of how to work with culturally diverse populations of students in order to be successful in working with the students now populating American schools.

Strategies for Teaching takes a broad approach to the multiple teaching models, skills, and techniques that are so necessary in working with culturally diverse student populations. American communities are becoming more pluralistic each year. This nation includes large numbers of people from many different cultures, ethnic and racial backgrounds, and lifestyles. We are increasingly becoming aware of these differences through our experiences in schools, in the workplace, and in our everyday lives. In Chapter 2, we describe the influence that culture exerts in determining an individual's learning style and the positions and values each individual holds concerning the various issues confronting our society. Throughout this text, we will offer ideas, activities, and directions that can be utilized in teaching culturally diverse populations of students—issues surrounding our becoming a more diverse nation that celebrates and values the diversity of America's people.

Further, *Strategies for Teaching* provides teachers with practical applications of the models presented from both fictional and "real-world" classroom settings. Whether the reader is an undergraduate student, a graduate student, or a staff-development participant, the lessons and activities found within this text will provide assistance in using the various instructional models. Furthermore, teachers will find valuable implementation suggestions, applicational examples, and evaluation criteria for each instructional model presented in this text. One disclaimer must be mentioned, however, before we proceed: given the numerous variables that go into instructional decision-making, we can honestly say that no one instructional model can or does address all student cognitive skills or styles within a given lesson. Curricular demands, student motivation, and student cognitive styles are among some of the considerations teachers must take into account when designing lessons. These considerations are identified and discussed within each chapter.

We have divided the text into three sections. Section A, "Contextualizing Instructional Model Usage," presents the conceptual framework for the text. In Chapter 1, "The Educational Context for Diversity," we document why the study of instructional models is necessary in the context of the changing demographic categories of race and gender in the United States and the effects of these demographic changes upon classroom instruction. We also describe how to foster student growth that is more responsive to the demands for greater teacher accountability. A critical component of this text is promoting and managing diversity in the classroom in order to develop individual student knowledge and skill. In Chapter 2, "Culturally Diverse Learners," we provide information concerning cognitive styles of learning; we present the major research findings concerning the relationship of gender, race, and cognitive styles; and we describe the implications of the research on cognitive styles for teacher use of alternative instructional models. Section B, "Effecting Instructional Model Usage," provides a thorough description of the planning process for instruction. In Chapter 3, "Instructional Models and the Planning Process," a brief description of the various instructional models and families presented in subsequent chapters is presented. Additionally, this chapter focuses upon the need for teachers to plan instructional lessons; the role of goals and objectives in planning; and how to develop performance objectives in the cognitive, affective, and psychomotor domains. Finally, ideas on how to evaluate student achievement of the performance objectives are presented.

In Chapters 4–11, we describe the characteristics of different models for presenting skills, content, and ideas to students. The chapters are divided into 10 components:

1. *Introduction* Each chapter begins with a brief anticipatory set relative to the model. The introductory ideas suggest how the model creates a richer environment for student learning.

2. *Case Study* Each chapter begins with a classroom episode demonstrating the usage of the model. This consists of a set of classroom interactions with the teacher implementing the instructional model.

3. *Theoretical Perspective* Each instructional model is described in detail along with supporting research data. This description provides the philosophical and psychological underpinnings behind each model, and the learning skills that are being developed and learned by students.

4. *Teaching Phases* Each chapter provides a detailed description of how to plan lessons and units utilizing the model. Examples of lessons including goals, objectives, and sample activities are provided. Once planning is complete, the reader encounters selected instructional alternatives. Useful and practical ideas on how to implement each model discussed are provided. Elementary and secondary school examples are presented so that the reader is aware of how each instructional model is implemented for each level of schooling.

5. *Applications to Diverse Classrooms* Each chapter provides a description of how the instructional model relates to the learning needs of diverse populations of students. The learning skills taught by using the instructional model are identified through the use of cognitive style strengths based upon gender and cultural group. Examples of the use of alternative cognitive styles are made available to the reader, especially regarding the use of relational and analytical cognitive skills.

6. *Prevalent Issues in Diverse Classrooms* Each chapter includes a discussion of those common issues that classroom teachers have experienced in implementing each instructional model. Particular attention is given to how the instructional model enhances the inclusiveness of the classroom teacher in embracing the ideas of all students.

7. *Evaluation Criteria* Each chapter includes evaluation processes and examples for the reader to use in assessing instructional model usage. A brief description of evaluation procedures is based upon the model underpinnings and skills to be developed by teachers.

8. *Sample Lessons* Each chapter (with the exception of chapter 11) includes a case study and a sample lesson plan in helping the reader understand how to implement the instructional model. Suggestions for using a coach, who would provide feedback, are also presented.

9. *Lesson Preparation* Each chapter offers suggestions on how to prepare lessons and includes a list of instructional resources—bibliography, videotapes, kits, etc.—which may be obtained by the reader for additional help in developing a repertoire of instructional skills.

10. *Summary* Each chapter concludes with a summary of the major components of the model and a brief discussion of the model's strengths and usage with diverse populations.

Section C, "Reflecting on Instructional Model Usage," consists of Chapter 12, "Developing Teachers for the Culturally Diverse." In this chapter emphasis is upon teachers as leaders of the instructional process, Fuller (1969) and Fuller and Bown's (1975) research on teacher career stages, the application of these stages to teacher decision making in terms of the purpose of schooling, inclusive and noninclusive teacher behaviors that determine student opportunity to learn, coaching as a vehicle for self-improvement, and the kind of society for which children are being prepared to live. The chapter concludes with an emphasis upon the importance of encouraging and supporting continuous improvement and the growth of school staffs through the use of an action planning format.

ⓇEFERENCES

Fuller, F. 1969. "Concerns of Teachers: A Developmental Perspective." *American Educational Research Journal* 6: 207–226.

————, **and O. H. Bown. 1975.** "Becoming a Teacher." Pp. 25–52 in K. Ryan (ed.), *Teacher Education.* 74th Yearbook of the National Society for the Study of Education. Chicago: University of Chicago Press.

Reed, I. 1988. "America: The Multinational Society." *Multi-Cultural Literacy.* St. Paul, MN: Graywolf Press.

Tyson, H. 1994. *Who Will Teach the Children?: Progress and Resistance in Teacher Education.* San Francisco: Jossey-Bass.

Acknowledgments

There are many individuals who have played a large part in the development and completion of this text. I would like to thank Bruce Joyce and Marsha Weil, who in the 1970s piqued my initial interest in the study and teaching of instructional models. Library research, proofreading, and checking reference accuracy are tedious and thankless jobs—thanks so much to Fr. Joe Massucci, Beverly Tillman, Carolyn Talbert-Johnson, Bickley Lucas, Jane Rafal, Dale Frederick, and Kristin Ross for their work, patience, and ideas.

Books do not appear unless an editor and publisher believe in them. I am very fortunate to have received the support and encouragement of Sabra Horne, our editor at Wadsworth. She has motivated us with her positive reactions to what we created, and has provided us with many useful suggestions to strengthen this endeavor.

Mentors, colleagues, and friends are rare! Joe Rogus has been all of these for approximately 30 years. Thanks for reacquainting me, after 15 years as an administrator, with the instructional models used in working with teachers. Ellis Joseph, our former dean, has provided me with the opportunities and resources to continue growing and learning personally and professionally. What a great leader he is—he enables and empowers individuals to achieve, to create, and to be critics of society.

In addition to editing, proofreading, indexing, and critiquing my work, my office colleague, Suzette Pico, impressively coordinated word processing, library research, and managing the work between two writers and innumerable draft versions that made this book possible. She rightfully earns accolades from all of our clients for her positive personality, caring and competent manner, and sharp administrative mind. Besides this book, she has managed and organized my teaching schedule, consulting practice, and work with the Dayton Public Schools. Thank you so much, Suzette—you are without peer!

I would like to thank my partner, Tom Lasley, from whom I have learned discipline, excellence, and integrity through our consulting practice and in the development of this text. Working with Tom has provided me a great opportunity to learn. Tom is a great teacher—he is also a great learner. His dedication to learning has been a personal source of motivation for me.

Finally, I wish to thank all those inner-city 8th grade youngsters I taught during the first 3 to 4 years of my career. These classes of predominantly African American students taught and gave me so much more than I provided them. Though I have not personally followed each of your lives, I know that many of you have achieved success and happiness, while others have passed from this life and are in His care. You taught me about caring, sensitivity, family relationships, and how to have fun and enjoy life. God bless each of you in life's journey!

T. J. M.

I, too, want to acknowledge the work of Bruce Joyce and Marsha Weil. Their book *Models of Teaching* fostered my initial interest in the topic of teaching models. My own students' struggles with the Joyce and Weil text was also the impetus for my desire to write this one. My hope is that this book will speak to some who are not able to connect with the ideas presented in the *Models of Teaching* text.

My greatest debt of gratitude goes to the hundreds of students who have used the models, taped their lessons, and allowed me to have a glimpse of their classroom life. I learned a lot by watching others teach—most of the classroom episodes described in Chapters 4–11 are based on, either directly or indirectly, lessons presented by my graduate students. To all, thank you.

A number of professional colleagues made this book possible. I especially want to thank Patricia Hart, Carolyn Talbert-Johnson, Beverly Tillman, Joe Rogus, Joe Massucci, Jane Rafal, Dale Frederick, Bickley Lucas, and Kristin Ross.

This is the first major writing project of this type I have undertaken with Tom Matczynski. Tom has been a friend for years, and this book has strengthened the ties of our friendship. Few people have his intellectual tenaciousness, and almost no one offers such unconditional support for friends.

Mea Maio, my office colleague, typed all of my portions of this text. No person I know evidences her patience and warmth in dealing with obsessive-compulsive behavior. She can also read my writing—although she has had to start wearing glasses. I hope the former was not the cause of the latter. For Mea's friendship, thoughtfulness, and caring support, I am most indebted!

Finally, I want to thank my family. Janet, my wife, is a teacher in an urban school. She caused me to see the need for the book, and she made me realize that many of the theoretical ideas had practical applications. My daughters, Elizabeth and Julianne, have spent a lot of time talking about their teachers—the good, the really good, and the "others." Their best teachers made them want to read when they came home and to seek knowledge even when outside the classroom. Janet, Elizabeth, and Julianne all influenced the way I thought about this book and helped shaped the ideas.

T. J. L.

Special Acknowledgment

The authors wish to express special thanks to the following teachers whose teaching episodes are the basis for many of the teaching episodes included in this book: Elaine Bennett, Judy Cox, Anne Futrell, Kerri Gayheart, Joyce Hayes, Stephanie Kortyna, Sarah Lloyd, David Morgan, Robin Root, Belinda Seagraves, Cheryl Skamfer, Debbie Tauber, Abby Taylor, Melissa Webb, Lori Yowler, and Mindy Cline.

The authors wish to express gratitude to the following colleagues for their thoughtful critiques of the text: Jo Alexander, Auburn University at Montgomery; Ann Anzalone, Educational Consultant, Dayton, Ohio; Jan E. Goings Covington, Gonzaga University; Katharine Cummings, North Dakota State University at Fargo; Judy Lehr Guarino, Furman University; John McIntyre, Southern Illinois University; Alice K. Mikovch, Western Kentucky University; Karen Cachevki Williams, University of Wyoming; and Donna Wiseman, Texas A & M University.

A Final Note

The teaching episodes in this text are in some instances fictional and in other instances variations on real classroom lessons. Pseudonyms are used for all the real classroom teachers involved; those teachers acknowledged above provided the essential ideas for the narratives presented to the readers in the numerous teaching cases.

- *Contextualizing Instructional Model Usage*

The Educational Context for Diversity

Today has not been a good day for Eduardo. His ear hurts and his stomach feels upset; but his mom is running late for work and he has to eat breakfast before she leaves. There is cold cereal to eat, but no milk to put on the cereal. Marguerite, his single mom, cannot take any more time off from work unless Eduardo is really sick; so he prepares to go to school alone. Before Marguerite leaves for work, she reminds Eduardo to return his library book, but by the time he leaves for school, 45 minutes later, he has forgotten it. Eduardo, who is a 2nd grader, arrives too late for the school breakfast program and can't get anything else to eat until lunchtime. It is very hard for Eduardo to concentrate, to listen to his teacher, or to become involved with group activities because his ear hurts so badly and his stomach aches for some food.

Eduardo's mom isn't having a good day herself! She can't concentrate on her work because she is constantly worrying about Eduardo. She wonders if he's gotten to school on time, if he's remembered his library book, and if he is concentrating on what the teacher is teaching. She is raising Eduardo alone. She is not receiving any support from his father and is having trouble making ends meet. She wants to be more involved in Eduardo's schooling, meet with his teacher, help with his homework, and get ideas on how best to help Eduardo, but she can't take time from work without losing the pay they both so badly need. Marguerite is working two minimum-wage jobs just to help pay for food, clothing,

And a pervasive spiritual impoverishment grows. The collapse of meaning in life—the eclipse of hope and absence of love of self and others, the breakdown of family and neighborhood bonds—leads to the social deracination and cultural denudement of urban dwellers, especially children. We have created rootless, dangling people with little link to the supportive networks—family, friends, and school—that sustain some sense of purpose in life. We have witnessed the collapse of the spiritual communities that in the past helped America face despair, disease, and death and that transmit through the generations dignity and decency, excellence and elegance.

CORNEL WEST

and their apartment. No matter what she tries to do to help, she never seems to get ahead. Bills keep piling up and no end is in sight! Marguerite knows Eduardo isn't doing his best in school, and wonders about how much of what they are going through as a family affects his school progress. She doesn't know what to do and doesn't know where to go for help! ∎

Eduardo is not alone in today's world. Many children and families are facing these very same complex issues. In recent monographs (Annie E. Casey Foundation, *Kids Count Data Book 1994: State Profiles of Child Well-Being*, 1994), 10 key factors were identified and described as affecting the future of America's children. One critical factor enumerated was: "Twenty percent of all U.S. children and 25% of those under age 6 live in poverty" ("U.S. Youth at Risk," 1994, p. 60). More families need at least two incomes in order to make ends meet, but more children are a part of single-parent families than ever before in the history of this nation. Presently, mothers of two-thirds of America's preschool children and three-fourths of all school-age children work outside of the home. Of the homes where there is only a single parent, 42 percent are at the poverty level compared with only 8 percent for two-parent families (Annie E. Casey Foundation, *Kids Count Data Book 1994: State Profiles of Child Well-Being*, 1994). It is quite clear that America's children are at risk. As we enter the twenty-first century, we need to focus on how schools can enhance life for students who come from a variety of families, racial and ethnic groups, economic situations, and multilingual environments. They are America's future!

❶HE CULTURALLY DIVERSE SCHOOL: A STATUS REPORT

Our nation's changing cultural demographics are playing a critical role in conversations concerning school success. The public school students of the future will be even more socially, economically, and educationally diverse than ever before; more students will come from backgrounds in which English is a second language, a circumstance that accounts for "15 percent of all children in urban schools" (Roberts, 1993, p. 63); and more will have a cultural and racial membership that is African, Hispanic (Latino), or Asian (Duckett, 1988; Kellogg, 1988; Rachal, 1989). In 1990, every state in the United States had a higher percentage of students of color than in 1980—every state increased in racial and ethnic diversity (Hodgkinson and Outtz, 1992). Unfortunately, these "diverse" students tend to be most affected by the directions and consequences of societal change because they have a limited voice in the content and direction of educational and social policy.

During this past decade, over eight million legal and illegal immigrants from all parts of the world—but primarily from Mexico, Central and South America, the Caribbean, and the Far East regions of the world—arrived on the shores of America (Ascher, 1993). According to the U.S. Census Bureau (1991), the United States increased by almost 10 percent from 1980 to a total of 248.7 million individuals in 1990. Roberts (1993) observes: "During the past decade, the

Asian population grew by 108 percent, the Hispanic by 53 percent, the black by 13 percent, and the white by only 6 percent" (p. 75). The racial groups in this country increased at vastly different rates, as depicted in Table 1.1. The sheer volume of new immigrants may demand that if inclusion is the goal of citizenship, then it will require much more tolerance by our present citizenry than has ever occurred in the past. Promoting and managing diverse populations may be the next great challenge facing American society and its schools.

With the arrival of a new immigrant population, a corresponding group of immigrant children—approximately two million—has entered our nation's classrooms. New immigrants to a country "typically arrive at the beginning of their prime childbearing years" (Riche, 1991, p. 28). Adding to this diversity is the reality that since 1980 women of color have been giving birth to more children proportionally than European American women. African Americans, who comprise 12 percent of the population, and Hispanic Americans, who are 9 percent of the total population, currently make up 15 and 12 percent, respectively, of American children under age 5 (Dunn, 1993).

According to all population projections, the face of America will become even more diverse in the decades ahead. The U.S. population will look quite different by 2010—the European American population will decrease from 75 percent in 1990 to 72 percent in 2000 and to 68 percent in 2010, whereas the Asian American population should continue to increase by 5 percent, the Hispanic American by 5 percent, and the African American by 1.3 percent (Exter, 1993).

The following information has been gathered from multiple sources and documents (Hodgkinson and Outtz, 1992; Roberts, 1993; U.S. Bureau of the Census, 1991; U.S. Department of Commerce, 1993) and reflects the dramatic changes in American demographics. This background information is suggestive of the type of society we are becoming and the kind of youngster the school will be serving, especially in the future. Indeed, some projections suggest that European Americans will become a "minority" group by the year 2050. Educators must make every effort to understand the diverse students who are coming to the schools, and they must be able to accept and value the gifts, talents, and background each child brings to the educational enterprise, and to

TABLE 1-1   Growth Rates of Racial and Ethnic Groups

	Growth 1980–1990 (%)	Number (M)	Percent of Total
European Americans	+6.0	187.2	75.2
African Americans	+13.2	29.2	12.1
Hispanic Americans	+53.6	22.3	9.0
Asian Americans	+107.8	7.2	2.9
Native Americans	+37.9	1.9	.8
United States	+9.8	248.7	100.0

Source: U.S. Bureau of the Census, 1991.

help each youngster become a contributing and successful citizen of America's new future. Those youngsters are America's future leaders.

The data listed below are categorized according to the cultural groups described in this text. Clearly each of these groups can be divided into multiple subgroups. Our point in making these observations is to illustrate the inherent and emerging diversity of American society.

Native Americans

- Native Americans grew by 38 percent since 1980 and now represent a total of almost 1 percent of the total U.S. population. This increase cannot be attributed to birthrate increases alone. For example, there is now a greater likelihood for individuals to report themselves as Native Americans than there was a decade ago.

- There were 2 million American Indians, Eskimos, and Aleuts living in the United States in 1990, with the great majority of the population living on 314 reservations. The poverty level for Native Americans living on reservations in 1989 was 51 percent.

- Almost one-half of Native Americans live in the West, 29 percent are in the South, 17 percent reside in the Midwest, and 6 percent live in the Northeast. The largest indigenous tribal nations are the Cherokee, Navajo, Chippewa, and Sioux. In 1990 more than one-half of the Native American population lived in just six states: Oklahoma, California, Arizona, New Mexico, Alaska, and Washington.

- In 1990, 39 percent of all Native Americans were under 20 years of age; compared with 29 percent of the total U.S. population. The median age of the Native American population was 26; that of the total U.S. population was 33.

- The proportion of Native American families maintained by a female head of household increased to 27 percent in 1990; this compares with 17 percent for the entire U.S. population. As a consequence, almost 31 percent of Native Americans (in 1990) lived below the poverty level compared with 13 percent of the total U.S. population.

- The educational achievement levels of Native Americans improved significantly during the 1980s but remained considerably below the national average: 66 percent of Native Americans over 25 years old were high school graduates. Only 9 percent of Native Americans completed a bachelor's degree, as compared with 20 percent of the total U.S. population.

African Americans

- African Americans now represent 12 percent of the U.S. population.
- African American populations are largely located in urban cities, with the following cities having the largest proportion: New York, Chicago, Detroit, Philadelphia, Los Angeles, Houston, Baltimore, Washington, D.C., Memphis, and New Orleans. African Americans represent 50 percent or

more of the population in Baltimore, Detroit, Memphis, New Orleans, and Washington, D.C.

- Over one-half of all African Americans lived in the South in 1990—a proportion that has not changed since 1979. The Midwest and Northeast each had 19 percent African Americans, and the smallest proportion (9 percent) lives in the West.

- African Americans are buying more homes in the suburbs—presently one-fourth of all African Americans live in the suburbs.

- The proportion of African Americans who are 25 years old and over and who completed high school rose from 51 percent in 1980 to 63 percent in 1990. Almost 12 percent of all African Americans have completed a bachelor's degree.

- There are more African American females than males in the civilian workforce.

- Nearly one-half of the African American families consisted of married (two-parent) couples as compared with more than four-fifths of the European American families. More than one-half of African American children under 18 years old lived in single-parent families in 1990—up from 46 percent in 1980.

Hispanic Americans

- The Hispanic American population grew more than all other cultural groups. It expanded to a total of 22.4 million individuals, or 9 percent of the total U.S. population.

- A tremendous increase in the Hispanic American population has occurred since 1970. Hispanic Americans have a higher birthrate than the rest of the U.S. population. The number of Hispanic Americans will surpass African, Asian, and Native Americans by 2020. They will represent 14 percent of the population in 2010, and 23 percent in 2050.

- Nearly 9 out of every 10 Hispanic Americans live in just 10 states, and the largest proportion reside in just four states: California, Texas, New York, and Florida, in that order. The remaining states with significant proportions of Hispanic Americans are: Illinois, New Jersey, Arizona, New Mexico, Colorado, and Massachusetts.

- In 1990, Mexicans were the largest Hispanic American group; they represented 61 percent of the Hispanic American population. Puerto Ricans were the second largest group with 12 percent; Cubans were 5 percent of the total Hispanic American population.

- In 1990, 7 out of 10 Hispanic Americans were younger than 35 years old; this compares with just 5 out of 10 non-Hispanic Americans. Forty percent of the Hispanic American population was under 20 years old, compared with 28 percent of non-Hispanic Americans.

- One-half of the Hispanic American population had at least a high school diploma. One in 10 individuals earned at least a bachelor's degree.

- Seventy percent of Hispanic American families were maintained by married (two-parent) couples. Thirty percent of all Hispanic American children are living with one parent—an increase of almost one-half since 1980.

Asian Americans

- Asian Americans now number over seven million individuals—a figure that represents a 100 percent increase in population since 1980. The total Asian American population is 3 percent of the entire U.S. population. The increases in population are the result of immigration from China, Korea, the Philippines, and other Asian and Pacific Island areas.
- In 1990, the largest proportion of Asian Americans were Chinese (24 percent), Filipino (20 percent), and Japanese (12 percent).
- Forty-four percent of the Asian American population live in the western states. Approximately 66 percent of the population live in five states: California, New York, Hawaii, Texas, and Illinois, in that order. And the majority of all Asian Americans live in just three states: California, New York, and Hawaii.
- Asian Americans had a median age of 30 years old in 1990, while the national median age was 33. Japanese Americans were the eldest at 36 years old; the Hmongs and Cambodians were the youngest at 13 and 19 years, respectively.
- Asian Americans had almost 4 persons per family as compared with 3.2 for the national average. Asian American families were larger partly because the percentage of youngsters under 18 who lived with parents was much higher (81 percent). Of the total U.S. population, 70 percent of all children live in two-parent families.
- Education is highly valued in Asian communities—yet the educational achievement of various ethnic groups varies widely. For example, the proportion of Japanese completing high school in 1990 was 88 percent; the figure for the Hmong was only 30 percent. Thirty-eight percent of Asian Americans graduated with a bachelor's degree (or higher), as compared with 20 percent of the total population.

Cultural group demographic changes, especially for Asian and Hispanic Americans, will continue to drastically modify the face of American schools from monoracial, monolingual environments, to multiracial, multilingual, multicultural institutions. In fact, more than six million children in America's schools speak a language other than English at home (Schnailberg, 1993), and over 150 languages are spoken throughout America's public schools (Sautter, 1994). By 2010, the 11 states (and Washington, D.C.) listed in Table 1.2 will comprise over one-half of the nation's 64.6 million non-European American youngsters.

In our nation's large urban areas, the changes have already arrived. Over one-half of all children of color are in public schools in the nation's cities. In only nine school districts (out of the 47 urban districts in the Council of Great City Schools) are European American students a majority of the student population (Casserly, 1992). Current estimates suggest that 42 percent of the

TABLE 1-2 Projected Percent of Non-European American Youth In Year 2010 by State

State	Percent Non-European American
Washington, D.C.	93.2
Hawaii	79.5
Texas	56.9
California	56.9
Florida	53.4
New York	52.8
Louisiana	50.3
Mississippi	49.9
New Jersey	45.7
Maryland	42.7
Illinois	41.7
South Carolina	40.1
United States	38.2

Source: *American Demographics*, May 1989.

Council's students are African American, 26 percent are Hispanic American, 25 percent are European American, 6 percent are Asian American, and 0.5 percent are Native American (Sautter, 1994). This trend is expected to continue well into the next century with projections indicating that before the year 2050, more than one-half of all K–12 students in this nation's schools will be children of color.

STATE OF EDUCATIONAL REFORM

While the schools' customers (that is, youngsters, parents, and employers) are changing dramatically, the school districts in this nation remain basically the same as they were well over 100 years ago. So, too, is our world changing—into a world increasingly based upon a global economy strongly undergirded by the need for citizens who are scientifically, mathematically, and technologically literate. Workers for tomorrow's world will be those who are able to think and solve complex problems, make decisions based upon consensus techniques, engage in a process of lifelong learning, tolerate ambiguity and uncertainty in a fast-paced global society, acknowledge cultural diversity and its value to the total community, and work cooperatively in teams to create and implement new ideas. Writers rightfully have noted that the issue of "global competitiveness" will involve the educational sector (Barker, 1992; Osborne and Gaebler, 1992). While school administrators worry about comparative test scores with neighboring school districts, policymakers and business leaders are focusing upon comparative performance studies with students in other parts of the world (Stevenson and Stigler, 1992). As a result, the need for a new workforce to educate America's youngsters in a more diverse and global society is critical.

Unfortunately, most American schools look just as they did at the turn of the century. For the most part, the following conditions still exist:

1. School calendars are organized around the assumption of agrarian lifestyles.

2. Schools operate based upon conditions that were more prevalent during the industrial age—mass production and employee conformity. American schools look and function like factories, which likely explains why the factory metaphor is so frequently used in describing schools.

3. Students follow a lockstep structure of 12 years of "schooling"; they "collect" a certain number of Carnegie units.

4. School schedules are structured as if mothers were home to greet their children in the mid-afternoon and as if nuclear families were the norm.

5. Student progress is measured through Carnegie unit accumulation—a practice designed at the beginning of the twentieth century. The number of units varies by state, but the practice is almost universal.

6. School curricula are sequenced or articulated from one grade level to another, but teachers determine what to teach and how to teach it.

7. Instruction occurs predominantly through the model of deductive pedagogy (lecturing)—a higher education anomaly. Rarely do teachers utilize instruction that draws upon what Howard Gardner (1985, 1991) calls students' multiple intelligences.

As a result of these conditions, students are still not realizing their full potential as learners. They have a constricted perception of both their own potential and their own abilities; they see education as something that happens *at school*; and they measure their performance by rather narrow criteria of success (knowing answers), rather than on a broader understanding of what it means to be a learner (knowing how to ask questions).

Adam Urbanski, Vice President of the American Federation of Teachers, stated it well when he reflected upon the nature of teaching and learning in American schools (Ribadeneira, 1990): "We know, based on research, that people remember about 10 percent of what they hear, 20 percent of what they see, 40 percent of what they discuss, and 90 percent of what they do. But we still largely use one teaching style: I talk, you listen, and you learn" (p. 1). Unfortunately, talking and teaching are considered synonymous.

The problem with schools is not that educators don't know what works. An abundance of research data exists concerning how the teaching–learning process works and what teachers can and should do that will stimulate motivation and learning in students. The problem is that many schools and teachers won't do what they should in terms of using the current research findings. As an example, many companies in the corporate world began writing software applications that could teach reading, writing, mathematics, and so on, yet only a small percentage of this nation's schools teach with a sensitivity to what is known relative to computer applications. In fact, few schools have the computer hardware available for students to use such software in the classroom. In the meantime, over the past 20 years, the corporate sector has not only drastically changed the way it does business (because of the computer), but it has radically changed its training methods based upon technology and alternative instructional models.

What have schools done to adopt the advances in the workforce and the corresponding technology? Very little! Despite an information-rich, biotechnology-oriented world, outmoded instructional approaches and conditions persist. Educators must begin addressing how the current educational paradigm influences students and how they function in an academic environment. This paradigm is based upon three antiquated beliefs:

Old Belief 1. Academic achievement is derived from innate ability;

Old Belief 2. Innate ability in youngsters is unevenly distributed among the population of students; and

Old Belief 3. The above two beliefs are unalterable.

Strategies for Teaching in a Diverse Society: Instructional Models directly challenges these beliefs. Educators must begin basing their instructional repertoire upon three fundamental new worldviews about schools and young people:

New Belief 1. All youngsters can learn at significantly higher levels if teacher instructional practice changes to accommodate the diverse learning styles of students.

New Belief 2. Teachers can learn how to teach more successfully if they are provided with the proper preparation experiences. (*Strategies for Teaching* concerns itself with operationalizing this assumption. This text describes how practicing teachers can acquire these instructional models and teach youngsters how to learn in alternative fashions.)

New Belief 3. Teachers must reflect considerably higher expectations for students. Substantial research has been conducted concerning the teaching–learning process and teacher expectations (see Brophy, 1983; Cooper and Good, 1983; Dusek, 1985; Marshall and Weinstein, 1984; Rosenthal and Jacobson, 1968). If students are to achieve their full academic potential, teachers must believe students can achieve more.

Educators must begin applying these research findings to instructional and curricular practices in a way that maximizes the learning of every student regardless of age, gender, racial and ethnic background, or physical ability. When students walk into classrooms, they need to be confronted with a teacher who sees the students' potential and helps students achieve their potential as learners. Rose (1995) describes one such teacher (Yvonne):

> Yvonne continued, "Teachers will say either 'We can't lower our standards' or 'This poor child is reading below grade level, so I'll need a third- or fourth-grade book.' But what you need to do is find a way to make that eighth-grade book *accessible*. You have to respect the child.... I used to give a speech to new teachers in which I began by enumerating all the adjectives used to describe our kids: *slow, poor, impoverished, deprived, oppressed*. We get so busy looking at children in terms of labels that we fail to look for the

potential—and to demand that kids live up to that potential. I tell these teachers, 'Do not think that because a child cannot read a text, he cannot read *you*.' Children can tell right off those people who believe in them and those who patronize them. They can tell once they come into the room— as if there's a smell in the air—they can tell right away if this teacher means business or if this teacher is, as they say, *jive*. They rise to whatever expectations are set. They rise or fail to rise. And when they rise, they can sometimes rise to great heights" (p. 17).

ⓡ ATIONALE FOR INSTRUCTIONAL REFORM

In 1983, the nation sounded the educational alarm with the now-famous report *A Nation at Risk* (National Commission on Excellence in Education, 1983). Since this report was released, over 300 national and state reports (for example, Carnegie Foundation for Advancement in Teaching, 1990; National Endowment for the Humanities, 1987; National Science Foundation, 1983; U.S. Department of Labor, 1991) have been written concerning the status of education in the United States. Most of the reports focus upon concepts such as lengthening the school day; increasing the standards for high school graduation, including an emphasis on the academic core and the "educational basics"; emphasizing mathematics, science, and technology; developing business and industrial partnerships; improving the pay and working conditions of teachers; emphasizing the use of technology, including computers in the education of youngsters; and implementing state legislative exit examinations for high school graduation. Many of these recommendations have been implemented at the state level through a regulatory process to mandate reforms. The authors of the reports, the state legislative bodies, and various local boards of education hold a set of assumptions concerning how schools should function given the current organizational structure. That structure is a bureaucratic model in which management decides what is to be accomplished, directs employees to accomplish what has been dictated, and monitors the work that is to be implemented. The problem with this bureaucratic description is that schools are loosely coupled organizations (Aldrich, 1979; Weick, 1976); or, as Deal and Celotti (1980) observe, the formal organization and administration of the school do not significantly affect the methods of instruction in the classroom. In similar fashion, research conducted by Meyer and Rowan (1983) identified that school bureaucratic structures and classroom instruction are disconnected. That is, schools are organizations with somewhat ambiguous goals (even when they do have clearly articulated mission statements!), fluid membership, unconnected activities, loosely connected structural components, and a structure that has little effect on the outcomes of schooling (Meyer and Scott, 1983). Thus, the notion that regulatory agencies and their mandates can "change" what schools do and how these ends are accomplished is fallacious. Only teachers can effect the kinds of change that will truly make a long-term difference in students' lives, and teachers can effect such changes only if they know how to work with parents and to build on the culture of the students.

Given the recommendations, mandates, and large sums of money that have been invested in reform, just what has been the progress to date? The impact of reform initiatives upon the youngsters in America's schools has been minimal. There have been lots of innovations, but a limited number of changes. Cuban (1988) noted that "innovation after innovation has been introduced into school after school, but the overwhelming number of them disappear without a fingerprint" (p. 86). In essence, there has been innovation but not great change. The school dropout rate in this country remains high (approximately 25 percent), and SAT and ACT scores are again declining after plateauing for a few years (U.S. Department of Education, 1994). America's best and brightest students continue to do poorly when compared with the best and brightest students from other countries (Stevenson, Chen, and Lee, 1993; U.S. Department of Education, 1991b). Not all the news is bad and not all the comparisons are negative, of course, but our point is that most of what has been suggested or mandated in terms of educational reform has had a minimal effect in terms of changing how educators function and students achieve. More and more school, business, and community leaders recognize that school reform has not worked, and they believe they know why: Reform efforts have been piecemeal, and the emphasis upon what occurs in the classroom with regard to teaching practices and behavior has not been highlighted. Furthermore, the basic problem with school structures is a failure to create at individual school sites a collaborative culture between the community, which includes parents and student peer cultures, and the school. The hierarchical school structures are efficient but ineffective in engendering educational programs that address the needs of diverse student communities. Noncollaborative structures cannot adjust to groups or individuals with needs different from the goals that the traditional organization defines. For this and other reasons that will be described later, there is an urgent need to reconceptualize how schools function collaboratively with a variety of significant others (for example, parents) and how teachers can work collegially to use and implement new instructional models. The focus of this text is on the latter, but the significance of the former cannot be dismissed. Stevenson, Chen, and Lee (1993) cogently note:

> We attribute the early superiority of American children to the greater cognitive stimulation provided by their parents, who indicated that they read more frequently to their young children, took them on more excursions, and accompanied them to more cultural events than did the Chinese or Japanese parents.... As American children grow older, parents appear to be less likely to provide the kinds of enriched out-of-school experiences that they did before the children entered first grade (p. 55).

Much of the Japanese success has been attributed to the collegial nature of the teachers' lives within schools (Stevenson and Stigler, 1992). Something similar can and must occur in American schools. In essence, American teachers need to work more collaboratively with both parents and their teacher colleagues—we will return to this topic in Chapter 12. More than 10 years have passed since *A Nation at Risk* (National Commission on Excellence in Education, 1983), thousands of meetings have been held, and the mass media has covered the reform subject with forums, special news editions, and television specials. Significant numbers of people are involved in the reform juggernaut, including the President of the United States, members of Congress, governors, state school officials, legislatures across the country, school boards, and executives from almost every large organization in the country. The need has been so pressing to the perceived survival of American society that the President and this nation's governors established a presidential commission to examine the problem and make recommendations. An outcome of their activities has been the establishment of an educational "Marshall Plan," with a concomitant set of national educational goals. The goals are both ambitious and comprehensive:

1. All children in America will start school ready to learn.

2. High school graduation rates will increase to at least 90 percent.

3. American students will leave grades four, eight, and twelve having demonstrated competency over challenging subject matter including English, mathematics, science, history, and geography. All students will learn to use their minds well, so that they may be prepared for responsible citizenship, future learning, and productive employment in our modern economy.

4. The nation's teaching force will have access to programs for the continued improvement of their professional skills and the opportunity to acquire the knowledge and skills needed in instructing students for the next century.

5. United States students will be first in the world in mathematics and science achievement.

6. Every adult American will be literate and will possess the knowledge and skills necessary to compete in a global economy and exercise the rights and responsibilities of citizenship.

7. Every school will be free of drugs and violence and offer a disciplined environment conducive to learning.

8. Every school will promote partnerships that will increase parental involvement and participation in promoting the social, emotional, and academic growth of children (U.S. Department of Education, 1994).

Governors and chief state school officers now have the challenge to develop strategies to reach these national goals. Some data suggest that progress is being made (see Table 1.3). Almost everyone believes these goals are critical to the survival of our nation; they also believe we need to reform schools. What they disagree about is how to achieve the goals. How can the overall progress toward goal achievement be made more positive? We emphasize the need to reinvent schools and the culture of the classroom because of the complex, changing demographics occurring in American society. American culture is dynamic and diverse. There is no prototypical American! And the diversity is most evident when considering facts about cultural groups and women, the welfare and prison systems, America's standard of living, school dropouts, and innovative technology.

TABLE 1-3   Progress in Meeting National Educational Goals

GOALS	Baseline	Most Recent Update	Overall Progress
GOAL 1 Ready to Learn			
1. **Children's Health Index:** Has the U.S. reduced the health risks? (1990, 1992)	37%	35%	↑
2. **Immunizations:** Has the U.S. increased the percentage of 2-year-olds who have been fully immunized against preventable childhood diseases? (1994)	75%	—	
3. **Family–Child Reading and Storytelling:** Has the U.S. increased the percentage of 3- to 5-year-olds whose parents read to them or tell them stories regularly? (1993, 1995)	66%	72%	↑
4. **Preschool Participation:** Has the U.S. reduced the gap in preschool participation between 3- to 5-year-olds from high- and low-income families? (1991, 1995)	28 pts	27 pts[ns]	↔
GOAL 2 School Completion			
5. **High School Completion:** Has the U.S. increased the percentage of 18- to 24-year-olds who have a high school credential? (1990, 1994)	86%	86%	↔
GOAL 3 Student Achievement and Citizenship			
6. **Reading Achievement:** Has the U.S. increased the percentage of students who meet the Goals Panel's performance standard in reading? (1992, 1994) ▲			
■ Grade 4	25%	25%	↔
■ Grade 8	28%	28%	↔
■ Grade 12	37%	34%	↓

(continued)

— Data not available.
[ns] Interpret with caution. Change was not statistically significant.
▲ Interpret with caution. Data are undergoing revision.

TABLE 1-3 Progress in Meeting National Educational Goals *(continued)*

GOALS	Baseline	Most Recent Update	Overall Progress
GOAL 3 Student Achievement and Citizenship *(continued)*			
7. Writing Achievement: *Has the U.S. increased the percentage of students who could produce basic, extended, developed, or elaborated responses to narrative writing tasks? (1992)*			
■ *Grade 4*	55%	—	
■ *Grade 8*	78%	—	
■ *Grade 12*	—	—	
8. Mathematics Achievement: *Has the U.S. increased the percentage of students who meet the Goals Panel's performance standard in mathematics? (1990, 1992)*			
■ *Grade 4*	13%	18%	↑
■ *Grade 8*	20%	25%	↑
■ *Grade 12*	13%	16%[ns]	↔
9. History Achievement: *Has the U.S. increased the percentage of students who meet the Goals Panel's performance standard in U.S. history? (1994)*			
■ *Grade 4*	17%	—	
■ *Grade 8*	14%	—	
■ *Grade 12*	11%	—	
10. Geography Achievement: *Has the U.S. increased the percentage of students who meet the Goals Panel's performance standard in geography? (1994)*			
■ *Grade 4*	22%	—	
■ *Grade 8*	28%	—	
■ *Grade 12*	27%	—	

(continued)

— Data not available.
[ns] Interpret with caution. Change was not statistically significant.
▲ Interpret with caution. Data are undergoing revision.

TABLE 1-3 Progress in Meeting National Educational Goals *(continued)*

GOALS	Baseline	Most Recent Update	Overall Progress
GOAL 4 Teacher Education and Professional Development			
11. Teacher Preparation: *Has the U.S. increased the percentage of secondary school teachers who held an undergraduate or graduate degree in their main teaching assignment? (1991, 1994)*	66%	63%	↓
12. Teacher Professional Development: *Has the U.S. increased the percentage of teachers reporting that they participated in various in-service or professional development programs on one or more topics since the end of the previous school year? (1994)*	85%	—	
GOAL 5 Mathematics and Science			
13. International Mathematics Achievement: *Has the U.S. improved its standing on international mathematics assessments of 13-year-olds? (1991)*	*U.S. below 5 out of 5 countries*	—	
14. International Science Achievement: *Has the U.S. improved its standing on international science assessments of 13-year-olds? (1991)*	*U.S. below 3 out of 5 countries*	—	
15. Mathematics and Science Degrees: *Has the U.S. increased mathematics and science degrees as a percentage of all degrees awarded to: (1991, 1993)*			
■ *all students?*	39%	40%	↑
■ *minorities (Blacks, Hispanics, American Indians/Alaskan Natives) ?*	39%	39%	↔
■ *females?*	35%	36%	↑

(continued)

— Data not available.
ns Interpret with caution. Change was not statistically significant.
▲ Interpret with caution. Data are undergoing revision.

TABLE 1-3   Progress in Meeting National Educational Goals *(continued)*

GOALS	Baseline	Most Recent Update	Overall Progress
GOAL 6 Adult Literacy and Lifelong Learning			
16. Adult Literacy: *Has the U.S. increased the percentage of adults who score at or above Level 3 in prose literacy? (1992)*	52%	—	
17. Participation in Adult Education: *Has the U.S. reduced the gap in adult education participation between adults who have a high school diploma or less, and those who have additional post-secondary education or technical training? (1991, 1995)*	27 pts	32 pts	↓
18. Participation in Higher Education: *Has the U.S. reduced the gap between White and Black high school graduates who:*			
■ *enroll in college? (1990, 1993)*	14 pts	13 pts[ns]	↔
■ *complete a college degree? (1992, 1994)*	16 pts	16 pts	↔
Has the U.S. reduced the gap between White and Hispanic high school graduates who:			
■ *enroll in college? (1990, 1993)*	11 pts	8 pts[ns]	↔
■ *complete a college degree? (1992, 1994)*	15 pts	18 pts[ns]	↔
GOAL 7 Safe, Disciplined, and Alcohol- and Drug-Free Schools			
19. Overall Student Drug and Alcohol Use: *Has the U.S. reduced the percentage of 10th graders reporting doing the following during the previous year:*			
■ *abusing any illicit drug? (1991, 1994)*	24%	33%	↓
■ *abusing alcohol? (1993, 1994)*	63%	64%[ns]	↔

(continued)

— Data not available.
[ns] Interpret with caution. Change was not statistically significant.
▲ Interpret with caution. Data are undergoing revision.

TABLE 1-3 Progress in Meeting National Educational Goals *(continued)*

GOALS	Baseline	Most Recent Update	Overall Progress
GOAL 7 Safe, Disciplined, and Alcohol- and Drug-Free Schools *(continued)*			
20. Sale of Drugs at School: Has the U.S. reduced the percentage of 10th graders reporting that someone offered to sell or give them an illegal drug at school during the previous year? *(1992, 1994)*	18%	24%	↓
21. Student and Teacher Victimization: Has the U.S. reduced the percentage of students and teachers reporting that they were threatened or injured at school during the previous year? *(1991, 1994)*			
■ *10th grade students*	40%	36%	↑
■ *public school teachers*	10%	15%	↓
22. Disruptions in Class by Students: Has the U.S. reduced the percentage of students and teachers reporting that disruptions often interfere with teaching and learning?			
■ *10th grade students (1992, 1994)*	17%	17%	
■ *secondary school teachers (1991, 1994)*	37%	46%	↔ ↓
GOAL 8 Parental Participation			
23. Teacher's Reports of Parent Involvement in School Activities: Has the U.S. increased the percentage of 8th grade public school students whose teachers reported that their parents attended parent-teacher conferences? *(1992)*	77%	—	
24. Principals' Reports of Parent Involvement in School Activities: Has the U.S. increased the percentage of 8th grade public school students whose principals reported that their parents participated in policy decisions? *(1992)*	62%	—	

(continued)

— Data not available.
ns Interpret with caution. Change was not statistically significant.
▲ Interpret with caution. Data are undergoing revision.

TABLE 1-3   Progress in Meeting National Educational Goals *(continued)*

GOALS	Baseline	Most Recent Update	Overall Progress
GOAL 8 Parental Participation *(continued)*			
25. Parents' Reports of Their Involvement in School Activities: Has the U.S. increased the percentage of students in Grades 3–12 whose parents reported that they participated in two or more activities in their child's school during the current school year? *(1993)*	63%	—	

Source: National Educational Goals Report Executive Summary, 1995.

— Data not available.

ns Interpret with caution. Change was not statistically significant.

▲ Interpret with caution. Data are undergoing revision.

Cultural Groups and Women

- School districts will experience a large increase of culturally diverse students. This population, especially Hispanic children, will not only be larger, but will be more diverse. At present, 23 of the 25 largest districts in this country have a majority of students of color (Baratz-Snowden, 1986; Hilliard, 1984; McNett, 1984).

- People of color, white women, and immigrants will account for 85 percent of the net growth in America's workforce in the 1990s (Johnston and Packer, 1987).

- People of color now make up the majority of the population in 16 of the top 25 urban markets throughout the United States (*D and B: Donnelly Demographics*, 1988).

- Over the next 20 years, the U.S. population is expected to grow by 42 million. Hispanic Americans will account for 47 percent of that growth; African Americans will account for 22 percent; Asian Americans and other people of color will make up 18 percent. European Americans will account for only 13 percent of the growth (Randle, 1990).

- Only 6 percent of the school-age population consists of the two-parent, multiple-child family (Select Committee on Children, Youth, and Families, 1988).

- The number of children born out of wedlock is increasing, and European American females are having a higher proportion of these children. In 1990, 55 percent of European American teenage mothers were single, and 19 percent of European American babies were born to single mothers (Roberts, 1993). Teenagers are having babies at an alarming rate, and part of that reality is that teenagers give birth more often to premature babies and low-birth-weight babies, thus there is a need for more special education programs because of poor diet, nutrition, and prenatal care (Hodgkinson, 1989).

Welfare and Prison Systems

- If America's children are not properly educated, there is a high probability that they will join the swelling ranks of the welfare and prison system populations. The current welfare and prison systems are growth industries. The cost to house a prisoner exceeds $20,000 a year, which is considerably more costly than a year of schooling nationally—$5,500. The data are positively correlated in favor of Head Start vs. non-Head Start participation relative to the percentage of individuals subsequently employed, enrolled in college, arrested, or on welfare (Hodgkinson, 1989).

Standard of Living

- Our country cannot maintain its standard of living if we as a nation have a second- or third-class education system. There are too many international studies that document U.S. inferiority in comparison studies of educational achievement (Bowsher, 1993).
- Without a qualified, high-achieving workforce that values diversity—in age, ethnic heritage, gender, physical ability, race, and sexual/affectional orientation—America's standard of living will decrease, jobs will transfer overseas, and more individuals will be dependent upon a bankrupt economy.

Dropouts

- One of every 10 individuals aged 16 to 19 was neither enrolled in school nor graduated from high school. This proportion was highest among Hispanics—22 percent—compared with 14 percent among African Americans, 10 percent of European Americans, and 5 percent of Asian Americans. Among adult Hispanics, only 49.8 percent have a high school diploma (Roberts, 1993).

- America is evolving toward two classes of citizens—one that is literate and relatively productive, and one that is illiterate, dependent upon social services, and a physical and moral threat to the other (Bowsher, 1993).

Technology

- America is an information-rich society. Almost 100 percent of U.S. households have radio and television, and about 95 percent have telephone service. Three-quarters of America's households contain a VCR, about 65 percent have cable television, and roughly 30 percent have personal computers (Gore, 1994).

- The current generation of students in our schools has acquired more information through the electronic media than through formal academic settings (Bowsher, 1993).

- When it comes to telecommunications services, schools are the most impoverished institutions in this society. Schools do not have the hardware and software to provide the educational opportunities to students so critical to living in this global economy (Gore, 1994).

Clearly some of the problems evidenced in schools relate to factors beyond teacher control. Indeed, Steinberg (1996) found that one of the primary reasons for the failure of school reform efforts was the diminution of adult involvement to reinforce the values and ideas taught at school. Because American parents become less involved as children get older, the burden on schools to counter the student culture of indifference becomes even more onerous. In Steinberg's words:

> National studies of American families show that parental involvement drops off precipitously between elementary and secondary school—precisely at the time when youngsters' susceptibility to peer influence is rapidly rising. Moreover, …evidence indicates that this sort of parental disengagement is not limited to school matters, but affects a whole range of issues, including monitoring and regulating the child's relationships with friends, the child's use of leisure time, and the child's choice of activities. To the extent that diminished involvement in their children's lives renders parents' influence less powerful, the door is opened for peers to step in and exert a significant impact on each other's behavior—including their behavior in school. And this is precisely what happens between the sixth and tenth grades. At this point, in fact, children's achievement is more easily influenced by their peers than at any other time in their school career (p. 142).

But many of the problems confronting schools are classroom based. Even if parents were supportive, schools would struggle to effectively transmit the requisite knowledge needed for students to succeed. As researchers (Boyer, 1983; Goodlad, 1990b; Goodlad, Soder, and Sirotnik, 1990b; Sizer, 1984, 1992) gather classroom data, it has become increasingly apparent that teachers have a very limited instructional repertoire and have limited knowledge about the kind of new world that is emerging, the kind of knowledge and skill demands needed in an international economy, and the way in which human resources—diverse groups of individuals not normally a part of the traditional organizational culture—can help fashion a new and better environment for all of us.

The current classroom paradigm of teacher-centered instruction has reached its limits of pedagogical usefulness, if it ever had such utility. Branson (1988) argues that the 100-year-old paradigm cannot be improved with programs such as "adopting-a-school," lengthening the school day, increasing teacher pay, offering leadership-development courses, or providing strategic-planning workshops. He asserts that we achieved 95 percent of the total possible educational performance using the current paradigm. Different instructional strategies are required if teachers are to educate effectively those diverse student populations who are enrolling in our nation's schools.

To make substantial and significant change in schools, educators must dramatically change the way students are taught. Americans cannot tolerate, nor can this nation afford, a society in which some children become fully educated and others do not. We must avoid creating a society of informational "haves" and "have nots." In a world of advanced technology, there will be new ways of communicating that will inform as well as entertain. Such communication vehicles will educate and increase productivity levels; they will also pose real problems if young people are unable to assimilate in a critical fashion all the new knowledge they have available.

Giroux (1992) described what he sees as the demise of democracy in the United States. He bases his claim upon three trends: the downward movement in voting patterns of the public, the polarization of the haves and have nots, and the vested interest groups (lobbyists) who tend to steer the government in ways that foster individual rather than group good. (The Montana Freemen may be the tip of this ideological iceberg.) Such assertions are very interesting in light of the increasing democratization of countries and regions around the world. These regions look to America as a beacon of democracy to emulate, and yet Giroux is pessimistic about our own country's future. The pessimism he describes stems from the notion that the basic purpose of schools is to prepare students as citizens in a democracy. Democracy demands full participation, and the latter is only possible if all students are fully educated to their potential, which means that they can think critically about the content they learn in schools. Democracies require educated citizens in order to maintain themselves, and educated citizens are those individuals who can explore, critique, and create ideas.

Strategies for Teaching focuses upon the culture of the classroom and the behaviors that teachers exhibit in working with youngsters. If teachers acquire and use a wider repertoire of instructional models, many of the problems confronting schools (as previously described) will be mitigated because students will be more active participants in the cultural realities of schools. This text will focus on the acquisition of the information and the application of appropriate teaching skills and styles:

- How diverse groups of students learn to use their different learning dispositions and intelligences (parts to wholes, wholes to parts, visual, auditory, kinesthetic/tactile) to make sense out of a complex social world.

- How using different instructional models draws upon the learning dispositions of diverse students and utilizes the natural power and skills that such students possess. This, in turn, helps motivate them to learn.

- How most of what students encounter in society involves an active engagement with ideas or people. It is only proper to utilize these same active processes in formal teaching/learning encounters. Such activity results in both the increased acquisition of knowledge, the enhanced retention of information, and the improved application and use of academic and social skills.

- How utilizing alternative instructional models will allow students to acquire and apply various thinking skills and problem-solving processes. Such skills are critical to an informed citizenry in a democratic society.

- How students who are challenged to learn in ways that are foreign to their natural dispositions will have an increased capacity to learn more easily as they encounter complex phenomena. As Hunter (1985) stated, "The more skilled the teacher is in using [an instructional] model, the more independent and successful learners can become and the greater the variety of teaching and learning styles that can be used" (p. 59). Students will acquire an increased capacity to learn by acquiring the various critical-thinking skills embedded within the different instructional models.

- How students will change in terms of their enthusiasm for learning, acquisition of information, and application of academic and social skills as their repertoire of learning strategies is enhanced. They will be able to accomplish more types of learning in various types of settings through the engagement of different phenomena.

❶EXT PURPOSES

Strategies for Teaching is based upon the belief that teachers want to be a part of the solution, not a part of the problem. Most teachers simply lack the opportunities, awareness, and/or skills to be critical players in the myriad solutions of educational reform. Teachers can actively engage in using the ideas and activities of this text; through this engagement they will gain the knowledge, skills, and attitudes required to join in the *re*invention of schools and the *re*-creation of classroom learning cultures. To this end, the following goals are identified for development throughout the remainder of this text:

1. To describe why the use of instructional models in the classroom is important in working with all students in America's schools.
2. To plan and organize instruction utilizing an appropriate instructional model.
3. To design lessons applying various instructional models.
4. To become skilled practitioners in utilizing alternative instructional models in Grades K–12.
5. To match a specific instructional model with specific learning skills and styles of students.
6. To provide experiences in utilizing alternative skills of learning.
7. To provide experiences in developing problem-solving and critical-thinking skills.

8. To provide examples of sample lessons that demonstrate the use and implementation of each instructional model.

9. To provide opportunities to practice and develop the skills necessary in living in a diverse, global society.

10. To identify examples of teacher career stages, the needs associated with each stage, and how staff development opportunities should be designed for professionals in order to maximize their instructional repertoire.

ⒸONCLUSION

Strategies for Teaching in a Diverse Society: Instructional Models provides numerous practical examples from various subject areas in order to demonstrate all of the instructional models. The context of this text is pedagogical and cultural—our diversity as a nation must be recognized, appreciated, and utilized if we as a nation are going to continue to sustain a world leadership position in the next millennium. This text has been written because educators can no longer ignore a vital untapped resource—student and cultural diversity. Ideas concerning how the classroom culture might be changed to be more flexible, hospitable, and supportive of diverse groups in our society will be described. One means to promote such a cultural change is to look critically, yet supportively, at what we do as educators, and to begin developing professional growth activities that can lead to new teaching approaches. This text provides a venue to help facilitate the instructional change that is so needed in our nation's schools.

ⓇEFERENCES

Aldrich, H. E. 1979. *Organizations and Environment.* Englewood Cliffs, NJ: Prentice-Hall.

"All Our Children." 1989. *American Demographics* (May).

Ascher, C. 1993. *The Changing Face of Racial Isolation and Desegregation in Urban Schools.* Report No. 91. ERIC/CUE Document Reproduction Service No. ED 358 199.

Baratz-Snowden, J. 1986. "Black Participation in the Teacher Pool." Prepared for the task force on Teaching as a Profession, Carnegie Forum on Education and the Economy.

Barker, J. A. 1992. *Future Edge: Discovering the New Paradigms of Success.* New York: William Morrow.

Bowsher, J. E. 1993. "Why and How to Restructure Education Systems." Paper presented at the meeting of the Association for Supervision and Curriculum Development, Washington, DC (March).

Boyer, E. L. 1983. *High School: A Report on Secondary Education in America.* New York: Harper & Row.

Branson, R. K. 1988. "Why Schools Can't Improve: The Upper Limit Hypothesis." *Journal of Instructional Development* 10(4): 15–26.

Brophy, J. 1983. "Research on the Self-Fulfilling Prophecy and Teacher Expectation." *Journal of Educational Psychology* 75: 631–661.

Carnegie Foundation for Advancement in Teaching. 1990. *The Condition of Teaching: A State-by-State Analysis.* Lawrenceville, NJ: Princeton University Press: 12, 34, 37–44.

Casserly, M. 1992. *National Urban Education Goals: Baseline Indicators 1990–91.* Washington, DC: Council of Great City

Schools. ERIC Document Reproduction Service No. ED 351 422.

Children and Families: Key Trends in the 1980s. 1988. Washington, DC: Select Committee on Children, Youth, and Families.

Cooper, H., and T. Good. 1983. *Pygmalion Grows Up: Studies in Expectation Communication Process.* New York: Longman.

Cuban, L. 1988. "Constancy and Change in Schools." Pp. 85–103 in P. W. Jackson (ed.), *Contributing to Educational Change: Perspectives on Research and Practice.* Berkeley: McCutchan.

D and B: Donnelly Demographics. 1988. Stamford, CT: Donnelly Marketing Information Services.

Deal, T. E., and L. D. Celotti. 1980. "How Much Influence Do (and Can) Educational Administrators Have on Classrooms?" *Phi Delta Kappan* 61: 471–473.

Duckett, W. 1988. "Using Demographic Data for Long-Range Planning." *Phi Delta Kappan* 70(2) (October): 166–170.

Dunn, W. 1993. "Educating Diversity." *American Demographics* (April): 40.

Dusek, J. (ed.). 1985. *Teacher Expectations.* Hillsdale, NJ: Erlbaum.

Exter, T. G. 1993. "The Declining Majority." *American Demographics* (January): 59.

Fuller, F., and O. H. Bown. 1975. "Becoming a Teacher." Pp. 25–52 in K. Ryan (ed.), *Teacher Education.* 74th Yearbook of the National Society for the Study of Education. Chicago: University of Chicago Press.

Gardner, H. 1985. *Frames of Mind* (rev. ed.). New York: Basic Books.

————. **1991.** *The Unschooled Mind: How Children Think and How Schools Should Teach.* New York: Basic Books.

Giroux, H. A. 1992. "Educational Leadership and the Crisis of Democratic Government." *Educational Researcher* 21(4): 4–11.

Good, T., and J. E. Brophy. 1991. *Looking in Classrooms* (5th ed.). New York: HarperCollins.

Goodlad, J. I. 1990b. *Teachers for our Nation's Schools.* San Francisco: Jossey-Bass.

————, **R. Soder, and K. A. Sirotnik.** 1990b. *Places Where Teachers Are Taught.* San Francisco: Jossey-Bass.

Gore, A. 1994. *National Telecommunications Reform: Bring the Information Revolution to Every Classroom, Hospital, and Library in the Nation by End of the Century.* A speech given by Vice President Al Gore at the University of California, Los Angeles.

Hilliard, A. G., III. 1984. *Saving the African-American Child.* Report of the National Alliance of Black School Educators, 14(11): 1–54.

Hodgkinson, H. L. 1989. *The Same Client: The Demographics of Education and Service Delivery Systems.* Washington, DC: Institute for Educational Leadership/Center for Demographic Policy.

————, **and J. Outtz.** 1992. *The Nation and the State: A Profile and Data Book of America's Diversity.* Washington, DC: Institute for Educational Leadership/Center for Demographic Policy.

Hunter, M. 1985. "What's Wrong with Madeline Hunter?" *Educational Leadership* 42(5): 57–60.

Johnston, W. B., and A. E. Packer. 1987. *Workforce 2000: Work and Workers for the Twenty-First Century.* Indianapolis, IN: Hudson Institute.

Kellogg, J. B. 1988. "Forces of Change." *Phi Delta Kappan* 70(3) (November): 199–204.

Kids Count Data Book 1994: State Profiles of Child Well-Being. 1994. Greenwich, CT: Annie E. Casey Foundation.

Marshall, H., and R. Weinstein. 1984. "Classrooms Where Students Perceive High and Low Amounts of Differential Teacher Treatment." Paper presented at the annual meeting of the American Educational Research Association, New Orleans, LA.

McNett, I. 1984. *Demographic Imperatives: Implications for Educational Policy.* Washington, DC: American Council on Education.

Meyer, J. W., and B. Rowan. 1983. "The Structure of Educational Organizations." Pp. 283–296 in J. W. Meyer and R. Scott, *Organizational Environments: Ritual and Rationality.* Beverly Hills, CA: Sage.

Meyer, J. W., and R. Scott. 1983. *Organizational Environments: Ritual and Rationality.* Beverly Hills, CA: Sage.

National Commission on Excellence in Education. 1983. *A Nation at Risk: The Imperative for Educational Reform.* Washington, DC: U.S. Department of Education.

National Education Association. 1987. *Status of the American Public School Teacher,*

1985–86. National Education Association Response. Washington, DC: National Education Association: 70.

National Endowment for the Humanities. 1987. *American Memory: A Report on the Humanities in the Nation's Public Schools.* Washington, DC: U.S. Government Printing Office.

National Science Foundation. 1983. *Educating Americans for the 21st Century: A Plan of Action for Improving Mathematics, Science and Technology Education for All American Elementary and Secondary Students So That Their Achievement Is the Best in the World by 1995.* Report to the American People and the National Science Board. Washington, DC: National Science Foundation.

Ogle, L. T., N. Alaalam, and G. T. Rogers. 1991. *The Condition of Education: Vol. 1. Elementary and Secondary Education.* Washington, DC: U.S. Department of Education, Office of Educational Research and Improvement, National Center for Educational Statistics. ERIC Document Reproduction Service No. ED 330 121.

Osborne, D., and T. Gaebler. 1992. *Reinventing Government.* Reading, MA: Addison-Wesley.

Rachel, J. R. 1989. "The Social Context of Adult and Continuing Education." In S. Merrian and P. Cunningham (eds.), *Handbook of Adult and Continuing Education.* San Francisco: Jossey-Bass.

Randle, W. 1990. "Some Firms Facing Facts on Workforce Diversity Dictates Major Changes." *Chicago Tribune* (January 2): C-1.

Ribadeneira, D. 1990. "Educators Say School Reform Is Not Enough." *Boston Globe* (1) (November 13): 1.

Riche, M. F. 1991. "We're All Minorities Now." *American Demographics* (October): 26–34.

Roberts, S. 1993. *Who We Are.* New York: Times Books.

Rose, M. 1995. *Possible Lives: The Promise of Public Education in America.* New York: Houghton-Mifflin.

Rosenthal, R., and L. Jacobson. 1968. *Pygmalion in the Classroom: Teacher Expectation and Pupils' Intellectual Development.* New York: Holt, Rinehart & Winston.

Sautter, R. C. 1994. "Who Are Today's City Kids?" *City Schools* (Fall–Winter): 6–10.

Schnailberg, L. 1993. "Immigration's Final Frontier." *Education Week* (February): 31.

Sizer, T. R. 1984. *Horace's Compromise: The Dilemma of the American High School: The First Report from a Study of High Schools.* Report co-sponsored by the National Association of Secondary School Principals and the Commission on Educational Issues of the National Association of Independent Schools. Boston: Houghton-Mifflin.

———. 1992. *Horace's School: Redesigning the American High School.* Boston: Houghton-Mifflin.

Steinberg, L.D. 1996. *Beyond the Classroom: Why School Reform Has Failed and What Parents Need to Do.* New York: Simon & Schuster.

Stevenson, H. W., and J. W. Stigler. 1992. *The Learning Gap.* New York: Summit.

Stevenson, H. W., C. Chen, and S. Lee. 1993. "Mathematics Achievement of Chinese, Japanese, and American Children: Ten Years Later." *Science* 259: 53–58.

U.S. Bureau of the Census, Economic and Statistics Administration. 1991. *1990 Census Profile: Race and Hispanic Origin.* Report No. 2.

———. **U.S. Department of Commerce, Economics and Statistics Administration, Bureau of the Census.** 1993a. *We, the American Asians.*

———. 1993b. *We, the American Blacks.*

———. 1993c. *We, the American Foreign Born.*

———. 1993d. *We, the American Hispanics.*

———. 1993e. *We, the American Pacific Islanders.*

———. 1993f. *We, the First Americans.*

U.S. Department of Education, National Center for Education Statistics. 1991a. *Digest of Education Statistics.* Washington, DC: U.S. Government Printing Office: 234, 276.

———. 1991b. *Trends in Academic Progress.* Washington, DC: U.S. Government Printing Office: 1–10.

———. 1992. *The Condition of Education.* Washington, DC: U.S. Government Printing Office: 144–145.

U.S. Department of Education, National Education Goals Report. 1994. *Building a Nation of Learners.* Washington, DC: U.S. Government Printing Office: 8–11.

————. Executive Summary. 1995. *Improving Education Through Family-School-Community Partnerships*. Washington, DC: U.S. Government Printing Office: 6–9.

U.S. Department of Labor. 1991. *The Secretary's Commission of Achiever Necessary Skills*. Washington, DC: U.S. Government Printing Office.

"U.S. Youth at Risk." 1994. *Futurist* 28(6) (November–December): 60.

Weick, K. E. 1976. "Educational Organizations as Loosely Coupled Systems." *Administrative Science Quarterly* 21: 1.

West, C. 1994. *Race Matters*. New York: Vintage Books.

Culturally Diverse Learners

The following objectives are identified for this chapter:

1. *To describe what is meant by cognitive styles of learning, and the constructs that have implications for improving the learning process.*
2. *To identify and describe the major research findings concerning cognitive style in terms of gender and the cultural groups examined in this chapter.*
3. *To identify and describe the implications of the research on cognitive styles for teacher use of alternative instructional models.*

DIVERSITY AND LEARNING

If we look at classrooms across America—whether in the urban centers of East Los Angeles, East Harlem, or East Cleveland; or the rural areas of Arkansas, Tennessee, or Kansas; or the suburbs of Atlanta, Miami, Phoenix, or Washington, D.C.—we can find students who represent all levels of diversity. In any one of these geographical locations, a visitor to a typical classroom has a better than 50–50 chance of encountering an almost equal split of students by gender (though females have the majority); students who bring various ability levels to the classroom table, including physical, emotional, and mental exceptionalities; students who come from various socioeconomic backgrounds, with their corresponding advantages and disadvantages; students who represent different religious preferences; students who evidence a wide range of racial and ethnic backgrounds, including those whose primary language is not English; students who do not come from traditional family environments; and an increasing number of students who resent what the school has to offer and how it is delivered to them by teachers. Given the diversity found within individual classrooms, is it any wonder that teachers throw up their arms and rhetorically plea: "What am I going to do with all of these kids?"

In addition to the primary characteristics of diversity (that is, gender, age, race, ethnicity, and physical disabilities), classrooms also have students who learn in various ways, at various times, and through various instructional approaches. The learning needs of students are varied and are based upon many factors such as past background and experiential development, as well as present and future opportunities to grow and excel.

> *All our children ought to be allowed a stake in the enormous richness of America. Whether they were born to poor white Appalachians or to wealthy Texans, to poor black people in the Bronx or to rich people in Manhasset or Winnetka, they are all quite wonderful and innocent when they are small. We soil them needlessly.*
>
> JONATHAN KOZOL

Students have different styles and preferences for learning. Some students learn best by taking the whole of an issue and breaking it into parts; others learn by taking the parts and creating a new whole. Some students work best in a very highly structured and teacher-directed manner; others learn best in a more open, nondirective classroom climate. Some students learn through deductive (field-dependent) thinking processes; others learn primarily through inductive (field-independent) processes. Some students learn visually; others use an auditory mode; still others acquire essential skills through kinesthetic/tactile (hands-on) experiences. Finally, some students learn best by working collaboratively with classmates, while other students learn best through independent activities. These diverse characteristics and corresponding cognitive styles require an answer to three questions:

- Should all students and all groups of students (by race, age, gender, and so on) be taught in the same manner?
- Do students have learning-style preferences that correspond to specific instructional models?
- Do student needs and past experiential development affect how students learn, and thus how teachers teach?

If teachers organize a learning environment based upon single characteristics of diversity (that is, age or race or ability level), only students who learn best deductively, or who learn best through an open and free classroom atmosphere, or who require collaborative learning processes will be successful. Teachers who are instructional "Johnny-one-notes" structure their classes to advantage one subset of students, and in the process they disadvantage other subsets of students.

Only teachers who utilize a variety of instructional models will be successful in maximizing the achievement of all students. Through the use of a variety of models, not only will students be more inclined to achieve the diverse goals established by teachers, but students will also acquire a variety of skills and approaches to personal learning that transcend their natural learning dispositions. Teachers need to "play to" students' strengths and to mitigate students' learning weaknesses. This can be done only through the use of instructional variety.

In the following chapter we indicate that there is no one best approach (a cookbook) for teaching all students in all situations. Further, there is no one cognitive style that can be attributed to all groups of students based upon age, ability level, gender, race, or ethnicity. Substantial research in the past 15 years has been conducted concerning the cognitive styles of culturally diverse groups in our society. As you will recognize from the literature review, no student group type (for example, racial group) can be classified and/or limited to a specific cognitive style and instructional model. That is, all African Americans are not field-dependent learners even if a significant subset of that population prefers field-dependent approaches. Caution is warranted here so that the reader does not generalize and/or stereotype the research findings that follow to all individual members within a cultural group. There are just too many individual exceptions within cultural groups that must be considered in an analysis of cultural group cognitive styles. In essence, we have what philosopher David Hume described as the "is" to "ought" problem. Because something is with *some* does not necessitate, by consequence, what ought to be for all. The teacher's task is to "read" the dispositions of students, and to vary instruction to accommodate different student needs.

COGNITIVE STYLE

There are three major types of learning domains: cognitive, affective, and psychomotor. The school, through its curriculum, instruction, testing, and physical resources, tends to emphasize almost exclusively the cognitive domain, and within that domain, the development of verbal and mathematical skills. The process of thought and its product—the acquisition of information and knowledge—is what is meant by *cognition*. The manner in which a student acquires and processes information characterizes a "cognitive style." Cognitive style is the manner in which children perceive, organize, and remember information (Ramirez, 1989b). Most research on the development of cognitive style (learning styles) indicates that family socialization practices play a major role in determining learning preferences in youngsters (Ramirez and Castaneda, 1974; Witkin et al., 1962). Thus, the significant role models in a child's life, the teaching styles of families, the types of learning encouraged, and the ways in which these learnings are encouraged, seem to contribute to the development of specific learning styles in children (Ramirez, 1989b).

Cognitive styles have been described as "information processing habits representing the learner's mode of perceiving, thinking, problem-solving, and remembering" (Messick, 1970, p. 11). Three constructs that relate to cognitive style and that have implications for improving the learning process have been identified by Keefe (1979):

1. Perceptual modality preferences
2. Field independence vs. field dependence
3. Conceptual tempo

Perceptual modalities refer to the senses (kinesthetic, visual, and auditory) that are used for organizing information and making sense out of the external environment. Students utilize these three senses in understanding the school environment and in learning new information within the school setting. Because this construct to learning is not absolute, many students also learn through a variety of other approaches (Dunn and Dunn, 1979). However, most educators rarely use the kinesthetic or visual approaches. The predominant style in schools is auditory because teachers do so much talking in the classroom. Teachers talk, students listen.

Field-dependence/sensitivity—field-independence approaches have been studied by Witkin et al. (1977) and refer to the way students approach the content material presented by the teacher. Field-dependent/sensitive students tend to be social, outgoing, and people-oriented; they view content in "wholes" or in a global manner. Such students have difficulty distinguishing the parts of a task from the whole. Field-independent students are more introspective and less socially oriented than field-sensitive students. In the classroom, such students are able to separate the parts from the whole and design new patterns and structures. These two approaches to learning are not mutually exclusive within any one person (that is, a student is not just field dependent or field independent), and neither is either approach necessarily the most desirable way to learn (Witkin et al., 1977). Most traditional educators tend to implicitly value the field-independent approach to learning (for example, teaching from abstractions to examples—if the reader doubts this, simply look at the way most textbook chapters are organized), and thus field-dependent students are often placed at a cognitive disadvantage. For example, field-dependent students often need more exact outcome definitions than field-independent students when they approach a task—they want to know what the outcome will be and why it is an important one to achieve: Why do I need to learn this? Field-dependent students are not as likely to do well in subjects such as math and science, especially given the way these subjects are taught by most teachers—lecture, recitation, assessment. Further, field-dependent individuals do not perform as efficiently as field-independent individuals on standardized tests (Saracho and Spodek, 1984; Witkin et al., 1977) because of the decontextualized nature of the tested material. In summary, field-independent students are more effective than field-dependent students in concept attainment, selective attention, and long-term memory process activities. Field-dependent students prefer and are more effective with instructional material that has personal content, involves collaborative and relationship-oriented activities, requires verbal and kinesthetic tasks, and provides role models for personal learning (Davis and Frank, 1979).

Conceptual tempo refers to the speed and accuracy of informational responses (Kagan, 1966). The experimental task to assess a student's cognitive approach utilizes hidden or embedded figures in an illustration. "Impulsive" individuals provide the first response that occurs to them; "reflective" individuals take longer to respond—they examine alternatives and attempt to validate an answer before responding. Kagan (1966) distinguishes between learners who are "analytical" or "thematic." The analytical learner identifies all component parts of a task and then forms a pattern; the thematic learner concentrates on the global dimensions of a task. Most educators tend to value the analytic over the thematic; but neither approach to learning is more correct and/or appropriate by itself.

The approaches described above provide a rich set of data concerning the learning processes that individuals choose in acquiring and understanding information. Such learning styles are sometimes cultural and sometimes biological, but they all refer to individual dispositions. In the next section, we examine cultural dispositions—that is, how various gender and racial groups approach learning tasks.

REVIEW OF RELATED RESEARCH

Any discussion of racial or ethnic dispositions is fraught with social and political complications. It is all too easy to move from an observation (for example, that Native Americans rely heavily on interpersonal cooperation) to a prescription (that is, that cooperative learning is the model of choice for all Native American students). As noted earlier, philosophers and psychologists have for years warned against such prescriptiveness. Facile prescriptions about how to teach Hispanic Americans or African Americans are the by-product of two *spurious assumptions:*

Assumption 1: That all members of one gender or of one racial or ethnic group learn in the same manner.

Assumption 2: That there is one best way to teach based upon an individual's gender and/or racial group membership.

Considerable support exists for the proposition that culture affects the learning style of various social, economic, and/or gender groups in our society (Hall, 1989). Yet, it is equally apparent from the literature on diversity that individuals within each cultural group vary in specific learning style. Some cultural groups excel well above other cultural groups in selected academic areas; others excel far less on other academic assessments (Gibson, 1987; Ogbu, 1987). These variations in learning style mean that we should not classify and thus stereotype all individuals within a cultural group as requiring a specific learning style. The basic premise of this chapter is that culture does affect the learning style of youngsters, but no clear research indicates that a specific learning style pattern is unique to everyone in a specific cultural group (Hall, 1989). We also take exception with the notion that any cultural or racial group possesses a genetic advantage. During the past several years, this topic has fostered acrimonious debate. Rather, we argue that *schools* advantage certain groups (and individuals). Our goal, as educators, is to create instructional programs that advantage all students. That can be accomplished only if teachers know how to vary their instructional approach to disciplinary concepts.

In this section, we identify and describe the research findings on learning styles for four cultural groups: Native Americans, African Americans, Hispanic Americans, and Asian Americans. Findings within any one of these groups may indicate that 55 to 70 percent of the cultural group learn in a specific manner. However, as noted earlier, the reader cannot generalize from these findings that all individuals within that cultural group learn in the same manner. Some consistencies have emerged for various cultural groups (Vernon et al., 1988), and we shall identify and describe these in this literature review. However, individual differences within each cultural group require cautious interpretation. There are no monolithic cultural approaches to learning. Indeed, there are just as many learning-style exceptions within European American groups as there are among and between other cultural groups in society (Dunn et al., 1990).

In the following sections, we provide general descriptions about learning dispositions for selected cultural groups. The reader needs to be aware of what the research says concerning how different cultural groups learn, and to understand the ways in which the various instructional models can enhance the overall performance of individual students. With such understandings, the reader can then use the extant research as a pedagogical tool for *thinking* about the learning potential of different students. This information should never be used as an instructional weapon with which to intellectually force all students to conform to some stereotypic image of how an African American or Hispanic American learns. As Sternberg (1994) notes: "There are different ways of capturing [or thinking about] children's learning styles. The important thing is to take them into account—to teach in a way that meets the needs of each child. In practice, I often teach the very same concept in different ways, and then assess that concept in various ways" (p. 565).

The purpose of this section is to explore the different ways students learn, with particular attention to the four cultural traditions (Native Americans, African Americans, Hispanic Americans, and Asian Americans) and to gender—the latter, of course, has received considerable attention because of research highlighting the inequitable participation of females in classrooms (Sadker and Sadker, 1994a). The purpose of Chapters 4–11 is to equip the reader with a better knowledge of the different instructional models that might be used to enhance the learning potential of students who exhibit different propensities for learning. The great variations among individuals within groups lend credence to the need for educators to begin using diverse instructional models with and for culturally diverse student populations. Two types of knowledge, one cultural and the other pedagogical, form a basis for achieving Sternberg's (1994) ideal result: "Children with different learning and thinking styles...[being] given the opportunity to show what they can learn and how they use it" (p. 565).

Native American Learners

One of the great difficulties in studying Native American learning styles has to do with the diversity among the various tribes within Native American culture. For example, the Sauk Fox, Navajo, Cherokee, and Seminole tribes are very different. However, Native American tribes share some similar cultural orientations. "A Native American identifies first with his clan, then with his tribe, and then as an Indian" (Bert and Bert, 1992, p. 4). For a Native American, culture and religion are powerful entities; they cannot be separated. They are interrelated systems that are conceptually integrated (Herring, 1989; Loftin, 1989). There are similar rites and traditions that most if not all Native Americans have in common:

1. The belief in a harmonious universe where everything has a sacred life. Religious symbols and rites are common across most tribes.
2. The belief that human beings are part of and not superior to nature.
3. The belief that every individual has rights and deserves dignity and respect.
4. The belief that individuals are a part of the whole group and are subjugative to the good of the group.
5. The belief that leadership is based on ability and earned respect (Loftin, 1989; Tooker, 1983).

Soldier (1985, 1989), using similar core values to those listed above, describes how the Native American youngster may need to interact with a teacher within the traditional classroom. One of the first values that Soldier describes is the emphasis upon the dignity of the individual—specifically, children are afforded the same respect as adults. Children are taught to seek the wisdom and counsel of their elders; at the same time, they are encouraged to be independent and to make their own decisions. The locus of control is more internal in Native American culture. Native American youngsters may respond, therefore, to a teacher (who represents external authority) with confusion and/or passivity when confronted with demands to recognize external control.

Philips (1972, 1993) sought to determine why Native American youngsters appeared more silent during classroom discussions than mainstream cultural students. She discovered, at the Warm Springs Indian Reservation in Central Oregon, that Native American youngsters were accustomed to a high degree of self-determination; that they carefully observed adults who were involved in completing daily tasks, especially how they performed ordinary tasks; and that Native American children were often taken care of by older siblings to whom they turned for help. Such approaches to learning placed Native American youngsters at a distinct disadvantage in the traditional American classroom: Traditional classroom teachers function in an authoritarian manner, they closely monitor student activities, and they rely heavily upon lecture and recitation as the dominant forms of instruction.

For the Native American student, teachers are not always considered leaders simply because of their position or authority. An individual in the Native American culture is a leader when others choose that individual because of his or her perceived abilities and/or knowledge. The teacher must learn to earn the student's respect before a student will follow and obey instructions from the teacher. Additionally, in traditional classrooms, youngsters are expected to display their knowledge in front of peers, and most classroom interactions are closely controlled by the teacher. For the Native American student, such classrooms are foreign to their cultural background and the manner in which they learned how to learn.

Native American youngsters at Warm Springs (the hunting and gathering bands of Tenino, Tygh, and Wy-am) responded best when provided with hands-on learning. In a science lesson on electricity using motors and batteries, the Warm Springs Indian children were much more energized when they had the opportunity to conduct projects and experiments rather than reading about electricity and answering workbook questions.

Native Americans value and develop acute visual discrimination. One of the common generalizations about Native American cultures is that information processing is conducted through the use of the visual mode—visual-spatial strength (Swisher and Deyhle, 1989). Native American children are taught to learn through careful observational techniques (for example, the nonverbal expressions of adults, changing weather conditions, the ecological alterations of earth, the behavioral changes and expressions of adults). Native American students approach learning through visual activity; they prefer to learn by observation before performance, and they seem to learn in their natural settings through experimentation (Swisher and Deyhle, 1987). Because of their visual perceptual strength, Native Americans demonstrate a high level of field independence. Studies by Dinges and Hollenbeck (1978), Halverson (1976), McShane (1980), and Utley (1983)—conducted with many different Native American tribes—suggest that Native Americans are just as field independent, if not more so, as European Americans. Another strength for Native Americans is the use of imagery as a tool for understanding complex concepts (Tafoya, 1982).

Anyone who doubts the rich imagery of Native American traditions should read popular fiction such as Leslie Silko's *Ceremony* or James Welch's *Fool's Crow*.

Further descriptions of Native American students emphasize the use of global processing skills over linear, sequential processes (Bryant, 1986; More, 1990). Global processing emphasizes the whole of phenomena; it makes use of overviews and placing phenomena within the context studied. Sequential learning emphasizes the "parts" and seeks to have learners divide phenomena into specific substructures. As a consequence, whole-language learning may be a more appropriate strategy in learning reading for a global learner (many Native Americans have this quality) than the usual phonetic approaches found in most schools (More, 1990). Indeed, the whole-language movement is an outgrowth, in part at least, of the work of Sylvia Ashton Warner, who worked with the Maori tribe in New Zealand.

Another core value for Native Americans is cooperation. Because the extended (clan or tribal) family is so important in the Native American culture (consider, for example, the Indian Child Welfare Act of 1978), youngsters tend to be group-oriented rather than self-centered. Personal property is not a familiar concept to many young Native Americans because of their cultural experience that emphasizes sharing what they have with others. Such sharing behavior often conflicts with the ethos created by a traditional teacher, who emphasizes respecting personal property, labeling possessions, taking care of one's own belongings, and being the best in the class (for example, a spelling bee champion). According to Soldier (1985), Native American children are "far more advanced than their non-Indian counterparts in such social behaviors as getting along with others, working in groups, taking turns, and sharing" (p. 187). The Native American student's culture traditionally teaches helping relationships rather than interpersonal competition.

It is very clear that the cognitive style of many Native Americans is somewhat different from what is valued and taught in most schools. Philips (1972) described how these structural and instructional differences can cause problems for Native American students:

> This process of Indian acquisition of competence may help to explain, in part, Indian children's reluctance to speak in front of their classmates. In the classroom, the processes of *acquisition* of knowledge and *demonstration* of knowledge are collapsed into the single act of answering questions or reciting when called upon to do so by the teacher, particularly in the lower grades. Here the assumption is that one will learn, and learn more effectively, through making mistakes in front of others. The Indian children have no opportunity to observe others performing successfully before they attempt it, except for their fellow classmates who precede them and are themselves uninitiated. They have no opportunity to "practice," and to decide for themselves when they know enough to demonstrate their knowledge; rather, their performances are determined by the teacher. And finally, their only channel for communicating competency is verbal, rather than non-verbal.
>
> Turning now from learning processes in the home to learning experiences outside the home, in social and ritual activities involving community members other than kinsmen, there is again considerable evidence that

Indian children's understanding of when and how one participates and performs individually, and thus demonstrates or communicates competence, differs considerably from what is expected of them in the classroom (pp. 387–388).

Philips (1972, 1983) indicates with this passage that Native American adults teach youngsters to listen, observe, pay close attention, and practice on their own (independently)—to learn by observing and watching adults, and to learn through listening to and observing those who are respected as elders. The only occasion when a public display would take place is when a new skill or knowledge is to be demonstrated or performed for others. This notion of "private learning" (Swisher and Deyhle, 1989) has been verified by other researchers for the Oglala Sioux children (Brewer, 1977), Navajo youngsters (Longstreet, 1978), and Yanqui youngsters (Appleton, 1983).

Current research concerning Native Americans has moved from an examination of student deficiencies related to language ability, cultural background, and cognitive development to studies focusing upon social and economic discrimination (Ogbu, 1983, 1987, 1989), which strongly criticizes the school as a central player of discriminatory practices. The latest research identifies the cognitive skills of Native Americans as strengths, not weaknesses (Benjamin et al., 1993; Grantham-Campbell, 1992; Macias, 1989; Shutiva, 1991). Thus, it is the responsibility of the school to alter its instructional practices and structure to utilize fully the cognitive skills and intellectual strengths of Native American children.

For those readers who doubt the power of cultural and individual genetic dispositions for Native Americans in terms of how they negotiate the world, consider the words of Linda Hodges (1996), a woman who adopted an Apache child in 1969 (prior to the Indian Child Welfare Act). At the age of 26, her adopted son returned to his tribe. She writes:

Andrew learned that both his parents died years ago in alcohol-related incidents, but he found a brother, grandmother, great-grandmother and dozens of aunts, uncles and cousins. They gave him a welcome-home party and showered him with gifts. He felt comfortable with them. Only the lan-

---

TABLE 2-1 Capitalizing on Native American Dispositions

Teachers need to:

- *Establish a conceptual context for new academic content.*

- *Provide time and space for thinking and personal reflection.*

- *Emphasize visual stimuli within the learning environment.*

- *Develop a warm and supportive classroom environment through the use of cooperative learning.*

- *Utilize imagery as a tool for understanding complex concepts.*

- *Provide an overview and rationale to help place academic content within a context to be studied.*

guage they usually spoke set him apart. He enrolled in the tribe, is thinking of moving to the reservation and wants to be buried in the cemetery where his birth parents rest.

He learned that his family never wanted his mother to sign him away. He was told that her decision to relinquish two of her three children for placement in non-Indian homes caused such a rift with her family that, while under the influence of alcohol, she took an overdose of sleeping pills and died. The family never stopped searching for the missing children.

Although Andrew grew up happy in our home, the positive change in my son once he touched his roots, and the ease into which he entered the lives of his large family, makes me think that the pull of the ingrained cultural memory is stronger than even the most loving adoptive bonds (p. A15).

African American Learners

For African American students the opportunity to use oral modes of expression (Goldstein, 1971; Kochman, 1972), to engage in kinesthetic/tactile activities, and to exhibit loyalty in interpersonal relationships are central to their intellectual growth (Hale-Benson, 1986; Hilliard, 1989; Shade, 1989). African Americans share a unique cultural heritage, and their learning styles are integrally linked with their historical culture (Hale-Benson, 1982). The influence of culture must be viewed by educators as a preferential or stylistic choice; it is not suggestive of intellectual inferiority or superiority. Hale-Benson (1986) believes that, as a result of their cultural heritage, African Americans are more affective, relational, and holistic in their orientation to learning than European American students. The issue of African American cultural heritage, however, has become problematic given the increasing cultural diversity present in African American communities (Slaughter-DeFoe et al., 1990). Children of color attending America's schools are now coming from Caribbean, South American, African, and, of course, African American families. While these individuals struggle with different social and economic circumstances, all are designing their own means of maintaining a personal and cultural identity.

Anderson (1988), like Hale-Benson (1986), noted that the African Americans' psychological orientation is more affective than that of European Americans: "The most characteristic feature of the African system is its focus on unity and connection" (p. 6). Cooper (1987) takes a similar position in her examination of language in the African American culture: "Black language is anchored in an aesthetic and a world view that are different from those of the Western tradition.... [It] reflects a holistic cognitive style and right-brain hemispheric dominance that is in diametric opposition to the Western ideal of analytic style and left hemispheric dominance" (p. 61).

Matthews (as cited in Cooper, 1987) elaborates:

The Black mind sees a thing as a connected whole, as against the view of the things as a build of isolated particulars.... The wholeness approach is a habit of seeing things whole before they are seen as broken apart. Instead of seeing 10 things as 10 separate units, the Black perspective tends to see

10 things as 10 parts of a single whole.... One wants to envision the ecology rather than the cell because the cell behaves one way outside of the ecology—and in a totally different way when put back into the ecology (p. 19).

Gilbert and Gay (1985) found that African American students grow up within a context that integrates the intellectual, physical, and emotional abilities and skills. African American students respond to a teacher's question using voice, emotion, and nonverbal characteristics. Usually African American students will respond orally, in unison, and in a choral manner based upon traditional modes of verbal expression—oral communication and group participation. If teachers are unaware of these cultural characteristics and historical antecedents, they may interpret this student responsiveness as unruly, disruptive, and unacceptable to the traditional decorum of the classroom.

The contributions of Anderson (1988), Cooper (1987), Hale-Benson (1986), and others bring into focus two different ways of knowing: one that is more analytical, where the learner studies phenomena in a detailed manner; and a second, which is more affective and relational, where the learner is more directly involved with what is to be known. Such a dichotomous view reinforces the research of Albas et al. (1976), LaFromboise et al. (1981), and Rollman (1978), which describes African American children's cognitive disposition to pay very close attention to the affective dimension in the school as well as to how the teacher relates to the students in the classroom.

Students of color tend to be more field dependent (Olstad et al., 1981; Ramirez, 1982)—that is, they contextualize knowledge and look for conceptual relationships. Shade (1984) noted that African Americans develop unique cultural patterns and have specific methods for organizing and processing information. The African American child is also more likely to be field sensitive (for example, to have the need for a warm and positive classroom setting, to use collaborative and cooperative instructional styles, to utilize kinesthetic activities, and to use people-oriented examples and role models) and less able to perceptually differentiate visual-spatial tasks than other groups (Kelly, 1984; Shade, 1981). Boykin (1994) and Tuck and Boykin (1989) have reinforced the research of Slavin (1977) and Slavin and Oickle (1981) concerning the use of cooperative learning strategies with African American youngsters. The youngsters in these studies achieved at a much higher level using cooperative learning strategies when compared with traditional classroom techniques. Boykin, in fact, asserts that African American students achieve at a higher level using cooperative learning strategies because of their cultural dispositions concerning affectional and relational learning (Boykin, 1994; Tuck and Boykin, 1989). Boykin consistently found that African American youngsters preferred to work cooperatively in groups even when external rewards were removed. He argues that this learning preference is an African American cultural norm; an argument that is consistent with Ladson-Billings's (1990, 1992) research concerning socialization and the distinctive ways of learning in African American communities.

The African American orientation to field sensitivity may also play a part in student abilities to interpret facial expressions (for example, how the student interprets the eye contact of a teacher). In studies concerning the gazing behavior of various cultural groups, LaFrance and Mayo (1976) found that European Americans tended to look away from the conversant when speaking, but to look at them when listening to the speaker. On the other hand, African Americans tended to look away when listening to someone but looked directly at the individual when speaking. This may help explain the frustrations of European American teachers who often view African American children as belligerent or inattentive based upon student-to-teacher eye contact.

Further, while the preferred modality for receiving information by European Americans is visual, many African Americans process information utilizing kinetic and tactile senses (Guttentag, 1972; Morgan, 1981). From studies focusing on the kinesthetic mode, it seems apparent that African Americans are much more skilled at utilizing kinesthetic processes as compared with European American children. The high degree of kinetic usage, especially for African American males, has led to negative perceptions by educators (Hale-Benson, 1986), as well as an inordinate amount of failing grades and special education placements (Harry, 1992; Obiakor, 1992).

African Americans are socialized to be person-oriented rather than object/thing-oriented (Prom, 1982; Shade, 1984; Young, 1970, 1974). Shade and Edwards (1987) found that African American households tended to have pictures or statues of people; European American families tended to have pictures or statues representing nature and/or abstract art. Damico (1983), in a comparison of black and white 6th grade youngsters, used photography as a vehicle of analysis and concluded that African American children chose to include people in their photos, while European American children were more inclined to depict objects or physical settings in their photos. The learning preference for African Americans tended to focus more on people and events as opposed to ideas and objects.

TABLE 2-2 Capitalizing on African American Dispositions

Teachers need to:

- *Develop a classroom climate characterized by warmth and encouragement.*
- *Utilize oral modes of expression within the classroom.*
- *Structure the classroom in formal rather than informal ways.*
- *Utilize collaborative work environments that promote social interaction.*
- *Provide overviews and rationale to help place academic content within a context to be studied.*
- *Provide concept learning that moves from the concrete to the abstract.*
- *Design learning activities that promote kinesthetic/tactile modalities.*
- *Be aware of the affective dimension of the classroom environment as well as how the teacher relates to all students.*
- *Utilize people-oriented examples and situations in the learning activities presented.*
- *Utilize as many positive role models as possible in the lessons presented to students.*

All too often the preferred cognitive style used by many African American children is incompatible with existing school practices (Olstad et al., 1981; Schimizzi, 1985). This incompatibility seems even greater in mathematics and science instruction, where analytical skills, abstract reasoning, and independent seatwork are more heavily utilized (Olstad et al., 1981).

Matthews (1981) found that African American students preferred a teacher who would 1) provide them with a second chance to pass tests, 2) stay after school to work with them, and 3) follow the textbook page-by-page. Further, Matthews concluded that African American youngsters responded better to instruction that required the use of global skills, a more personal orientation (content material that included relationships with real-world people and/or issues), the use of hands-on learning, and group work to facilitate positive, social interactions.

Hispanic American Learners

Classifying all people of Spanish descent as Hispanic Americans is fraught with difficulties, especially when one considers the myriad of potential ethnic groups—Colombian, Cuban, Mexican, Puerto Rican, and so on—normally classified as Hispanic American. Roberts (1993), in his review of 1990 U.S. Census data, found that among all people who identified themselves as of Hispanic origin, 61 percent were Mexican, 12 percent were Puerto Rican, 5 percent were Cuban, with the remaining 22 percent from the various countries in Central and South America. Additionally, there is the problem of labeling the racial/ethnic group—*Hispanic* is favored in Florida and Texas and by Cubans; *Latino* is preferred in California. Most of the research cited below has been conducted with children who are described by the researchers as Mexican American. Because most multicultural education texts and the U.S. Census Bureau utilize the term *Hispanic Americans*, we will use this descriptor.

There are considerable differences between and among Puerto Ricans, Cubans, Mexicans, Colombians, and other ethnic groups who are referred to as Hispanic Americans. Because this descriptor embraces so many ethnic groups, there is little appreciation for the characteristics of diversity within and among the groups. Within each group there are differences related to language (dialect differences), social class, acculturation, and educational background. Newly arrived immigrants differ greatly from individuals who may be third- or fourth-generation U.S. citizens. Older-generation Hispanic Americans may call themselves Spanish Americans, speak a different form of Spanish, and differ in their customs and the foods they eat (Keefe and Padilla, 1987). The early Cuban immigrants to the United States after Castro took power came from a highly educated and socially mobile economic class compared with the more recent Cuban immigrants (Suarez, 1993). Furthermore, there are black Cubans and Puerto Ricans who have a common culture with white Cubans and Puerto Ricans even though they are often misnamed as *African Americans.*

Compared with African Americans and European Americans, Hispanic Americans enter school later, leave school earlier, and are less likely to complete a high school education (Howe, 1994). Hispanic Americans remain the most undereducated racial group in the United States (De La Rosa and Maw, 1990).

Hispanic American students regard family and personal relationships as important and are comfortable with cognitive generalities and patterns (Cox and Ramirez, 1981; Vasquez, 1991). These qualities help explain why Hispanic American students often seek a personal relationship with a teacher and are more comfortable with broad concepts rather than component facts and specific information.

Ramirez (1973) reports that European American students do better in competitive situations; Hispanic American students perform better when members of the family are in a position to benefit from their performance. Further, "the traditional Mexican American is encouraged to always view themselves as an integral part of the family. The child is reared in an atmosphere which emphasizes the importance of interpersonal relationships. Consequently, the child develops greater sensitivity to social cues, and to the human environment in general" (p. 902).

Ramirez (1982) further reported that Hispanic American youngsters are much more group-oriented than European Americans, flourish at academic tasks when cooperative learning is the instructional strategy, and are much more sensitive to the social environment of the classroom. He found that Hispanic American students tended to be much more responsive to adult role models, less comfortable with trial-and-error instructional strategies, and less interested in the details of academic, abstract tasks.

An interesting pair of studies focusing upon child-rearing practices was conducted by Ramirez and Castaneda (1974) and Cox and Ramirez (1981). Each study utilized both observations of students and interviews with mothers and the observation of their mothering skills. The authors compared Hispanic American and non-Hispanic American elementary students and collected data around two child-rearing practices—"traditional" and "modern." Traditional child-rearing practices were oriented toward encouraging children to work cooperatively and learn by modeling; traditional parents were motivated through the use of social rewards. Modern child-rearing practices, on the other hand, utilized trial-and-error learning, encouraged children to work individually, and focused on motivation through nonsocial rewards. Both studies noted that youngsters reared in families using *both* traditional and modern child-rearing practices were more flexible in learning disciplinary concepts, social skills, and academic content than those children raised with a single approach. Such "dual" children, regardless of ethnicity, could work either individually or in groups, cooperate or compete, function in field-sensitive or field-independent situations, and were motivated by both social and nonsocial rewards. The more flexible children in the study were labeled *bicognitive*, because they could function in both field-independent and field-sensitive cognitive styles. In other words, "dual" children could adapt to different situations and teaching styles. The educational strengths of these children emerged because of their bicognitive abilities.

In research conducted on cognitive style, Cohen (1969), Messick (1970), and Ramirez (1973, 1982) found that most Hispanic American children tended to be field dependent and to do their best work on verbal tasks. The children in these studies also learned material more easily when it included the use of humor, social content (for example, the use of issues that affected the community), and some fantasy and the opportunity for creative expression. The children were also extremely sensitive to the opinions of others. European American children, on the other hand, did best on analytical tasks; they were able to learn material that was inanimate and impersonal more easily; and their performance was not greatly affected by the opinion of others. These data are reinforced by Kagan and Buriel (1977), Keogh, Welles, and Weiss (1972), and Ramirez and Castaneda (1974), who indicated that Hispanic American children were more group-oriented, more field sensitive to the outside environment, and more positively responsive to role modeling than European American students. Such data support similar conclusions found in studies dealing with Native Americans and African Americans. Hispanic American youngsters tend to be less competitive; less sensitive to spatial relationships; less tolerant of trial-and-error tasks; and less interested in details, isolated factual information, and nonsocial academic situations.

Kagan and Madsen (1971) studied the motivational styles of Hispanic American children. They found that Hispanic American children were less competitive than European American children, and that Hispanic American children were also more highly motivated in the cooperative setting than in the competitive setting. Ramirez and Price-Williams (1974) demonstrated that Hispanic American children scored higher than European American children on need affiliation and the need to be comforted.

This research was further confirmed by a number of other research studies. Kagan and Zahn (1976), in a study comparing Mexican American and Anglo American (as labeled by Kagan) youngsters on reading and mathematics achievement, found that Mexican Americans were more field sensitive/dependent, which is quite different from the way schools tend to be structured. Knight and Kagan (1977), in an analysis of Anglo American and Mexican American 5- to 9-year-old children, found that Anglo American children tended to be much more competitive, made fewer choices related to equality, and exhibited superiority behaviors. Prosocial, altruistic, and group involvement tended to be exhibited by Mexican American youngsters. Finally, in a study by Kagan and Knight (1981), confirmation was made with all of the previous studies—Anglo American children were more competitive than Mexican American children and exhibited higher levels of achievement motivation than Mexican American youngsters.

The final aspect of analysis we shall consider about Hispanic Americans—language issues—also applies in the next section to Asian Americans. There are schools in this nation where a myriad of different languages are spoken daily by students. If the schools and teachers do not help students maintain and utilize their first language, educators are, for all intents and purposes, indicating to youngsters that they are not valued. The language a person speaks is part of who that person really is. If schools try to strip youngsters of their primary language, educators are telling these youngsters that the school does not respect them as whole individuals. As America's student population grows more diverse, the question of how to address non-English youngster learning needs becomes more complicated. Good teachers in multicultural contexts are, of necessity, bicultural—they know how to mediate between the students' past experiential development and the school's expectations. Good teachers are also language sensitive. Even those who are English-first advocates must be sensitive to how words in English might be better understood by non-English-speaking students.

Teachers need to remember that students are not just learning academic skills at school, they are learning the value of education. Clayton (1996) writes:

> The process of acculturation is not just learning a language; it is also learning the values that underlie the culture or the behaviors that make sense in the culture. As such, it can involve a profound change in a person, particularly in children who want so much to be accepted by their peers. Value systems come into conflict, and the cross-cultural student and family are often the battleground (p. 62).

Case study analyses by Carter and Chatfield (1986), Delgado-Gaitan (1992), Lucas, Henze, and Donato (1990), Moll (1988), and Pease-Alvarez, Garcia, and Espinoza (1991) provide insight into instructional management, skill development, language development, and academic achievement of Mexican American students. Each of these studies begins by rejecting the historical notion that Mexican American families are inferior to European American families with respect to social values, family organization, and concern for education.

Moll (1988) found in her observations of classrooms that students who were classified as "limited-English-proficient" were as bright and achieving as was allowed by the teacher. Effective teachers in these settings emphasized the active use of language to obtain or achieve academic content and skills; they sought to understand the students, not just impose cultural information. Teachers taught their students to examine one's own and others' use of language and thinking. In many cases this meant that "students could read a book in English but write their analysis of the book in Spanish" (p. 468).

Pease-Alvarez, Garcia, and Espinoza (1991) found similar results in their case study analyses. Pedagogical practices elicited experimental instructional practices, opportunities to use active student learning, use of cooperative learning strategies, the development of a caring and nurturing community of classroom learners, and a commitment to bilingual education and the integration of the cultural background of students into the classroom. This meant that teachers instructed in both English and the native language when difficult and complex academic concepts were being learned by non-English-speaking students. Permitting students to speak in their native languages allowed them to better understand the academic content and phenomena being taught. For those who

TABLE 2-3 Capitalizing on Hispanic American Dispositions

Teachers need to:

- *Emphasize the use of social interaction within the classroom.*
- *Utilize collaborative work environments that promote verbal tasks.*
- *Provide overviews and rationale to help place academic content within a context to be studied.*
- *Utilize the family, its role, and its importance in the lives of youngsters.*
- *Develop a more personal relationship with students.*
- *Utilize positive role models in all classroom activities.*

doubt the merit of bilingualism and biculturalism, we encourage a simple (yet costly) test—travel in a foreign country where you do not know the language. Anyone who has had such an experience knows the pleasure of meeting someone who can communicate with them.

In each of these studies, the researchers found that effective teachers encouraged students to actively seek support in their academic studies from other students. Language instruction was no different! Primary-grade teachers utilized both Spanish and English to teach academic content and assigned tasks that helped students apply that content in different contexts, while upper-grade teachers tended to use mainly English in their assignments and instruction. Students, however, were allowed to use either language, and to interchange the languages when development and understanding of concepts and skills were being learned and when higher-order thinking processes were being developed.

Research findings support the notion that if teachers are cognizant of the cognitive dispositions of their students and utilize culturally congruent content and instruction (including, where possible, the use of the student's native language), students and their families will respond in a very positive manner. As Clayton (1996) observes:

> Learning styles are influenced by culture in the socialization process within the family and community and by ecological adaptations, and as such, are somewhat a reflection of the larger culture.... One or another learning style is not better; there is no value judgment involved. It is simply a fact of difference. A continuous clash of styles between teacher and student can mean frustration for both. Identification, recognition, and understanding of the difference can help both cross-cultural student and teacher (p. 54).

Asian American Learners

The Asian American population more than doubled in the United States between 1980 and 1990 to about 3 percent of the total population (Roberts, 1993). This increase in population has been due primarily to the enactment of the Immigration Act of 1965. Though a majority of Asian Americans live in just three states—California, Hawaii, and New York—they are less isolated geographically than ever before. Asian Americans are also very diverse—23 percent of all Asian Americans are Chinese, 19 percent are Filipinos, 11.7 percent are Japanese, with the remainder coming from various other Asian countries (Roberts, 1993). Koreans are also increasing as a percentage of the American population, as are Vietnamese, Asian Indians, and the Hmong.

Because of the relaxation of immigration laws, there are two groups of Asian Americans—those born in the United States, some as long as 200 years ago, and those who are immigrants (Cordova, 1983). Asian Americans born in the United States are much more likely to be assimilated into the mainstream culture (Cabezas, 1981), speak English fluently, live in middle-class neighborhoods, and tend not to identify themselves along ethnic lines. Immigrant Asian Americans clearly demonstrate a wide range of backgrounds. In search of political and economic stability, these individuals tend to identify along ethnic lines, have a limited English-speaking ability, and bring with them to this country the concomitant characteristics of poverty and despair.

Research findings concerning Asian American students' cognitive styles are relatively sparse. This is partly because until only recently there were so few Asian Americans in American schools that researchers had not taken seriously any need to study this group of students. The research that does exist has indicated that many Asian Americans are extremely hardworking, high achieving, and nonverbal, and seek careers in science and mathematics (Yoshiwara, 1983). However, the data that do exist are dated. New studies are needed in order to understand and help Asian American students, especially those recent immigrants who have entered our nation's schools. Whatever the reason for the dearth of research, the data thus far lean in the direction of field-independent styles for Asian Americans (Dunn, 1993). This may be one reason why Asian American students do so well in American schools—the structure, the instructional approaches, and the adherence to authoritarian methods (high teacher control) are congruent with Asian American teaching–learning approaches. There is also growing evidence that the more assimilated the Asian American students are, the more their performance mirrors that of other American cultural groups. For example, Shanker (1996) indicates that "the more Asian-American students become Americanized, the less will they perform—which, incidentally, disposes of the idea that their success is based on genetic superiority. Assimilated, Asian-American students are no more successful than anyone else (p. 17)."

Yu and Bain (1985) studied the cognitive styles of Chinese and Chinese-English 8- to 11-year-old students in Hong Kong and Alberta, Canada. They found that the Chinese and Chinese-English students in both Hong Kong and Canada performed much more in a field-independent manner than did Anglo students; recall that Anglo students tend to be more field independent then other racial and ethnic groups.

The results of Enright (1987) and Hansen (1984) also confirm the results of Yu and Bain (1985). Chinese students in both Hong Kong and North America perform in a field-independent manner. One reason for this finding may be the strong visual-spatial skill development of Chinese students as reported by Flaugher and Roch (1977) and Vernon (1984).

Two studies, one by Hansen (1984) and the other by Hansen-Strain (1987), are worth examining. Hansen (1984) compared Filipino and South Pacific Island students. She found that the Filipino students functioned in a field-independent manner as compared with South Pacific Island students, and that the males were more field independent than the female students.

Hansen-Strain (1987) compared Hawaiian with South Pacific Island students. She, too, found that the Hawaiian students were more field independent; and, once again, the males of all groups were more field independent than the females.

Relative to the socialization of Asian American (Chinese, Japanese, Korean, and Vietnamese) children, Cabezas (1981) found that the mothers utilized a variety of question-asking behaviors in their child-rearing practices, especially in comparison with the direct commands, modeling, or cuing found in more traditional homes. Because of these child-rearing practices, the youngsters in this study interacted positively with and sought verbal approval from their mothers. This research is in direct opposition to the view held by many American teachers that many Asian American youngsters are shy and withdrawn, and do not possess the requisite verbal skills necessary to be successful in school. In actuality, Asian American students' reluctance to interact in class discussions probably has more to do with the lack of teacher encouragement to engage in verbal interactions than to any innate lack of verbal ability (Pang, 1990).

Au and Kawakami (1985) also identified the importance of verbal interactions in their research with Hawaiian American students. They found that by structuring reading lessons around culturally affirming and compatible learning styles, students would concentrate on reading lessons twice as much as they would with traditional teaching approaches. The approach used in the Au and Kawakami study used a culturally familiar interactional pattern labeled "talk story"—a process in which the children tell a story together. Group, rather than individual, performance is the emphasis of this culturally congruent form of communication. As the story is told, teachers allowed their students to break in when they wanted to, rather than calling upon individual students to participate and contribute to the discussion. This culturally affirming teaching approach creates a style of teaching and learning that engenders a sense of caring, a family atmosphere, and the sharing of reading responses.

Because so few research studies concerning Asian American students have been conducted, educators tend to stereotype all members of this cultural group. Suzuki (1983) reinforces this observation by stating:

> Many teachers stereotype Asian and Pacific American students as quiet, hardworking, and docile, which tends to reinforce conformity and stifle creativity. Asian and Pacific American students, therefore, frequently do not develop the ability to assert and express themselves verbally and are channeled in disproportionate numbers into the technical/scientific fields. As a consequence, many Asian and Pacific American students undergo traumatic family/school discontinuities, suffer from low self-esteem, are overly conforming, and have their academic and social development narrowly circumscribed (p. 23).

The current literature base needs to be expanded to include more recent research on immigrants from Southeast Asia and how their performance fares in our nation's schools. Very little data on the cognitive dispositions of these immi-

---

TABLE 2-4   Capitalizing on Asian American Dispositions

Teachers need to:

- *Emphasize visual-spatial skills within classroom lessons.*
- *Utilize analytic skills in the tasks designed for students.*
- *Provide learning activities that provide opportunities for students to take parts and/or components and design new wholes and/or solutions.*
- *Provide time and space for thinking and personal reflection.*

grants are currently available (see Worthley, 1987). As Pang (1990) has cautioned, researchers must be cognizant of the limited research findings concerning Asian Americans in explaining the behavior of all Asian Americans. The inaccurate "model minority" myth relative to the homogeneity of all Asian Americans has limited the educational development of students and the design of programs needed by Asian American youngsters (Pang, 1990).

Gender

The notion that males and females process information differently raises serious and controversial questions, just as it has for most non-European American groups. Whether a hierarchy of male and female learning characteristics exists is an issue that sparks a heated debate. Whether girls and boys receive differential treatments in classrooms, though, is without question (Bailey, 1996). The notion of hierarchical cognitive differences is bothersome to many women's groups and to us because it implies national differences that some use as justification for prejudicial practice. We will not promote such a hierarchy or indicate that either a male learning style or a female learning style is preferred. Rather, this discussion of gender cognitive style is presented similar to those provided for the other cultural groups presented in this chapter. The research findings are provided to help teachers consider the possibilities for how to organize instruction, identify and utilize student cognitive dispositions, and enhance student cognition by providing experience in alternative styles of learning.

McCaulley et al. (1985) classified learners as either "thinkers" or "feelers." In their research, those learners who utilized the thinking mode—approximately three-fourths of whom were male—preferred instruction that was objective (more field independent), and utilized the skills of analysis, evaluation, and discourse. Individuals who preferred the feeling mode—approximately two-thirds of whom were female—learned best through instruction that was personal and caring, focused on issues of human values, utilized collaboration and cooperative learning, and was designed around academic material that stressed the improvement of people's lives and the relevance of ideas to the real world. The findings of McCaulley et al. ring true to previous research cited in other sections of this chapter that classified learners as feelers (field-sensitive learners) or thinkers (field-independent learners).

Kolb (1984) and Smith and Kolb (1986) reinforce McCaulley et al.'s findings by critiquing how males and females process information. Although the two groups were equally distributed, the researchers found that 59 percent of females preferred the processing of information through concrete, hands-on experiences (field dependent). Of the males in the study, 59 percent preferred processing information through abstract conceptualization (field independent).

Belenky et al. (1986) extended the research further through a lucid description of women's ways of knowing. Belenky's "ways of knowing" classification is of two types. The first type is preferred predominantly by women and is classified as "connected knowing." Through this knowing type, information is processed in an integrative, involved, empathetic, and subjective manner. The focus is upon understanding in the sense that the learner has a personal acquaintance with the thing (idea) or person being studied. It requires that the learner place herself/himself in the other person's place or context. The second type of knowing is preferred mostly by men and is classified as "separated knowing." This knowing type is conducted through an abstract, objective, and removed process. In other words, it requires a separation between the thing or person studied and the knower/information processor. This way of knowing follows strict rules by which data or an issue are evaluated. Belenky et al. (1986) state that neither way of knowing is necessarily better or worse than the alternative, but in understanding how children learn (whether male or female), teachers are in a better position to help youngsters reach their full potential.

The cognitive style differences among European American women are not unique. There are also cognitive style differences among women of non-European American cultures. The research findings indicate that educational environments tend to be biased by gender as well as by culture (Howard, 1987). As we found previously in our analyses of several selected cultural groups, women also tend to value cooperation rather than competition, working together in teams, and helping others achieve tasks and fulfill responsibilities.

Belenky et al. (1986) and other research findings are very similar to a recent report released by the National Foundation for Women Business Owners (1994) concerning women's leadership behavior. The report identifies a number of characteristics that women tend to exhibit in their interactions with others—for example, an emphasis upon intuition, upon values and feelings in dealing with others, and upon relationships with others built over time. Women tend to see success through building relationships with people, developing strong team-oriented groups, reaching decisions through the use of consensus techniques, and accomplishing something worthwhile for themselves and others. Men, on the other hand, tend to rely on logic and rational thinking processes, and find success by achieving goals and tasks for their own sake.

Gilligan (1982) and Baker Miller (1986) found similar and recurrent differences between men and women in terms of field independence–field sensitivity. Women, who tend to be classified as field sensitive in cognitive style, were found to value affiliation with their coworkers, tended to develop a personality or style oriented toward relationships rather than autonomy, and exhibited a preference for cooperative interaction or collaboration rather than competition. Similarly, Baxter Magolda (1989) found the same type of difference when college-age men

TABLE 2-5 Capitalizing on Female Dispositions

Teachers need to:

- *Develop a warm and supportive classroom environment through the use of cooperative learning.*

- *Provide an overview and rationale to help place academic content within a context to be studied.*

- *Relate what is to be studied to a context in the "real world."*

- *Develop a classroom climate characterized by caring and personal environments.*

- *Facilitate classroom discussions and interactions.*

and women were studied. The most important finding identified was women's preference for cooperative, relationship-oriented interaction with themselves, peers, and their college instructors (Baxter Magolda, 1989).

Teachers need to be aware of the learning preferences evidenced by men and women, but many educators quite rightly express frustration with what to do with that knowledge. How does the teacher act on it? Gender equity, similar to racial or ethnic equity, requires awareness and action (Bailey, 1996). By being aware of the fact that people are different, regardless of their racial, ethnic, or gender affiliation, teachers can accommodate those differences by varying instructional strategies so that students have opportunities to use their strengths. The teacher's responsibility is also related to modifying the curriculum to ensure that the materials used and content covered are reflective of the richness of the human family. History is not simply a white, male experience; it is something that all people, regardless of race or gender, have experienced. As a consequence, teachers need to provide a curriculum that embraces that richness and helps students see their "face" in our country's past and its future.

❷ UMMARY OF THE FINDINGS

We have examined and presented the salient research findings concerning cognitive styles by gender and by selected cultural groups. We will now identify some broader cognitive characteristics among those various groups, and we will use primarily the research of Anderson (1988) and Hilliard (1976). Reliance on broader categories is fraught with difficulties, especially if teachers use the knowledge to narrowly define how to teach each child. But such categories can help immeasurably if they are used as a way of considering the importance of variability in instructional approach. We are going to take all the diverse ideas about how different cultural groups learn and fit them into a couple of different categories. This approach will enable the reader to think through the complexities of teaching in a way that is more instructionally manageable. Our approach is not without conceptual support. Educational anthropologist Edward Hall (1989) argues: "Over thirty years of teaching students and learning from them have convinced me that no two people learn in exactly the same way. I am also convinced that there are major categories into which learning styles can be fitted" (p. 32).

Anderson (1988) assessed the learning disposition of different cultural groups based upon a worldview that was either Western or non-Western in outlook (see Table 2.6). Anderson warns that such worldviews exist on a continuum rather than as polar extremes. Cultural groups cluster somewhere along the continuum based upon the issue or circumstance confronting them at any given point in time.

Anderson (1988) categorized the same cultural groups based upon how they perceive reality, how they choose to function within the world in which they live, and how they choose to think about that same world. As Table 2.7 illustrates, many of the same concepts discussed previously in this chapter (that is, cooperation vs. competition, extended family vs. nuclear family, relationship-oriented vs. task-oriented behavior, and holistic thinking vs. dualistic thinking) are also prominently presented as part of Anderson's analysis.

In Table 2.8, Hilliard (1976) has differentiated the cognitive styles of the various cultural groups. The reader will notice how Hilliard has distinguished the groups based upon the bipolar classifications of field-dependent vs. field-independent learners. The characteristics identified for the two groupings are

TABLE 2-6   Worldviews of Cultural Groups

Non-Western	*Western*
■ *American Indians*	■ *Euro-Americans (primarily males)*
■ *Mexican Americans*	■ *Minorities with a high degree of acculturation*
■ *African Americans*	
■ *Vietnamese Americans*	
■ *Puerto Rican Americans*	
■ *Chinese Americans*	
■ *Japanese Americans*	
■ *Many European American females*	

Source: James Anderson. 1988. "Cognitive Styles and Multicultural Populations." *Journal of Teacher Education* 39: 6.

TABLE 2-7   Some Fundamental Dimensions of Non-Western vs. Western Worldviews

Non-Western	*Western*
■ *Emphasize group cooperation*	■ *Emphasize individual competition*
■ *Achievement as it reflects group*	■ *Achievement for the individual*
■ *Value harmony with nature*	■ *Must master and control nature*
■ *Time is relative*	■ *Adhere to rigid time schedule*
■ *Accept affective expression*	■ *Limit affective expression*
■ *Extended family*	■ *Nuclear family*
■ *Holistic thinking*	■ *Dualistic thinking*
■ *Religion permeates culture*	■ *Religion distinct from other parts of culture*
■ *Accept worldviews of other cultures*	■ *Feel their worldview is superior*
■ *Socially oriented*	■ *Task oriented*

Source: James Anderson. 1988. "Cognitive Styles and Multicultural Populations." *Journal of Teacher Education* 39: 6.

also very familiar based on the previous discussions of each cultural group's learning style preferences (for example, perception based upon wholes vs. parts, achieves best on verbal vs. analytical tasks, influenced by role models vs. not influenced by others, and learning style conflicts vs. learning style suited to school structure).

Hilliard's (1976) model differentiates instructional strategies based upon two styles of learning—an analytical as opposed to a relational style. Hilliard's model can help teachers develop a sensitivity toward the various learners in the class-

TABLE 2-8   Cognitive Style Comparison

Field-Dependent Relational	Field-Independent Analytic
Students:	**Students:**
1. Perceive elements as part of a total picture.	1. Perceive elements as discrete from their background.
2. Do best on verbal tasks.	2. Do best on analytic tasks.
3. Learn material that has a human social content and that is characterized by fantasy and humor.	3. Learn material that is inanimate and impersonal more easily.
4. Performance influenced by authority figure's expression of confidence or doubt.	4. Performance not greatly affected by the opinions of others.

Source: James Anderson. 1988. "Cognitive Styles and Multicultural Populations." *Journal of Teacher Education* 39: 6.

Teacher focus on:	**Teacher focus on:**
1. Creativity.	1. Conformity.
2. Memory for essence.	2. Memory for specific facts.
3. Global views.	3. Atomistic views.
4. Divergent thinking.	4. Convergent thinking.
5. Expressive.	5. Controlled.
6. Meanings are contextual.	6. Meanings are universal.
7. Indirect.	7. Direct.
8. Holistic.	8. Linear.
9. Inductive.	9. Deductive.
10. Evolving.	10. Constancy.
11. People-oriented.	11. Object-oriented.

Source: A. G. Hilliard, III. 1976. *Alternatives to IQ Testing: An Approach to the Identification of Gifted Minority Children* as cited in J. Hale-Benson, 1982. *Black Children: Their Roots, Culture, and Learning Styles.* Baltimore, MD: Johns Hopkins Unversity Press.

room and the need for individualistic, multicultural instruction—that is, instruction that is sufficiently varied, in which students have an opportunity to exhibit their cognitive dispositions. We will draw extensively on the analytical–relational conceptualization in our analysis of when to use each of the instructional models. Indeed, each chapter that follows will include a table that conceptually describes the relative strengths and weaknesses of an instructional model vis-à-vis the analytical and relational modes.

It is important to note that we are not saying that if a teacher works predominantly with African American students that the teacher should use only teaching strategies that foster field-dependent student dispositions. Our point is that by knowing that students are different, the teacher purposefully varies instruction to draw upon student strengths and develop student weaknesses in ways that reflect intentionality—the teacher knows the purpose of the instructional strategy and how that strategy will work to the benefit of all students.

Our own classifications have been adapted from Anderson (1988) and Hilliard (1976) and are further extended based upon selected research findings that have emerged during the past 10 years. Table 2.9 presents our classification of the cultural groups analyzed in this chapter and their cognitive style dispositions—field sensitive/dependent or field independent. Table 2.10 consists of our illustration, with examples of cognitive style characteristics, of the research findings of field-sensitive and field-independent learners. Notice that for each column of learners, a "disposition to be" descriptor is identified. This descriptor suggests that individuals often fall on a continuum between the two extremes of field sensitivity–field independent or relational–analytical. This illustration should not be interpreted literally as two opposite extremes. Once again, all learners, regardless of their racial or gender affiliation, have acquired, through experience, other cognitive style characteristics and utilize these characteristics throughout the continuum of field sensitivity–field independence.

Numerous efforts have been made to help teachers individualize instruction and develop instrumentation to facilitate the teaching–learning process. The instruments designed to identify learning style preferences are numerous and exist to help teachers identify how individual students learn. Each of the instruments helps assess a variety of learning styles and provides a profile of the student's strengths and weaknesses. Appendix A provides a listing and brief description of the learning-style instruments available to teachers. The data

TABLE 2-9 Cultural Group Classification by Cognitive Style

Field Sensitive	Field Independent
■ Hispanic Americans	■ European American males
■ African Americans	■ Asian Americans
■ European American females	■ Native Americans
■ Recent Asian American immigrants	■ Other cultural groups with a high degree of assimilation

TABLE 2-10 Cognitive Style Differences

Field Sensitive	Field Independent
Traditional Child-Rearing	**Modern Child-Rearing**
Non-Western Styles	**Western Styles**
Disposition to be:	Disposition to be:

Field Sensitive	Field Independent
■ Relationship-oriented	■ Task-oriented
■ A processor of information using kinetic/tactile and/or aural senses	■ A processor of information using the auditory senses
■ Person-oriented	■ Object-oriented
■ Interested in viewing reality or phenomena in a global manner	■ Interested in viewing reality or phenomena in parts or components of a whole
■ Interested in concrete/tangible reality	■ Interested in abstractions or ideas
■ Responsive to the use of role models	■ Uninterested in learning through the use of role models
■ Group-oriented in behavior	■ Individually oriented in behavior
■ Effective in collaborative relationships	■ Effective in competitive relationships
■ Socially oriented	■ Not as socially oriented
■ Interested in interpersonal thoughts and values	■ Interested in introspective thoughts and values
■ Relationally and affectively oriented	■ Rationally and analytically oriented
■ Motivated by academic material that uses humor and has a social context	■ Motivated by academic material that is inanimate and impersonal
■ Sensitive to the outside environment and easily distracted	■ Reflective—long attention and concentration span
■ Oriented toward others	■ Oriented toward self
■ Motivated by lessons that utilize collaboration, oral discussions, direct instruction, hands-on learning, and personalized subject matter	■ Motivated by lessons that utilize concept attainment and development, long-term memory processes, and trial-and-error learning
■ Interested in achievement as it reflects the group	■ Interested in achievement as it reflects the self through standardized measures
■ Motivated by holistic approaches to learning	■ Motivated by linear, sequential approaches to learning
■ Effective at oral learning experiences	■ Effective at visual-spatial learning experiences

Source: J. A. Anderson. 1988. Cognitive Styles and Multicultural Populations. *Journal of Teacher Education* 39: 2–9, A. G. Hilliard, III. 1976. *Alternatives to IQ Testing: An Approach to the Identification of Gifted Minority Children*, M. Ramirez, III, and A. Castaneda. 1974. *Cultural Democracy, Bicognitive Development and Education*. New York: Academic Press.

derived from these instruments can help in identifying student style preferences, creating instructional strategies that are congruent with student learning styles, and choosing instructional models that not only match student learning preferences but also help enhance the academic and social skills needed by all students.

IMPLICATIONS FOR CLASSROOM PRACTICE

In the previous sections of this chapter, we provided the reader with a synopsis of selected research findings for women and cultural groups. This synopsis provided data that were both unique to and common among the various groups examined. We found that women and most cultural groups tend to be field dependent/sensitive in their cognitive styles, more group rather than individually oriented, more sensitive to the social environment around them, and more responsive to adult role models. Additionally, these cultural groups tended to be less competitive, less sensitive to spatial incursions by others, less comfortable in trial-and-error situations, and less interested in the details of nonsocial tasks (Ramirez, 1982). The question that most classroom teachers may now ask would be: "What do all of these findings mean to me in working with diverse student populations?" The question is appropriate in terms of how these findings can affect classroom practice.

The first implication that can be drawn from our previous discussion relates to the attitudes and expectations teachers may have toward culturally diverse learners. When teachers misunderstand (or fail to understand!) the cultural behaviors, nonverbal cues, and verbal interactions of culturally diverse students, they sell such students short. This underestimation of intellectual power and potential, failure to challenge young people's minds, and the ridiculous labels placed upon students do irreparable harm. Teachers who are unaware or unappreciative of the rich cultural and cognitive backgrounds that diverse students bring to the classroom underestimate students' cognitive potential, academic achievement, and complex language abilities. Through his research contrasting African and African American cultures with European and European American cultures, Hilliard (1992) found that teachers who had low expectations for students would slow the pace of instruction, fragment instruction, and fail to offer conceptually oriented instruction. Hilliard (1992) elaborates:

> Thus, we see that it is not the learning style of the child that prevents the child from learning; it is the perception by the teacher of the child's style as a sign of incapacity that causes the teacher to reduce the quality of instruction offered (p. 373).

The second implication we can draw from the research relates to the need for teachers to acquire a repertoire of instructional models for use in their classrooms. To identify an instructional model for use in teaching a lesson is of little value unless that model is specifically appropriate in teaching the lesson objectives. Teachers must have a repertoire of models to draw from rather than rely solely on one teaching approach—which is often the way they were taught. The teacher of the future must be skilled in using several instructional models in order to accommodate the diverse student cognitive styles in a classroom. By varying the instructional model, the teacher can be more assured the students will have an opportunity to "play to" their learning strengths. Further, future teachers must provide students with opportunities to learn through the use of alternative cognitive styles—some with which students have had much practical experience, and others with which students have had little or no practical experience.

As educators, our responsibility is not only to help youngsters experience and learn about new phenomena, but to also help fashion new ideas and to assist youngsters in discovering their own intellectual abilities. Through the use of alternative instructional models (which are presented in a step-by-step, deliberate manner) students will have access to multiple learning experiences that provide them with new learning approaches and the corresponding intellectual skills. By becoming better informed about their own learning/cognitive styles, students will increase their ability to develop their total intellectual potential. We see a real value in helping students identify and understand their dominant and supporting styles of learning. Through such a process, and the corresponding explanation of why the teacher is approaching learning in a specific manner, the student will be able to recognize the relationship between what is to be learned and how such a study is to be approached.

The consideration of various student learning styles leads to another implication that calls for new ways to organize and implement learning for youngsters. The alternative teaching approaches, which this text emphasizes, foster the cognitive style dispositions of women and cultural groups such as oral discussion, collaborative learning, interpersonal situations and relationships, hands-on learning, laboratory work, and projects that involve individuals and/or groups more directly in their own learning. Education is not something teachers *do to* students; it is, instead, something teachers do *with them*. Good teachers learn as they teach because they become intellectually engaged with the students.

A final implication that arises from the research findings emphasizes learning within a natural, rich environment. When students learn in ways that are natural for them, a number of positive outcomes result—increased academic achievement, increased social acceptance by others, improved self-concept, an enhanced (and more positive) feeling toward the notion of learning, increased creative energy, increased self-direction, and improved basic skill development (Dunn and Dunn, 1979; Olstad et al., 1981; Saracho and Spodek, 1984; Shade, 1984). When teachers utilize a combination of visual, auditory, and kinesthetic modes, all students learn more easily. Although each of us exhibits a preferred learning style, students who learn through more than one learning modality develop richer understandings of new concepts and acquire a larger repertoire of academic and social skills. When any one of us is in the process of acquiring either new information or new skills, we learn by using alternative learning modalities. In fact, many of us use "coaches" to help us learn new skills in such activities as golfing, sewing, cooking, playing bridge, or painting. Because we practice this principle in our personal lives, it is time we begin utilizing this same principle in our professional lives—we will return to this idea in Chapter 12.

Care must be taken by the reader to critically utilize the concepts and ideas discussed in this chapter. That is, the ideas are tools to help in the creation of individualized classroom environments—not facile labels to classify whole groups of people. No cognitive style is better or worse than any other style. The only judgment that can be made is that different cognitive styles exist because of the multiplicity of cultural influences and personal dispositions. Cultural groups and male and female students do learn differently from one another (the research supports this). However, individuals within each group learn differently mainly because of either their involvement within the mainstream culture or the complex child-rearing practices they experience within the "home" culture in which they grow up.

All youngsters can learn, but they need to be taught in ways that warrant them as learners so they can more fully achieve their potential. By varying their instruction and recognizing the intellectual gifts of the learners, teachers can be more assured that each student's needs are being met. An important educational initiative for the classroom teacher is to: recognize and implement what is known from the research, acquire a repertoire of instructional alternatives to be used with youngsters, and organize and implement a system of individualization in order to better serve America's culturally diverse student populations. Mike Rose (1995), in his description of successful teachers in diverse cultural settings, powerfully reinforces this perspective:

> But two things seemed to hold across classrooms [in multicultural settings]. First, a teacher's authority came from multiple sources—knowledge, care, the construction of safe and respectful space, solidarity with students' background—rather than solely from age or role. Though there were times when our teachers asserted authority in a direct and unilateral way, in general, authority was not expressed or experienced as a blunt exercise of power. As one of Stephanie Terry's first-graders put it, "She doesn't fuss a lot."
>
> The second thing to note was that even in classrooms that were run in a relatively traditional manner, authority was distributed. In various ways, students contributed to the flow of events, shaped the direction of discussion, became authorities on their own experience and on the work they were doing. Think of Stephanie Terry's students reporting on their observations of the tree frog and hermit crab and Michelle Taigue's Navajo and Hopi students explaining slang and dialect on the reservation. There were multiple pathways of authority, multiple opportunities for members of the class to assume authority. And since authority and the generation of knowledge are intimately connected—those who can speak affect what is known—there were multiple opportunities to shape the knowledge emerging in the classroom (pp. 414–415).

CONCLUSION

Most of the current literature in leadership and in organizational theory emphasizes a new type of worldview. Every few hundred years the world begins a transformation wherein society rearranges its values; its views of reality; its social, political, and economic structures; its incorporation of peoples; and its manner of conducting business. We are in the midst of such a process—a transformation of the world's scientific, educational, and political paradigms. One of the most noticeable of these transformations is that historically disenfranchised groups (that is, women, Native Americans, Africans, Asians, and Hispanics) are now seeking to play a more active role in setting a direction for the global, economic society. They want to be included, not excluded!

As a consequence, a new set of demands is being placed upon schools to provide and produce a workforce that meets the demands of an international society (Drucker, 1993; Kanter, 1989; Toffler, 1990). In discussions at national and international conferences, and in the literature of sociology, management, and political science, critical characteristics are identified as being required by this new workforce. Individuals in this society will need to:

1. Value diversity in the workplace both in terms of the primary characteristics of diversity (for example, age, gender, race, physically challenged) and in terms of diversity of thought.
2. Exhibit a willingness to continue learning and growing throughout their lives.
3. Value collaborative, team-oriented work relationships.
4. Function in consensus-reaching structures rather than hierarchical, bureaucratic structures.
5. Exhibit a willingness to focus on relationship-oriented behavior by which individuals are empowered in the decision-making process.
6. Think globally in the use of knowledge, skills, and attitudes.
7. Exhibit knowledge and the use of the various forms of technology (that is, computers, videotapes, distance learning, and so on) to communicate, learn, and work.
8. Function in a more personal rather than formal manner in interactions with others.
9. Energize others through charisma, knowledge, and conviction.
10. Empower others to function in creative and innovative ways to perform work and/or discover new ways of working.

Ironically, many of these same traits are similar to the qualities attributed to women and the various cultural groups in our society. The characteristics summarized in the "Review of Related Research" section illustrate what is needed by this new society: the ability to accept and appreciate cultural and gender diversity; the ability to conceptualize problems in both a whole and linear, sequential manner; the ability to function in cooperative work teams that value interaction and alternatives; and the ability to utilize kinesthetic/tactile, hands-on learning and experimentation. Such skills, dispositions, and capacities need to not only be developed and enhanced among women and the disenfranchised cultural groups of society, but be promoted and developed within our total society.

If our citizens are to be contributing members in this knowledge society, educators will need to encourage student participation, share information and power, enhance student self-worth, and energize student excitement in learning and being a critical player in this global society. These characteristics can be developed in our schools if we begin looking critically at what we do in schools and how we function with youngsters in their preparation for world participation. Let us now examine and apply the new instructional models that can help teachers develop the skills and attitudes needed by this new workforce so that they can discover and translate this new knowledge in the continuing development of our people and nation.

ⓇEFERENCES

Albas, D. D., K. W. McCluskey, and C. A. Albas. 1976. "Perception of the Emotional Content of Speech." *Journal of Cross-Cultural Psychology* 7: 481–490.

Anderson, J. A. 1988. "Cognitive Styles and Multicultural Populations." *Journal of Teacher Education* 39: 2–9.

Appleton, N. 1983. *Cultural Pluralism in Education: Theoretical Foundations.* New York: Longman.

Au, K., and A. Kawakami. 1985. "Research Currents: Talk Story and Learning to Read." *Language Arts* 62(4): 406–411.

Bailey, S. M. 1996. "Shortchanging Girls and Boys." *Educational Leadership* 53(8): 75–79.

Baker Miller, J. 1986. *Toward a New Psychology of Women* (2d ed.). Boston: Beacon.

Baxter Magolda, M. B. 1989. "Gender Differences in Cognitive Development: An Analysis of Cognitive Complexity and Learning Styles." *Journal of College Student Development* 30(3): 213–220.

———. 1990. "Gender Differences in Epistemological Development." *Journal of College Student Development* 31(4): 555–561.

Belenky, M. F., B. M. Clinchy, M. R. Goldberger, and J. M. Tarule. 1986. *Women's Ways of Knowing: The Development of Self, Voice, and Mind.* New York: Basic Books.

Benjamin, D. P., S. Chambers, and G. Reiterman. 1993. "A Focus on American Indian College Persistence." *Journal of American Indian Education* 32(2): 24–40.

Bennett, C. I. 1986. *Comprehensive Multicultural Education, Theory and Practice.* Boston: Allyn & Bacon.

Bert, C. R. G., and M. Bert. 1992. *The Native American: An Exceptionality in Education and Counseling.* ERIC Document Reproduction Service No. ED 351 168.

Boykin, A. W. 1994. "Harvesting Culture and Talent: African-American Children." Pp. 324–371 in J. Spencer (ed.), *Achievement and Achievement Motives.* Boston: W. H. Freeman.

Brewer, A. 1977. "An Indian Education." *Integrated Education* 15: 21–23.

Bryant, H. W. 1986. "An Investigation into the Effectiveness of Two Strategy Training Approaches on the Reading Achievement of Grade One Native Indian Children." Unpublished doctoral dissertation. Vancouver: University of British Columbia.

Cabezas, A. 1981. *Early Childhood Development in Asian and Pacific American Families: Families in Transition.* San Francisco: Asian.

Carter, T. P., and M. L. Chatfield. 1986. "Effective Bilingual Schools: Implications for Policy and Practice." *American Journal of Education* 95(1): 200–232.

Clayton, J. B. 1996. *Your Land, My Land: Children in the Process of Acculturation.* Portsmouth, NH: Heinemann.

Cohen, R. A. 1969. "Conceptual Styles, Culture Conflict, and Nonverbal Tests of Intelligence." *American Anthropologist* 71: 838–856.

Cooper, G. C. 1987. "Right Hemispheric Dominance, Holistic Cognitive Style, and Black Language." Pp. 61–86 in J. A. Anderson (ed.), *Benjamin E. Mays Monograph Series* 1(1).

Cordova, F. 1983. *Filipinos: Forgotten Asian Americans.* Dubuque, IA: Kendell and Hunt.

Cox, B., and M. Ramirez III. 1981. "Cognitive Styles: Implications for Multiethnic Education." Pp. 61–71 in J. Banks et al. (eds.),

Education in the 80s: Multiethnic Education. Washington, DC: National Education Association.

Damico, S. B. 1983. "The Two Worlds of School: Differences in the Photographs of Black and White Adolescents." Paper presented at annual meeting of American Educational Research Association, Montreal.

Davis, J. K., and B. M. Frank. 1979. "Learning and Memory of Field Independent-Dependent Individuals." *Journal of Research in Personality* 13: 469–479.

De La Rosa, D., and C. E. Maw. 1990. *Hispanic Education: A Statistical Portrait 1990.* Washington, DC: National Council of La Rosa.

Delgado-Gaitan, C. 1992. "School Matters in the Mexican-American Home: Socializing Children to Education." *American Educational Research Journal* 29(3): 495–513.

Dinges, N. C., and A. R. Hollenbeck. 1978. "Field-Dependence-Independence in Navajo Children." *International Journal of Psychology* 13: 215–220.

Drucker, Peter F. 1993. *Post-Capitalist Society.* New York: HarperCollins.

Dunn, R. 1993. "Learning Styles of the Multiculturally Diverse." *Emergency Librarian* 20(4): 24–30.

———, and K. Dunn. 1979. "Using Learning Style Data to Develop Student Prescriptions." Pp. 109–122 in National Association of Secondary School Principals, *Student Learning Styles: Diagnosing and Prescribing Programs.* Reston, VA: NASSP.

Dunn, R., J. Gemake, F. Jalali, R. Zenhausern, P. Quinn, and J. Spiridakis. 1990. "Cross-Cultural Differences in Learning Styles of Elementary-Age Students from Four Ethnic Backgrounds." *Journal of Multicultural Counseling and Development* 18(2): 68–93.

Enright, D. S. 1987. "Cognitive Style and First Language Background in Second Language Test Performance." *TESOL Quarterly* 21: 565–569.

Flaugher, R. L., and D. A. Roch. 1977. "Patterns of Ability Factors Among Four Ethnic Groups." Research Memorandum No. 7. Princeton, NJ: Educational Testing Service.

Garcia, E. 1991. "Effective Instruction for Language Minority Students: The Teacher." *Journal of Education* 173(2): 130–141.

Gibson, M. A. 1987. "The School Performance of Immigrant Minorities: A Comparative View." *Anthropology and Education Quarterly* 18(4): 262–275.

Gilbert, S., and G. Gay. 1985. "Improving the Success in School of Poor Black Children." *Phi Delta Kappan* 67(2): 133–137.

Gilligan, C. 1982. *In a Different Voice: Psychological Theory and Women's Development.* Cambridge, MA: Harvard University Press.

Goldstein, R. 1971. *Black Life and Culture in the United States.* New York: Thomas Crowell.

Grantham-Campbell, M. 1992. "Successful Alaska Native Students: Implications 500 Years After Columbus." Paper presented at the meeting of the American Anthropological Association, San Francisco (December).

Guild, P., and S. Garger. 1985. *Marching to Different Drummers.* Alexandria, VA: Association for Supervision and Curriculum Development.

Guttentag, M. 1972. "Negro-White Differences in Children's Movement." *Perceptual and Motor Skills* 35: 435–436.

Hale-Benson, J. 1982. *Black Children: Their Roots, Culture, and Learning Styles.* Baltimore, MD: Johns Hopkins University Press.

———. 1986. *Black Children: Their Roots, Culture, and Learning Styles* (rev. ed.). Baltimore, MD: Johns Hopkins University Press.

Hall, E. 1989. "Unstated Features of the Cultural Context of Learning." *Educational Forum* 54(1): 21–34.

Halverson, B. 1976. "Cognitive Style of Preschool Seminole Indian Children." Unpublished doctoral dissertation, Florida State University, Tallahassee.

Hansen, L. 1984. "Field Dependence-Independence and Language Testing: Evidence from Six Pacific Island Cultures." *TESOL Quarterly* 18: 311–324.

Hansen-Strain, L. 1987. "Cognitive Style and First Language Background in Second Language Test Performance." *TESOL Quarterly* 21: 565–569.

Harry, B. 1992. *Cultural Diversity, Families, and the Special Education System.* New York: Teachers College Press.

Herring, R. D. 1989. "Counseling Native American Children." *Implications for Elementary School Guidance and Counseling* 23(April): 272–281.

Hilliard, A. G., III. 1976. *Alternatives to IQ Testing: An Approach to the Identification of Gifted*

Minority Children. Final report to the California State Department of Education.

————. 1989. "Teachers and Cultural Styles in a Pluralistic Society." *NEA Today* 1: 65–69.

————. 1992. "Behavioral Style, Culture, and Teaching and Learning." *Journal of Negro Education* 61(3): 370–373.

Hodges, L. 1996. "Blood Ties." *New York Times* (July 19): A15.

Howard, B. C. 1987. *Learning to Persist/Persisting to Learn*. Washington, DC: Mid-Atlantic Center for Race Equity, American University.

Howe, C. 1994. "Improving the Achievement of Hispanic Students." *Educational Leadership* 51(8): 42–44.

Hunter, M. 1984. "Knowing, Teaching and Supervising." Pp. 175–176 in P. L. Hosford (ed.), *Using What We Know About Teaching*. Alexandria, VA: Association for Supervision and Curriculum Development.

Kagan, J. 1966. "Reflection-Impulsivity: The Generality and Dynamics of Conceptual Tempo." *Journal of Abnormal Psychology* 71: 17–24.

Kagan, S., and R. Buriel. 1977. "Field Dependence-Independence and Mexican-American Culture and Education." Pp. 279–328 in J. L. Martinez, Jr. (ed.), *Chicano Psychology*. Orlando, FL: Academic Press.

Kagan, S., and G. P. Knight. 1981. "Social Motives Among Anglo American and Mexican American Children: Experimental and Projective Measures." *Journal of Research in Personality* 15(1): 93–106.

Kagan, S., and M. C. Madsen. 1971. "Cooperation and Competition of Mexican, Mexican-American, and Anglo-American Children of Two Ages Under Four Instruction Sets." *Developmental Psychology* 5: 32–39.

Kagan, S., and G. L. Zahn. 1976. "Field Dependence and the School Achievement Gap Between Anglo-American and Mexican-American Children." *Journal of Educational Psychology* 67: 643–650.

Kanter, R. M. 1989. *When Giants Learn to Dance*. New York: Simon & Schuster.

Keefe, J. W. 1979. "Learning Styles: An Overview." Pp. 1–17 in *Student Learning Styles: Diagnosing and Prescribing Programs*. Reston, VA: National Association of Secondary School Principals.

Keefe, S. E., and A. M. Padilla. 1987. *Chicano Ethnicity*. Albuquerque, NM: University of New Mexico Press.

Kelly, J. A. 1984. "Influence of Culture, Gender and Academic Experience on Cognitive Style." Unpublished dissertation, Vanderbilt University, Memphis, TN.

Keogh, B. K., M. F. Welles, and A. Weiss. 1972. "Field Dependence-Independence and Problem-Solving Styles of Preschool Children." Technical Report. Los Angeles: University of California.

Knight, G. P., and S. Kagan. 1977. "Development of Prosocial and Competitive Behaviors in Anglo-American and Mexican-American Children." *Child Development* 48(4): 1385–1394.

Kochman, T. 1972. *Rappin' and Stylin' Out: Communication in Urban Black America*. Urbana, IL: University of Illinois Press.

Kolb, D. 1984. *Experiential Learning*. Englewood Cliffs, NJ: Prentice-Hall.

Ladson-Billings, G. 1990. "Like Lightning in a Bottle: Attempting to Capture the Pedagogical Excellence of Successful Teachers of Black Students." *International Journal of Qualitative Studies in Education* 3(4): 335–344.

————. 1992. "Liberatory Consequences of Literacy: A Case of Culturally Relevant Instruction for African American Students." *Journal of Negro Education* 61(3): 378–391.

LaFrance, M., and C. Mayo. 1976. "Racial Differences in Gaze Behavior During Conversation." *Journal of Personality and Social Psychology* 33: 258–285.

LaFromboise, T., P. Dauphinais, and P. Lujan. 1981. "Verbal Indicators of Insincerity as Perceived by American Indians." *Journal of Nonwhite Concerns in Personnel and Guidance* 9: 87–94.

Laosa, L. M. 1982. "School, Occupation, Culture, and Family: The Impact of Parental Schooling on the Parent-Child Relationship." *Journal of Educational Psychology* 74(6): 791–827.

Loftin, J. D. 1989. "Anglo American Jurisprudence and the Native American Tribal Quest for Religious Freedom." *American Indian Culture and Research Journal* 13(1): 1–52.

Longstreet, W. S. 1978. *Aspects of Ethnicity*. New York: Teachers College Press.

Lucas, T., R. Henze, and R. Donato. 1990. "Promoting the Success of Latino Language-Minority Students: An Exploratory

Study of Six High Schools." *Harvard Educational Review* 60(3): 315–340.

Macias, C. J. 1989. "American Indian Academic Success: The Role of Indigenous Learning Strategies." *Journal of American Indian Education* (August, special issue): 43–52.

Matthews, W. 1981. "Race- and Sex-Related Differences in High School Mathematics Enrollment." Doctoral dissertation, University of Chicago, 1980. *Dissertation Abstracts International* 41: 3934A.

McCaulley, M. H., G. P. MacDaid, and R. E. Kainz. 1985. "Estimated Frequencies of the MBTI Types." *Journal of Psychological Type* 9: 3–8.

McShane, D. 1980. "A Review of Scores of American Indian Children on the Weschler Intelligence Scales." *White Cloud Journal* 1: 3–10.

Messick, S. 1970. "The Criterion Problem in the Evaluation of Instruction: Assessing Possible, Not Just Intended, Outcomes." Pp. 183–202 in M. C. Wittrock and G. D. E. Wiley (eds.), *The Evaluation of Instruction: Issues and Problems*. New York: Holt.

Moll, L. C. 1988. "Some Key Issues in Teaching Latino Students." *Language Arts* 65(5): 465–472.

More, A. J. 1990. "Learning Styles of Native Americans and Asians." Paper presented at the annual meeting of the American Psychological Association, Boston. ERIC Document Reproduction Service No. ED 330 535.

Morgan, H. 1981. "Factors Concerning Cognitive Development and Learning Differentiation Among Black Children." In A. E. Harrison (ed.), *Conference on Empirical Research in Black Psychology* 6: 14–22.

National Foundation for Women Business Owners. 1994. *Styles of Success: The Thinking and Management Styles of Women and Men Entrepreneurs*. Washington, DC: National Foundation for Women Business Owners (July).

Obiakor, F. E. 1992. "A Cultural Ecology of Competence Among Inner-City Blacks." Pp. 45–60 in M. Spencer, G. Brookins, and W. Allen (eds.), *Beginnings: The Social and Affective Development of Black Children*. Hillsdale, NJ: Lawrence Erlbaum Associates.

Ogbu, J. U. 1978. *Minority Education and Caste: The American System in Cross-Cultural Perspective*. New York: Academic Press.

———. 1983. "Cultural Discontinuities and Schooling." *Anthropology and Education Quarterly* 13: 290–307.

———. 1987. "Variability in Minority School Performance: A Problem in Search of an Explanation." *Anthropology and Education Quarterly* 18(4): 312–334.

———. 1989. "The Individual in Collective Adaptation: A Framework for Focusing on Academic Underperformance and Dropping Out Among Involuntary Minorities." Pp. 181–204 in L. Weis, E. Farran, and H. Petrie (eds.), *Dropouts from School: Issues, Dilemmas, and Solutions*. Albany, NY: State University of New York Press.

Olstad, R., J. Juarez, L. Davenport, and D. Haury. 1981. *Inhibitors to Achievement in Science and Mathematics by Ethnic Minorities*. Bethesda, MD: ERIC Document Reproduction Service No. ED 223 404.

Pang, V. 1990. "Asian-American Children: A Diverse Population." *Educational Forum* 55(1): 49–66.

———. 1995. "Asian Pacific American Students: A Diverse and Complex Population." Pp. 412–424 in J. Banks and C. Banks (eds.), *Handbook of Research on Multicultural Education*. New York: Macmillan.

Pease-Alvarez, L., E. Garcia, and P. Espinoza. 1991. "Effective Instruction for Language Minority Students: An Early Childhood Case Study." *Early Childhood Research Quarterly* 6(3): 347–363.

Philips, S. 1972. "Participant Structures and Communicative Competence: Warm Springs Children in Community and Classroom." Pp. 370–394 in C. Cazden, V. John, and D. Hymes (eds.), *Functions of Language in the Classroom*. New York: Teachers College Press.

———. 1983. *The Invisible Culture: Communication in Classroom and Community on the Warm Springs Indian Reservation*. New York: Longman.

———. 1993. *The Invisible Culture*. Prospect Heights, IL: Waveland Press.

Prom, S. E. 1982. "Salient Content and Cognitive Performance of Person- and Thing-Oriented Low Income Afro-American Children in Kindergarten and Second Grade." Doctoral dissertation, Howard University, Washington, DC.

Ramirez, M., III. 1973. "Cognitive Styles and Cultural Democracy in Education." *Social Science Quarterly* 53: 895–904.

———. 1982. "Cognitive Styles and Cultural Diversity." Paper presented at the annual meeting of the American Educational Research Association, New York City (May).

———. 1989b. "Pluralistic Education: A Bicognitive-Multicultural Model." *Clearinghouse Bulletin* 3: 4–5.

———, and A. Castaneda. 1974. *Cultural Democracy, Bicognitive Development and Education.* New York: Academic Press.

Ramirez, M., III, and D. R. Price-Williams. 1974. "Cognitive Style of Three Ethnic Groups in the U.S." *Journal of Cross-Cultural Psychology* 5(2): 212–219.

Roberts, S. 1993. *Who We Are.* New York: Times Books.

Rollman, S. A. 1978. "The Sensitivity of Black and White Americans to Nonverbal Cues of Prejudice." *Journal of Social Psychology* 105: 73–77.

Rose, M. 1995. *Possible Lives: The Promise of Public Education in America.* New York: Houghton-Mifflin.

Rumbaut, R., and K. Ima. 1988. "The Adaptation of Southeast Asian Refugee Youth: A Comparative Study." Report prepared for the U.S. Department of Health and Human Services, Family Support Administration, Office of Refugee Resettlement, Washington, DC.

Sadker, M., and D. Sadker. 1994. *Failing at Fairness.* New York: Charles Scribner's Sons.

Saracho, O. N., and B. Spodek. 1984. *Cognitive Style and Children's Learning: Individual Variation in Cognitive Processes.* ERIC Document Reproduction Service No. ED 247 037.

Schimizzi, N. V. 1985. *Mathematics Achievement Scores in High School: Are They Related to the Way We Teach in the Earlier Grades?* ERIC Document Reproduction Service No. ED 265 012.

Shade, B. J. 1981. "Racial Variation in Perceptual Differentiation." *Perceptual and Motor Skills* 52: 243–248.

———. 1984. "Afro-American Patterns of Cognition: A Review of the Research." Paper presented at annual meeting of American Educational Research Association, New Orleans, LA.

———. 1989. "The Influence of Perceptual Development on Cognitive Style: Cross Ethnic Comparisons." *Early Child Development and Care* 51: 137–155.

———, and P. A. Edwards. 1987. "Ecological Correlates of the Educative Style of Afro-American Children." *Journal of Negro Education* 86: 88–99.

Shanker, A. 1996. "Succeeding in School." *New Republic* (July 1): 17.

Shutiva, C. 1991. "Creativity Difference Between Reservation and Urban American Indians." *Journal of American Indian Education* 31(1): 33–52.

Slaughter-DeFoe, D. T., K. Nakagawa, R. Takanishi, and D. J. Johnson. 1990. "Toward Cultural/Ecological Perspectives on Schooling and Achievement in African- and Asian-American Children." *Child Development* 61: 363–383.

Slavin, R. E. 1977. *Student Team Learning Techniques: Narrowing the Achievement Gap, Between the Races.* Report No. 228. Baltimore, MD: Johns Hopkins University, Center for the Study of Social Organization of Schools.

———, and E. Oickle. 1981. "Effects of Cooperative Learning Teams on Student Achievement and Race Relations: Treatment by Race Interactions." *Sociology of Education* 54: 174–180.

Smith, D. M., and D. Kolb. 1986. *Users Guide for the Learning Style Inventory: A Manual for Teachers and Trainers.* Boston: McBer.

Soldier, L. 1985. "To Soar with Eagles: Enculturation and Acculturation of Indian Children." *Childhood Education* 61: 185–191.

———. 1989. "Cooperative Learning and the Native American Student." *Phi Delta Kappan* 71(2): 161–163.

Sternberg, R. J. 1994. "Commentary: Reforming School Reform: Comments on Multiple Intelligences: The Theory in Practice." *Teachers College Record* 95(4): 561–568.

Suarez, Z. E. 1993. "Cuban Americans: From Golden Exiles to Social Undesirables." Pp. 164–176 in H. P. McAdoo (ed.), *Family Ethnicity: Strength in Diversity.* Newbury Park, CA: Sage.

Suzuki, B. H. 1983. "The Education of Asian and Pacific Americans: An Introductory Overview." In D. T. Nakanishi and M. Hirano-Nakanishi (eds.), *Education of Asian and Pacific Americans: Historical Perspectives and Prescriptions for the Future.* Phoenix, AZ: Oryx Press.

Swisher, K., and D. Deyhle. 1987. "Styles of Learning and Learning Styles: Educational Conflicts for American Indian/Alaskan Native Youth." *Journal of Multilingual and Multicultural Development* 8(4): 350.

———. 1989. "The Styles of Learning Are Different, but the Teaching Is Just the Same: Suggestions for Teachers of American Indian Youth." *Journal of American Indian Education* (August, special issue): 1–14.

Tafoya, T. 1982. "Coyote Eyes: Native Cognition Styles." *Journal of American Indian Education* 21(2): 21–33.

Toffler, Alvin. 1990. *Powershift.* New York: Bantam Books.

Tooker, E. 1983. *The Development of Political Organization in Native North America.* Washington, DC: American Ethnological Society.

Tuck, K., and A. Boykin. 1989. "Verve Effects: The Relationship of Task Performance to Stimulus Preference and Variability in Low-Income Black and White Children." Pp. 84–85 in A. Harrison (ed.), *The Eleventh Conference on Empirical Research in Black Psychology.* Washington, DC: NIMH.

Utley, C. A. 1983. "A Cross-Cultural Investigation of Field-Independent/Field-Dependent as a Psychological Variable in Menominees Native American and Euro-American Grade School Children." Madison, WI: Wisconsin Center for Education and Research.

Vasquez, J. A. 1991. "Cognitive Style and Academic Attainment." Pp. 163–179 in J. Lynch, C. Modgil, and S. Modgil (eds.), *Cultural Diversity and the Schools: Consensus and Controversy.* London: Falconer Press.

Vernon, P. A., D. N. Jackson, and S. Messick. 1988. "Cultural Influences on Patterns of Abilities in North America." Pp. 208–231 in S. H. Irvine and J. W. Berry (eds.), *Human Abilities in Cultural Context.* Cambridge, MA: Cambridge University Press.

Vernon, P. E. 1984. "Abilities and Achievements of Ethnic Groups in Canada with Special Reference to Canadian Natives and Orientals." Pp. 382–395 in R. Samuda, J. Berry, and M. Laferriere (eds.), *Multiculturalism in Canada: Social and Educational Perspectives.* Toronto: Allyn & Bacon.

Witkin, H. A., R. B. Dyk, H. F. Faterson, D. R. Goodenough, and S. A. Karp. 1962. *Psychological Differentiation.* New York: Wiley.

Witkin, H. A., C. A. Moore, D. R. Goodenough, and P. W. Cox. 1977. "Field-Dependent and Field-Independent Cognitive Style and Their Educational Implications." *Review of Educational Research* 47: 1–64.

Worthley, K. M. 1987. "Learning Style Factor of Field Dependence/Independence and Refugee Students." Master's Thesis, University of Wisconsin, Stout (July).

Yoshiwara, F. M. 1983. "Shattering Myths: Japanese American Educational Issues." P. 23 in D. T. Nakanishi and M. Hirano-Nakanishi (eds.), *Education of Asian and Pacific Americans: Historical Perspectives and Prescriptions for the Future.* Phoenix, AZ: Oryx.

Young, V. H. 1970. "Family and Childhood in a Southern Negro Community." *American Anthropologist* 72: 269–288.

———. 1974. "A Black American Socialization Pattern." *American Ethnologist* 1: 405–413.

Yu, A., and B. Bain. 1985. *Language, Social Class and Cognitive Style: A Comparative Study of Unilingual and Bilingual Education in Hong Kong and Alberta.* Hong Kong: Hong Kong Teachers' Association.

B

Effecting Instructional Model Usage

Instructional Models and the Planning Process

The following objectives are identified as targets in presenting the basic concepts of this chapter:

1. *To identify and describe what an instructional model is and how it can be used by teachers.*
2. *To identify and describe what is meant by an instructional model category.*
3. *To identify and briefly describe eight different instructional models.*
4. *To describe the purpose of instructional planning.*
5. *To differentiate between goals and objectives.*
6. *To differentiate between the cognitive, affective, and psychomotor learning domains.*
7. *To design objectives utilizing the different taxonomical learning levels.*

❶ NTRODUCTION

Do you recall when you first learned how to play golf, made an afghan for a family member, used a computer to be more productive at work, or played backgammon as a leisure-time activity? In each case, there was some critical information necessary to understand the new skills; there were specific cognitive and psychomotor skills you had to learn in order to apply the information previously learned; there were feelings elicited from applying the cognitive and psychomotor learning; and there were activities that helped you acquire a satisfactory level of proficiency. New tasks or skills are difficult to acquire because there is so much information to deal with, so many subskills to learn and apply, and so much practice required for satisfactory performance.

Two examples illustrate our point. Approximately 25 years ago, both of the authors of this text began learning how to play the game of golf. We say "began learning" because after all of these years, countless rounds of golf, and many thousands of dollars, we each continue to look for and seek the "perfect" round of golf. As we look back on our golfing odyssey, we learned some basic information about the game: its terminology, its rules and regulations, its means of scoring, and even a little about its history. In addition, we practiced how to

> *The way to real growth is not to become more powerful or more famous, but to become more human and more tolerant.*
>
> HELEN STEINER RICE

hold a golf club, how to either prevent a slice or promote a fade, how to prevent a hook or promote a draw, how to position the body and feet depending upon the club used, how to chip—getting the golf ball up and down to the hole, and how to putt, perhaps the most critical activity in lowering one's score. The information and skills needed to play the game effectively are complex—from head position, to keeping the left arm straight (if a right-handed golfer), to the follow-through. We learned that applying appropriate rules and skills is situational; the game requires constant learning, practice, and coaching.

Let's look at another example of acquiring information and skills to illustrate our point about the connection between learning, practice, and coaching—making an afghan. To make an afghan, the apprentice needs to know how to read and follow a pattern, how to differentiate the various types of pattern styles and yarn textures available, how to determine the different types of yarn (baby vs. wool vs. acrylic yarn), and how to choose between the different weights of yarn (3 oz. vs. 4 oz.). The information needed to make an afghan depends upon the type of afghan being made. In addition, there are various types of stitches that the apprentice needs to know and practice (for example, the chain stitch, the double or triple crochet stitch, and the shell stitch). Each pattern chosen calls for specific stitches to be used, and thus the need for higher levels of proficiency. As a side note, if you have ever made an afghan, whether for a twin- or king-size bed, you know from experience that the information and crocheting skills needed for success take much time, practice, patience, perseverance, and coaching. With information, skill, practice, and help from others, the results are astounding! Whether to play golf or make an afghan effectively, each task calls for the acquisition of information and skill, the use of logical thinking, some understanding of mathematical probability, and the application of all of this in some form of guided practice.

Similarly, information, practice, and coaching are absolutely requisite to learning alternative instructional models. The learner must acquire basic information about each model in order to understand how it operates; specific instructional skills relative to each model must be practiced in order to implement the model effectively. Once the various subskills are acquired, the learner must engage in a cycle of practice, coaching, and more practice before the knowledge and skills acquired previously can be used comfortably. Only through the application of this knowledge and the corresponding skills and steps inherent in each instructional model will each learner achieve some level of proficiency and make the model a part of an instructional repertoire.

Strategies for Teaching in a Diverse Society: Instructional Models presents eight teaching models that expand the instructional repertoire of teachers and enable teachers to create more culturally relevant instruction. To use the models, a teacher will need basic theoretical information about each model, technical skills relative to the effective use of each model, and opportunities to apply the knowledge and skills to everyday practice. The teacher also needs a substantial level of subject matter mastery. Good teachers know a lot about what they teach. For teachers of diverse student populations, this requirement is especially essential because they have to know how to adjust instruction based on the unique learning needs of students. Consider Ladson-Billings's (1994) account of one successful teacher of African American students:

On one particular day, when the students had finished reading a Greek myth about a princess, Devereaux asked, "How would you describe the princess?" Her question was designed to elicit responses about the princess's character, but the first student to respond began with a physical description. "She was beautiful, with long blond hair," said the student. Nowhere in the story was there a description that matched this response. "What makes you say that?" Devereaux asked. "Because that's the way princesses always are," the student replied. "I don't have long blond hair and neither does anyone else in here. Does that mean that none of us could be a princess?" Devereaux asked. The student and several others seemed resigned to the fact that that was the case. Devereaux feigned disbelief that they were unaware of black princesses.

Slowly, without fanfare, Devereaux walked to her bookshelf and selected a book, John Steptoe's *Mufaro's Beautiful Daughters* (1987), about two African sisters, one good and one evil. After reading the fourth graders the book, Devereaux asked how many students still believed that a princess had to have long blond hair. No one raised a hand (p. 92).

Knowing about the availability of additional resources or the applicability of ancillary concepts requires that teachers possess more than a superficial understanding of curriculum materials and disciplinary ideas. Teachers need depth in their content background in order to help ground the learning process for the students they teach. Ms. Devereaux exhibits such depth in the previous example.

❶ NSTRUCTIONAL MODELS AND FAMILIES

Learning an instructional model is, in many respects, very similar to learning to play golf or make an afghan. If you recall, one of the critical components of making an afghan was the utilization of patterns, whether commercially prepared or created by the afghan-maker. Without a pattern, blueprint, or outline, neither the afghan-maker nor the teacher will be able to achieve the desired ends. Similarly, the selection of an instructional model is critical because it is based upon the desired objective(s) of the teacher. Thus, the instructional procedures (the instructional model) for teaching a concept, academic content, and/or an academic or social skill will depend upon what the students are expected to learn as a result of the instructional model chosen by the teacher (see Figure 3.1).

When planning to cook lobster bouillabaisse, a chef does not use a recipe for sourdough bread; a blueprint for a log cabin home will not result in a brick colonial; and neither will use of an 18-foot runabout be appropriate to cross one of America's Great Lakes, even though a pilot has appropriate nautical maps. So, too, instructional models have varying purposes. Some are designed to organize information, others to develop critical thinking skills, and still others to help students work in a collaborative manner. The appropriate teacher instructional model will be determined based upon the student instructional objectives the teacher seeks to develop. The approach that teachers take in working with

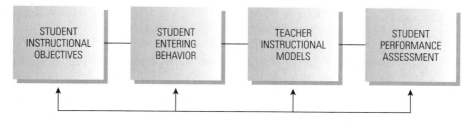

```
STUDENT          STUDENT          TEACHER          STUDENT
INSTRUCTIONAL ── ENTERING    ──  INSTRUCTIONAL ──  PERFORMANCE
OBJECTIVES       BEHAVIOR         MODELS           ASSESSMENT
```

FIGURE 3-1   Generic Teaching–Learning Model

students is dependent upon the teachers' thinking regarding the process of teaching, not just the content of lessons.

Content issues are receiving much more attention today because of the poor performance of American students on international comparative tests. Content, as Ladson-Billings (1994) poignantly illustrates, is extremely important, but how teachers present and organize content also has significant implications for how students learn. If the American public—specifically corporate America—wants students to engage in critical thinking, not just recite facts, then they need students who have been engaged in solving problems and thinking through the complex nature of ideas.

The critical-thinking skills that teachers seek to foster will occur only if they have identified what is expected from students (for example, the recall of facts, creative thinking, organization of information, team-generated solutions, problem-solving, critical thinking, collaboration, and so on). As Figure 3.1 illustrates, once instructional objectives are identified, a corresponding teacher instructional model is matched to develop the intended student instructional objectives. The instructional models presented in this book cover a wide range of potential instructional objectives (for example, recalling and organizing information, utilizing critical thinking, identifying and describing concepts and generalizations, or experiencing collaborative work environments). These instructional models have been chosen not only to help teachers recognize how to use new teaching approaches, but also to help them determine when to use such models as they relate to specific learner outcomes.

RESEARCH ON TEACHING MODELS

The Joyce and Weil Model

Joyce and Weil (1986, 1992) described approximately 20 models of teaching for use in the classroom. In their search for appropriate teaching strategies, they drew upon many sources: classroom practice, group process procedures, philosophers, psychologists, the military, and the ideas of other educators. Their conclusions led them to emphasize the need for varying approaches to teaching based upon identified student outcomes; the organizational framework for their applications were four families of teaching models: information processing, social interaction, behavioral, and personal.

Information Processing Family   This family emphasizes how students acquire and use information. The models in this family focus on recalling information, teaching concepts both deductively and inductively, and solving problems.

Social Interaction Family   This family emphasizes the relationships between individuals and groups in order to build more positive learning communities. The models in this family emphasize problem-solving approaches, cooperative learning procedures, and experiences in working through the democratic process.

Behavioral Family   This family emphasizes changing the behavior of students by utilizing behavioral psychology. The models in this family focus on training and therapeutic approaches in order to achieve specific behavioral changes.

Personal Family   This family emphasizes the development of each individual's talents and interests. The models in this family focus on personal growth and creative process approaches to individual fulfillment.

The Hanson, Silver, and Strong Model

Joyce and Weil's work may represent one of the more popular theoretical discussions concerning instructional models, but it most certainly is not the only perspective on how teachers present content to students. For example, Hanson, Silver, and Strong (1986), drawing from the psychological research of Myers (1962) and Jung (1971), developed four basic teaching styles that hinge upon the personality (learning-style) archetypes of individuals. As originally developed by Jung (1971), with modifications by Hanson, Silver, and Strong (1986), the following are the learning-style archetypes:

Sensing-Thinker   The sensing-thinker is characterized as good at working with and remembering facts and details; is realistic, practical, and matter-of-fact; tends to be results-oriented; approaches tasks in a logical and sequential fashion; and is interested in immediate and tangible outcomes.

Sensing-Feeler   The sensing-feeler is characterized as sympathetic, friendly, and interpersonally oriented; is sensitive to people's feelings; works for group harmony; prefers to learn about things that directly affect people's lives; makes judgments based upon personal likes and dislikes; and is spontaneous and open to impulses.

Intuitive-Thinker   The intuitive-thinker is characterized as theoretical, knowledge-oriented, and intellectual; is curious about abstractions and thought processes; tends to be logical, analytical, and impersonal; is able to organize and synthesize information; and retains large amounts of information.

Intuitive-Feeler   The intuitive-feeler is characterized as curious, imaginative, and creative; is concerned with beauty, symmetry, and form; is committed to values and artistic expression; approaches tasks in a variety of ways; and is interested in both the future and solving the problems of human beings.

According to Hanson, Silver, and Strong (1986) these four learning styles can be translated into four educational goals: mastery, understanding, synthesis, and involvement.

The teacher is the one who fosters the translation process, but the students are the ones who genuinely benefit from the teacher's efforts. With the *mastery* goal, the student is asked to remember and recall important information and skills. The major purpose of this goal is to have students develop a high level of competence in the basic skills—reading, mathematics, and the language arts. Further, this goal helps students with skills such as following directions, sequencing, and matching. It utilizes approaches that require practice by students, and the objectives for this goal emphasize previously presented concrete skills. The mastery goal is matched with the *sensing-thinking learning style*.

The *understanding* goal focuses on developing students' reasoning skills and helping them think critically about major ideas and issues. The main purpose of this goal is the development of higher-order thinking skills, and an understanding of concepts, patterns, and proof for ideas using different content vehicles. It utilizes approaches that require the processing of information into new forms or patterns. Further, this goal helps develop the skills of comparing and contrasting, hypothesizing, and the testing of alternative choices. The understanding goal is matched with the *intuitive-thinking learning style*.

The *synthesis* goal has as its major purpose either the reorganization of knowledge or the creation of new or original work and the application of all skill levels to new contexts. This goal utilizes approaches that call for a problem-solving style of thinking. Further, the synthesis goal helps develop problem-solving strategies that emphasize the thinking operations of defining a problem, generating alternative solutions, utilizing metaphors, and formulating conclusions. The synthesis goal is matched with the *intuitive-feeling learning style*.

Finally, the *involvement* goal has as its purpose the ability to find personal meaning and relevance in what is being learned. The major purposes of this goal are the development of a positive self-concept and healthy social relationships. This goal emphasizes the skills of introspecting, empathizing, evaluating, and decision making. The involvement goal is matched with the *sensing-feeling learning style*.

Hanson, Silver, and Strong (1986) connect each teaching model with a teaching family and thus with a specific learning style. A teaching model, a set of learning styles, and a set of curriculum objectives are all closely related in terms of the teaching–learning process. As we identified previously, the teacher needs to identify what outcomes are expected of the youngsters, and then use the appropriate teaching strategies to help students achieve the outcomes.

Out of all the approaches to the teaching–learning process—and there are many (Eggen and Kauchak, 1988; Gunter et al., 1990; Joyce and Weil, 1986, 1992)—the Hanson, Silver, and Strong (1986) approach makes the most sense in terms of understanding the teaching–learning process because it more directly connects the various elements of the instructional process.

Unfortunately, Hanson, Silver, and Strong (1986) fail to adequately address issues of diversity, especially as related to race and gender. In essence, both Joyce and Weil (1986, 1992) and Hanson, Silver, and Strong (1986) describe models of teaching, but an eclectic approach, similar to theirs, does little to help teachers choose which alternative model to use in multicultural situations (Donmoyer, 1996). They place an emphasis on what the learner (the individual) will learn (the outcomes), but they limit their discussion of the ways in which student diversity might influence teacher decision making.

The Lasley and Matczynski Model

Our own instructional model classification also uses four instructional categories. Drawing on the work of Hanson, Silver, and Strong (1986) and Joyce and Weil (1986, 1992), and building on the growing body of research on diversity, we attempt to classify the instructional models presented in this text around four broad categories. The four categories (*reasoning, reorganizing, remembering,* and *relating*) deal with the range of intellectual skills students must exhibit in order to experience success in schools composed of diverse student populations. Two instructional models are discussed within each of the four categories. The two instructional models are not the only examples for each instructional category, but they do represent models that best achieve the student learning goals for each category. Figure 3.2 presents a graphic representation of the four model categories and the corresponding instructional models we shall describe within each of the categories. A brief description of the instructional categories and the eight instructional models follow:

REASONING CATEGORY

- Concept Attainment
- Inquiry

REORGANIZING CATEGORY

- Concept Formation
- Synectics

REMEMBERING CATEGORY

- Mnemonics
- Direct Instruction

RELATING CATEGORY

- Cooperative Learning
- Oral Discussion

FIGURE 3-2 Teaching Categories and Models

Category I: Models that Foster Reasoning Skills Models that foster reasoning skills provide students with opportunities to acquire concepts from various disciplines and the skills involved in critical thinking and problem-solving. Such models expose students to strategies that elicit the styles of thinking necessary to process information, formulate conclusions, identify hypotheses, and test alternative solutions. The focus of reasoning models is not only acquiring thinking skills, but also enabling students to defend their choices when they use data.

- *Concept Attainment* Based on the work of Jerome Bruner et al. (1959), concept attainment was designed to teach concepts to students and the corresponding thinking skills of categorizing concepts. Through the use of positive and negative examples, students are able to define a concept and determine the concept's essential attributes. The model is very useful in teaching the skills of comparison and contrast, differentiation, and interpretation.

- *Inquiry* Based on the work of Richard Suchman (1962), inquiry was designed to teach students to form questions, create hypotheses, and test theories. Using a discrepant event or puzzling situation as a basis for discussion with students, this model helps students become more skilled at problem-solving. Students generate hypotheses as they collect and analyze data. Through the use of this model, the skills of hypothesizing, evaluating, and problem-solving are acquired by students.

Category II: Models that Foster Reorganizing Skills Models that foster reorganizing skills help students reexamine what they have learned or understand, and to apply this knowledge to new situations. Further, these models help develop intellectual skills such as inquisitiveness and metaphorical thinking; and they also foster the student's imagination, personal insight, and inductive processes.

- *Concept Formation* Created by Hilda Taba (1971), concept formation (some describe it as concept development) was designed to help students organize information, make connections among data, and create and test hypotheses. Through the use of this model, students will learn how to group data on the basis of similarities, and form categories and labels based on those data. The model is useful in teaching the skills of comparing and contrasting, categorizing, applying, analyzing, and synthesizing data.

- *Synectics* Created by William Gordon (1961), synectics was designed to use analogies, metaphors, and the power of personal imagination as tools for problem-solving. The model helps in the development of creativity in learners and is very useful in fostering collaboration, exploration, analogies, and creative thinking.

Category III: Models that Foster Remembering Skills   Models that foster remembering skills help students acquire information and skills through practice, drill, and memorization. In this category the teacher determines what is important for students to learn and designs instruction that helps students learn and remember discrete facts and skills. The emphasis is upon the retention of information and the performance appraisal of students in determining the retention of knowledge.

- *Mnemonics*   Based on the work of Pressley, Levin, and Delaney (1982) and Lorayne and Lucas (1966), mnemonics was designed to help students memorize and acquire information. Mnemonics can be used to help students learn both low-level information (facts) as well as more complex concepts from different disciplines.

- *Direct Instruction*   Based on the work of Anderson, Evertson, and Brophy (1979), Good and Grouws (1979), Hunter (1984), and Rosenshine (1983), direct instruction was designed to help students learn basic skills and/or discrete pieces of information. The model is especially effective in mathematics, reading, and language arts. Further, this model is useful in learning not only cognitive skills/information but also psychomotor skills such as playing golf, sewing, holding a pencil, and so on. Direct instruction utilizes a step-by-step sequence of teaching to help students recall and recognize facts and data.

Category IV: Models that Foster Relating Skills   Models that foster relating skills provide students with an opportunity to understand others and themselves through enhanced interpersonal communication and group process approaches. The purposes of these models are the development of a positive self-concept, an increase in communication skills, the development of team-oriented skills, and the acquisition of knowledge.

- *Cooperative Learning*   Created by Slavin (1980, 1987a) and Johnson et al. (1984), cooperative learning was designed to help students develop team-building skills by the experience of working with others in cognitive task situations. Through formal cooperative learning strategies such as STAD and JIGSAW, and informal strategies such as "peer group teaching," students are able to experience different leadership roles, learn the skills necessary in building collaborative cultures in the classroom, and acquire the communication skills needed to work effectively with other group members.

- *Oral Discussion*   Originally made famous by Socrates, oral discussion utilizes a questioning format to enhance classroom discussions. Teacher questions are used to check student understanding. Classroom interactions that enhance higher-order thinking processes (factual, interpretative, and evaluative) in students are encouraged and directed by the teacher.

These eight instructional models are neither specific to any particular age group, student ability level, or student grade level, nor subject-matter specific. Each instructional model can be utilized, within reason, with any age youngster and within the framework of teaching any academic discipline. Each model has been used with a variety of K–12 students and with various types of student ability groups. In presenting each instructional model, we provide examples of both elementary and secondary education case studies and lesson plans from a variety of academic disciplines (that is, mathematics, language arts, science, art, and social studies). Additionally, a section entitled "Applications to Diverse Classrooms" will be used to describe the appropriateness of each model for culturally diverse students.

The instructional models presented in this text are predicated on the idea that there is no "best" way to teach all youngsters in all situations. As we described the teaching–learning model depicted in Figure 3.1, there are many learning goals: recalling facts, forming generalizations, working in teams, identifying concepts, and solving problems through various thinking processes. The choice of an instructional model is based upon the complex educational goal(s) established by the teacher for students and *by the depth of understanding that teachers have of the students in their classrooms*. Further, these goal choices are based not only upon a knowledge of how to use a specific instructional model, but also upon an understanding of what cognitive skills each model will engender in students. Teachers of diverse student populations understand that knowledge is dynamic and evolving, and that students are complex. Teachers who are instructionally limited commit a form of pedagogical malpractice—they teach in ways that mitigate student growth and "academically damage" students in succeeding subsequently in school. A first step toward eliminating this circumstance would be for a teacher to reflect upon the following types of "self-directed" questions in designing culturally relevant instruction for students:

1. What specific knowledge and skills (academic and social) do I want students to achieve at the completion of a lesson or unit?

2. What specific interests, prior experiences, and cognitive styles do my students bring to the classroom learning environment?

3. Which instructional models best help me explore the concepts and teach the skills I want my students to learn?

4. Which instructional models are most appropriate given my students' interests, prior experiences, and learning styles?

This last point is critical in implementing, adapting, and evaluating instructional models. To choose culturally relevant instructional models, teachers must know the students they teach, know how to instructionally approach culturally diverse student populations, and know how to utilize various instructional models. This needs to occur in order both to match teaching and learning styles, and to provide all students with the opportunities to learn and experience phenomena in varying educational contexts. As we will describe in the following chapters, such knowledge of instructional models and the concomitant skills necessary to implement these models are critical in opening the minds and souls of culturally diverse learners to be contributing members of American democracy and the new global economic society.

❶HE PLANNING PROCESS

The place to begin anything—whether it is reading a book, watching a movie, or teaching youngsters about the world in general—is at the beginning. In the teaching–learning process this means that teachers need to decide what their students must accomplish, what their students need to do, and what is expected of students once instruction by teachers is completed. Successful people in society have a game plan for their personal and professional lives. Such people know where they are going on a day-to-day basis. They set goals! The human system is goal seeking by design and may be compared with an airplane's autopilot. Once the target (goal) is locked on, all efforts are focused on the target in order to attain the desired end (goal). Winners have definite purposes in life—losers wander aimlessly and generally self-destruct! Even when goal-directed individuals are not actively pursuing a set of goals, they are thinking about them. *Purpose* (a goal) is the motivator that powers a winner's life. In fact, as winners are about to achieve goals, they begin identifying other goals to pursue. They are never satisfied with achieving one set of goals as an end—they continually redefine new goals that motivate them even further in life.

Successful people can describe where they are going and why, approximately how long it will take, what they plan to do on the way, and who will share the journey with them. They have a plan for their lives! Similarly, effective teachers have game plans—plans that indicate what they expect from students, how they plan to help students reach these expectations, and what students are expected to do after the instructional process is completed. Such plans turn teacher thoughts and goals into new opportunities for students. The planning process is a key factor in successful teaching, whether that teaching requires students to recall information, perform specific skills, formulate new concepts and use them with phenomena, utilize problem-solving practices in addressing community issues, or apply collaborative skills in working with other human beings. In order to be successful in utilizing the instructional models, effective teachers plan their strategies by identifying student goals and objectives. The focus for successful teachers is on an instructional plan and the accomplishment of goals and objectives.

The intent of the planning process is to decide what is expected of students—goals and objectives—and to identify what the teacher will do—instructional activities, strategies, and materials—that will help teachers facilitate student achievement. The result of planning either a lesson or unit of instruction consists of a series of instructional strategies that have a common purpose or focus. The following chapters in this text will provide these strategies in the form of instructional models. Sometimes the instructional model revolves around a series of questions to promote student inquiry, others focus upon formulating concepts and generalizations, while still other models teach social as well as academic skills.

One of the more unique examples we have come across concerning goals, destinations, and directions is the fabled sea horse story created by Mager

(1984). Its theme is simple: If you don't know where you are going, how will you know if you've arrived there?

The Fable of the Sea Horse

Once upon a time a Sea Horse gathered up his seven pieces of eight and cantered out to find his fortune. Before he had traveled very far he met an Eel, who said, "Psst. Hey, bud. Where 'ya goin'?"

"I'm going to find my fortune," replied the Sea Horse proudly.

"You're in luck," said the Eel. "For four pieces of eight you can have this speedy flipper, and then you'll be able to get there a lot faster."

"Gee, that's swell," said the Sea Horse, and paid the money and put on the flipper, and slithered off at twice the speed. Soon he came upon a Sponge, who said,

"Psst. Hey, bud. Where 'ya goin'?"

"I'm going to find my fortune," replied the Sea Horse.

"You're in luck," said the Sponge. "For a small fee I will let you have this jet-propelled scooter so that you will be able to travel a lot faster."

So the Sea Horse bought the scooter with his remaining money and he went zooming through the sea five times as fast. Soon he came upon a Shark, who said, "Psst. Hey, bud. Where 'ya goin'?"

"I'm going out to find my fortune," replied the Sea Horse.

"You're in luck. If you'll take this short cut," said the Shark, pointing to his open mouth, "you'll save yourself a lot of time."

"Gee, thanks," said the Sea Horse, and zoomed off into the interior of the Shark, there to be devoured (p. vii).

The problem with some classrooms today is that neither teachers nor students know where they are going. For many people, including teachers, just getting through the day is their goal. As a result, they generate just enough energy and just enough motivation from their students to get through that day. Effective teachers know where they are going and where they are leading their students, and that's why they are successful! Successful individuals turn imagination into reality, turn fantasy into fact, and turn dreams into actual goals. Such individuals seem to have a game plan for life—they know where they are going on a day-to-day basis. Someone unknown once said, "Whatever the mind can conceive—and truly believe—can be achieved." We can make amazing things happen for ourselves and others if we let ourselves dream (develop a plan) and make it come true (develop a set of strategies).

Because we tend to move in the direction of our dominant thoughts—whatever we are thinking about—we unconsciously move toward the achievement of those thoughts. Another way of putting it is: One must have a dream if one is going to make dreams come true. And your dreams, your directions, and your destinations need to be translated into a plan in the form of goals and objectives—goals for life, goals for the day, and goals for instruction. Let's now take a look at what we mean through the examination of a definition and examples of *instructional goals.*

Ⓦ HAT IS AN INSTRUCTIONAL GOAL?

In most classrooms across America, youngsters are expected to know something about academic content—facts, concepts, and generalizations. Further, youngsters are expected to acquire and apply skills unique to an academic subject by applying these skills in the study of academic information. Youngsters are also expected to adopt various attitudes and values that American society considers important in terms of our culture, and that are a derivation of the knowledge and skills acquired in the examination and utilization of the academic content.

Determining an instructional purpose is an initial step in the instructional planning process. This takes the form of identifying instructional goals and objectives. This step of the planning model (Figure 3.3) emphasizes what the students will be expected to do after the teacher has implemented an instructional model. Once the teacher has identified instructional goals and converted these into performance objectives, there is no prescribed sequence in implementing the planning model. The process becomes interactive in that different steps or elements of the model interact with one another.

The instructional planning process model in Figure 3.3 involves three general steps that all teachers need to take in planning lessons or units of instruction. The three steps are:

- Identifying what students will achieve or accomplish after the lesson or unit is completed. This will involve the first two steps of the model: identifying student goals and identifying student performance objectives. (Both of these will be discussed in the next section of this chapter.)

- Identifying how the teacher will help students achieve the goals and objectives of the instructional lesson or unit. (This will be described in Chapters 4–11 of this text.)

- Identifying how well the students have achieved or accomplished the instructional performance objectives identified in the second step of the planning model. (This will be discussed in the remaining sections of this chapter.)

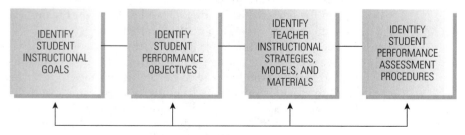

FIGURE 3-3   Instructional Planning Process Model

All steps in the instructional planning process model are important and interact with one another. Curriculum evaluators call this interaction the *concept of internal consistency:* Objectives, instructional strategies, and performance assessment must all relate to one another and be congruent based upon what has been developed previously in the model. However, the essential step in implementing the planning process is the first: identifying instructional goals and converting them into student performance objectives. Without these, instructional models and strategies will not provide you the means to arrive at your pedagogical destinations.

Knowledge, skills, and attitudes are what we expect students to acquire and apply in their academic studies. In order for teachers to design plans for students to accomplish these expectations, a variety of directional statements need to be written by teachers. Some of these statements are written very broadly with verbs such as *understand, appreciate, aware,* or *believe.* Other statements are more performance-oriented and utilize such verbs as *list, differentiate, share,* or *defend.*

Instructional goals, especially as we will define them here, are broad statements of direction that identify what is expected of students. Goals serve as initial organizers and provide direction for educational participants, including teachers, who plan and write curricular programs, guides, or courses. They are written broadly and in general terms because they cover a breadth of content over longer periods of time. Examples of broad goal statements are:

- To understand the causes of the Civil War.
- To appreciate the works of Edgar Allan Poe.
- To use effective personal health practices.
- To understand and appreciate the human experience.
- To understand how human resources are influenced by social and political systems.
- To describe how the multicultural composition of American society enhances the quality of life for all Americans.
- To know the primary colors.

In the planning process, goals provide a general direction for instruction. However, goals such as "producing effective consumers" or "appreciating the literary works of Walter Mosley" or "being sensitive to the dignity of all human beings" are so general that they leave the teacher and the student wondering where to begin instructionally, and what is expected in terms of accountability and achievement (see Table 3.1). Because of this, the next step in the planning process is to take each goal and convert it into specific student performance terminology. In other words, the teacher needs to determine what is expected of students in specific ways that can be assessed in terms of performance.

TABLE 3-1   Verbs Associated with Goals: Words and Phrases Open to Many Interpretations

To understand

To appreciate

To grasp the significance of

To have faith in

To realize

To enjoy

To believe in

To recognize

To fully sense

To take satisfaction in

What Are Performance Objectives?

The intent of instructional planning is to determine what students should accomplish, and then to plot a course of action (instructional models and strategies) that facilitates student accomplishment of objectives. Performance objectives are an outgrowth of the goals discussed in the previous section. They are written in order to provide specific direction and meaning for what is expected from students. Objectives are important in teacher planning because they help facilitate: 1) an identification of what is expected of students at the conclusion of the study; 2) a basis for organizing instructional activities and materials; 3) a means for determining ways to assess student performance; and 4) a performance level of accountability for students. For purposes of this text, performance objectives are defined in terms of student outcomes—what the *student* will be able to do. They are written in terms that clearly delineate the student behavior that will be evaluated. Examples of broadly defined performance objectives are:

- To list three statements of fact and three statements of opinion.
- To solve at least seven radical equations.
- To run the 100-yard dash.
- To convert data on hunger in selected developing countries to a bar graph.
- To identify Maya Angelou's primary life choices in *Gather Together in My Name* and to identify how she resolved each decision situation.

- To predict the height of a plant on the 21st day of growth, given appropriate light and water.

For many "expert" teachers, such broadly defined objectives are more than adequate. But for novice teachers, more precision may be necessary to ensure that the teacher and students know precisely the goal to be attained.

Readers who take time to examine these performance objectives will notice that these statements seem reasonably clear but they are not specific. These performance objectives provide direction to teachers as to what instructional models to employ in helping students achieve these outcomes, but they don't provide some essential information. For example, what type of plant will the students grow? What will be the source of the facts and opinions—the students' imagination or a teacher resource? Also apparent with this examination of objectives is the notion that assessment is not as clearly defined as it might be. Performance objectives utilize precise verbs in identifying what is expected of students after instruction has been completed (see Table 3.2 for a list of such verbs).

Performance objectives written to communicate the student outcomes and the means of goal assessment exhibit three essential characteristics—the instructional conditions under which the student performance will occur; the student behavior expected after instruction is completed; and the standard, criterion, or performance level that each student is expected to demonstrate (Mager, 1984).

TABLE 3-2 Verbs Associated with Objectives

To list

To compare and contrast

To construct

To differentiate

To identify

To write

To speak

To assemble

To describe verbally

To describe in writing

To float

To construct

- *Instructional conditions under which the student performance will occur.*

The instructional conditions are strategies that the teacher will employ in helping students exhibit the performance expected. The following examples are conditions that could be components of a performance objective:

- Given a three-place subtraction problem with regrouping,...
- Given a standard set of tools,...
- Without the aid of a calculator or computer,...
- When the student is describing a poem by Langston Hughes,...

Each condition is written after consideration of the appropriate instructional strategies necessary to achieve the outcome. The next characteristic of performance objectives is:

- *Student behavior expected after instruction is completed.*

The student behavior is identified in performance terms that will be acceptable as evidence that the student has achieved the objective. Further, this student behavior is written in specific language so that few, if any, interpretations are apparent in terms of what is expected to be performed. This student behavior is then attached to the instructional conditions as described in the previous step. The following are examples of the two characteristics of performance objectives—conditions and student behavior—put together in proper form:

- Given a linear algebraic equation with one unknown, the student will be able to solve for the unknown without the aid of tables, references, or calculating devices.
- Given a list and discussion of factors leading to significant historical events, the student will be able to select and justify at least three economic factors contributing to the influx of immigrants to the United States since 1980.
- Given a description and demonstration of the first 10 numbers of the numerical system, the student will be able to print these 10 numbers in order.

The final characteristic of performance objectives is:

- *A standard, criterion, or performance level that each student is expected to demonstrate.*

The performance level provides the teacher with a standard by which to assess instructional effectiveness as well as student achievement. This characteristic defines for the student what is expected and what level of performance is required. Through standards, the teacher will have a measure to determine the depth, breadth, and complexity by which to judge students and to judge the teacher's instructional effectiveness. The following examples are provided to demonstrate this final characteristic of performance objectives:

- Given linear algebraic equations with one unknown, the student will be able to solve 8 out of 10 of these equations without the aid of tables, references, or calculating devices.

- Given the knowledge of how to run a dash, the student will be able to run the 100-yard dash within a period of 14 seconds.

- Given both a description of how to float on water and a viewing of videotapes concerning floating positions, students will be able to float on their backs for at least 1 minute.

- Given knowledge of measurement and weights, the student must be able to use the chemical balance well enough to weigh materials accurately to the nearest milligram.

In summary, performance objectives should consist of an instructional condition, an expected student behavior, and a standard by which to judge achievement. After a teacher has completed a listing of all performance objectives for a lesson or unit of instruction, the teacher can evaluate each planned objective based upon the following three questions:

1. Does the performance objective describe what students will be doing when they demonstrate that they have achieved the objective?

2. Does the performance objective describe the conditions under which students will be expected to demonstrate achievement?

3. Does the performance objective indicate how the students will be evaluated?

If the reader will take into consideration these three questions when designing performance objectives, then students and the teacher will be very clear in terms of the performance expected and how evaluation will occur.

Though we have spent time describing the characteristics of performance objectives, we believe that the most important component is the identification of the behavior expected from the students. Remember that performance objectives are written for students, in student terms, and for what is expected of students. That is why the remainder of this text emphasizes what students will be expected to accomplish.

Thus far, we have described how classroom teachers can use performance objectives in a very mechanistic manner. Many of the examples provided previously in this discussion have elicited low-level, convergent thinking processes—right or wrong/correct or incorrect responses. Schooling in America, especially in its best forms, provides youngsters with more than just correct or incorrect responses! As you will recognize in the following chapters, a good number of instructional models (that is, concept attainment, synectics, inquiry, oral discussion) facilitate the development of youngsters' minds through the use of thinking skill development and the application of these skills to culturally relevant curricula and materials.

One system that can be used to write performance objectives and develop higher-order thinking skills was originally created by Bloom et al. (1956) and is referred to as the Taxonomy of Educational Objectives. There are three types of learning objectives (cognitive, affective, and psychomotor) that teachers need to utilize and students need to develop; Bloom has become best known for his work in the cognitive domain.

1. Cognitive Objectives—those that use academic knowledge to develop the intellectual abilities of youngsters.

2. Affective Objectives—those that help youngsters develop values, attitudes, and feelings.

3. Psychomotor Objectives—those that help youngsters develop large and small muscle coordination and manipulative skills.

COGNITIVE DOMAIN

Cognitive objectives deal with academic information and knowledge. Objectives in this domain focus upon what students will accomplish intellectually from the following perspectives: recalling facts, concepts, and generalizations; applying information and concepts; synthesizing various concepts and generalizations; and making judgments according to standards and criteria. Originally designed by Bloom et al. (1956), this taxonomical domain is a system for classifying cognitive educational objectives into a hierarchy of thinking levels. This categorical taxonomy has been designed from the most simple form of thinking to the most complex—convergent to divergent thinking processes. Therefore, the importance of using this taxonomy, or one of the other cognitive schemas developed by Sanders (1966) or Hunkins (1972), is to promote higher levels of thinking and development for America's students. Research by Henry (1955) first documented that most teachers in schools tend to utilize convergent thinking (that is, correct or incorrect responses, one way of answering questions) rather than divergent thinking (that is, many possible responses, problems that are not immediately solvable). More recent discussion of the problem suggests that the tendency toward low-level objectives and convergent questions is still evident in schools of the 1990s (Good and Brophy, 1994). Convergent thinking is promoted in most of America's schools based upon an examination of typical classroom instructional objectives, teacher-made test items, the types of questions asked in class discussions, and the types of questions found at the end of chapters of textbooks. The result of this is student passivity, or in Henry's (1955) terms, student docility.

In order for students to utilize higher-order thinking skills (divergent thinking levels), they must be taught the skills needed in using each taxonomical level. As we shall point out in a later chapter, fostering critical thinking requires that teachers become more subversive in their thinking—teaching students to question more and accept less. Teacher use of different cognitive levels should be evidenced in the types of questions used in class discussions, the types of tests given to students, and the types of performance assessments utilized to assess student knowledge. Each cognitive level is described below along with sample performance objectives for each level in the taxonomy. The sample performance objectives focus only upon expected student behaviors in order to emphasize what students will be doing at each level of the taxonomy.

Knowledge

This level of the cognitive taxonomy requires students to acquire knowledge of factual information. It seeks to have students recall facts, concepts, and generalizations from an academic discipline.

Examples:

- The student will be able to cite at least three causes of the Civil War.
- The student will be able to identify the earth's distance from the sun.
- The student will be able to list three essential criteria for judging the effectiveness of a surrealistic painting.
- The student will define, based upon the class lecture, what is meant by the term *electricity*.

Comprehension

The comprehension level checks whether students understand the information learned at the knowledge level. This is demonstrated by one or more of the following processes: translating material from one form of communication to another (that is, using one's own words, role playing, simulations, charting and graphing), interpreting material (that is, comparing and contrasting, drawing relationships), and estimating and extrapolating (that is, predicting effects, drawing implications).

Examples:

- The student will be able to paraphrase the Gettysburg Address in six sentences or less.
- The student will be able to paraphrase Martin Luther King, Jr.'s "I Have a Dream" speech in six sentences or less.
- The student will be able to compare and contrast the economic system of the South in 1860 with the economic system of the South in 1996.
- After a study of Edgar Allan Poe's poem "The Raven," students will describe in their own words the symbolism of the phrase "Quoth the Raven, 'Nevermore.'"
- Given a graph of the growth of a plant over 10 days, the student will predict the growth of the plant on the 25th day, assuming a steady rate of growth. The student will further predict growth rates given different light and water applications.

If you examine the objectives listed above, you should be able to recognize that the knowledge and comprehension levels of the taxonomy elicit only convergent thinking by students. The behavior expected from these levels asks students to perform tasks that lead to correct or incorrect responses. From those teachers using these taxonomical levels, students will acquire information concerning a topic or concept and perform the task required (that is, recall information, translate information or ideas into another form of communication, compare and contrast information, and/or draw relationships or implications). Each of these tasks calls for the use of convergent thinking processes. Though information and the understanding of ideas and concepts are important, it is also necessary to develop higher-order thinking skills in youngsters. The taxonomical levels described below promote student learning through the use of more divergent thinking processes.

Application

The application level deals with taking information that has been studied and understood at the previous levels (knowledge and comprehension) and applying concepts or generalizations to new situations. Application objectives and thinking involve the solving of problems through the identification of issues, and the selection and use of skills and generalizations.

Examples:

- The student will be able to describe three ways in which the Civil War could have been averted.

- After a lesson on the preservation of food, the student will be able to demonstrate a procedure for retarding or preventing the growth of mold on bread.

- Mr. Jones is going to locate a new steel plant in a midwestern state. The student will identify three possible locations where steel can be produced and transported economically.

As you will recognize, these objectives promote divergent thinking because the tasks presented are not immediately solvable. They take much more student reflection, and they require that students use facts, concepts, and generalizations to draw their conclusions.

Analysis

Analysis objectives are used when the teacher wants students to systematically examine factual content in order to solve problems. For this taxonomical level, students are required to take whole issues (that is, conclusions or generalizations) and to divide these wholes into their component parts (that is, examine whether factual information supports conclusions). Analysis tasks require students to utilize inductive and deductive thinking, recognize assumptions, and identify common mistakes in the reasoning process.

Examples:

- The student will be able to analyze the following assumption: "If the South had successfully seceded from the Union, the United States would never have become a world power."

- The student will identify and describe some of the significant reasons why blacks in South Africa, who comprised a majority, lacked the power to vote prior to 1993.

- The student will be able to either accept or reject the following statements and conclusion:
  a. "Ms. Cortez uses X detergent to wash her clothes."
  b. "Ms. Cortez has found that X detergent gets her clothes whiter than new."
  c. "Therefore, X detergent is the best detergent made!"

Synthesis

Synthesis objectives require students to put together discrete elements (that is, factual material) into a pattern or structure that the elements did not previously form. This taxonomical level offers more freedom of thought (that is, original and creative thinking) than any of the previous levels and truly requires divergent thinking on the part of students.

Examples:

- Given the idea that conflicts in ideologies still exist between the North and South, the student will be able to devise ways of resolving these conflicts.
- Given various information concerning the types and structures of poetic compositions, the student will create a poem using one of these types and structures.
- The student will devise a set of standards that would be useful in defining the proper division of decision-making power between automobile workers and management.
- Because drug abuse is a widespread and growing problem today, the student will write and orally present a plan to decrease the use of drugs by teenagers.

Evaluation

The evaluation level elicits from students a judgment regarding the value of procedures and the imposition of criteria by either the teacher or students. With synthesis, the student creatively puts together different elements or ideas in order to create a new pattern; in evaluation, the student uses decision-making skills and must make decisions that are grounded on sound facts or ideas.

Examples:

- The student will be able to write an essay on the following question: Do you think the Civil War was justified? Why or why not?
- Given newspaper and scientific articles for or against the fluoridation of water, the student will be able to take a position (pro or con) on fluoridation and write three scientific reasons in defense of the position.
- The student will write a short essay defending or opposing the use of Standard English in all American classrooms.

The major purpose of describing and providing examples of each of the levels of the cognitive taxonomy is to provide the reader with a systematic process for designing objectives according to the levels of thinking. As you will recognize from the descriptions and examples for each taxonomical level, a hierarchy of thinking processes and levels moves from the most simple—knowledge—to the most complex—evaluation. The teacher who utilizes the cognitive taxonomy requires students to acquire information and skills and to apply these to problem situations utilizing both convergent and divergent thinking processes. It is certainly possible, and perhaps even ideal, to use the same academic content and have students move through all the thinking levels, as in the Civil War examples. Tables 3.3 and 3.4 provide additional examples of applying the same content/concept through the cognitive levels. As you analyze these examples, you will notice that each performance objective, similar to the previous examples, emphasizes the resulting student behavior. This is done to emphasize that the student behavior is what the teacher must clearly delimit in terms of what is expected. The conditions under which the behavior will occur and the performance level that the student will evidence are important in the planning

TABLE 3-3 English Literature

Knowledge:

The student will be able to list five distinguishing physical characteristics of the monster Grendel.

Comprehension:

The student will be able to compare and contrast the physical characteristics of the monster Grendel in the poem "Beowulf" and the film Grendel, Grendel, Grendel.

Application:

Based upon the viewing of the film Grendel, Grendel, Grendel, the student will suggest three ways that King Hrothgar and his people might have changed Grendel's attitude toward them.

Analysis:

The student will analyze the following assumption:

"If Cain had not killed Abel, Grendel would not have terrorized King Hrothgar's kingdom."

The student will critique this statement based upon the reading of the heroic poem "Beowulf" and the viewing of the film Grendel, Grendel, Grendel.

Synthesis:

The student will write a modern heroic epic poem that relates the heroic activities of at least one character, and reflects at least two values of modern society.

Evaluation:

The student will write a short essay on the following: "Which character do you believe to be more heroic, Beowulf or Grendel? Why?"

process. However, in this discussion of writing performance objectives, our emphasis is upon writing objectives that are clear and specific in terms of what behavior is expected of students. Readers will note that the levels are, in the words of Orlich et al. (1985), "cumulative and inclusive." As students develop understandings at one taxonomical level, these understandings can subsequently be used for tasks involved in more complex levels of cognitive processing.

We also readily acknowledge that many expert teachers do not have a need for defining specific objectives they hope to achieve, but they do plan. Expert teachers engage in complex planning (which includes thinking through what objectives will be achieved and how they will be accomplished) and in anticipating the events that might mitigate lesson effectiveness (Carter, 1990). They also have the benefit of past experience. Expert teachers design future lessons based on past experiences; novice teachers have few or no past classroom experiences, so the level and depth of their planning (including stating the conditions of objectives) become more important for success.

TABLE 3-4   Biology—Cells

Knowledge:

The student will identify three components of red blood cells and their specific functions.

Comprehension:

The student will compare and contrast a red blood cell and its various functions with a bone marrow cell and its various functions.

Application:

Given a list of chemicals and the cellular components they interact with, the student will identify which chemicals will clot blood and which will break up or dissolve clots in the least amount of time.

Analysis:

Given a medical procedure and the knowledge that it did not work, the student will determine what steps in the procedure were probably responsible for its failure and describe why.

Synthesis:

The student will be able to construct a model cell containing all necessary components of a cell, eliminating all wasted space and materials, and determine what specific function this cell might fulfill.

Evaluation:

Dr. Jeffrey Geiger of Chicago Hope has one heart donor and two candidates for the heart. He has one-half hour to decide who will receive the heart: a 12-year-old child or an otherwise healthy 55-year-old Nobel Prize winner (for solar engine designs) renowned for her scientific achievements. The student will choose who will receive the heart and describe how and why the choice was made.

Affective Domain

The cognitive domain, as just discussed, dealt with intellectual abilities—the use of the mind in understanding and using knowledge from the different disciplines. The affective domain involves one's feelings, emotions, interests, attitudes, and values. Developed by Krathwohl, Bloom, and Masis (1964), the affective domain was a natural follow-up to the design of the cognitive taxonomy of educational objectives.

The affective domain deals with how students are affected by their learning, as well as how their feelings and interests affect their learning. In addition, the teacher's attitude toward an academic subject or topic—like or dislike—affects the student's disposition toward what is to be learned. In other words, the teacher's feelings toward what is to be taught or learned has an affective relationship upon the student. The implication for teachers is that students receive/pick up feelings of interest or disinterest for the subject and model these same attitudes or interests. Thus, the more teachers are enthusiastic and love what it is that they teach youngsters, the more positively students will react to the teacher and the subject under discussion.

For purposes of describing these taxonomies, it may be necessary to analyze and plan lessons in which the cognitive (knowledge) and the affective (feelings) domains are separated. In fact, many teachers, because of their fear of evaluation in the affective domain (to be addressed later), frequently disregard planning or teaching within this taxonomy. However, in practice—both consciously and unconsciously—the cognitive and affective domains tend to merge together. Think of a youngster who is learning how to use a pencil for the first time. There are some specific cognitive understandings that should occur—how to hold the pencil, where to position the fingers, or how to make either letters or numbers. There are also some affective learnings that occur—feelings of comfort or discomfort, interest in being like mommy or daddy in learning how to write, or feelings of success or failure in either holding the pencil or making letters or numbers. The knowledge of what is worth knowing and the feelings that emanate from this pursuit of knowledge consistently commingle in phenomena that students explore. Most learning occurs in this manner!

Krathwohl et al.'s (1964) taxonomy offers a system for planning and organizing objectives in the affective domain. Recall that the cognitive domain is based upon a hierarchy of objectives from the most simple form of thinking—knowledge—to the most complex form of thinking—evaluation. Further, as phenomena are explored, the hierarchy is utilized so that the thinking skills involved in each of the previous levels of the taxonomy are considered—there is a logical progression of the students' thinking. This is not necessarily the case in using the affective domain. The affective domain is based upon the degree to which an individual has internalized and organized attitudes and values. The affective domain is structured around how strongly individuals feel about and are willing to stand up for and defend their attitudes and values. The lowest taxonomical level is *receiving*—the willingness to listen to varying views, whereas the highest level is *characterization of a value*—the willingness to openly profess their attitudes or values. The following descriptions of the five levels of the affective taxonomy of educational objectives provide a clearer explanation of this idea.

Receiving

This level of the taxonomy refers to an individual's willingness to attend to particular classroom stimuli or phenomena. It involves a teacher acquiring, holding, and directing the student's attention, but it requires that a student willingly and consciously consider some phenomenon or idea.

Examples:

- The student will listen attentively to the pros and cons of capital punishment.
- The student will develop an awareness of the impact of homelessness upon young children.
- The student will demonstrate an awareness of the five classroom rules listed on the chalkboard.
- The student will be able to differentiate nonverbally the sounds of the major instruments in a classical orchestra.

Responding

This level requires active participation on the part of students. The student does something (performs, participates, reacts, speaks, and so on) based upon the stimuli that were presented at the previous level. In essence, the student must act on some new awareness. Real internalization requires that students take action on what they know.

Examples:

- The student will understand the causes of hunger and identify two ways to become personally involved with helping the hungry.
- The student will appreciate the causes of homelessness so that the student can identify social policies that need to be changed to reduce homelessness.
- The student will demonstrate an interest in reading poetry.
- The student will follow simple verbal requests.

Valuing

Valuing emphasizes the worth an individual attaches to phenomena, things, or behaviors. It is based upon an internal set of values but is operationalized by the open behavior of individuals. With valuing, the student is not just acquiescing to some feeling, but rather is intentionally deciding to make a personal commitment to some idea (value).

Examples:

- The student will demonstrate a belief in housing for the poor and homeless by helping construct homes through Habitat for Humanity.
- The student will demonstrate an acceptance of individuals of other races by joining groups that are racially mixed.
- The student will demonstrate an appreciation for the role that science plays in our everyday lives.

- The student will attempt to interest peers that conflict-resolution strategies have value as methods to deal with interpersonal conflict.

Organization

Organization is the process by which individuals begin to formulate value systems. This level is concerned with synthesizing different values, resolving conflicts between values, and constructing an internally congruent value system. This is the level where individuals begin developing a philosophy to live by, and to determine what it is that they will be committed to as individuals.

Examples:

- The student will learn about personal responsibility and consistently accept responsibility for personal behavior and the consequences derived from that behavior.

- The student will acquire an understanding of ecological issues and will demonstrate this by describing the effects of industrial pollution in urban environments.

- The student will appreciate the importance of long-range plans and will formulate a 5-year plan for life after high school based upon interests, abilities, and beliefs.

Characterization by a Value or Value Complex

Within this level of the taxonomy, an individual internalizes and personalizes a value system. Because this individual has lived by this value system for a long time, a lifestyle of behavior is practiced. Value systems are actualized by individuals at this level through persuasive, consistent, and predictable behavior. In essence, the individual is able to "walk the talk" and to reconcile personal actions with personal convictions.

Examples:

- The student will display safety-conscious behaviors when working in a science laboratory.

- The student will practice cooperation and collaboration when involved in group and team activities.

- The student will demonstrate good health habits through a balanced diet and a regimen of exercise.

The affective taxonomy is based upon how individuals feel about or are willing to defend the values and beliefs that they hold dear. Though it is possible to write affective objectives for all levels of the taxonomy, it is difficult to write them with the same precision of cognitive objectives. Teachers can also write affective objectives from the simplest level—receiving—to the most complex level—characterization—using the same content or concept. However, as one uses this taxonomy, it becomes more difficult to evaluate student progress because of the time it takes to make a determination of progress and the imprecision that occurs in writing and assessing these objectives. This statement is not an excuse to disregard the use of the affective taxonomy. Affective domain objectives will take more time to develop and evaluate, and attitudinal changes call for even more time and development by teachers and students.

Ⓟsychomotor Domain

Psychomotor domain objectives emphasize the development of muscular or motor skills. Further, such objectives can be used in the manipulation of instructional materials most often used in hands-on science or mathematics programs. Psychomotor learning can take the form of learning how to hold and use a pencil, throwing or catching a football, climbing a rope, playing a musical instrument, or using scientific laboratory equipment.

Bloom (1956) and his colleagues did not prepare a taxonomy for the psychomotor domain; however, others like Harrow (1972) and Moore (1972) have provided their versions of a psychomotor taxonomy. Though the psychomotor domain is important in the overall learning of youngsters, especially in activity-oriented courses (for example, physical education, human ecology, industrial technology), this text and the instructional models focus more on the cognitive domain than the affective or psychomotor. Teachers in activity-oriented courses are able to use the various models, but they tend to do so when teaching specific cognitive skills and understandings. Readers should examine the taxonomical references by Harrow (1972) and Moore (1972) to fully explore the psychomotor domain. Table 3.5 illustrates Harrow's six levels and also provides an example of skills at each level.

TABLE 3-5 Harrow's Taxonomy of the Psychomotor Domain

Level	*Example*
1. Reflex movement	Knee-jerk and other reflex movements innate at birth
2. Basic fundamental movements	Visual tracking of an object, crawling, walking, grasping an object
3. Perceptual abilities	Body awareness, figure-ground differentiation, auditory awareness, memory
4. Physical abilities	Muscular endurance, agility, strength
5. Skilled movement	Simple behaviors such as sawing wood and complex behaviors such as playing tennis
6. Nondiscursive communication	Moving interpretatively and using the body creatively to express ideas or emotions

Reprinted from D. C. Orlich et al. 1985. *Teaching Strategies: A Guide to Better Instruction* (2d ed.). Toronto, Canada: D. C. Heath.

ⒺVALUATION IDEAS

Most of the content in this chapter focuses on establishing clear goals for instruction and knowing what students are expected to achieve. Most of the rest of this book examines the means for achieving those defined goals. The only missing element is knowing if a goal has been achieved—evaluation.

The following ideas are presented to help teachers better evaluate student achievement of performance objectives. Some teacher-defined goals will be relatively easy to evaluate because they call for simple forms of thinking—convergent processes. Divergent thinking objectives, however, are more difficult to evaluate because students are required to think through problems; such objectives take more time to develop in students and more time to evaluate by teachers. Good evaluation requires thoughtful planning and attention to the following elements:

1. *Write performance objectives in a precise manner.* Avoid writing objectives that are vague, general, or nebulous. Utilize the verbs and examples presented for each level of the cognitive and affective taxonomies. Write objectives in performance terms that are specific and can be evaluated.

2. *Decide upon the content, materials, instructional strategies, and evaluation procedures.* The content, materials, and instructional strategies will be used to help students achieve the performance objectives. The evaluation procedures are important in helping assess the degree of achievement.

3. *Select a variety of evaluation procedures.* Choose from many sources and types of evaluation, depending upon the performance objective and the taxonomical level being implemented. Avoid an overreliance on a few evaluation procedures (for example, paper and pencil tests). Besides the typical objective tests found in most classrooms, include such assessment devices as: short-answer essays, case studies, student self-evaluation, simulations, role playing, observational analysis, journals and logs, oral and group discussion, portfolios, and others.

4. *Be sure your evaluation procedures assess what is taught.* Assess only those skills, concepts, and factual information that students were taught or can be expected to know. Too often educators assess ideas that are not fully examined and explored in the lesson. Avoid doing this!

5. *Evaluate frequently.* Students should be evaluated often because these experiences can lessen anxiety and fear. The frequency of assessment should be based upon instructional decisions instead of punishment, and this concept should be communicated to students. Testing is one form of learning—not the goal of instruction. Teacher evaluation should be objective and subjective, and as teachers get to know students better, more attention should be given to how (and what) students learn than to testing everything they learn.

6. *Evaluation demonstrates what you value.* Testing of students is very revealing to observers—by looking at the form of tests and the items on tests, an observer

can begin to determine what teachers value in the learning process. Through such observations a determination can be made whether a teacher stresses recall of information or higher-level cognitive and affective thinking. Teacher assessments communicate to outside observers what the teacher believes is worth knowing!

ⓈUMMARY

In this chapter, we have presented a brief analysis of instructional model building and the psychological underpinnings associated with instructional models. In addition to the analysis, we have described our own system of categorizing the instructional models, and have identified and provided a description of the eight instructional models that this text emphasizes.

This chapter has also provided readers with a description of the instructional planning process and why planning is so very critical in presenting instructional lessons and units to youngsters. One important aspect of the planning process is the use of goals and objectives. Performance objectives become the teacher's targets toward which instruction aims. The objectives become the focal point of lessons because these objectives are the behaviors that students are expected to perform.

We now are ready to move on to an examination and description of eight instructional models. These models are organized around four categories for classification purposes. The models enable students to use facts and concepts in different ways, and those variations result in enhanced cognitive achievement. Students learn best what they use and what they acquire in different ways. In our presentation of these models, we provide a theoretical description of each model, the phases of planning and implementing each model, at least two case studies and a lesson plan to demonstrate how each model is implemented, and evaluative criteria to assess the degree of proficiency in implementing each model. Each chapter that follows also has a discussion of how the instructional model is implemented with culturally diverse students. Applications of cognitive-style research are utilized within each of the instructional model chapters. The emphasis of this text is on the instructional models, but as clearly articulated in this chapter, the models cannot be separated from the instructional goals and student evaluation. If the teacher does not recognize how goals suggest instructional possibilities and how instructional practices dictate evaluative techniques, the teacher will not have an impact on student learning, but instead will be either entertaining students or keeping them busy. Process without content is meaningless, and content without process is unlearned.

ⓇEFERENCES

Anderson, L. M., C. M. Evertson, and J. E. Brophy. 1979. "An Experimental Study of Effective Teaching in First Grade Reading Groups." *Elementary School Journal* 79: 193–223.

Bloom, B., M. Englehart, E. Furst, W. Hill, and D. Krathwohl. 1956. *Taxonomy of Educational Objectives: The Classification of Educational Goals, Handbook I: Cognitive Domain.* New York: David McKay.

Bruner, J. S., J. J. Goodnow, and G. A. Austin. 1959. *A Study of Thinking.* New York: John Wiley and Sons.

Carter, K. 1990. "Teachers' Knowledge and Learning to Teach." Pp. 291–310 in W. R. Houston (ed.), *Handbook of Research on Teacher Education.* New York: Macmillan.

Donmoyer, R. 1996. "The Concept of a Knowledge Base." Pp. 92–115 in F. B. Murray (ed.), *The Teacher Educator's Handbook.* San Francisco: Jossey-Bass.

Eggen, P., and D. Kauchak. 1988. *Strategies for Teachers.* Englewood Cliffs, NJ: Prentice-Hall.

Good, T., and J. E. Brophy. 1994. *Looking in Classrooms* (6th ed.). New York: Harper-Collins.

Good, T., and D. Grouws. 1979. "The Missouri Mathematics Effectiveness Project: An Experimental Study in Fourth-Grade Classrooms." *Journal of Educational Psychology* 71: 355–362.

Gordon, W. 1961. *Synectics: The Development of Creative Capacity.* New York: Harper & Row.

Gunter, M. A., T. H. Estes, and J. H. Schwab. 1990. *Instruction: A Models Approach.* Boston: Allyn & Bacon.

Hanson, H., H. Silver, and R. Strong. 1986. *Teaching Styles and Strategies.* Moorestown, NJ: Hanson, Silver, Strong and Associates.

Harrow, A. J. 1972. *A Taxonomy of the Psychomotor Domain.* New York: David McKay.

Henry, J. 1955. "Docility, or Giving Teacher What She Wants." *Journal of Social Issues* 11(1): 33–41.

Hunkins, F. P. 1972. *Questioning Strategies and Techniques.* Boston: Allyn & Bacon.

Hunter, M. 1984. "Knowing, Teaching, and Supervising." Pp. 169–192 in P. L. Hosford (ed.), *Using What We Know About Teaching.* Alexandria, VA: Association for Supervision and Curriculum Development.

Johnson, D. W., R. T. Johnson, E. J. Holubec, and P. Roy. 1984. *Circles of Learning.* Alexandria, VA: Association for Supervision and Curriculum Development.

Joyce, B., and M. Weil. 1986. *Models of Teaching* (3d ed.). Englewood Cliffs, NJ: Prentice-Hall.

————. 1992. *Models of Teaching* (4th ed.). Boston: Allyn & Bacon.

Jung, C. G. 1971. *Psychological Types.* Bollinger Series, Vol. 6. Princeton, NJ: Princeton Press.

Krathwohl, D., B. Bloom, and B. Masis. 1964. *Taxonomy of Educational Objectives, Handbook II: Affective Domain.* New York: David McKay.

Ladson-Billings, G. 1994. *The Dreamkeepers.* San Francisco: Jossey-Bass.

Lorayne, H., and J. Lucas. 1966. *The Memory Book.* New York: Briercliff Manor.

Mager, R. 1984. *Preparing Instructional Objectives* (3d ed.). Palo Alto, CA: Fearon.

Moore, M. R. 1972. "Consideration of the Perceptual Process in the Evaluation of Musical Performance." *Journal of Research on Music Education* 20: 273–279.

Myers, I. B. 1962. *The Myers-Briggs Type Indicator Manual.* Palo Alto, CA: Consulting Psychologists Press.

Orlich, D. C., R. J. Harder, R. C. Callahan, C. H. Kravas, D. P. Kauchak, R. A. Pendergrass, and A. J. Keogh. 1985. *Teaching Strategies: A Guide to Better Instruction* (2d ed.). Toronto, Canada: D. C. Heath.

Pressley, M., J. R. Levin, and H. Delaney. 1982. "The Mnemonic Keyword Method." *Review of Educational Research* 52: 61–91.

Rosenshine, B. 1983. "Teaching Functions in Instructional Programs." *Elementary School Journal* 83(4): 335–350.

Sanders, N. M. 1966. *Classroom Questions: What Kinds?* New York: Harper & Row.

Slavin, R. E. 1980. *Using Student Team Learning* (rev. ed.). Baltimore, MD: Johns Hopkins University, Center for Social Organization of Schools.

———. 1987a. "Cooperative Learning and Cooperative School." *Educational Leadership* 45(3): 7–13.

Suchman, R. J. 1962. *The Elementary School Training Program in Scientific Inquiry.* Report to the U.S. Office of Education, Project Title VII.

Project no. 216. Project of the Illinois Studies of Inquiry. Urbana, IL: University of Illinois Press.

Taba, H. 1971. *Hilda Taba Teaching Strategies Program.* Miami, FL: Institute for Staff Development.

Many states are now requiring proficiency exams for students seeking to graduate from high school. Whether such tests are good for education is arguable, but that they are an emerging reality is without doubt. A review of selected tests in one state revealed that many of the items required students to think through a problem and discern an answer. The answer was not something stored in short-term memory; rather it was derived only after students used what they knew in order to make sense out of some "new" problem. In essence, the test item required the student to use reasoning skills.

The two chapters in this section focus on two instructional strategies for students to think through a problem. The first, concept attainment, focuses on teaching significant concepts to students, but the students must use their personal powers of reasoning in order to define the concept's salient attributes. In the second model, inquiry, the students use their observational skills to analyze a phenomenon in a way that enables them to induce a logical explanation for events.

These strategies are not gimmicks for teachers to use. Instead, they represent part of what should constitute the instructional repertoire of every teacher. How and when to use them is a matter of personal preference. But why one would use these instructional models is clear—to make students *think!* ■

Models that Foster Reasoning Skills

Concept Attainment

The purpose of this chapter is to expand the reader's understanding of how and when to use the concept attainment model. More specifically, readers will be able to:

1. *Identify the specific phases of the concept attainment model.*
2. *Identify strengths and weaknesses of the model.*
3. *Understand the theoretical basis for the model.*
4. *Evaluate sample lessons that utilize the concept attainment strategy.*
5. *Identify ways in which concept attainment enhances the learning abilities of culturally diverse students.*
6. *Create a plan for a personally developed concept attainment lesson.*

❶ NTRODUCTION

The model presented in this chapter is an inductive approach to help students critically think through the meaning of a particular concept (for example, symmetry, verbs, balance of power, gravity). Perhaps in an "ideal" world teachers would not need to seriously consider and plan for the types of instruction that may occur in classrooms—students would learn, in essence, despite the instructional model. Indeed, Rousseau once observed that for a child who wanted to learn to read, any teaching technique would work; the child's natural interests would lead him or her to decode the written word. If absolutely every student in a classroom exhibited an insatiable desire for knowledge or came from the same cultural (and family) circumstance, then using alternative instructional models might not be an absolute necessity. Because each student is different and because classrooms, regardless of context, are inherently diverse, it is imperative that teachers create lessons that tap the natural interests and inquisitiveness of students.

> It is the consensus of virtually all the men and women who have been working on curriculum projects that making material interesting is in no way incompatible with presenting it soundly.
>
> JEROME S. BRUNER

Several instructional dynamics frame the way in which the teaching process occurs in the classroom (Ornstein, 1995)—understanding student differences, determining the length of instruction, identifying how to foster student participation, and evaluating student understanding. These dynamics focus not only on how bright students learn, but also on how every student can be engaged to think through ideas. Concept attainment creates an environment where the teacher has frequent access to student knowledge (a necessary precursor for quality instruction), where teachers visibly see the ways in which students are thinking through ideas, where the natural interests and cognitive styles of culturally diverse students are the incentive for student involvement, and where the teacher decides which concepts are significant to warrant in-depth attention and analysis.

One of the prominent concerns of educational reformers is that classroom instruction is too traditional—teacher controlled and teacher centered. Lessons are organized around specific correct and incorrect responses, and students, especially students from culturally diverse backgrounds, have too few opportunities to use their cognitive style dispositions and to explore their own thinking skills. As a consequence, many students, especially those who lack the necessary "academic skills," begin to psychologically exit the system. Such students subsequently become a part of the great mosaic that makes up America—a mosaic that now includes almost 30 million adults who are functionally illiterate (Roberts, 1993; U.S. Bureau of the Census, 1991).

The concept attainment model enables each student to construct and justify an answer to questions that make personal sense. The teacher begins to "shape" the students' thinking by adding new data. Concept attainment is grounded on how students view the world and construct ideas, or in the language of Gregory Cajete (1994), a Tewa Indian educator and writer, it is learning that focuses on "seeing the whole through the parts" (p. 31). This instructional model also enhances motivation because students are required to search for ideas that make conceptual sense to them; they can personally invest themselves in the ideas. Because all inductive models have "the search" element in common, they build effectively on the natural curiosity of children regardless of their cultural or social background.

CASE STUDY

Maria Sanchez is preparing to teach the concept of mixed numbers to her 5th grade students. The students already possess a good understanding of proper and improper fractions. Typically Maria uses direct instruction when teaching new skills to students. Today she wants to use a strategy that engenders more active hypothesizing and critical thinking. She starts the lesson by emphasizing the gamelike nature of a concept attainment lesson.

"Today, class, we are going to play a game. It's not a complicated game or even a competitive game. Rather, it's a type of guessing game. I want to see if you can guess what idea I am thinking about when you see some examples I place on the board. Over here you see a smiling face—that face represents 'yes' examples. The 'yes' examples all have the characteristics or attributes of the concept I am thinking of. You will also notice a frowning face. The examples under that face do not have the required attributes—they are 'no' examples."

Maria then places one "yes" and one "no" example on the board:

$1\frac{1}{2}$ 55

"Now, based on the 'yes' example and 'no' example I provided, can you guess or hypothesize my idea? Lupe."

"Small numbers?" Lupe's guess is written down under a third category, labeled "student hypotheses."

"Any other ideas? José, what do you think?"

"I think you want numbers that have a whole number and a fraction."

"Good. I'll write that down along with Lupe's."

Mrs. Sanchez looks around for other responses and then continues. "My next examples are $22\frac{1}{2}$, which is a 'yes,' and $\frac{4}{5}$, which is a 'no.' Now, what additional ideas do you have?"

LaShanda's hand goes up quickly. "I think the 'yes' examples have to have either a number 1 or 2 in them."

Mrs. Sanchez writes LaShanda's hypothesis on the board.

Mike responds, "I agree with José's hypothesis. The 'yes' examples are terms with a whole number and a fraction."

Mrs. Sanchez looks around for other volunteers. Several students respond by agreeing with one of the first three hypotheses. Some suggest even other ideas that make sense given the examples provided by Mrs. Sanchez.

"OK. Let me give you another 'yes' and 'no' example. The 'yes' is $131\frac{1}{3}$ and the 'no' is $\frac{4}{3}$."

"Based on these, can I eliminate any of the hypotheses that you generated? Mia?"

"Yes, we can eliminate LaShanda's hypothesis. The 'yes' you just gave us has a 4 and 3, not just a 1 and 2."

"Good. Does everyone agree?" The students all nod affirmatively.

The lesson proceeds with additional 'yes' and 'no' examples until approximately eight positive and negative exemplars are on the board. The students have now eliminated all the hypotheses except "numbers that have a whole number and a proper fraction."

As the lesson concludes, Mrs. Sanchez confirms that the attribute identified by the students is in fact essential to defining the concept.

She then adds, "Does anyone know the technical name for what we call numbers with this attribute? That is, what do we call numbers that have a whole number and a proper fraction? Tonya?"

"Mixed numbers?"

"Excellent. That's right. Mixed numbers are numbers that have a whole number and a proper fraction. Now I want you to generate 10 more 'yes' and 'no' examples that we can add to our list. Do that on your own, then I will ask for volunteers to share their 'yes' and 'no' examples with the class, and we will see if everyone agrees with your classification."

The preceding case is an example of a concept attainment lesson. ■

Theoretical Perspective

The concept attainment model has deep, rich historical and philosophical roots. Aristotle, over 2,000 years ago, was concerned with how humans discern or "make sense of" the world in which they live. Within the context of that discerning process, people begin to classify the objects and ideas that they perceive. Indeed, Aristotle was the quintessential scientific organizer; his goal was to clarify concepts and order the world he experienced. He did this by creating his own broad categories (living and nonliving things) and then showing how these categories could be further subdivided. Aristotle used characteristics of an object to make the categorization. As Gardner (1996) notes:

> When Aristotle divides natural phenomena into various categories, his criterion is the object's characteristics, or more specifically, what it can do or what it does.
>
> All living things (plants, animals, humans) have the ability to absorb nourishment, to grow, and to propagate. All living creatures (animals and humans) have in addition the ability to perceive the world around them and to move about. Moreover, all humans have the ability to think—or otherwise to order their perceptions into various categories and classes (p. 114).

The twentieth-century version of the model is based largely on the research of Bruner, Goodnow, and Austin (1956), and it has been subsequently popularized and identified as a teaching strategy by a number of different authors, most especially Joyce and Weil (1972, 1992, 1996). The learning of concepts from various academic disciplines is important to understanding the world. Concepts help make the complex and often abstract nature of diverse ideas much more understandable to students. Without concepts, people would have no way of categorizing new ideas efficiently and effectively; they would have to engage in constant learning and could not use past experience to frame new experiences.

At the most basic level, concepts can be either concrete (simple) or abstract (complex). The level of complexity is dictated by the number of inherent attributes within the concept. Concrete concepts (see Figure 4.1) are those things that can be seen, felt, heard, smelled, or tasted on some direct, experiential level; they can be evidenced by the senses and observed in reality. A car, horse, or whole number can be identified using direct experience—the teacher can point to a Ford, or a stallion, or the number 5. On the other hand, abstract concepts (see Figure 4.1) represent nonobservable instances of a larger, complex idea; they are a collection of meanings that cannot be adequately defined by a single or sometimes even several examples or attributes. The concept of *democracy* is one such abstract concept that is often taught in school. Other examples include ecology, literary criticism, or interdependence.

The concept attainment model can be used by elementary school teachers to teach concrete concepts such as mixed numbers, which is the focus of Maria Sanchez's lesson. With high school teachers, the concepts taught will often be more abstract, and in many instances the appropriateness of the concept attainment model must be carefully assessed before teachers consider using it. In gen-

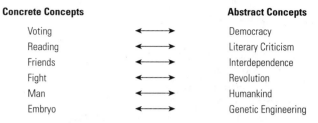

Concrete Concepts		Abstract Concepts
Voting	←——→	Democracy
Reading	←——→	Literary Criticism
Friends	←——→	Interdependence
Fight	←——→	Revolution
Man	←——→	Humankind
Embryo	←——→	Genetic Engineering

FIGURE 4-1   Types of Concepts

eral, concept attainment (CA) is used most effectively by teachers who are teaching concrete concepts; but, as a teacher's skills grow in using the CA model, so, too, can the teacher manifest an ability to transform the model's usage to include a greater variety of complex and abstract concepts.

Concepts are characterized by three elements: a concept name, the essential and nonessential concept attributes, and the attribute value within a concept (Joyce and Weil, 1992). The *concept name* is its common identifier—the term given to the myriad examples within a concept category. Hence, the common identifier for a word that represents a person, place, or thing is *noun*. The term *noun*, in turn, has selected essential and nonessential attributes.

An *attribute* is, according to Bruner, Goodnow, and Austin (1990), "any discriminable feature of an event that is susceptible of some discriminable variation from event to event.... When some discriminable feature of the environment is used as a basis for 'going beyond' by inference, it serves as a signal. When such a discriminable feature is used as a means of inferring the identity of something, ...it is a criterial attribute" (p. 26). In essence, a criterial attribute parallels Joyce and Weil's (1992) notion of essential attribute. If an attribute is changed in value and that change makes it impossible to classify the object, the attribute is essential or criterial for categorizing the object. Changing the color of apples is not criterial; changing their shape would be.

Essential attributes are those characteristics that enable a person to make specific classifications within particular categories. Any term that is a person (Thomas Jefferson), a place (Chicago), or a thing (chair) is labeled a noun. Of course, it can also be labeled a particular type of noun (proper or common), but the type of noun is nonessential to its classification as a noun. *Nonessential attributes* are those characteristics that are evident in a concept but are not needed for accurate concept identification. Hence, crayons are nouns, but the actual color of the crayons is not needed (color is a nonessential attribute) to make an appropriate designation as a noun. Chicago is a city and is classified as a (proper) noun—where it is located and its size are nonessential to its identification as a noun.

Attribute value is the degree to which some characteristic is manifested in order to accurately categorize a concept (Joyce and Weil, 1992). Attribute value is typically less pedagogically evident with concrete concepts than it is with abstract concepts. The presence of seeds (not the number of seeds) represents one essential attribute of fruit. The presence of four wooden legs and a seat (not the quality of the wooden materials) characterizes a chair. For abstract concepts, attribute value plays a more prominent role in the categorization process. As an example, for the concept of democracy, the type of participation of the citizens and the choices they have available are important definitional qualities. A citizen in one country may be able to participate in the political process (when the government dictates) and make choices (for candidates the government specifies) yet live in a dictatorship. In another country, the type of participation and choices may be sufficiently different to qualify as a democracy (that is, citizens have full participation in the political process; they can vote for a range of candidates; and political candidates do not require governmental approval in order to appear on a ballot). Attribute value—the degree to which an attribute is manifested in teacher-identified exemplars—is critical to the identification of abstract concepts.

Concepts can also be *superordinate, subordinate,* or *coordinate.* Indeed, one concept can represent or fit definitionally within all of these descriptors. In Figure 4.2, historical fiction is superordinate to political fiction, subordinate to fiction, and coordinate with romantic fiction. The different levels become important as teachers begin to select examples of concepts for concept attainment lessons. In Figure 4.3, apples are subordinate (in a subcategory) to fruit but coordinate (within the same category) with bananas and oranges. Finally, apples are superordinate to the apple types of Macintosh or Granny Smith.

Providing such examples to students is critical in teaching concept attainment lessons. Equally important, especially as the concept attainment lessons are implemented, is the use of nonexamples. It is through the use of both examples and nonexamples that students learn to fully explore the attributes of concepts.

Examples must possess the essential attributes of a concept, while nonexamples will not have one or more of the essential attributes. Concept attainment lessons rely heavily on both examples and nonexamples, though how the examples are actually presented to students may vary significantly depending on the type of hypothesizing desired by the teacher.

Concept attainment strategies are intended to frame the essential attributes of a concept while expanding the thinking skills of students. Students in schools are expected to acquire content information and to actively think about that content. Most schools place students in the position of learning content information without critically thinking about how that content is organized or structured—the teacher provides the schema rather than requiring students to

FIGURE 4-2 The Hierarchical Structure of Fiction (Superordinate to Subordinate Concepts)

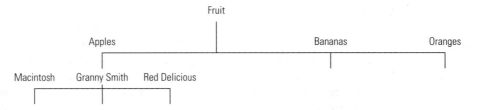

FIGURE 4-3 The Hierarchical Structure of Fruit (Superordinate to Subordinate Concepts)

independently generate their own conceptual organization. Concept attainment requires that the teacher identify a significant concept and then structure a lesson so that students identify the salient aspects of that concept. Students must engage in higher-order thinking to determine the concept name and the specific attributes that the teacher predetermines as focal points of a concept attainment lesson.

Teachers usually implement the curriculum by identifying in lessons a salient concept, providing a definition of the concept (with the appropriate attributes), and then providing examples of the concept (see Figure 4.4). Such a deductive approach is an efficacious one, especially for teaching certain types of functional skills (for example, how to divide or add fractions). But such an approach to teaching also has limitations because it fails to create within students the type of critical-thinking skills students need once they enter the world of work. As examples, doctors work from symptoms to diagnosis; lawyers work from a client's problem to an understanding of applicable legal codes; and students retain more when they work from observing and classifying data to defining and articulating concepts. Tennyson and Cocchiarella (1986) compared the effectiveness of treatments in which students induce attributes and definitions as compared with deductive instances where definitions are presented by the teacher and then followed by exemplars. They found that students consistently developed better concept understandings and retained concepts longer when inductive rather than deductive instructional approaches were used.

FIGURE 4-4 A Comparison of Deductive and Inductive Pedagogical Structures

Concept attainment is an instructional model that utilizes inductive thinking strategies. The teacher moves from specific instances and examples to general ideas and concepts. This instructional process requires that students think through what the teacher-generated examples have in common (how the exemplars are alike) and how to synthesize those attributes (consider them in combination) to determine a specific concept name.

CONCEPT ATTAINMENT: TEACHING PHASES

Phase I: Concept Identification

Not every concept can or should be taught using the concept attainment approach. Concepts taught using the concept attainment model should be significant and have relatively clear and specific attributes, especially when the teacher is first utilizing this instructional model. Teachers who first use the model should probably start with simple, concrete concepts and then move to more complex, abstract concepts after they have some understanding and comfort level in using this instructional model.

The beauty of the concept attainment model is that although a teacher has a clear concept in mind, the students must identify the essential attributes by thinking about the exemplars the teacher provides. Students become active participants in the construction of the lesson. They must carefully think about what the positive examples have in common (how they are the same) and eventually determine a concept name that has been predetermined by the teacher. The model works best when a concept has several different defining attributes (for example, a fruit or a part of speech) because student thinking can be expanded upon as the lesson progresses.

Once the teacher identifies the concept for the lesson, by examining a textbook, by following a district prescribed course of study, or by assessing a need for students to acquire the concept, students then actually participate in the concept attainment instructional model. Students, in essence, become active participants in constructing their own understandings.

Phase II: Exemplar Identification

Providing exemplars to students is at the heart of the concept attainment model. Exemplars consist of positive and negative examples of a concept. Positive exemplars contain all the necessary critical attributes of a concept. In Maria Sanchez's lesson, the positive example ($1\frac{1}{2}$) has all the requisite attributes of a mixed number (that is, a whole number and a fraction). Negative exemplars do not contain a necessary critical attribute—Mrs. Sanchez's example of 55 has a whole number but not a fraction.

The positive and negative exemplars can be presented in several different ways to students. In a later section of this chapter, we will describe an alternative concept attainment strategy that can be used to help students acquire the necessary understandings of the critical attributes.

The first set of positive exemplars provided in the lesson should be relatively clear and specific. The emphasis should not be on tricking students but rather on helping students identify the requisite essential attributes. Eggen and Kauchak (1988) suggest that "examples [should be] selected so that each contains the combination of essential characteristics and none of the nonexamples contain the same combination" (p. 136). Tennyson and Park (1980) suggest that a set of exemplars should contain at least "three examples and five nonexamples which…[reflect] the number of critical and variable attributes of the concept" (p. 57).

In selecting positive exemplars, each should illustrate the requisite characteristics. In providing negative exemplars, care should be taken to ensure that nonessential attributes are varied and substantially represent *what the concept is not*. Tennyson and Park (1980) argue that "nonexamples help the student concentrate on critical attributes [especially] when presented in a matched set of examples and nonexamples…[but] nonexamples may not facilitate concept learning unless they are matched to examples having similar variable attributes" (p. 59). For Mrs. Sanchez's lesson the nonexamples might include the following: 55 (a whole number), $4/5$ (a proper fraction), $4/3$ (an improper fraction), and .33 (a decimal). The positive examples for her lesson are all mixed numbers: $1\frac{1}{2}$, $22\frac{1}{2}$, $131\frac{1}{3}$, but they are not the same type of mixed numbers (that is, $1\frac{1}{2}$, $2\frac{1}{3}$, $3\frac{1}{4}$, and so on). Correct classification occurs most readily when the examples are ordered from easy to difficult (simple to complex), when they differ in essential attributes, and when nonexamples differ from examples in a minimum number of critical attributes.

Some teachers attempt to "match" examples and nonexamples. Matched exemplars contain similar elements, except each nonexample lacks an essential attribute necessary for accurate concept identification. McKinney (1985) writes: "As an illustration, when teaching the concept of 'domesticated animal,' a teacher may show a picture of a house cat (example) and a tiger (nonexample). They are matched because both are types of cats" (p. 66).

After the students see a variety of positive and negative exemplars (whether matched or unmatched), they can begin to differentiate the exemplars and to engage in the third phase of the concept attainment model: hypothesizing.

Phase III: Hypothesizing

With the concept attainment model, the student is asked to identify the common attributes and eventually identify a label (or name) for the examples provided by the teacher. Phases II and III are cyclical, with the student observing some examples and then hypothesizing. The teacher then shares some additional positive and negative examples, which are followed by additional hypothesizing. At some point in the class discussion, the students will have all the critical attributes identified and all the false hypotheses eliminated. False hypotheses occur early in the process when a limited number of exemplars are available for student review. They are eliminated as a result of the cyclical process, with students identifying those hypotheses that remain valid after all exemplars are available for review. In the case study provided above, recall that after the third set of exemplars is provided by Mrs. Sanchez, she asks: *"Based on these, can I eliminate any of the hypotheses that you generated?"* And Mia responds, *"Yes, we can eliminate LaShanda's hypothesis. The 'yes' you just gave us has a 4 and 3, not just a 1 and 2."*

The cyclical process helps students compare items and see how the various exemplars are both similar and different. One problem that some teachers encounter at the early stages of this phase is that a student will guess the correct concept very quickly—"I think it's mixed numbers." If students accurately identify the concept, the teacher should avoid immediately confirming the guess as correct with "Right! You have it!" Instead, the teacher should treat each guess (hypothesis) as equally valid until most or all of the exemplars are identified. Remember the purpose is to foster thinking and to learn the teacher-defined concept. In concept attainment, the thinking process is just as important as the correct identification of the concept.

In essence, the cyclical process entails the following steps:

1. Teacher presents (matched or unmatched) exemplars
2. Students analyze exemplars and generate hypotheses
3. Teacher presents additional exemplars
4. Students add additional hypotheses and eliminate invalid hypotheses
5. Teacher and students confirm all valid hypotheses and eliminate all invalid hypotheses.

Once all valid hypotheses have been confirmed and all invalid hypotheses eliminated, the teacher then prepares for closure.

One final note: The actual level or amount of hypothesizing will be dictated by the number of attributes and the concomitant discriminable values of the examples or instances presented by the teacher. Bruner, Goodnow, and Austin (1990) observe:

> The larger the number of attributes exhibited by instances and the larger the number of discriminable values they exhibit, the greater will be the number of hypotheses to be entertained. This is the first constraining factor imposed on problem-solving by the nature of instances encountered (p. 61).

Phase IV: Closure

The closure phase requires the least amount of teaching time. In this phase of the lesson the teacher reviews the hypotheses that remain after all the exemplars have been presented, and helps the students isolate a working concept name. Recall that Mrs. Sanchez asks, *"What do we call numbers that have a whole number and a proper fraction?"* Some students may recognize the term *mixed number.* If so, the teacher accepts the response, *"That's right. Mixed numbers are numbers that have a whole number and a proper fraction."* However, the teacher also reviews and demonstrates why the concept attributes define whether an item is a positive example or a negative example. For example: *"Let's review the examples. The number $1^{1}/2$ is a mixed number because 1 is a whole number and $^{1}/2$ is a proper fraction—the two together ($1^{1}/2$) create a mixed number. The number 55 is not a mixed* *number because there is no fraction with the whole number 55.*" If students cannot identify the correct concept name, the teacher should provide it: "*You have identified the essential attributes of a number in mathematics we call a* mixed number." This response is perfectly acceptable, especially with elementary-age youngsters who do not have a prior history with concepts being presented by the teacher.

Many teachers prematurely stop lessons once students identify the concept. They fail to review with students the reasons for the positive and negative exemplar labels. This is a mistake! Even if the very first student guesses the concept name, keep the lesson going until the students begin to hone in on the critical attributes and the specific concept. The reinforcement of having students recognize why each exemplar is either positive or negative is extremely important in fostering enhanced student understanding. Further, such reinforcement enables students to proceed more easily to the application phase of the model. Some teachers have students write down the concept name and critical attributes (valid hypotheses) before proceeding. Other teachers just leave the concept name and attributes displayed on an overhead projector or on a chalkboard. Either way, it is important to make certain that the critical attributes are clearly identified before students proceed to the application phase.

Phase V: Application

The application phase enables students to fully explore their understanding of the concept. Students demonstrate an understanding of the concept by creating their own exemplars. Actually, students may be asked to generate their own positive and negative examples. This process allows the teacher to explore the ability of students to define the concept's essential attributes. Mrs. Sanchez said to her students, "*Now I want you to generate 10 more 'yes' and 'no' examples that we can add to our list.*" The students then generate their own examples and must be prepared to accurately describe each exemplar based on the critical attributes. One student may respond that $4\frac{1}{2}$ is a positive example because it has a whole number and fraction and that .46 is not an example because it is a decimal number. The teacher at this point can more fully explore the difference between essential attributes and nonessential attributes. For example, it is essential that mixed numbers have a whole number and a proper fraction. A nonessential attribute is the actual value of the different numbers (for example, for a mixed number the actual value of a whole number or proper fraction is irrelevant to making an accurate classification; or, for a car, a nonessential attribute is the car's color).

❶NSTRUCTIONAL VARIATIONS

Teachers who introduce concept attainment approaches in the classroom may find students initially confused by the use of exemplars (especially nonexamples) as a way of inducing definitions. We suggest that when teachers first start to use the model they play a simple concept attainment game to help students understand the teaching strategy that will be used. One that we have used and found to be successful follows:

"Class, in preparing for today's lesson I need to have you play a little game with me. This game focuses on your ability to identify the physical attribute I am thinking of when I call on one of you to stand. For instance, Nguyen [a brown-haired boy with glasses], I want you to stand. Nguyen is a positive example of my idea. Stephanie [a redheaded girl without glasses], I want you to stand. Stephanie is a nonexample of my idea. Based on these two examples, what idea do you think I have in mind?"

The students now begin to hypothesize. Some students think the teacher's idea is "boys." Others think it has something to do with hair color. And still others guess glasses. After all the hypothesizing is completed, the teacher proceeds with more positive and negative examples.

"Marion is an example of my idea [a brown-haired girl with glasses] and Bob is a nonexample [a blond-haired boy without glasses]."

As the lesson progresses, the students eliminate all hypotheses except "students with glasses."

The high school teacher we originally saw use this "introduction" then proceeded to teach a lesson on parts of speech. He complimented the students on identifying the correct physical characteristic and then asked them to see if they could do the same thing with a more abstract concept.

Teachers might use such introductory activities as a way of orienting students to the nature of concept attainment procedures. Such a preparation activity can help students begin to understand the concept attainment model.

Variations on concept attainment mainly focus on how phases II and III are implemented. Teachers who use concept attainment at different times in the school year may want to alter the manner in which the positive and negative examples are provided and the hypothesizing is conducted. The following variation is provided so that teachers, utilizing this instructional model, can more effectively vary their approaches throughout the school year.

Concept Attainment I

In Concept Attainment I (CAI) the teacher provides one or two positive and negative examples and then asks the student to begin hypothesizing. By limiting the number of initial exemplars, the teacher maximizes the number of hypotheses that will be generated by the students. After the students create a tentative set of hypotheses, the teacher continues by placing another set of positive and negative examples on the board. After each set is provided, the students add or delete hypotheses based on their analyses of the new exemplars. The following is a listing of the example (phase II) and hypothesizing (phase III) steps with which students will be involved within a concept attainment lesson:

Concept: Natural Resources

Step I: Teacher presents first set of exemplars
    trees—yes
    paper—no
    animals—yes
    gasoline—no

Step II: Students generate hypotheses
- things that are living
- things that are abundant
- things that can be used by humans to do work
- things that end in the letter *s*
- things you can touch

Step III: Teacher presents second set of exemplars
sunlight—yes
electricity—no
limestone—yes
cars—no

Step IV: Students add and delete hypotheses
- ~~things that are living~~
- things that are abundant
- things that can be used by humans to do work
- ~~things that end in the letter *s*~~
- things you can touch

Step V: Teacher presents third set of exemplars
crude oil—yes
kerosene—no
rivers—yes
paper bags—no

Step VI: Students refine hypotheses until all invalid ideas are eliminated

The teacher provides as many exemplars as is necessary to identify the appropriate concept attributes (valid hypotheses). The actual number of desired exemplars will vary according to the concept taught. Tennyson and Park (1980) note: "The optimal number of examples is probably not an absolute number. It will vary depending upon the characteristics of the concept such as the number of attributes" (p. 61). In the previous example the teacher is teaching the concept of natural resources and completes the lesson once the students identify the salient attributes of the positive examples (for example, occur naturally, are used to make products for humans, have value, and so on). The invalid hypotheses (for example, things that end in *s*, and things you can touch) are eliminated.

Concept Attainment II

In Concept Attainment II (CAII) the students are provided with all positive and negative examples before the lesson begins. The teacher starts with one positive and one negative example of the concept to be taught, and then lists the other exemplars, without classifying them as either positive or negative, that will be used as part of the lesson. Hypothesizing starts once students recognize the range of available exemplars. The following is an example of how Concept Attainment II is implemented:

Concept: Natural Resources

Step I: Teacher presents one positive and one negative example of the concept

    trees—yes

    paper—no

Step II: Teacher presents a variety of other exemplars

animal	kerosene
gasoline	cars
sunlight	rivers
electricity	limestone
crude oil	paper bags

Step III: Students hypothesize

    Student 1: "I think your idea is things needed to make paper. To make paper you need trees, electricity, and probably gasoline [to run machines]."

    Student 2: "I think your idea is things that grow in a forest."

    Student 3: "I think your idea is things that are living."

The teacher listens to different student ideas and methodically classifies the other exemplars based on each hypothesis presented. For example, after the first student hypothesis, the teacher might respond: *"If you are right about things needed to make paper, which of the other exemplars would you group with trees?"* The teacher should record all hypotheses, though not all need to be fully developed. (Indeed, teachers may want to list all the potential hypotheses and then "revisit" those that match or are close to the one selected by the teacher.) As students provide exemplars (positive and negative) for a "selected" hypothesis, only those that fit the category as the teacher defines it should be listed. As a result of this process, each student begins to rethink the validity of his or her original hypothesis (for example, things needed to make paper) as the teacher reveals which items are in fact "yes" and "no" examples. A student may include electricity under "things to make paper," but need to eliminate the proposed hypothesis once the teacher labels electricity as a "no." (In this instance the teacher is teaching the concept of natural resources.) Once the students identify the correct hypothesis (or attributes), and all teacher-generated exemplars are labeled, the teacher then asks students to generate their own additional exemplars.

Eggen and Kauchak (1988) propose another variation. They suggest that teachers provide the first two exemplars (one positive and one negative) and then ask the students to generate their own exemplars (and appropriate hypotheses) that they would classify under the original two exemplars. Students must defend each example based on either an implied or a defined hypothesis. Students would then provide additional examples and defend them. At this stage of the instructional variation, the teacher indicates whether the student's example (as a "yes" or "no") is accurate. Hypotheses are added, refined, or eliminated as a result of this iterative process on the part of the students. As students add more and more examples, the valid hypotheses or attributes are more clearly identified. This technique places the cognitive load on students to defend an idea—it places students in the position of having to think critically about ideas and create their own schema relative to the concepts being taught by the teacher.

Concept Attainment I is more appropriate for younger students or for students who are just learning how to use this approach. *Concept Attainment II* is more effective with older students who have the verbal and critical-thinking skills necessary to analyze concepts from several different perspectives. Thus, the efficacy of the different approaches is often dictated by the developmental needs of the students and the pedagogical proficiency of the teacher.

Ⓐpplications to Diverse Classrooms

As the student population in American schools becomes more diverse, it is increasingly important that teachers vary the instructional approaches they use to teach essential content. The use of alternative instructional models is important for several reasons. Such variation enables teachers to match appropriate instructional models with corresponding student cognitive styles and learning modalities. This matching is critical in order to teach students other forms of learning so that they may draw upon alternative styles of information processing when confronted with unfamiliar phenomena, and to vary instructional approaches to teaching and learning in order to sustain the interest and motivation of today's multimedia/sensory students.

As we noted in Chapter 2, American schools tend to favor analytical (field-independent) forms of thinking. This type of schooling for the most part is teacher-centered and is oriented toward deductive thinking processes (deductive teaching requires linear, sequential thinking on the part of students). Indeed, Hale-Benson (1982) contends that "not only does the school reward the development of the analytic style of processing information, but its overall ideology and environment reinforces behaviors associated with...[the analytical] style" (p. 34). Clayton (1996), in her work with cross-cultural students (students from other cultures who enter U.S. schools), reinforces Hale-Benson's point: "In the United States, there is emphasis, for example, on the task to be accomplished, on linear thinking, on decontextualized information, on 'the facts' rather than feelings, on details rather than the whole, on ways of presenting the self to others, on ways of asking questions, and on the attention given to activities" (p. 7).

Analytical thinkers, according to Hale-Benson (1982), view attributes "of a stimulus as having significance in themselves; ...[relational thinkers] think they [attributes] have significance only in reference to some total context" (p. 31). Hilliard (1976) and others suggest that many culturally diverse students approach cognitive tasks through the use of more relational, field-sensitive modes. That is, their cognitive style is one that is oriented toward divergent thinking, inductive learning, and creative processing. Concept attainment fosters divergent thinking (through hypothesizing), engenders inductive thinking (through student examination of specific instances before a general definition is provided), and enhances creative processing (through the ability of students to create their own patterns for the specific exemplars provided by the teacher). Because the concept attainment model utilizes relational processes to teach concepts, it plays to the cognitive strengths of many Native, African, and Hispanic Americans as well as to cross-cultural and female students. The model seeks to develop the skills of comparing and contrasting phenomena. Students are not told the answer in CA approaches; rather they are expected to create their own hypotheses based upon the exemplars presented to them by the teacher. In the early phases of CAI and CAII, it is almost impossible for students to have an incorrect response as long as they can offer a logical explanation for each hypothesis.

Table 4.1 more clearly suggests how the concept attainment instructional model fosters relational skills (as opposed to analytical skills). All students, and especially culturally diverse students, need opportunities to demonstrate their conceptualizations rather than simply recite back to the teacher what the teacher defines as correct. With concept attainment the teacher "sees" the thinking of the students—how they organize ideas and how they define concepts prior to seeing the teacher's cognitive structure. In Maria Sanchez's lesson, readers should assess the number of different ways in which divergent thinking was fostered and how an evolving definition of the concept occurred. Mrs. Sanchez required, for example, the students to look for patterns (she does not tell them the pattern), and she fostered meaning by having the students justify their answers.

TABLE 4-1 Relationship of Model to Cognitive Skills

Model	Relational Skills	Analytical Skills
■ Concept Attainment	■ Creativity	■ Examining parts in relation to whole
	■ Divergent thinking	
	■ Inductive thinking	
	■ Evolving definition of concept	
	■ Flexible participation (limited number of teacher-defined right answers)	
	■ Improvising with ideas and the relationships between ideas	

PREVALENT ISSUES IN DIVERSE CLASSROOMS

Several issues preclude teachers from using concept attainment effectively. The following section focuses on a set of common issues that teachers confront when they use concept attainment for the first time. After each question, we have highlighted some possible responses that may prove useful to those attempting to use the technique effectively, especially with the diverse learners that constitute a growing part of America's classrooms.

Q: *How do I deal with those students who do not want to participate in a lesson?*

A: It is quite common for some students to be apprehensive about participating in and to think creatively about generating hypotheses—especially students who are part of cultural groups where competition is considered inappropriate (see Chapter 2; Cooper et al., 1980; Cox and Ramirez, 1981; Hale-Benson, 1986; Ramirez and Castaneda, 1974; Shade, 1984; Shade and Edwards, 1987; Soldier, 1989; Vasquez, 1991). Inductive strategies have an implicitly open quality. As students use the inductive approach, they will learn to appreciate the inherent ambiguity of ideas; however, initially the teacher may need to call on a variety of nonvolunteers to offer answers. Teachers should call on students who may, at times, be reticent to respond—but teachers must be comfortable in waiting for student responses. One cooperative learning technique (numbered heads together, NHT, to be described in Chapter 10) may be especially useful in helping reticent students generate ideas. In this approach, the teacher forms the students into groups of three and then has the students in each group count off by threes (that is, one student is assigned the number 1, another 2, and another 3). The teacher then asks the different groups to generate ideas in response to specific teacher questions. For instance, in the example at the beginning of this chapter, Mrs. Sanchez could have asked students to do the hypothesizing in NHT groups instead of just calling out individual ideas. Once the NHT students have completed their group hypothesizing in response to a question, the teacher calls for all number "2s" to raise their hands, and then calls on one of the 2s to share the group's ideas. NHT lowers the personal risks associated with each student generating ideas. In essence, the ideas are more representative of the group's thinking.

Q: *How do I deal with students who dominate and have a need to be* right *all of the time?*

A: One of the biggest problems with inductive strategies emerges when some "gifted" students try to dominate the lesson. These students "know" the answers, and all too often teachers inadvertently play into their hands. The purpose of inductive teaching is to expand student thinking—everyone's thinking. As a consequence, it is absolutely imperative that teachers do not intentionally acknowledge some responses as better than others. Explore all the students' ideas. Instead of praising each response with a "great" or "wonderful," spend more time examining why the response makes sense to the student or how the student sees the response as relevant. Ask quite a few "how," "what," and "why" questions as students think through the possibilities of a hypothesis. The beauty of inductive strategies is that teachers "see" more of the students' thinking. The problem with traditional approaches (for example, lecture) is that teachers expect students to assimilate ideas in precisely the same way as the teacher, and then the teacher has a tendency to call on a narrow range of students to respond (Sadker and Sadker, 1994a).

Q: *Do my exemplars really make that much difference in who participates?*

A: Yes! Some teachers create exemplars for each lesson that require just one representation of an idea. That is, they consistently use words or pictures to represent an idea. For students who come from cultural backgrounds where linguistic intelligence is valued and fostered, such narrowness may seem efficacious—the approach plays to their strengths. Unfortunately, many students have other types of intelligence that teachers fail to tap in a way that allows for individual expression of creativity and cognitive exploration. Teachers at all grade levels who use concept attainment need to utilize a variety of exemplars to communicate ideas—objects, pictures, words, music, metaphorical expressions, and even the students themselves (for example, recall the sample activity earlier in this chapter where the students with and without glasses were asked to stand). Concept attainment fosters what Cajete (1994) describes as a type of indigenous teaching (that is, teaching that builds on the natural dispositions of children) because the teacher can use larger ideas and because students are required "to listen, to look, to create, and to reflect…[in a way that enables them] to see things deeply" (p. 227).

One of the greatest stimuli to enhanced student self-esteem is success; and one of the best ways to foster success is to vary how ideas are presented so that students from different social, cultural, and personal backgrounds can, at times, play to their cognitive style dispositions.

Q: *Is it important to vary learning modalities when using the concept attainment model?*

A: Very definitely yes! Teachers at all grade levels and content areas who use this instructional model need to vary choices of modalities—visual, auditory, kinesthetic—within a concept attainment lesson. The more alternative modalities presented within the lesson, the more likely it is that the teacher will reach all youngsters in the learning process. Recall from Chapter 2 that a number of unique attributes were discussed regarding how individuals within cultural groups process information; these attributes have implications for designing instruction for students. The research conducted by Damico (1983) and by Shade and Edwards (1987) concerning the use of people-oriented pictures and statues has use in planning concept attainment lessons. Their research findings indicate that when working with African American youngsters, as opposed to European American youngsters, people-oriented examples tended to have a greater impact on student learning. African American, and Hispanic American youngsters as well, tended to relate positively when people-oriented examples were used within classroom lessons. The learning principle is clear: whenever possible, especially when teaching concrete concepts, use both animate and inanimate examples in concept attainment lessons. Teacher use of nonverbal expressions, the use of imagery in understanding complex concepts, changing environmental conditions, and the use of warm, cooperative environments can play an important role in the success of implementing this model (Loftin, 1989; Soldier, 1985; Swisher and Deyhle, 1989). The use of a wide variety of examples that utilize alternative styles of modality (visual, kinesthetic, and auditory) in the form of objects, pictures, words, music analogies and metaphors, and role playing will have a profoundly positive effect upon the development of student thinking.

ⒺVALUATION CRITERIA

Teachers who first use the concept attainment strategy will struggle to make certain they include all the phases of the lesson, and they may need to refer to notes or other resources to keep the direction and flow of the lesson on target. As instructional proficiency with the model increases, so, too, will the teacher's flexibility in organizing the lesson. In general, the following types of questions need to be asked in understanding whether a lesson has been properly developed and sequenced.

Phase I: Concept Identification

1. Is the concept a significant frame of reference for additional student learning? Is the concept important?

   ○ Yes ○ No
   ○ Yes ○ No

2. What type of concept (concrete or abstract) has the teacher decided to emphasize?

   Concept name: _____

   What are the superordinate, subordinate, and coordinate concepts that students may need to know?

   Superordinate: _____
   Subordinate: _____
   Coordinate: _____

Phase II: Exemplar Identification

1. What type of concept attainment strategy did the teacher choose to use (CAI, CAII)?

   CAI _____ CAII _____

2. Are the positive examples clear prototypes for the concept?

   ○ Yes ○ No

3. Does the teacher allow for substantial amounts of student hypothesizing (that is, attempt to explore a broad range of possibilities)?

   ○ Yes ○ No

4. Does the teacher eliminate invalid student hypotheses as the lesson progresses? ○ Yes ○ No

5. Are equal numbers of positive and negative examples provided? ○ Yes ○ No

6. Are a sufficient number of exemplars provided (approximately 8 to 10 exemplar pairs)? ○ Yes ○ No

7. Are students asked to defend their hypotheses? (Students often guess without thinking—teachers need to focus the students' thoughts on the *validity* of proposed ideas.) ○ Yes ○ No

Phase III: Hypothesizing

1. Does the teacher clearly define the concept so that identified attributes are presented? ○ Yes ○ No

2. Does the teacher review why "yes" and "no" examples received the classification they were given? ○ Yes ○ No

3. Do the students know the technical name for the concept? ○ Yes ○ No

Phase IV: Closure

1. Do the students have an opportunity to generate their own exemplars? ○ Yes ○ No

2. Are students required to defend their exemplars? ○ Yes ○ No

3. What types of relational and analytical skills are emphasized in the lesson (see Table 4.1)?

List:

_____ _____

_____ _____

❂ SAMPLE LESSONS

The following classroom episodes are intended to help readers fully understand the concept attainment model. The first scenario is a concept attainment lesson that focuses on object weight; the second example is a proposed lesson plan that will utilize the concept attainment approach with high school pupils. Read each scenario and respond to the questions that follow.

CASE STUDY

Joyce Sampson is preparing her 1st grade students to understand the concepts of big and little for a science lesson. She teaches in an inner-city elementary school in a midwestern city. Today she wants to focus on the concept of heavy objects.

She begins by placing a 5-pound bag of sugar in front of a big sign labeled "yes" and putting a cotton ball in front of a sign that reads "no."

"Class, you know the game we sometimes play where you attempt to guess the idea I am thinking of? Well, today we are going to play that game again. The 5-pound bag of sugar is an example of my idea. The cotton ball is not an example. What do you think my idea is? Aoki?"

"I think it is stuff you can eat. I eat sugar. I don't eat cotton."

Ms. Sampson places the phrase "things you eat" on the board under the label "student guesses."

"OK, who is next? Jeremy."

"I think it's stuff you use in cooking. My mom uses a lot of sugar when she makes cookies."

"Great. I'll write 'things needed for cooking' right under Aoki's guess. What else? Rosetta?"

"I think it's something that has lots of little parts. The bag has lots of tiny pieces of sugar."

Ms. Sampson looks at the bag and the cotton and before she writes down 'things made up of lots of small pieces,' she asks Rosetta to take a small magnifying lens and look at the cotton ball.

"Doesn't the cotton have a lot of little parts?"

"Yes, but they are connected," responds Rosetta. "I am thinking of things that are tiny but not connected."

"OK, you've convinced me." Ms. Sampson writes Rosetta's guess on the board.

The students generate about four more ideas before Ms. Sampson says, "Let's look at a second set of 'yes' and 'no' examples. This gallon of water is a 'yes' and this little pillow is a 'no.' The two new exemplars are placed in front of the signs.

"Now what new guesses do you have? And does the water eliminate any of our previous guesses?"

Almost all of the first set of guesses still stand. The students argue a bit about whether to keep "things that are tiny and not connected" on the board. One or two students believe that it should stay. Most believe that water is *one* substance and therefore Rosetta's guess should be eliminated. Jack raises his hand and says, "I think your 'yeses' are all heavy."

The students now have six guesses on the board. They include:

- things you eat
- things used in cooking
- things that are heavy
- things that you use with food
- things that you find in a kitchen
- things that are good for you

"Let me give you one more set of examples. This [unabridged] dictionary is a 'yes.' And this paperback book is a 'no.'"

The students all raise their hands.

"Before you respond," says Ms. Sampson, "I want you to think about your current guesses. If this [unabridged dictionary] is a 'yes,' then can we keep 'things you eat'?"

The students respond in unison, "No."

"How about 'things used in cooking'?"

Again, "No!"

"How about 'things that are heavy'?"

"Yes!" (Though a couple of students yell "Not for me.")

Ms. Sampson proceeds until only "things that are heavy" is left. She then asks students to look at four more examples that she has available: a slipper, a big boot, a puzzle piece, and a big, framed picture.

"Tell me which of these is a 'yes' and which is a 'no.'" The students correctly label each item.

"Now work with your partner and develop your own list of 'yes' and 'no' examples. I will have each one of you share your examples with the class. Let's see if your friends can indicate whether your examples are 'yes' or 'no' examples." ■

Follow-up questions

1. Is the concept "heavy" an appropriate one for concept attainment?

2. What type of concept attainment strategy (CAI or CAII) did the teacher use in presenting the lesson?

3. Are the examples and nonexamples clear and appropriate for the students' age level?

4. Identify how you might have taught the concept "heavy" using concept attainment. What other instructional strategy might be used to teach this concept?

5. Identify other examples and nonexamples you might provide to the students. What other examples would you include to ensure that all students' needs would be met?

6. What should Ms. Sampson have done differently in teaching this concept to the class?

LESSON PLAN

The lesson plan provided below is for a high school teacher who is preparing to teach a concept attainment lesson to a 9th grade physical science class. Look over the lesson plan and answer the follow-up questions.

Concept: Potential Energy

The *potential energy* of an object is the work possible by the object as a result of its relative position (for example, water at the top of a dam has potential energy).

Objectives:
1. To develop a working definition of potential energy
2. To enable students to generate and identify examples of potential energy in their everyday lives

Methods:
- Teacher will divide the chalkboard into two equal sections. One section is to be labeled "yes" and the other is to be labeled "no."
- Teacher will illustrate pictures of each example and place the exemplar in the appropriate category.

Yes	*No*
1. Ball at the top of stairs.	1. Ball bouncing down the steps.
2. Rocks at the top of slope.	2. Rockslide down a slope.
3. Magnet/nail (apart).	3. Magnet/nail (together).

- Teacher will ask students to identify common characteristics of each of the positive examples.
- Teacher will ask students to compare and contrast positive and negative examples.
- Teacher will ask students to formulate tentative hypotheses.
- Teacher will ask students to test each hypothesis by examining more exemplars.

4. Food.	4. Athlete running.
5. Battery/open circuit.	5. Battery/closed circuit.
6. Gasoline.	6. Car running.

- Students will revise hypotheses.
- Teacher and students will define the concept of *potential energy.*
- Students will practice identifying examples of potential energy by examining additional exemplars.

7. Water behind a dam.	7. Water flowing out from a dam.
8. Ice.	8. Boiling water.
9. Radio tower.	9. Radio playing.

Closure: Students will bring in 10 pictures illustrating potential energy.

Follow-up questions

1. Is the concept *potential energy* an appropriate one for a concept attainment lesson? Why or why not?

2. Are the positive and negative exemplars appropriate? Describe. Which ones are not appropriate? Why?

3. What needs to be added to the teacher's lesson plan? What changes would you suggest? (For example, do you think the teacher should begin with four sets of exemplars?)

4. Do the first positive examples adequately exhibit the essential attributes of the concept? Why or why not?

5. Does the sequence of examples appear logical for both the positive and negative exemplars? Why? How would you sequence the positive examples? The negative examples?

❶ESSON PREPARATION

Using concept attainment requires that teachers fully understand the theoretical basis for the concept attainment model. In preparing a lesson plan, teachers may need to do further reading about how and when to use the model. They may also want to watch videos of other teachers who are using the model in their own classrooms. In preparation for the lesson plan process, teachers should consider using the following readings and videotapes.

Suggested readings

Lasley, T. J., S. J. Williams, and P. M. Hart. 1991. "Nonexamples: Why Teachers Don't Use Them and Why Teacher Educators Should." *Mid-Western Educational Researcher* 4(3): 2–6.

McKinney, C. W. 1985. "A Comparison of the Effects of a Definition, Examples, and Nonexamples on Student Acquisition of the Concept of 'Teacher Propaganda.'" *Social Education* 49: 66–70.

Tennyson, R. D., and O. Park. 1980. "The Teaching of Concepts: A Review of Instructional Design Research Literature." *Review of Educational Research* 50(1): 55–70.

Suggested videotapes

"Concept Attainment." Booksend Laboratories, 652 St. Andrews Drive, Rio Del Mar, Aptos, CA 95003.

Episode Number 2: "Symmetry." Video Library of Teaching Episodes. Association for Supervision and Curriculum Development.

Episode Number 3: "Ways to Make 10." Video Library of Teaching Episodes. Association for Supervision and Curriculum Development.

Suggested lesson development

Once teachers have a reasonably good understanding of how and when to use the model, they need to develop their own lesson plan. The steps to follow are:

1. Determine the concept to be taught.
2. Identify the essential concept attributes that students need to learn.
3. Select positive and negative concept exemplars—be especially concerned with using a variety of perspectives (visual, kinesthetic) to represent the idea or concept.
4. Determine whether CAI or CAII approach will be used.
5. Identify follow-up activities for students once they identify the concept.

SUMMARY

Concept attainment is a strategy that teachers can use periodically to enhance the motivation of students to learn and to foster greater use of relational rather than analytical skills. Because the strategy has a gamelike quality, students actively participate in the hypothesizing phase. Teachers who use the model note that one of the distinct advantages of the model is that students who within traditional classroom structures fail to participate are much more readily involved in the hypothesizing phase. The reason for this circumstance is simple: Every hypothesis that can be defended is acceptable. Many of the students' ideas will be creative—they will look at the phenomena presented by the teacher in very different ways. Such creativity is a positive possibility for all students, but especially for culturally diverse students.

Students in schools are generally very aware that they must make certain they have the correct answer before they respond. For many students, this fact becomes the primary reason they choose not to participate—they either do not want to be wrong, or they do not want to be right at the expense of a fellow student.

Arriving at the correct concept attributes and concept name are important in concept attainment. But the hypothesizing process of CAI and CAII are sufficiently open so that students will feel more willing to participate and to take the chance of proffering their ideas. Indeed, some of the best hypotheses will often be offered by "nonparticipant" students who have learned not to be actively engaged—they have learned that teachers want "correct" answers, not defensible hypotheses. One strength of concept attainment is its ability as an instructional model to help students fully explore and develop their own thinking skills—to take intellectual risks.

REFERENCES

Bruner, J. S., J. J. Goodnow, and G. A. Austin. 1956. *A Study of Thinking.* New York: John Wiley.

———. 1990. *A Study of Thinking.* New Brunswick, NJ: Transaction.

Cajete, G. 1994. *Look to the Mountain: An Ecology of Indigenous Education.* Durango, CO: Kivaki Press.

Clayton, J. B. 1996. *Your Land, My Land: Children in the Process of Acculturation.* Portsmouth, NH: Heinemann.

Cooper, L., D. Johnson, R. Johnson, and F. Wilderson. 1980. "Effects of Cooperative, Competitive, and Individualistic Experiences of Interpersonal Attraction Among Heterogeneous Peers." *Journal of Social Psychology* 111(2): 243–252.

Cox, B., and M. Ramirez III. 1981. "Cognitive Styles: Implications for Multiethnic Education." Pp. 61–71 in J. Banks et al. (eds.), *Education in the 80s: Multiethnic Education.* Washington, DC: National Education Association.

Damico, S. B. 1983. "The Two Worlds of School: Differences in the Photographs of Black and White Adolescents." Paper presented at annual meeting of American Educational Research Association, Montreal.

Eggen, P. D., and D. P. Kauchak. 1988. *Strategies for Teachers.* Englewood Cliffs, NJ: Prentice-Hall.

Gardner, J. 1996. *Sophie's World.* New York: Berkley.

Gunter, M. A., T. H. Estes, and J. H. Schwab. 1990. *Instruction: A Models Approach.* Boston: Allyn & Bacon.

Hale-Benson, J. 1982. *Black Children: Their Roots, Culture, and Learning Styles.* Baltimore, MD: Johns Hopkins University Press.

———. 1986. *Black Children: Their Roots, Culture, and Learning Styles* (rev. ed.). Baltimore, MD: Johns Hopkins University Press.

Hilliard, A. G., III. 1976. *Alternatives to IQ Testing: An Approach to the Identification of Gifted Minority Children.* Final report to the California State Department of Education.

Jarolimek, J. 1990. *Social Studies in Elementary Education.* New York: Macmillan.

Joyce, B., and M. Weil. 1972. *Models of Teaching.* Boston: Allyn & Bacon.

———. 1992. *Models of Teaching* (4th ed.). Boston: Allyn & Bacon.

———. 1996. *Models of Teaching* (5th ed.). Boston: Allyn & Bacon.

Lasley, T. J., S. J. Williams, and P. M. Hart. 1991. "Nonexamples: Why Teachers Don't Use Them and Why Teacher Educators Should." *Mid-Western Educational Researcher* 4(3): 2–6.

Loftin, J. D. 1989. "Anglo American Jurisprudence and the Native American Tribal Quest for Religious Freedom." *American Indian Culture and Research Journal* 13(1): 1–52.

McKinney, C. W. 1985. "A Comparison of the Effects of a Definition, Examples, and Nonexamples on Student Acquisition of the Concept of 'Teacher Propaganda.'" *Social Education* 49: 66–70.

Ornstein, A. C. 1995. *Strategies for Effective Teaching.* Madison, WI: Brown and Benchmark.

Ramirez, M., III. 1973. "Cognitive Styles and Cultural Democracy in Education." *Social Science Quarterly* 53: 895–904.

———, **and A. Castaneda.** 1974. *Cultural Democracy, Bicognitive Development and Education.* New York: Academic Press.

Roberts, S. 1993. *Who We Are.* New York: Times Books.

Sadker, M., and D. Sadker. 1994a. *Failing at Fairness.* New York: Charles Scribner's Sons.

Shade, B. J. 1984. "Afro-American Patterns of Cognition: A Review of the Research." Paper presented at the annual meeting of the American Educational Research Association, New Orleans, LA.

———, **and P. A. Edwards.** 1987. "Ecological Correlates of the Educative Style of Afro-American Children." *Journal of Negro Education* 86: 88–99.

Soldier, L. 1985. "To Soar with Eagles: Enculturation and Acculturation of Indian Children." *Childhood Education* 61: 185–191.

———. 1989. "Cooperative Learning and the Native American Student." *Phi Delta Kappan* 71(2): 161–163.

Swisher, K., and D. Deyhle. 1987. "Styles of Learning and Learning Styles: Educational Conflicts for American Indian/Alaskan Native Youth." *Journal of Multilingual and Multicultural Development* 8(4): 350.

————. 1989. "The Styles of Learning Are Different, But the Teaching Is Just the Same: Suggestions for Teachers of American Indian Youth." *Journal of American Indian Education* (special issue, August): 1–14.

Tennyson, R. D., and M. Cocchiarella. 1986. "An Empirically Based Instructional Design Theory for Teaching Concepts." *Review of Educational Research* 56: 40–71.

Tennyson, R. D., and O. Park. 1980. "The Teaching of Concepts: A Review of Instructional Design Research Literature." *Review of Educational Research* 50(1): 55–70.

U.S. Bureau of the Census, Economic and Statistics Administration. 1991. *1990 Census Profile: Race and Hispanic Origin.* Report No. 2.

Vasquez, J. A. 1991. "Cognitive Style and Academic Attainment." Pp. 163–179 in J. Lynch, C. Modgil, and S. Modgil (eds.), *Cultural Diversity and the Schools: Consensus and Controversy.* London: Falconer Press.

FIVE

• *Inquiry*

At the completion of this chapter, the reader will be able to:
1. *Understand the theoretical basis for the model.*
2. *Identify the essential phases of the inquiry model.*
3. *Identify the strengths and weaknesses of the model.*
4. *Describe ways in which the inquiry model enhances the learning opportunities for culturally diverse student populations.*
5. *Create an inquiry lesson for personal use in a classroom.*

❶NTRODUCTION

American schools are instructionally organized more for the transmission of discrete knowledge than they are for student construction of personal knowledge. The former assumes that knowledge is fixed and that the teacher is the source of that knowledge. Students, as a consequence, work independently to acquire necessary, teacher-defined information. Because of this orientation, students exit the school environment often knowing lots of disconnected facts but not fully understanding what they have acquired. Let's look at an example to illustrate the point. Most readers of this text know how to divide $1\frac{1}{3}$ by $\frac{1}{2}$. The division of fractions (learning how to invert and multiply) is rather standard fare in the intermediate grades. If you know how to divide these numbers, let's now go another step by asking the question: "Why does one invert the $\frac{1}{2}$ to derive the correct answer?" If you don't know the reason for inverting, perhaps you can tackle a "simpler" problem: "Think up a story problem for $1\frac{1}{3}$ divided by $\frac{1}{2}$." If you are struggling with the examples, don't feel as though you are alone. Borko and her colleagues (1990) found that almost 70 percent of all elementary education majors were unable to develop a story problem for this simple algorithm.

Some of the reasons for the above circumstance are related to the fact that prospective teachers do not have the academic background knowledge required to fully understand requisite mathematical concepts. Tyson (1994) writes that "many subjects that teachers are expected to teach in public school aren't taught in college.... [For example] mathematics majors are rarely exposed to fractions, at least not as students in the math-

> *Inquiry is a method of teaching; nothing more, nothing less. It is an approach to learning which is based on sound and established concepts, and it is directed toward achievement in content areas as well as toward development of the rational powers.*
>
> Robert F. Bibens

ematics department..." (p. 11). Another reason for this lack of conceptual understanding is due to the fact that elementary and secondary school students are rarely required to think, to question, and to explore ideas. Most questions asked in a classroom are teacher-initiated. Those that do originate with students typically deal with procedural issues (that is, how should an assignment be accomplished?). Hyman (1980) described two research studies, one involving 43,531 classroom behavior incidents, of which only 728 were student questions; the other involved an ethnographic study in which student questions accounted for only 4 percent of the classroom instructional time. Is it any wonder that American students lack depth in what they have studied? Teachers are performing most of the intellectual work; they are doing the thinking for the students.

Inquiry requires that the teacher engage students with content material in a way that fosters exploration, discovery, and critical thought (Good and Brophy, 1994). Students become active participants in the learning process because they can use what they already know to explore the reasons for what they sense. As a consequence, the inquiry instructional model utilizes student past experiences (cultural and intellectual) to become a part of the teaching–learning process. Inquiry also has two inherent advantages over more didactic approaches. First, it builds on the natural curiosity of students and, hence, is more motivational, especially for students who feel disenfranchised within classrooms because they seldom are the first to know the *right* answer. With inquiry, student success is based on good questions, not right answers. Second, because the assumptions of inquiry methods are different from those of more traditional, teacher-directed approaches, many students can experience success who were unable to achieve at a higher level using more traditional instructional approaches. Formulating a question is far different from knowing an answer. Ironically, many high-achieving students are very good at the latter, but quite weak with respect to the former. On the other hand, many students from dysfunctional family environments who are suspicious of the school as an advocate for their learning have learned how to ask difficult, and at times contentious, questions; these same students have spent much less time memorizing correct answers. Even though inquiry builds upon the natural curiosity of students, the teacher's role is to channel the students' interests and ideas in ways that develop their critical reasoning abilities.

❻ASE STUDY

Sarah Lange teaches 5th grade in a midwestern school district. She wants her students to engage in critical thinking about vertebrates. Her lesson today focuses on the interrelationship of animals—how they often work together to secure food.

"Class, today we are going to act like scientists. I want you to observe a phenomenon (an event) and then hypothesize (or guess) what you think is happening. Because you are scientists your role is to ask me a lot of questions. The only unique thing about this approach is that I can respond to your questions only with either a 'yes' or a 'no' response. So your questions must be designed so that you only get a 'yes' or 'no' response from me.

"I'm going to show you many pictures, and your job is to ask me questions about what you see. If my answer is positive, I'll put the information in the 'yes' column [Ms. Lange points to a column on the board with a "yes" in the heading. See Figure 5.1.] If my response is negative, I'll put the information in the 'no' column. Once we have enough information, I'll ask you to start making some hypotheses or guesses. I'll put that in the third column labeled 'hypotheses.' Everyone ready?"

The students respond with a choral "Yes."

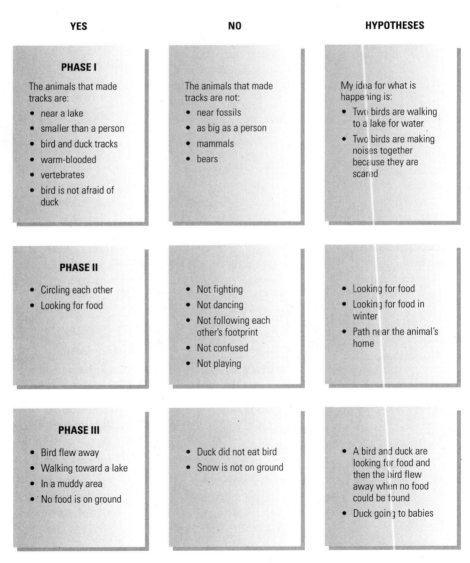

YES	NO	HYPOTHESES
PHASE I The animals that made tracks are: • near a lake • smaller than a person • bird and duck tracks • warm-blooded • vertebrates • bird is not afraid of duck	The animals that made tracks are not: • near fossils • as big as a person • mammals • bears	My idea for what is happening is: • Two birds are walking to a lake for water • Two birds are making noises together because they are scared
PHASE II • Circling each other • Looking for food	• Not fighting • Not dancing • Not following each other's footprint • Not confused • Not playing	• Looking for food • Looking for food in winter • Path near the animal's home
PHASE III • Bird flew away • Walking toward a lake • In a muddy area • No food is on ground	• Duck did not eat bird • Snow is not on ground	• A bird and duck are looking for food and then the bird flew away when no food could be found • Duck going to babies

FIGURE 5-1 Data for Inquiry Lesson on Animal Tracks

"I want you to know that the first set of questions you ask should focus specifically on what you see in this picture (see phase I of Figure 5.2). Basically, class, I want your questions to focus on what is obvious—on facts about what you see rather than on a theory about what is happening. The tracks you see in this figure were left in the mud, and scientists have found them. Now, what questions do you have? Nick?"

"Is there a lake nearby?"

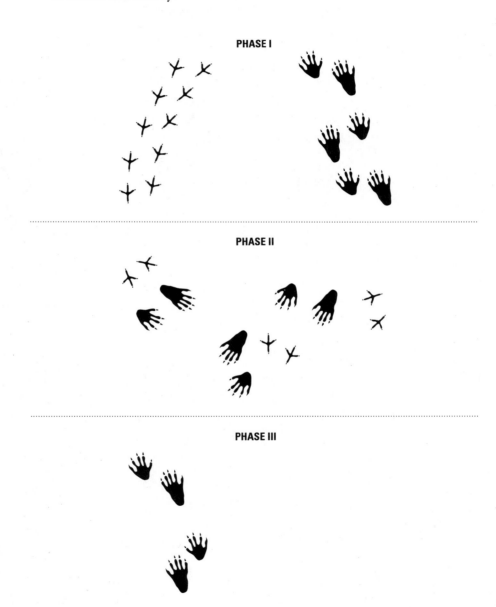

FIGURE 5-2 Phases of Animal Tracks

"Yes, Nick, there is." Ms. Lange walks to the board and in the "yes" column writes the phrase "near a lake." (See Figure 5.1.)

Ms. Lange turns to the class, and Reuben asks whether fossils are nearby. Ms. Lange says "No" and writes "near fossils" in the "no" column right under her lead sentence that reads "The animals that made tracks are not:…"

The next student asks whether one of the animals that made the tracks was as big as a human, and Ms. Lange writes that it is not. This question is followed by a query regarding whether one of the animals is smaller than a person and Ms. Lange notes that it is. Ms. Lange then has the students ask a series of questions on the size of the animals that made the tracks.

Then a student, Suzette, asks, "Are they bird and duck tracks?"

Ms. Lange responds, "Yes, they are. That's excellent! Some of you probably assumed they were bird and duck tracks. Suzette has verified that they are."

The students continue to ask questions, all of which can be answered with a "yes" or "no," and Ms. Lange writes the information on the board as it is gathered. At the end of this phase of the lesson, Ms. Lange asks the students to begin forming hypotheses. How would they make sense out of what they see? One student, Javier, suggests, "Two birds are walking to a lake to get water," and a second student, Milagros, offers "Two birds are making noises together." A third student hypothesizes about the duck.

"Class, before I accept more hypotheses, I want you to look at my next picture." (See phase II of Figure 5.2.) The students express various forms of excitement as they look at the second picture.

"OK, now that you see this picture, what new questions do you have? Seong."

"Are the birds fighting?"

"No," responds Ms. Lange. "That's an excellent question. However, the answer is in the negative." She writes "not fighting" in the "no" column.

Another student asks, "Are they dancing?"

Again Ms. Lange responds with a "No." She turns and writes "not dancing" in the "no" column.

Almost all student hands are raised in the class. Students ask a variety of questions, but all have the common feature of allowing Ms. Lange to respond with a "yes" or "no." After several minutes of questioning, Ms. Lange says, "Class, let's stop again and do some more hypothesizing about what you think is happening in the picture. Your 'yes' responses are going to be the best clues for you to consider." She then calls on Fumiko.

"I think that the birds are really looking for food."

Ms. Lange writes Fumiko's hypothesis on the board and then calls on Esther.

Esther adds that she thinks Fumiko's hypothesis is correct except she believes that it's wintertime. Ms. Lange writes Esther's idea on the board.

A couple of students create hypotheses that are not at all related to the data generated in the "yes" or "no" column. Ms. Lange listens to their comments and then asks them to identify the existing data that supports their conclusions. When they are unable to provide support, she comments, 'We need to make certain that our hypotheses are related to our data."

"Let's look at a third picture, class, and see if that provides you with some other ideas." Ms. Lange then unfolds the poster paper and reveals another picture (see phase III of Figure 5.2). The students excitedly gasp and raise their hands.

"Class, quiet. I need to be able to hear. OK, Jean, what question do you have?"

"Did the duck eat the bird?"

"No." Ms. Lange then writes "Duck did not eat bird" on the board and turns to the class and asks, "What other ideas do you have?

Jonathan asks, "Did the bird fly away?"

"Yes," says Ms. Lange. She then writes "Bird flew away" on the poster paper.

The students continue asking questions. Some ask questions about the duck, and others inquire about the feelings of the bird ("Is the bird afraid of the duck?"). Ms. Lange writes down information and then reviews all the "yes" and "no" responses.

"Let's do some additional hypothesizing, class. I want you to create one or two more hypotheses, and then let's consider which hypothesis makes the most sense."

The students do some additional hypothesizing, and then Ms. Lange has the students begin a discussion to determine which hypothesis makes the most sense. The students begin the final phase of this lesson by eliminating invalid hypotheses that make little sense given the data in the "no" column. Ms. Lange draws a line through the invalid hypotheses.

The students consider each of the remaining hypotheses and decide on what they view as the most logical hypothesis: "A bird and duck are looking for food, and the bird flew away when no food could be found." This hypothesis, according to the students, seems to make the most sense given the known data. Ms. Lange then confirms that, in fact, that is what occurs.

Ms. Lange asks, "Class, what data from the 'yes' and 'no' columns was the most helpful to you in reaching your conclusion?" The students share their ideas and complete the lesson by doing research on the feeding behavior of different birds and on how animals often compete for food sources. ∎

Ms. Lange's lesson is an example of inquiry instruction. The students are asking questions to identify data that subsequently will be used to create workable hypotheses. The model is an inductive one, but its real power is associated with requiring students to critically think about data—data that they generate themselves.

THEORETICAL PERSPECTIVE

In Chapter 6 of this text (Concept Formation) we will argue, as did Hilda Taba (1966), that thinking can be taught, but that students need to follow a careful sequence of steps in order to maximize the power of a learning experience. The inquiry model is one structured method of helping students learn to think. The technique is not new; it is, in fact, as old as Western culture. Socrates used inquiry to enable his pupils to reach thoughtful conclusions. Although he did not use the type of guided ("yes" and "no" question) approach used by Ms. Lange, he did work with his students as they made observations, synthesized information, generated hypotheses, and explored ideas. Socrates attempted to shape students' thinking as they searched for *truth*. Indeed, he was so good at using questions that he ultimately was perceived as impious and paid the price with his life.

Inquiry requires many more intellectual skills of a student than merely knowing content; the student must also be able to understand the dynamics that ground that academic content. Schools place tremendous emphasis on knowing content and far too little on developing thinking skills. The consequence is that students leave schools with much misinformation. Tyson (1994) describes, for example, a study conducted in the early 1990s when students at Harvard University were asked about the phases of the moon—Harvard students clearly understood that there were phases, but they were unable to explain correctly what caused those phases. Tyson writes: "When asked to explain the phases, virtually everyone cheerfully [explained] that a partial moon occurs when the earth gets between the sun and the moon and casts a shadow" (p. 6). Such misunderstandings are not unusual. Teachers frequently reach the conclusion of a lesson only to discover through some student question or explanation that the students have an erroneous cognitive structure for the facts that were presented.

Inquiry, whether guided or unguided, has three general stages: exploration, invention, and discovery (Bibens, 1980). In the exploration phase, students attempt to clearly understand the pertinent information related to a specific topic. Ms. Lange does not begin by having students offer hypotheses; rather, she initiates the activity by having students identify, through "yes" or "no" questions, the pertinent information that subsequently can be used to generate hypotheses. Bibens writes:

> They [students] are asked to locate pertinent information which has a bearing on the topic. They may draw on what has been found in earlier investigations...or even presentations made by the teacher. Once they are satisfied that they have the necessary data, they are asked to arrange their findings in some kind of reasonable pattern (p. 89).

In the second stage, invention, students are expected to begin to make sense out of the data they generated in the first phase. Students look for patterns and attempt to pull together those ideas that represent reasonable explanations for whatever phenomenon they have observed. They use the pertinent information to form synthesized conceptual representations (or hypotheses). Those hypotheses set the stage for a very important third stage in the inquiry process—discovery.

Bibens notes that it is during the discovery process that students "discover the inadequacies of what they have invented" (p. 90). The discovery stage occurs as the students explore whether the hypotheses really make sense given the array of pertinent data available to them. Once Ms. Lange, for example, had students generate some hypotheses, she had the students examine whether their ideas (hypotheses) could accurately describe the data (in the "yes" column).

The inquiry instructional model presented in this chapter is inductive in nature. The structure given to the inquiry lesson, however, can be either guided or unguided. Most of the attention in this chapter will be on guided inquiry, which is a more defined pedagogical structure for having students generate data. Guided inquiry moves the students from observations to inferences and then to generalizations (Orlich et al., 1985), but the teacher controls the way in which questions are worded (that is, they must be answerable with a "yes" or "no") and in which hypotheses are generated. The teacher controls what the students observe, but the students are free to explore any ideas that they feel relate to the phenomenon they are observing. Many different models of guided inquiry exist in the literature (Orlich et al., 1985; Shulman and Tamir, 1973). How we use the inquiry model relates specifically to a teacher-controlled process (the requirement of convergent student questions) for having students make observations, and then proceed from those observations to the stage of hypothesizing.

Unguided inquiry, on the other hand, enables students to be more creative. The teacher still controls the overall dynamics of the classroom situation, but the students are given much more latitude in the types of questions they ask during the lesson. In addition, the teacher is not attempting to position students toward a specific hypothesis to explain a phenomenon. Ms. Lange, using guided inquiry, knew which hypothesis was correct. Ms. Lange clarified students' ideas in an effort to position them toward a logical explanation. (Sometimes there is absolutely no correct explanation, and the teacher fosters student thinking regarding the *most workable* hypothesis.) Similar closure is not required for unguided inquiry. If a teacher has students read a Pat Conroy novel (for example, *Beach Music*) and then asks, "What observations about the South do you have that might explain the protagonist's relationship with his parents?" the teacher is not attempting to derive one specific set of ideas. Rather, the teacher is looking at how the students use their observations of characters in *Beach Music* to support generalizations about how Conroy grew up in the South.

Orlich and his colleagues (1985) argue that unguided inquiry works best once students understand the guided inquiry process. Though he used a slightly different definition of guided inquiry than the one we use, we basically agree with his assertion. Students need practice in the process of making careful observations. Such practice is probably monitored best through guided inquiry approaches in which teachers subtly influence the direction of student thought.

GUIDED INQUIRY: TEACHING PHASES

Phase I: Discrepant Event

Guided inquiry lessons begin by having the teacher create an event or present a problem that cannot be easily explained or immediately solved. Wright (1981) provides one of the best definitions of a discrepant event—"a phenomenon which occurs that seems to run contrary to our first line of reasoning" (p. 575). The students in Ms. Lange's class were asked to look at the various duck and bird tracks and make some sort of sense out of what they observed. The third phase of the discrepant event created particular excitement because it was at this point that students saw duck tracks, but no bird tracks.

The key to a good inquiry lesson is an effective discrepant event. Teachers who have experimented with the inquiry model will quickly note that the more powerful the discrepant event, the better the student participation in a lesson. A weak discrepant event is one that can be explained quickly and that has very few competing ideas that represent possible explanations for the event. A powerful discrepant event is one that engenders a tremendous number of student questions and can potentially be explained in several different ways. The following examples are from three classroom lessons the authors have observed, and Table 5.1 is an example of several others identified by Wright and Govindarajan (1992).

1st grade: The teacher takes two eggs (one soft-boiled and the other hard-boiled) and asks the students to explain why one egg would spin for a long time and the other just a couple of times.

7th grade: The teacher uses tongs and takes an empty pop can that has been heated on a hot plate and places it in cold water. Once in the cold water, the pop can implodes. Students are asked to explain why the implosion occurs.

11th grade: The teacher takes raisins and places them in a jar of carbonated water. Once in the water, the raisins begin to "dance" or move up and down in the jar. Students are asked to describe why this movement occurs.

All three of these discrepant events focus on science, but a discrepant event is possible in every disciplinary area. The only disciplinary area that often proves problematic for teachers is mathematics. Because of the very nature of traditional mathematics (that is, mathematicians describe behavior in order to predict behavior and they use mathematical theory to accomplish this), mathematics teachers, especially high school mathematics teachers, often express frustration when attempting to generate good discrepant events. The most natural areas for using the inquiry technique are social studies, science, and language arts. In general, the more content depth a teacher has acquired in the academic discipline, the easier it is to recognize complex relationships and to determine what discrepant events are possible in a discipline.

One additional note regarding discrepant events is needed. It is imperative, especially for guided inquiry, that teachers have some reasonable knowledge of the phenomenon the students are observing. Several years ago, one of the authors watched a dry ice lesson for an intermediate-level class. The teacher uncovered the dry ice, and the vapor that emerged looked like smoke; the students were, to say the least, very engaged. Her discrepant event was, "How can something so cold create something that looks so hot?" There was only one difficulty. As the students asked questions (and they were truly excited about what they saw!), the teacher repeatedly had to answer, "I don't know." After several minutes, the frustration of the students became apparent. The teacher does not need to know everything about a phenomenon, but the teacher should possess sufficient knowledge to sustain the momentum of an inquiry lesson.

TABLE 5-1 Sample Discrepant Events

Phenomenon, Event, or Question	Probable Student Response	Conceptual Discrepancy	Scientific Principle or Concept Illustrated by Conceptual Discrepancy
1. An amoeba could theoretically become as large as an elephant if it were in a liquid medium of suitable temperature and nutrients.	True	False	In general, volume increases by the power of three, while surface area increases by the power of two. The area/volume ratio decreases as size increases. Eventually, the surface area would become too small to accommodate the needs of the organism.
2. Can two individuals who are both brown-eyed, whose forefathers all had brown eyes, become the biological parents of a child with blue eyes?	No	Possible	The possibility exists when a mutation of the dominant brown-eyed gene takes place in both the sperm and the egg that produced the zygote with the recessive trait of blue eyes.
3. Girls are physically stronger than boys.	False, at least as indicated by boys.	True. Have both sexes face a wall and pace back three steps. Place a chair between each student and the wall. Ask students to bend over with their head against the wall, take hold of the chair, and in one motion stand up straight. Girls can do this easily. Boys will find it impossible. The superior aperture of the pelvis is greater and wider in females, allowing greater flexibility. Also, the pubic arch in females forms an angle greater than 90 degrees, causing the female to have a greater freedom of movement. In males, both the above features are not as prominent.	

(continued)

TABLE 5-1 Sample Discrepant Events *(continued)*

Phenomenon, Event, or Question	Probable Student Response	Conceptual Discrepancy	Scientific Principle or Concept Illustrated by Conceptual Discrepancy
4. It is not possible to light sugar cubes with a match. What will happen if you sprinkle burnt cigarette ash on a cube before lighting it with a match?	Nothing	It will burn.	Cigarette ash acts as a catalyst. The scientific concepts of catalyst and catalytic functions in biochemical systems should be stressed. An interdisciplinary extension into the study of physiological chemistry of glucose (in sugar cubes) and its metabolism in the body will interest students.
5. A man's weight went from 190 lbs. to 0 lbs. and back to 190 lbs. in one day and he lived. Is this biologically possible?	No	Yes	Introduce concepts of mass and weight in anti-gravity conditions by informing students about the phenomenon; also, this serves as an excellent interdisciplinary focus when aspects of physics and biology are discussed. If the man traveled to and returned from space in one day, his mass would remain constant but he would be weightless in space.

Reduced and reprinted from E. L. Wright and G. Govindarajan. 1992. "Stirring the Biology Teaching Pot with Discrepant Events." *American Biology Teacher* 54(4) (April): 205–210.

Phase II: Question Sequence

Once students have observed a discrepant event, the next step is to have students ask questions about what they have observed. The questions they ask, though, should be structured so that the teacher can answer with either a "yes" or "no" response. The teacher first asks students to identify pertinent information. Students have a tendency to jump ahead and identify possible hypotheses—they attempt to develop theories before they fully understand the facts. Students should generate hypotheses (phase III of the inquiry process) only after all available pertinent information (facts) are identified. Ms. Lange, for example, should have tried to elicit some specific data about the types of animal tracks students saw in the picture. (*"Class, ask me questions about the types of animals who made these tracks, and then ask questions about the patterns of the tracks."*)

There is absolutely nothing wrong with focusing students' attention on what types of questions to ask.

If a student asks a question, and it cannot be answered with a "yes" or "no" response, then ask the student to reword the question: "Please reword that so I can answer it with a 'yes' or 'no.'" This is a very common problem! Some teachers try to help students understand how to engage in inquiry by playing 20 Questions with the students. The "20 Questions" game enables the students to practice the "yes" and "no" questioning skills and to understand the guided inquiry process.

Teachers who have used this strategy also have found it useful to record data generated by the students as the students ask the questions. Ms. Lange created a chart for the students (see Figure 5.1). Other teachers have found it useful to use a handout similar to the one in Figure 5.3. As students generate questions

?   **WHAT IS HAPPENING?**   **?**

My "Yes" Information Is	My "No" Information Is

My guess is: _____

Explain why this is your guess: _____

_____

_____

_____

_____

FIGURE 5-3 Record Data Chart

that can be answered with a "yes," they place the appropriate information in the "yes" column. If a "no," then they use the "no" column. Such a strategy is especially useful with young children, but it is potentially helpful for all students, especially when a substantial amount of data are to be generated and the students are not accustomed to this type of critical-thinking experience.

After the students have generated many basic "yes" and "no" pieces of information, the teacher can then ask the students to move on to the next stage, which requires student hypothesizing.

Phase III: Generating Hypotheses

In the hypothesizing phase, the teacher attempts to have students synthesize the "yes" column information in a way that will enable them to create a logical explanation of what they see. As the students provide their guesses or hypotheses, it is imperative that the teacher continue to ask clarifying questions such as: *"What facts in the 'yes' column were most useful in forming your hypothesis? Are there any 'no' facts that would eliminate or contradict your hypothesis?"* In essence, the teacher writes down all student ideas but also challenges students to defend their ideas and conceptually ground their hypotheses. Teachers should attempt to solicit as many hypotheses as possible. The goal during this phase is to see how each student is synthesizing the information in order to formulate a hypothesis that can be defended with the use of data.

Phase IV: Closure

Once all hypotheses have been generated, the teacher begins to focus the students' attention on eliminating invalid hypotheses. At this point some teachers find it very useful to analyze each hypothesis relative to the "yes" column data. Ms. Lange did not do this in her "bird track" lesson. If she had, she would have taken the first hypothesis and asked something like, *"Class, let's look at each fact we have and see if it supports the various hypotheses you have generated. Our first hypothesis is, 'Two birds are walking to a lake.' Given what we know at this point (our "yes" data), is this hypothesis valid? First, is there a lake nearby? [Students are directed to the chart (Figure 5.1) and to notice that 'lake' is, in fact, listed.] Second, are the tracks smaller than those that might be made by humans?..."* The teacher would then continue through the "yes" column data and either retain a hypothesis (if all the "yes" data applies) or eliminate it (if the pieces of "yes" data *conflict* with a hypothesis). Such systematic checking of the data is particularly important for students who are experiencing the technique for the first time. It forces students to closely consider each piece of data.

A common scenario in implementing the inquiry model is for students to conclude the lesson with several workable hypotheses. If the hypotheses are variations on the same idea, then the teacher can work with the class to synthesize the wording and create one workable hypothesis. If, however, the hypotheses represent very different explanations of the same phenomenon, the teacher should have students return to the previous discussion and gather more data. More "yes" and "no" questions need to be asked until the students can either validate or reject each one of the hypotheses.

Phase V: Analysis

At the completion of the inquiry lesson, once a valid hypothesis is agreed upon by the class, the teacher asks the students to evaluate which data helped them determine the valid hypothesis. The teacher, through phase V, is attempting to focus the students' attention in a way that makes them more critical consumers of information. Recall that Ms. Lange asked, *"Class, what data from the 'yes' and 'no' columns was the most helpful to you in reaching your conclusion?"* Students generally will identify two or three key prior questions that really helped them understand the phenomenon. A common student response might be something like, *"Nick's question was the one that really did it for me. When you answered 'yes' to his question about the lake, that's when I knew what was occurring."*

Phase VI: Extension

Once students have a working hypothesis and know the relevant data that supports that hypothesis, the teacher then needs to identify ways of extending the students' thinking. Ms. Lange had students do research on the feeding behavior of birds, but other variations might also be considered. As we will discuss in the next section, it is at this point that the natural interests of the students can be nurtured and the teacher can foster a more culturally responsive classroom atmosphere.

UNGUIDED INQUIRY: TEACHING PHASES

Unguided inquiry, at least the way we present the model, involves many of the same cognitive tasks as Taba's (1966) "interpretation of data." That is, in unguided inquiry the students are looking at raw data and then evolving personal theories to explain how that data can be logically connected.

Phase I: Provide Data

The teacher begins an unguided inquiry lesson similar to a guided inquiry lesson, by providing some type of discrepant event or unstructured data. As an example, Orlich and his colleagues (1985) describe how some teachers use discarded phone directories from different cities and then ask students to discuss what they see in the directory. In unguided inquiry, the teacher is not looking for a particular explanation, a single workable hypothesis. Rather, the teacher is attempting to see how students synthesize information and make sense out of what they observe. Other types of data that might be provided include charts or graphs that require students to analyze and then ask questions about the data provided. Table 5.2 provides data on garbage disposal and collection for several

TABLE 5-2 Cost of Garbage Collection and Disposal in Selected Ohio Cities

CITY	YEAR	TOTAL NET COST	COST PER CAPITA	COST PER TON
Cincinnati	1909	$90,000	$.25	$2.59
Cleveland	1909	38,989	.07	0.87
Columbus	1909	40,706	.23	2.46
Dayton	1908	21,000	.19	2.11
Zanesville	1909	5,695	.21	4.71

Source: *Investigating Solid Waste Issues*, Ohio Department of Natural Resources, 1994

Observations: What do you notice? (Write down facts.)

1. _____

2. _____

3. _____

Questions: What additional information do you need? (Write down your additional questions.)

1. _____

2. _____

3. _____

Generalizations: What significant relationships are evident?

1. _____

2. _____

3. _____

Ohio cities. Based on the data provided, the students would then be asked to generate observations (possible questions and/or hypotheses) that they perceive as relevant given the data in the chart. The observations could be declarative statements (*"Cincinnati's costs were greater than Cleveland's"*) or questions that require them to collect more information (for example, what was the population of each city in 1908 or 1909?). Another example can be found in Table 5.3. In this instance, students would make observations about the way in which two households spend money and consume resources.

TABLE 5-3   Household Resource Uses: Two Cases
Annual Income and Expense Figures

Case: Wesley and Wilma

Wesley and Wilma enjoy the benefits of having two children and two incomes. If they monitor their spending carefully, they have a few dollars left over for emergencies or special occasions. Working leaves Wilma with little free time. It also requires that everyone in the family contribute to housework to make sure all the necessary chores are accomplished.

Average trash disposal per week: 20 pounds

Income before taxes:	$38,262
Total expenditures:	32,753
Food at home:	3,066
Food away from home:	1,987
Shelter:	7,951
Clothing:	1,985
Transportation:	6,384
Health care and pension:	3,959
Personal taxes:	3,761
Other expenses:	5,004
Utilities including sanitation and waste collection:	2,114

Case: Horace

Horace is a college graduate with a degree in business. He was recently hired for his first job as assistant manager at Big's Warehouse. Horace leads an active single life. He spends little time at home in his small apartment, except to eat microwave dinners and watch TV. His active single lifestyle leaves him with little cash. He uses credit to finance his independent lifestyle and to make sure his telephone answering machine is in good working order.

Average trash disposal per week: 3.5 pounds

Income before taxes:	$18,551
Total expenditures:	18,726
Food at home:	1,794
Food away from home:	1,288
Shelter:	5,875
Clothing:	1,353
Transportation:	5,623
Health care and pension:	3,291
Personal taxes:	2,980
Other expenses:	4,232
Utilities including sanitation and waste collection:	1,749

Source: *Investigating Solid Waste Issues*, Ohio Department of Natural Resources, 1994.

Observations: What do you notice? (Write down facts.)

1. _____

2. _____

3. _____

Questions: What additional information do you need? (Write down your additional questions.)

1. _____

2. _____

3. _____

Generalizations: What significant relationships are evident?

1. _____

2. _____

3. _____

Phase II: Make Observations and Ask Questions

Once the students have had an opportunity to examine the data, the next phase in unguided inquiry is to make relevant observations. Some of the students may make declarative, factual statements about the data: *"Cincinnati spent more per capita in 1909 for garbage disposal than did Cleveland."* With declarative statements the teacher attempts to focus students' attention on why this might have been the case. The teacher may or may not know the answer—that is relatively unimportant. The key issue is to enable students to make thoughtful observations and to determine what other data they might need in order to answer specific questions. Indeed, as a follow-up, students might be asked to do research on some of the unanswered questions.

As the students make observations, the teacher keeps track of what observations have validity and what questions need answers. Similar to guided inquiry, it is probably best to write the information on the board (or on notepaper) as the students generate ideas. In some cases the teacher might find it useful to place sections on the data sheet for students to make their observations, write questions, and prepare generalizations.

Phase III: Create Generalizations

After a substantial amount of data are generated, the next step is to determine what generalizations make sense relative to the ideas the students have enumerated. A generalization is nothing more than the relationship between two or more concepts. One generalization might be *"The size of a city influences directly the costs of collecting and disposing of garbage."* Any generalization is acceptable as long as students can show what data they used to formulate and support their ideas. The teacher at this phase in the lesson is literally teaching the students how to learn, to be critical consumers of ideas, and to recognize how to support an argument with data. In this phase of the lesson, the teacher needs to ask plenty of questions such as, *"What ideas that we have on the board support your generalization?"* or *"What additional data would you need to make your generalization even stronger?"* All student generalizations should be written on the board so that students can clearly identify the conceptual relationships. It may be useful to then review each generalization and assess the degree to which students perceive that data are available to support each of the students' statements.

Phase IV: Follow-Up

In the final phase of the lesson, the teacher can ask students to engage in several different types of activities. Each of these activities (for example, defending generalizations and predicting alternatives) is intended to enable students to refine their thinking and to consider what additional information might be required.

Defending a Generalization   Ask students to select the generalization they like the best and then describe (in one or two paragraphs) why that statement is the best representation for their ideas.

Predicting Alternatives   Ask students to make "what if" predictions based on the generalizations and data they have available. For example, one generalization for Table 5.1 might be "Cities on lakes have lower disposal costs than do cities that are situated on rivers." As a consequence, a prediction the students might make is "Chicago had lower disposal costs in 1909 than did Indianapolis." The students can then do research on their hypotheses to determine the level of support for their ideas.

Of course, not all the predictions can be analyzed. But unguided inquiry lessons are enhanced when some of the predictions are examined to determine if the students' ideas can be verified.

Ⓐ PPLICATIONS TO DIVERSE CLASSROOMS

Inquiry approaches play to the natural interests and curiosity of students; and in terms of dealing with diverse learners, there is no better academic equalizer than the intrinsic interests of students. Teachers who know how to engender student involvement based on intrinsic interests create, according to Wlodkowski and Ginsberg (1995), "culturally responsive" classrooms. In essence, culturally responsive teaching does not create circumstances in which the teacher imposes knowledge on students, but rather it is teaching that enables students to deepen their understanding of and enthusiasm for ideas that have personal meaning and relevance.

Inquiry fosters substantial intragroup student cooperation to solve an intellectual problem. The students work together as a group to determine what data are relevant and which hypotheses are most viable. Intrinsic motivation is not an idea that is oriented toward only African American or Hispanic American students—it is a disposition that helps all students regardless of their cultural backgrounds.

Wlodkowski and Ginsberg (1995) describe four conditions that are essential for culturally responsive teaching: establishing inclusion, developing attitude, enhancing meaning, and engendering competence. We'll examine how two of these interplay within the context of an inquiry lesson. First, inquiry as an instructional model fosters inclusion—it is an inclusionary process. Every student question has inherent worth—inquiry reveals something about how a student is understanding content material. Even a "no" response by the teacher helps in the inquiry process. American children are oriented toward knowing the correct answers, and certainly in most situations correct answers have fundamental importance. But many students get turned off to learning when they discover they cannot always give the answer that the teacher wants on demand. With inquiry, all questions have merit and all answers have importance! All student contributions have significance! More important, when the teacher creates lessons that are inclusionary and meaningful, the lesson embraces students' cultural differences (Wlodkowski and Ginsberg, 1995). It is a culturally inclusive process because it values and accepts all student observations, ideas, and generalizations.

Second, by observing phenomena and attempting to make sense out of the ideas, students experience enhanced meaning and enhanced motivation. That is, they can construct their own questions and their own meaning about the discrepant event they observed. Their ideas are then combined with the thinking of the other students in the classroom. The teacher constructs inquiry in order for students to ask "why" something is true. The "why" becomes the motivating force according to Wlodkowski and Jaynes (1990) because the

> ...students feel a little perplexed and wondering. This will cause them to think harder and reflect more deeply. Ask questions like "Why is it that the world can produce enough food to feed everyone, yet starvation runs rampant even in countries with the highest standards of living?" or "If you look at a mirror your image reverses from left to right; why not from top to bottom?" Introducing contradictions, using experiments, and playing the devil's advocate are instructional processes that bring unusual and different information to students in an exciting way (p. 92).

Table 5.4 describes the relationship of the inquiry model to the cognitive skills of students. The inquiry model places much more emphasis on relational skills than on analytical skills. Students examine an event or phenomenon and inductively attempt to determine a plausible explanation. That inductive process fosters substantial levels of creative thought and forces students to examine ideas from a holistic perspective. Ms. Lange's teaching is especially powerful in this regard because she continued to expand the complexity of the phenomenon. As a consequence, new meanings emerge based on new facts that the teacher presents.

Not only does the relational nature of inquiry enable culturally diverse learners to participate, but it also enables a type of co-learning (between teachers and students) that enhances learning possibilities for female students; students have an opportunity to *see* the thinking of the teacher. Indeed, Polling (1995) notes that alternative assessment strategies "that do work well for girls include *embedded assessments*—activities in which students, usually in groups, per-

TABLE 5-4   Relationship of Inquiry Model to Cognitive Skills

Model	Relational	Analytical
■ Inquiry	■ Creativity	■ Object-oriented
	■ Divergent thinking	
	■ Inductive	
	■ Evolving	
	■ Meanings are contextual	
	■ Expressive	
	■ Holistic	

form experiments, discover patterns, and arrive at hypotheses" (p. 32). Female students benefit when the teacher structures lessons to maximize student thinking and creativity; but all students, regardless of their gender or cultural background, benefit when the teacher structures lessons that build on students' intrinsic interests and when the teacher recognizes the worth of each student's contributions.

PREVALENT ISSUES IN DIVERSE CLASSROOMS

The inquiry approach requires real teacher skill and lots of teacher "on-the-spot" thinking. Because students are controlling the questions, the teacher becomes much more vulnerable to the feeling of losing instructional control. The questions that follow are typical of the issues teachers have confronted when they first use the inquiry strategy.

Q: *What happens when students ask questions that are "yes" or "no" oriented, but that require a more descriptive response by the teacher?*

A: It is not at all uncommon for students to ask a question that is worded to elicit a "yes" or "no" response but that, if answered with a "yes" or "no," would create conceptual confusion. In essence, a clear "yes" or clear "no" would communicate misinformation about what happens in the discrepant event. When this occurs, the teacher has two choices. First, the teacher can request that students either rephrase the question or ask another question that is narrower in scope. One of the weaknesses of Ms. Lange's lesson, in fact, is that she does not provide enough clarifying information to the students. When one of the students asks about the bird flying away, Ms. Lange responded "Yes." She might have said something like, "Yes, but ask me specific questions about why the bird flew away." With inquiry, it is perfectly legitimate for the teacher to encourage students to focus on a specific aspect of an event. Quite obviously, the teacher needs to limit the degree to which this occurs. If the teacher's descriptive responses and requests for rephrasing questions are done too much, the open-ended, creative aspect of inquiry is destroyed. But if teachers provide no direction, it is also possible that students will fail to develop a clear picture of all the variables evident in a discrepant event.

A second option available is for the teacher to respond with a "yes" or "no" and then provide additional information to make certain that students clearly understand what the "yes" or "no" means. At times it is just too difficult to move the students toward the questions the teacher believes need to be asked, especially when the questions are intended to clarify an idea. The authors have seen teachers literally destroy the flow of a lesson because the teacher spends 5 minutes trying to get students to ask a particular question. A good inquiry lesson demands that teachers know when to ask clarifying questions and when to simply provide information that students need.

Q: *How can I make certain that all students participate? Some students just want to dominate the process; others do not want to be involved at all!*

A: The so-called "bright" students immediately want to provide the "right" answer. Darling-Hammond (1995) writes, "Today's schools were designed when the goal of education was not to educate all students well but [rather] to process a great many efficiently, selecting and supporting only a few for 'thinking work'" (p. 153). The objective of inquiry is to enable all students to think and perform in an inquiring mode. Strategies for accomplishing maximum student participation include the following:

1. Begin the lesson by having all students jot down three questions, and then have each student in the class ask one question of the teacher. Students need to have three questions available in order to ensure that they have alternatives to questions that might be asked by peers.

2. Use a "numbered heads together" technique (see Chapters 4 and 10) that enables students to work in groups of three to generate ideas. This technique enables everyone to participate, even if some students are having difficulty thinking of good questions.

Q: *You indicated that elements of cooperative learning can be used in implementing the inquiry model. Will cooperative learning work in all cases using this model?*

A: Cooperative learning strategies are effective as an instructional model for all students, but particularly with those students from African American and Hispanic American communities and cross-gender groups (Hale-Benson, 1986; Hilliard, 1989; Shade, 1989). This model must also be gauged by knowledge of the students served by the teacher. Caution should be exercised based upon the students' cultural affiliation. Not all Asian American or Hispanic American ethnic groups are necessarily receptive to working with one another (Pang, 1995). Historical animosities continue to be resurrected and promulgated within some Asian American or Hispanic American communities. In those cultures that perpetuate male dominant roles or nationalistic attitudes, cooperative learning strategies may cause strong feelings of concern, animosity, and even anger. This source of conflict emanates from historical antagonisms. Pang (1995) describes how a teacher had a Vietnamese American and Cambodian American student working in cooperative group strategies. The teacher asked the Vietnamese student to work with the Cambodian student assuming that each would be happy with this arrangement because they had similar immigrant experiences. Pang describes that the Vietnamese student "...explained diplomatically that he did not think the other student would accept his help. This greatly surprised the teacher, but the prediction of the student was confirmed when the Cambodian student said, 'I do not want to accept help from a Vietnamese'" (p. 414). We mention this in order to make teachers aware of the sensitivities needed in designing group work situations (see Chapter 10) for culturally diverse student populations.

❷ VALUATION CRITERIA

The inquiry instructional model is often very difficult for teachers to use because they are unaccustomed to allowing students to ask questions. Because the students have more control of an inquiry lesson, teachers often feel as though the lesson lacks structure and definition. That sense of not having control is one of the most difficult aspects of using this instructional model. Teachers must be comfortable with allowing students to dictate how the content is sequenced (after all, the order of their questions will determine the sequence with which different concepts are addressed). The teacher's responsibility is to enable students to structure and synthesize the ideas meaningfully. The following questions are presented so that teachers (and perhaps a peer coach) can design and critique inquiry lessons presented to students.

Phase I: Discrepant Event

1. Does the discrepant event present students with a problem that is not immediately solvable?　　○ Yes　○ No

2. Are students intrigued and interested by the problem/discrepant event?　　○ Yes　○ No

3. Does the teacher clearly present the discrepant event in a way that enables students to see all dimensions of the phenomenon?　　○ Yes　○ No

Phase II: Question Sequence

1. Does the teacher begin the questioning phase by having students identify all the pertinent data (that is, verify the nature of the objects involved in the event)? ○ Yes ○ No

2. Are all student questions worded to elicit a "yes" or "no" teacher response? ○ Yes ○ No

3. Does the teacher distinguish the difference between fact-oriented questions (questions oriented toward specific data) and theory-oriented questions (questions focused more on a defined hypothesis)? (Recall that the first set of questions should focus on eliciting factual information.) ○ Yes ○ No

4. Does the teacher help students keep track of what data are being generated (that is, the teacher uses some system like a grid or matrix)? ○ Yes ○ No

5. Are *all* students participating in the data-generation process? (Teachers should call on volunteers and nonvolunteers to ensure full student participation.) ○ Yes ○ No

Phase III: Generating Hypotheses

1. Do the students have ample opportunities to create workable hypotheses? ○ Yes ○ No

2. Are students required to identify what data supports their proposed hypothesis? ○ Yes ○ No

3. Are students required to critically discuss the viability of the different hypotheses? ○ Yes ○ No

Phase IV: Closure

1. Are students able to eliminate invalid hypotheses by specifically describing why a particular hypothesis is unworkable?   ○ Yes   ○ No

2. Are students able to generate more "yes"/"no" questions that enable them to narrow the number of possible hypotheses?   ○ Yes   ○ No

3. Are students able to refine existing hypotheses so that each statement (hypothesis) is conceptually clear?   ○ Yes   ○ No

Phase V: Analysis

1. Are students able to identify the best working hypothesis?   ○ Yes   ○ No

2. Are students required to make predictions based on each hypothesis?   ○ Yes   ○ No

Phase VI: Extension

1. Is there a logical follow-up activity that extends the students' thinking regarding the event?   ○ Yes   ○ No

SAMPLE LESSONS

The following sample lessons illustrate the variety that is possible with regard to inquiry teaching. In the first lesson, a whole-language teacher demonstrates how it is possible to use inquiry in a language arts lesson. The second case (lesson plan) is one of the most creative inquiry lessons that the authors ever observed.

CASE STUDY

Ms. Kline teaches 1st grade at Wilson Elementary School. She begins the class by talking to the students about what it means to be an author. She also reviews with them the names of some of their favorite authors and illustrators. At this point she tells them that she has written a book that she wants them to read along with her. The teacher-made picture book is titled "A Day in the

Barnyard." She begins reading the book and has the students read (as they are able) the text with her:

"Cockadoodle-doo," said the rooster. It was a beautiful sunny morning on the farm. Daffney Duck had an early start as she bathed in the cool lake.

Benny Bluebird went out to catch his breakfast. A plump red bird said, "Chirp, Chirp," as he enjoyed this glorious morning.

"Oink, Oink," said Penny Pig. She slowly left the barn in search of some sticky mud.

"Oink, Oink, Oink," she said as she slipped deep into the brown muck.

Suddenly Linda Lamb stuck her head out the barn door. "Stop all that racket," she yelled. Benny dropped his breakfast. Daffney stopped in mid-stroke, but Penny continued to play. "Oink, Oink," Penny snorted as she continued sloshing in the mud. She got so carried away that her back feet slipped out from under her and she fell with a splat! Mud sprayed up and hit Linda square in the face! Linda came storming out of the barn and went right up to Penny.

"Let's go," Linda said.

"Where?" asked Penny.

"We're going out to the forest alone," she answered.

Penny reluctantly followed Linda into the muddy, shady forest. Penny thought Linda must have gotten up on the wrong side of the bed.

Back in the barnyard, hours had passed and the animals were worried about Penny and Linda. They decided to go into the forest and look for them. When they reached the edge of the forest, they stopped suddenly. "What's this?" asked Daffney. "What happened here?" asked Benny.

When Ms. Kline turns to the last page, she drops her voice and asks, "What happens here?" (It appears that Penny Pig has disappeared.) The students are hushed by her voice change, but they are also excited as they look at Linda Lamb's footprints and see that Penny's have disappeared.

"To find out what occurs, we are going to play 20 Questions." She then turns to a large piece of poster paper and tells the students to ask questions so that they can discover what really happens in the story. Because Ms. Kline has played 20 Questions with the students several times in the past, she tells them to ask questions in exactly the same way as they have when they played the game before.

"Before we start, I'm going to ask someone to tally the number of questions that we ask. We'll keep track of that as well as the information that you are able to generate. OK, let's begin. Who wants to ask the first question? Gregory."

"Were they fighting?"

Ms. Kline responds "Yes" and writes on the poster board, "They were fighting." She turns to Melissa and asks, "What's your question?"

Melissa asks, "Did one of them die?"

Ms. Kline responds with a "No" and shares with the students that because the answer is "no" she will not put any information on the board. She is only putting "yes" information on the board.

Another student asks, "Are those bear footprints that I see?" Ms. Kline indicates that they are and writes, "The footprints were made by a bear" on the poster paper. (See Table 5.5.)

The lesson progresses for another 10 or 15 minutes, and the chart paper is full of "yes" ideas. At several points in the lesson, the students respond with "ohs" or "ahs" as they think they understand what happened at the end of the story. The students ask almost 30 questions in their search for an answer to the story's ending.

She then says, "Based on the information we have, what do you think happened?" The first student says, "I think they became friends." Another responds, "I think the pig jumped on the lamb's back and got out." A third student gives a long explanation but draws on ideas that have no support from the "yes" data board. Ms. Kline reminds the students that their ideas must support the conclusions that appear on the "yes" board.

A total of five hypotheses (or guesses) are offered (see Table 5.5). Ms. Kline takes several minutes to review each hypothesis and asks all the students to critically think about whether each "hypothesis" has support from the "yes" data. The students eliminate a couple of the hypotheses. A lot of discussion ensues as students explore the viability of each hypothesis. Ms. Kline carefully reviews each piece of data to determine if each hypothesis works. The students end up with two possible hypotheses.

Ms. Kline says, "You have done a great job. Now let's finish the story and find out whose explanation is correct." She turns back to her picture book and reads the conclusion to the story.

> As Benny and Daffney puzzled over this question, they saw Linda and Penny slowly coming out of the woods. What! Penny is on Linda's back.
>
> Linda sat down to let Penny off her back. Then she explained, "Penny and I were off to a mud fight when she got completely stuck in the mud. She couldn't even move, so I offered her a Piggy-back ride."
>
> Benny and Daffney were so glad that their friends were all right that they hurried back to the barnyard to eat.

Ms. Kline completes the lesson by analyzing what data were most useful and identifying which hypothesis was the best explanation. ■

TABLE 5-5   Chart from Ms. Kline's Lesson

Yes	*Guesses*
■ *They were fighting*	■ *They became friends*
■ *One walked out*	■ *The pig jumped on the lamb's back and snuck out*
■ *The footprints were made by a bear*	■ *The lamb got lost*
■ *The lamb walked out*	■ *The pig went back to the barn*
■ *The lamb ran at the pig*	■ *The lamb stayed in the woods*
■ *Penny got on the lamb's back*	

Follow-up questions

1. What type of inquiry lesson is this—guided or unguided?
2. Is the question "What happened to Penny?" an appropriate discrepant event?
3. What might Ms. Kline have done at the end of the lesson to foster additional critical thought?

LESSON PLAN

The teacher who taught the following lesson used inquiry as a follow-up to a unit on mysteries. The students had read several mystery novels and discussed some real-life mysteries that they knew about based on personal experiences.

Concept: Mysteries (in the fictional and physical world)

Discrepant Event: The 8th grade teacher shows the students a blown-up balloon that has a skewer through the middle of it—the skewer enters the balloon near its knot. Students are asked how a skewer can go through a balloon without breaking it. They are told that three basic materials are required to do the experiment: an inflated balloon, a skewer, and oil.

Methods:
- Teacher walks around the room with a balloon and skewer.
- Teacher asks students to draw an example of the balloon and skewer on a piece of paper.

   Teacher distributes to students the required materials to conduct the experiment: oil, balloon, and skewer. She tells students they will have one opportunity to try the experiment.

   Students inflate balloons and are asked to think of information they need so that when they attempt the experiment they will be successful.

   Students ask questions and obtain the following types of "yes" information: Examples:

   "Do you put oil on the skewer?"

   "Do you blow up the balloons?"

- Students attempt the experiment based on the limited information provided by the teacher.
- Students are told to ask more questions. Additional "yes" information is generated. Examples:

   "Yes, you put oil on the skewer before putting the skewer through the balloon."

   "Yes, you put the skewer through the tied knot of the balloon."

   "Yes, the pointed end of the skewer is the one that is used."

"Yes, you push the skewer through very slowly."

- Teacher reviews the "yes" data and provides students with more materials and asks them to try the experiment again.
- Students generate more "yes" data based on their second attempt. New information includes:

"Yes, oil should be placed on both the balloon and skewer."

"Yes, the balloon should be only partially inflated."

Closure: A couple of students who successfully complete the experiment are asked to come to the front of the room and help the other students solve the problem. After all the pertinent "yes" data are generated, the students are asked to attempt the experiment one additional time. As students experience success, they are allowed to work with others who are still experimenting, but they can help only by answering "yes" and "no" questions.

Follow-up questions

1. Is the discrepant event appropriate for eliciting a curious student response?
2. What process could the teacher use to help students discover the specific sequence that needs to be followed so the balloon does not burst?
3. Is it sufficient to collect just "yes" information? Under what circumstances would the "no" information be included as well?
4. Most of this lesson is organized around the questioning sequence. How could the teacher have fostered more hypothesizing?

LESSON PREPARATION

Inquiry instruction fosters the natural curiosity of students. Perhaps the most difficult aspect to implementing the inquiry model is creating a good discrepant event. The following materials will enable teachers to better understand the inquiry model and the theoretical basis for the approach.

Suggested readings

Bibens, R. F. 1980. "Using Inquiry Effectively." *Theory Into Practice* 19(2): 87–92.

Henson, K. T. 1986. "Inquiry Learning: A New Look." *Contemporary Education* 57(4): 181–183.

Vye, N. J., and J. D. Bransford. 1981. "Programs for Teaching Thinking." *Educational Leadership* 26: 26–28.

Wright, E. L., and G. Govindarajan. 1992. "Stirring the Biology Teaching Pot with Discrepant Events." *American Biology Teacher* 54(4) (April): 205–210.

Zevin, J. 1969. "Mystery Island: A Lesson in Inquiry." *Today's Education* 58: 42–43.

Suggested videotapes

"Inquiry Training I: Demonstration." Booksend Laboratories, 3830 Vine Maple Drive, Eugene, Oregon 97405.

Suggested lesson development

Once teachers understand the theoretical basis of inquiry and know how to foster student questioning in the classroom, they should develop their own classroom lesson. The following suggestions are offered as a guide:

1. Identify a phenomenon or idea that students should explore and would interest them.
2. Identify an appropriate discrepant event that is related to the phenomenon.
3. Determine whether guided or unguided inquiry should be used.
4. Create a data-collection device for keeping track of the information that students generate.
5. Identify a process for collecting hypotheses.
6. Determine an appropriate follow-up or closure activity for helping students synthesize material.

....

Ⓢ UMMARY

Gunter, Estes, and Schwab (1995) observe that "good questions are more important than right answers" (p. 135). Although many educators may embrace the spirit of this phrase, few structure their classroom practice in ways that validate the statement. Through the exams given, the assessments provided, and the dialogue fostered, teachers tend to communicate to students that deriving right answers is the goal of the educational enterprise. Good schools are often defined as those that enable students to learn factual knowledge. Conservative syndicated columnist Thomas Sowell recently wrote about one "good" school—Hillsdale Academy. According to Sowell, this school is one where students learn the facts. They know who Julius Caesar, Constantine, and Augustus were, and they can describe in some detail the legacy of the Roman Empire. Clearly, facts are important. But the putative ignorance of American students is vastly overemphasized, especially when students in today's schools are compared with earlier generations of Americans—those who claim that after they walked 10 miles to school in the snow they had to learn much more than today's students. Indeed, considerable research exists that suggests that, if anything, current student populations are more knowledgeable than were those in the past (Whittington, 1991). Whittington observes:

> Advocates for reform of education and excellence in public schooling should refrain from harkening to a halcyon past (or allowing the perception of a halcyon past) to garner support for their views. Such action, or inaction, is dishonest and unnecessary. Indeed, excellence is a goal that

should be advocated on its own merits, as should the advocacy for higher standards than those of the past (p. 778).

What is missing in far too many classrooms is instruction that requires students to both *think* and *know*. The inquiry instructional model fosters both of these dimensions! A good question requires knowledge, just as a correct answer requires understanding. A student who is going to be successful in school and in life must possess both abilities. As Gunter, Estes, and Schwab (1995) comment: "Although it is true that those who succeed in school are often those who can remember the 'correct' answer, those who succeed in life are usually those who are willing to ask questions and search for solutions" (p. 165).

Ⓡ EFERENCES

Bibens, R. F. 1980. "Using Inquiry Effectively." *Theory Into Practice* 19(2): 87–92.

Borko, H., C. Brown, R. Underhill, M. Eisenhart, P. Jones, and P. Agard. 1990. *Learning to Teach Mathematics for Understanding.* College Park, MD: University of Maryland.

Darling-Hammond, L. 1995. "Restructuring Schools for Student Success." *Daedalus* 124(4): 153–162.

Good, T., and J. E. Brophy. 1994. *Looking in Classrooms* (6th ed.). New York: HarperCollins.

Gunter, M. A., T. H. Estes, and J. Schwab. 1995. *Instruction: A Models Approach* (2d ed.). Boston: Allyn & Bacon.

Hale-Benson, J. 1986. *Black Children: Their Roots, Culture, and Learning Styles* (rev. ed.). Baltimore, MD: Johns Hopkins University Press.

Henson, K. T. 1986. "Inquiry Learning: A New Look." *Contemporary Education* 57(4): 181–183.

Hilliard, A. G., III. 1989. "Teachers and Cultural Styles in a Pluralistic Society." *NEA Today* 1: 65–69.

Hyman, R. T. 1980. "Fielding Student Questions." *Theory Into Practice* 19(1): 38–44.

Investigating Solid Waste Issues. 1994. Columbus, OH: Ohio Department of Natural Resources.

Orlich, D. C., R. J. Harder, R. C. Callahan, C. H. Kravas, D. P. Kauchak, R. A. Pendergrass, and A. J. Keogh. 1985. *Teaching Strategies: A Guide to Better Instruction* (2d ed.). Lexington, MA: D. C. Heath.

Pang, V. 1995. "Asian Pacific American Students: A Diverse and Complex Population." Pp. 412–424 in J. Banks and C. Banks (eds.), *Handbook of Research on Multicultural Education.* New York: Macmillan.

Polling, A. 1995. "Gender Balance: Lessons from Girls in Science and Mathematics." *Educational Leadership* 53(1): 30–33.

Shade, B. J. 1989. "The Influence of Perceptual Development on Cognitive Style: Cross Ethnic Comparisons." *Early Child Development and Care* 51: 137–155.

Shulman, L., and P. Tamir. 1973. "Research on Teaching in the Natural Sciences." Pp. 1098–1148 in R. M. W. Travers (ed.), *Second Handbook of Research on Teaching.* Chicago: Rand McNally.

Taba, H. 1966. *Teaching Strategies and Cognitive Functioning in Elementary School Children.* Cooperative Research Project 2404. San Francisco: San Francisco State College.

Tyson, H. 1994. *Who Will Teach the Children?: Progress and Resistance in Teacher Education.* San Francisco: Jossey-Bass.

Vye, N. J., and J. D. Bransford. 1981. "Programs for Teaching Thinking." *Educational Leadership* 26: 26–28.

Whittington, D. 1991. "What Have 17-Year-Olds Known in the Past?" *American Educational Research Journal* 28(4): 759–780.

Wlodkowski, R. J., and M. B. Ginsberg. 1995. "A Framework for Culturally Responsive Teaching." *Educational Leadership* 53(1): 17–21.

Wlodkowski, R. J., and J. H. Jaynes. 1990. *Eager to Learn.* San Francisco: Jossey-Bass.

Wright, E. L. 1981. "Fifteen Simple Discrepant Events that Teach Science Principles and Concepts." *School Science and Mathematics* 81: 575–580.

———, and G. Govindarajan. 1992. "Stirring the Biology Teaching Pot with Discrepant Events." *American Biology Teacher* 54(4) (April): 205–210.

Zevin, J. 1969. "Mystery Island: A Lesson in Inquiry." *Today's Education* 58: 42–43.

The history of ideas is replete with examples of how people constructed and then reshaped ideas. For example, in the early 1800s, the earth was thought to be 6,000 years old. The generations from Adam and Eve to the present were meticulously documented by theologians. Then along came Charles Darwin, who in 1859, with his publication of *The Origin of Species*, caused people to rethink how humankind came to inhabit the earth. Darwin was trained as a theologian (indeed he graduated from Cambridge, with a degree in theology in 1831), but he challenged the thinking of the clergy. Darwin built on the ideas of other scientists, such as Sir Charles Lyell and Jean Baptiste de Lamarck, both of whom had created their own organizational schema about animal behavior and geologic phenomena—Lyell was a biologist and Lamarck was a zoologist. Darwin's work revolutionized how people thought about the evolution of human beings—he "reordered" scientific ideas. Subsequently, of course, Darwin's work itself has been reordered and challenged—to the point, in fact, that many have intellectually cycled back to the original creationist perspectives that dominated in the 1800s.

The beauty of the human experience is the ability to look at the complexity of the universe in ways that make multiple interpretations possible. The evolution of ideas is really a reordering and reorganizing of what others, who lived earlier, have accomplished. Socrates, who was concerned with man's place in society, juxtaposed his ideas with those of the sophists and the natural philosophers. Plato relied heavily on Socrates; and Aristotle, the master scientific organizer, evolved the ideas of his predecessors even further. Over the past couple thousand years, people have been creating new frontiers of knowledge using what is known—the boundaries of the unknown have been pushed back, and the area that constitutes the "known" is constantly being restructured.

In the next two chapters, two techniques are provided that make it possible for students within classrooms to engage in their own forms of intellectual reordering. Both models require that students actively engage themselves with data, and both enable the creative capacities of students to be extended. Students can see, therefore, that they have a capacity to generate their own meanings and that some of those meanings might even make more sense than what they have learned previously. ∎

Models that Foster Reorganizing Skills

SIX

• *Concept Formation*

At the completion of this chapter, readers will be able to:
1. *Understand the theoretical basis of the model.*
2. *Identify the essential phases of a concept formation lesson.*
3. *Identify the strengths and weaknesses of the model.*
4. *Evaluate lessons that use the concept formation model.*
5. *Describe ways in which concept formation enhances learning opportunities for students from culturally diverse backgrounds.*
6. *Create a concept formation lesson for classroom use.*

❶ NTRODUCTION

The purpose of concept formation is to "see" the thinking processes and conceptual schema of students. In far too many classrooms, what students experience is the reality of the teacher's thinking. That is, the teacher does the thinking for the students. The teacher determines what concept is going to be taught, provides the students with a definition of that concept, gives a variety of examples that illustrate the definition, and then provides practice activities (homework) to ensure that students learn the material. Parker (1987) described this as the content mastery approach. Such an approach is disadvantageous when it occurs with such regularity that students have no opportunity to critique what they are learning.

> *So you might say that the challenge of education is, on the one hand, to preserve the imagination and the questioning and the theoretical stance of a 5-year-old, but on the other hand—gradually but decisively—to replace those ideas that are not well-founded with theories, ideas, conceptions, stories, which are more accurate.*
>
> HOWARD GARDNER

The content approach is not necessarily educationally unsound. Indeed, in many instances, such a deductive strategy has real efficacy as the reader will recognize in Chapter 8 when we will discuss direct instruction as an instructional model. However, the direct, teacher-controlled approach to learning becomes a barrier to student growth when students are not provided with instructional alternatives. The ideal instructional system eliminates the use of one model exclusively; the ideal system utilizes many different instructional strategies as a means of tapping the full intellectual potential of students.

Concept formation is an instructional model that places the *emphasis on student thinking, not teacher thinking.* This focus upon who is thinking is a very important distinction and must be kept in mind when using this instructional model. In order for this model to have maximum impact, teachers need to sequence and plan the way in which students approach the prescribed learning activities. In essence, teachers create the conditions (set the stage), but the students are given latitude in terms of how to respond and think (create their own "play"). Whimbey (1977) asserts that to teach students how to think, teachers must carefully demonstrate to students how to process information, and then provide students with an opportunity to practice what they have learned.

Concept formation, according to Parker (1987), enables students to systematically examine data in a way that 1) fosters an understanding of how a label for a concept is just that, a "label"; 2) engenders more complex thinking "about the content, [and creates] further sense making as learners try to capture with a single term [determined by them] the similarities' essence" (p. 52); and 3) enables students to connect their experiences with the available data. As Parker notes, "Student generated labels are more likely to be connected meaningfully to students' present experiencing than are conventional [teacher provided] labels..." (p. 52).

This last characteristic of concept formation is perhaps most important for teachers of culturally diverse youngsters. Because students come to school with such varied backgrounds due to child-rearing practices, the concept formation model enables teachers to build on the existing cognitive schema and life experiences of students. It also fosters a respect for what students know. Rather than having students sit in classrooms where they are *"being done to,"* students are in a position to *create their own meaning*, to warrant their own backgrounds, and to compare what they know with what is already known (Haberman and Post, 1995).

⬤ASE STUDY

Lou Tripodi is preparing to teach an earth science unit on the different types of resources that human beings use. Lou typically uses the direct instruction model in introducing concepts and ideas, but because he believes his students have a reasonable understanding of the available resources, he decides to use a different instructional model to introduce the concept. He wants to see how his students have organized ideas associated with the way resources are used by people to lead a quality life.

"Today, class, we are going to begin a unit on resources that people use to sustain and enhance the quality of their lives. I'm going to list some resources on the board as examples. I then want you to add additional terms of your own."

Mr. Tripodi proceeds by listing on the board the following terms:

1. crude oil
2. paper
3. rain
4. trains
5. chemicals
6. minerals
7. trucks
8. gasoline
9. forests
10. water
11. fish
12. coal
13. factories
14. electricity
15. atomic energy
16. natural gas

After he completes the listing, he asks the students to add other resources that they feel are important to people's quality of life. The students provide additional examples such as trees, wildlife, soil, lakes, rivers, plants…. When the list grows to approximately 50 terms, he asks them to stop.

"Well, we have a nice listing of items here. Are there any terms you don't understand? For example, does everyone know what crude oil is? Robin, let's make sure we all know what that term means."

Robin responds, "Crude oil is the stuff in the ground that oil companies pump out and use to make gasoline."

"That's right," responds Mr. Tripodi. "Actually, there are many more by-products than gasoline, but gasoline is most likely what you would think of first. Now, are there any other terms that you want to discuss before we start?"

The students nonverbally respond that they understand all the terms, and Mr. Tripodi checks by questioning them on some of the terms listed.

Mr. Tripodi continues the lesson. "I am going to provide each one of you with a sheet of paper that has three circles on it. I want you to work in your peer pairs [he has each student paired with a fellow student] and group these terms in a way that makes the most sense to each of you. For example, if I select one term, such as 'paper,' what item(s) or term(s) would you put with it?"

"I would select trees," reacts Huan-Kun.

"Why?" questions Mr. Tripodi.

"Because you make paper from tree pulp. I learned that a while ago when I had Ms. Kunjufu in social studies."

"Excellent. Now, let's see how many other items we can put with the two terms, paper and trees."

The students expand the category to eight items—some of which are from the original listing of 50 terms. Others are new items that the students believe fit and that they thought of as the lesson progressed. After about 5 minutes Mr. Tripodi stops further categorization and labels the grouping, "Things needed to make paper."

He states: "Using the same process we used here, I now want you to create your own groups of items. Select one item, any item, and then see what other terms fit with the one you selected. Then after you have as many terms placed together in the circle as you can think of, label the group. Think of a name that is appropriate for all the items you have grouped together."

The students work for 15 minutes creating their own word groupings. Mr. Tripodi walks around the room, checks on the students' progress, and then draws three large circles on the board.

"Let's see how you did," states Mr. Tripodi. "Lucinda, give me one of your groupings."

Lucinda lists all the items from one category, and Mr. Tripodi writes them down in a circle as follows:

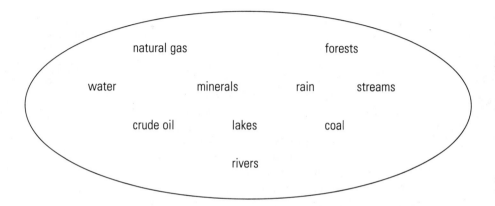

"Lucinda, what descriptor do you have for this group?"

Lucinda responds, "Natural resources that people use."

"Good," responds Mr. Tripodi. "Now, class, what other items might we put into this grouping that Lucinda's group left out? You may even be able to identify some that were not on our original list."

The students add six additional terms before Mr. Tripodi stops the process and goes to the next peer group and asks them for one of their word groups.

The students create 10 different groupings before Mr. Tripodi stops the lesson. Many of the groupings focus on natural resources. Mr. Tripodi has the students regroup the terms into large concept groupings and some into smaller groupings.

"Class, let's go back to Lucinda's grouping. What I want to do now is look more carefully at the interrelationship of the natural resources we've identified and the actual products that result from those resources. I want you to read Chapter 4 in your text and then select two resources from Lucinda's grouping and identify some products that result from each resource. I also want you to write a generalization about why resources are important to people." ■

The preceding case is one type of inductive lesson titled "concept formation"—the students are forming major concepts from a smaller subset of concrete and abstract items. In this chapter, we will explore the concept formation model, and focus on how and when this model can be used to expand student critical thinking.

Theoretical Perspective

The concept formation model is one of several teaching strategies first popularized by Hilda Taba (1966). Actually, Taba identified several different strategies (or cognitive tasks) that teachers could use to enhance the thinking skills of students. Concept formation is one approach in the use of inductive models, and in many respects it represents one of the most uncomplicated strategies for classroom teachers.

The purpose of concept formation is to enable students to differentiate a set of ideas presented by the teacher. Students move from a specific set of exemplars to broader conceptual categories that have the characteristics of those exemplars. Students engage in more higher-order thinking when they are required "to manipulate information or ideas in ways that transform their meaning and implications...[and] arrive at some conclusion or interpretation" (Newmann and Wehlage, 1993, p. 9). The manipulation of concept exemplars enables students to compare and contrast different interpretations of the ideas that are available for categorization and classification.

In traditional classrooms that emphasize teacher-centered pedagogy, teachers identify the categorizations for students and students become relatively passive learners who are expected to learn the teachers' categorizations. That is, the teacher starts by stating something like, *"Today we are going to study natural resources. A natural resource is something that is not made by humans but is used by people to enhance the quality of their lives. An example would be crude oil...."* In essence, the teacher tells the student the idea and then defines that idea for students. The question is: Does telling students an idea, teach an idea? Parker (1987) asserts that it does not: "[Telling an idea does not teach an idea] except of course for the few students in the room who will do the necessary thinking whether or not the teacher encourages it. That makes it [teacher telling] a very weak strategy.... Teachers have often heard themselves say 'I told them and told them and told them, and they still didn't learn it!'" (p. 52).

In utilizing the concept formation model, students become active participants in the learning process because they construct their own academic meanings for their own categorizations. The students make a series of decisions that influence how the ideas (or exemplars) will be organized, and the teacher is positioned to monitor how students are thinking about selected concepts. In essence, both teachers and students become active participants in the learning process. Teachers become active participants because they must continually monitor the students' thinking, and the students are actively engaged because they create their own schema from the available data (the exemplars provided).

The concept formation model uses a very active instructional pattern between individual students and the data. That pattern is important because it requires students to use information-processing skills in observing and interpreting data (examples) provided by the teacher. If it is true, as Taba (1966) postulated, that there "is a sequence in the development of abstract and symbolically mediated thought" (p. ii), then students need to be provided with opportunities to explore how to structure ideas on their own rather than to have that structure created for them by the teacher. The concept formation model requires that students make observations, compare and contrast data, and then draw conclusions about the interrelationships of that data. As Borich (1988) asserts, the approach is used when "students are asked to draw a conclusion, make a generalization, or develop a pattern of relationship from data. It is a process in which students observe specific facts and then generalize to other circumstances to which the facts apply" (p. 174).

CONCEPT FORMATION: TEACHING PHASES

Phase I: Data Generation

The first phase of concept formation requires that students examine a data set. That data set can be either teacher- or student-generated. With teacher-generated data, the teacher makes a determination regarding what ideas to present to students, and each student in turn categorizes the data into "concept groupings." For example, a teacher of social studies may use a set of terms associated with the continent of Africa (for example, *Nile River, Zulu, Sahara, nomads,* and so on). The students would take these terms and inductively create categories such as *landforms* or *tribes* or *cultural groups.* An English teacher might give the students an extensive set of words such as *yellow, beautiful, fire, store, box,* and so on. The students would then be asked to create groupings that might include the various parts of speech—*adjectives, nouns, verbs.* The actual labels of *noun, verb,* and so on would not be imposed on the students by the teacher. Rather, the labels would emerge from the students' understandings of the concept—parts of speech. The students, however, may or may not use the actual terms *noun, verb, adjective.* With an inductive strategy such as concept formation, the actual category label that students generate may not be the category that the teacher expects. The category label is the students' to formulate, not the teacher's to dictate. However, the teacher can help shape the emergent categories by sharing with the students the focus of a lesson: *"See how many categories you can create that deal with important features of Africa"* or *"Put together groupings that focus on parts of speech."*

Student-generated data are created by students, not the teacher. As an example of this, we once observed a teacher who had just completed a unit on the Revolutionary War. The teacher asked the students to go to the chalkboard and write down a word or phrase that captured something about the Revolutionary War that was important to them. The process was iterative. After every student listed one term on the board, the teacher asked the students to carefully read what terms were listed and add any other terms they thought deserved inclusion. After some time passed, a large number of additional terms were added to the board. This process continued until the chalkboard was literally covered with a wide variety of words and phrases. From this point the teacher began the process by having the students sort, categorize, and label the data. Another example we witnessed involved a high school science teacher conducting a unit on water resources. This teacher asked the students to identify all the items they could think of related to water usage. As each student responded, the teacher wrote the term on the chalkboard. The students created over 100 water-related terms, which formed the basis for a concept formation lesson. Such lessons enable teachers to literally recognize (to "see") the schema used by students. With such information, the teacher is in a better position to identify student understandings and misunderstandings.

In the teaching scenario that introduced this chapter, the teacher used a combination of student- and teacher-generated data. Mr. Tripodi began by listing 16 resources that he thought students should consider. The students then provided additional items of their own using the conceptual lead provided by Mr. Tripodi. With younger children, a combination of teacher- and student-generated data may be necessary, especially if the unit material being covered is not well known by students. Teachers should not hesitate to add data to the data set, especially if students are inadvertently leaving out certain critical terms.

Essentially, there are many appropriate alternatives to generate data. The teacher's goals for a lesson, coupled with the background knowledge of the students, will dictate which approach—teacher-generated or student-generated data or some combination of each—is most efficacious for helping students subsequently construct categories that make conceptual sense.

Phase II: Data Grouping

In phase II of the model, students take all the data and begin to create groupings of conceptually similar terms. There are several ways to accomplish this successfully. Before beginning the grouping process, the teacher needs to carefully check and make certain that all of the students understand the meanings associated with each listed term. This can be accomplished by asking students to define selected terms, randomly asking students to define terms, or asking students if they need specific terms defined before the lesson begins. Once all terms are defined and clarified, the teacher can begin the grouping process, usually through the use of a teacher-generated example. That is, the teacher can ask a student to pick any term from the available list and to place that term in a large circle. (Incidentally, there is nothing magical about circles. The circle is nothing more than a symbolic way of "enclosing" or defining a concept.) Recall that Mr. Tripodi began the grouping process as follows: *"I am going to provide each one of you with a sheet of paper that has three circles on it. I want you to work in your peer pairs and group these terms in a way that makes the most sense to each of you. For example, if I select one term, such as 'paper,' what item or term would you put with it?"*

The students construct the groupings based upon their own perceptions of how the terms fit with one another. They place as many terms together in one circle (or group) as they feel logically and conceptually fit. Once they "fill a circle," they then pick another term at random, place it in the next circle, and the grouping process begins again. Remind students that terms can be placed in several different circles. Once a term is used in one circle it is not excluded from use in other groups.

Some students tend to label the groups before they begin the categorization. This needs to be discouraged by the teacher. Teachers should encourage students to randomly select a "first" item and then conduct the grouping process based on that first selection: What item is similar to the first item? Students should be cautioned, in essence, not to label a group too quickly.

Phase III: Labeling

Once students have created their groupings, they then determine the best concept label for that grouping of items. Recall that for Mr. Tripodi's class a 10-item group emerged (*natural gas, forests, water, minerals,* and so on), and one of the students (Lucinda) provided the label, *"Natural resources that people use."* Parker (1987) notes that "by letting students label the concept...we accomplish several things. First, we want students to learn that the name is just that, a name for the idea, not to be confused with the idea itself.... Second, the naming act involves further thinking about the content..." (p. 52).

The labels should be simple conceptual descriptors that connect and embrace all the terms listed within the circle. The students are the ones who have responsibility for creating the labels, not the teacher. The teacher can have a preconceived concept that needs to be taught, but that concept should not be imposed on the students. Some teachers become very intrusive because they believe they know what labels are best suited for the item groupings. The teacher's concept should emerge from the lesson just as naturally as do the students'. Teacher conceptual intrusiveness is instructionally undesirable because such teaching behavior mitigates the intellectual power of the learner. Remember, one of the goals of the concept formation model is to provide students with opportunities to create or construct their own meaning relative to the enumerated terms. The teacher also needs to require that students justify the categories. Students should be able to explain why each item is included in a grouping.

Teachers should not hesitate to challenge student thinking by asking plenty of "why" questions. Students should be able to defend each item within each group by describing why and by what criteria they categorized each item.

Phase IV: Expanding the Category

Once students have grouped and labeled the terms, the teacher reviews each grouping to determine how students thought through the categorization process. Some teachers have each student pair describe one of its label groupings for the entire class. Peer pairs may describe the grouping category on a transparency, or they may write the terms and category label on the chalkboard. As each label grouping is described by a peer pair, the teacher and the students have responsibility for determining what additional items could logically be placed in that grouping. The teacher also checks the understandings of the other students in the class. Recall that Mr. Tripodi asked, after the first grouping was presented, *"Now, class, what other items might we put into this grouping that Lucinda's group left out? You may even be able to identify some that were not on our original list."*

Expanding the category is necessary to fully explore the meanings and interrelationships of the identified terms. Some teachers just have students present their categories; they provide no critique of what else makes sense to add to each grouping. One of the salient goals of concept formation is to enhance the thinking skills of students, and for that to occur, teachers need to extend and expand student understanding of concepts by identifying additional terms and by delineating the rationale for including the additional terms within the various groupings.

Phase V: Closure

The final phase of the concept formation model varies depending on the objectives of the unit and/or the purposes of the teacher. For those teachers who use the technique to introduce units of instruction (that is, the teacher wants to see how students are thinking about an idea and to explore their schema before content coverage occurs), the closure process may include nothing more than collecting the groupings and explaining to students that they will reexamine the "groupings" once the unit is completed. Students will then have a "before and after" perspective on a concept—they will be able to see their schema before a unit of instruction is presented and after the unit is completed.

Other teachers use concept formation as a unit review—at the conclusion of a unit. They want to see how students have developed and organized their understandings of the key concepts that the teacher presented during the unit of instruction. Once students present categories in this way, the teacher may have them do one or more of the following: 1) create a generalization relative to each of their categories, 2) describe how different terms within a category relate to one another, or 3) create an assignment from the listed terms that enables students to fully explore the meanings of the different terms in that category. Recall that Mr. Tripodi used the third approach when he stated: *"Class, let's go back to Lucinda's grouping. What I want to do now is look more carefully at the interrelationship of the natural resources we've identified and the actual products that result from those resources. I want you to read Chapter 4 in your text and then select two resources from Lucinda's grouping and identify some products that result from each resource."*

If the generalization (or first) option were to have been selected, Mr. Tripodi might have requested the following: *"Class, for each one of your categories, I want you to create a generalization that indicates the relationship of the items you selected and the title you developed. For example, for Lucinda's grouping I might develop the generalization, 'Resources such as crude oil are found naturally in the earth and are used to make products that we use in our homes.' Then I want you to support that generalization by providing an example. In this instance you will actually identify a product that is used in your home."*

The second option, showing how terms interrelate, can be accomplished through the creation of "webs." Students would select a conceptually broad item to use as the title for their category and to serve as the conceptual focus; they would then develop a web such as the one in Figure 6.1. The teacher might have the students extend the web in each area until an item appears that is synthetic or manufactured rather than naturally occurring. Hyerle (1966) observes that "practiced with depth, ...webs offer students the opportunity to break the stiff intellectual molds of the 'behavioralist' classroom and to spin new interpretations and construct new forms of knowledge" (p. 37). Webs help students develop a measure of fluency with the ideas offered by the teacher. As students

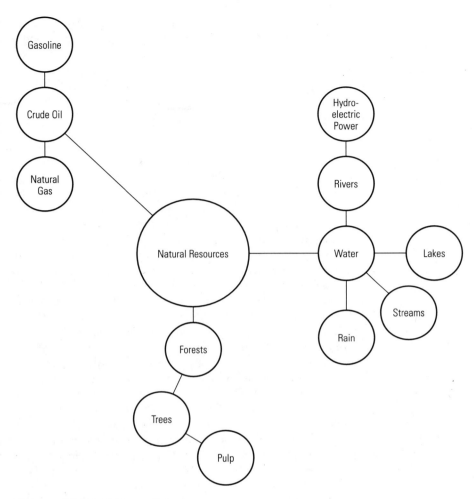

FIGURE 6-1 Concept Web for Natural Resources

brainstorm the various conceptual relationships, they develop a better and deeper understanding of requisite content area concepts.

Ⓐ PPLICATIONS TO DIVERSE CLASSROOMS

For too many teachers and schools, multicultural issues are addressed through isolated "set-aside" programs: "African-American Studies Week," "Women Heroes," and so on. The problem with the set-aside approach is that students all too often are able to dismiss ideas about African Americans or Hispanic Americans or women because they view them out of any meaningful context.

Because teachers control the curriculum and students have limited opportunities to infuse their own directions and views, the likelihood that set-aside perspectives will occur is even further enhanced. Textbooks and curriculum materials, until very recently, have been very male and very "white"—some teachers attempted to correct this problem by highlighting a few persons of color during Black History Month. Such an approach is well meaning but counterproductive. It tends to isolate, hierarchically, people in history rather than to integrate them in ways that warrant their contributions on an equal basis. Concept formation and other inductive strategies provide some measure of assurance that students can begin to use their own frames of reference (their own cultural schema) to shape personal learning. They can use what they know to enhance what the teacher wants them to know. Teachers who use concept formation are often fascinated by the number of student ideas that they (the teachers) never thought of—or if they thought of them, never perceived their relevance to the larger set of ideas being studied.

Concept formation enhances the relational thinking skills of students. As Table 6.1 illustrates, students who engage in inductive (concept formation) activities are able to create a meaningful (personal) context for their ideas, exhibit divergent thinking processes, use their own creative sense of how ideas fit together, and creatively think about how concepts interface with one another.

These types of learning opportunities support relational cognitive styles more than analytical ones. Further, they enable students to use their verbal abilities and refine their reasoning skills to defend ideas that they provide in defense of hypotheses. Variability in classroom instructional approaches is best illustrated through analysis of Table 6.2. As you will notice, verbal and reasoning skills represent significant strengths for African American students but areas of potential weakness for Chinese American students. Teachers who rely heavily on one instructional approach disadvantage subsets of students whose preferred styles are not compatible with a particular teacher's preferred approach. Remember, instructional variability is one of the best palliatives for addressing the needs of diverse student populations in the classroom.

As one begins reflecting upon the alternative learning styles, some readers may be inclined to assume that because they teach in an affluent or suburban setting, the performance characteristics of the students will not be the same as evi-

TABLE 6-1   Relationship of Concept Formation Model to Cognitive Skills

Model	Relational Skills	Analytical Skills
■ Concept Formation	■ Divergent thinking (phase I)	■ Convergent thinking (phases II, III, and IV)
	■ Flexibility	
	■ Creativity	■ Linear thinking (especially in webbing activities)
	■ Patterning of ideas	
	■ Meaning-orientation of ideas	

TABLE 6-2 Order of Performance for Various Ethnic Groups

African Americans:	verbal ability, reasoning, space conceptualization, number ability
Chinese Americans:	space conceptualization, number ability, reasoning, verbal
Jewish Americans:	verbal, number ability, reasoning, space conceptualization
Puerto Rican Americans:	space conceptualization, number ability, reasoning, verbal

Source: Janice Hale-Benson. 1982. *Black Children: Thin Roots, Culture, and Learning Styles.* Baltimore, MD: John Hopkins University Press: 29.

denced by students in lower socioeconomic neighborhoods. In other words, they may believe that social class is a more important factor than ethnic affiliation (for example, that poor, at-risk students think alike because of the similar socialization process they experience). The literature fails to support this view. In fact, ethnicity may be more important than social class. That means teachers should know just as much, if not more, about the racial and cultural dimensions of student learning as they do about a student's socioeconomic circumstances. Hale-Benson (1982) notes:

> Each [racial or ethnic] group was markedly different both in the *level* of each mental ability and in the *pattern* of these abilities. The most interesting finding...was that social class variation within the ethnic group does not alter the basic organization or pattern of mental abilities peculiar to that group.... Social class is a factor; but ethnicity emerged as the primary factor (pp. 29–30).

Table 6.3 is a question matrix that can be used to help teachers foster enhanced student reasoning. Effective teachers ask a range of questions (what, how, why, and so on). They want to see if students know the material and if they can then defend what they know. "What" questions focus on knowledge; "why" questions foster the reasoning that grounds that knowledge. As the teacher moves beyond the "what is?" question, students are required to use higher-level thinking skills (see Wiederhold and Kagan, 1992). They are also required to consider more complex conceptual relationships. The use of "why," "what," and "how" questions is absolutely essential to enable students to think through their categories and their ideas. Although the matrix questions were originally designed for student use (that is, students in cooperative groups would use the word pairs of "what is?" or "what might?" in cooperative learning settings), we offer them here as a guide for teachers to use as they consider how to facilitate better student thinking during concept development work: "Class, *which* of these terms *might* be grouped together? *Why would* these terms be grouped together?"

Stephanie Kovina is an inner-city teacher who uses concept formation as an instructional model in order to provide her students with an opportunity to explore their own reasoning skills. Notice how many higher-order questions she asks as the students explore the topic of sea creatures.

TABLE 6-3   Question Matrix

WHAT IS?	*WHERE/ WHEN IS?*	*WHICH IS?*	*WHO IS?*	*WHY IS?*	*HOW IS?*
WHAT DID?	*WHERE/ WHEN DID?*	*WHICH DID?*	*WHO DID?*	*WHY DID?*	*HOW DID?*
WHAT CAN?	*WHERE/ WHEN CAN?*	*WHICH CAN?*	*WHO CAN?*	*WHY CAN?*	*HOW CAN?*
WHAT WOULD?	*WHERE/ WHEN WOULD?*	*WHICH WOULD?*	*WHO WOULD?*	*WHY WOULD?*	*HOW WOULD?*
WHAT WILL?	*WHERE/ WHEN WILL?*	*WHICH WILL?*	*WHO WILL?*	*WHY WILL?*	*HOW WILL?*
WHAT MIGHT?	*WHERE/ WHEN MIGHT?*	*WHICH MIGHT?*	*WHO MIGHT?*	*WHY MIGHT?*	*HOW MIGHT?*

Source: C. Wiederhold and S. Kagan. 1992. "Cooperative Questioning and Critical Thinking." P. 203 in N. Davidson and T. Worsham (eds.), *Enhancing Thinking Through Cooperative Learning.* New York: Teacher's College Press.

Ⓒase Study

Stephanie Kovina is presenting a lesson on "Creatures of the Sea" to her 3rd grade students. She is near the end of this unit of instruction. She begins the lesson by gathering the students around a bulletin board that has pictures of 40 or 50 sea creatures—crabs, otters, sea horses, and so on. The students spend several minutes identifying the different creatures the teacher selects. The students call out creatures' names, and Ms. Kovina writes the names as they are identified: penguin, sea horse, dolphin, whale, crab, walrus, fish, otter, shark, starfish, jellyfish, pelican, seagull, and so on.

After the students complete the identification process, Ms. Kovina asks that they turn around and look at the chalkboard where she has drawn two large circles. Next to the circles are individual pictures of the various sea creatures the students have previously identified. She asks the students to look carefully at the pictures, and for a third time, she identifies each sea creature's name.

"Class, HOW COULD I separate these pictures into two groups? Think about what we have been studying and decide on how the different pictures could be divided."

Latoya responds by indicating that she would put two penguins in one circle and a lobster and crab in the other.

"Good answer, Latoya," responds Ms. Kovina. "Now WHAT PICTURES WOULD you put with these? What would go with penguins and what would go with the lobster and crab?"

Another student, Mariko, shares that the whale and dolphin would fit with the penguin.

"Does everyone agree?" asks Ms. Kovina. "WHERE DO YOU think they should go? Leroy?"

Leroy wants them with the lobster and crab.

Ms. Kovina asks why Leroy would make that classification. Rashid provides another reason for the classification.

The students proceed through the classification process until all the sea creatures are categorized. When there is any disagreement, Ms. Kovina asks WHY THE STUDENTS ARE MAKING the classification. They have to defend their answers. She asks a large number of "why" questions to force the students to think in more depth. The students develop two groupings, A and B.

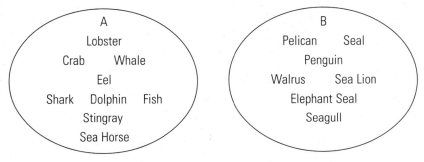

The toughest single item classification occurs for the "turtle." The students are divided regarding whether it should go in group A or group B. Ms. Kovina finally has the students vote, and the sea turtle is placed in group B.

She then asks the students to determine how each category could be labeled. "CLASS, WHAT NAME DO YOU THINK WOULD be appropriate for each of these groupings?"

Takesha responds by saying that if the sea creatures in group A are out of the water for a very long period of time they will die.

"Excellent. WHAT COULD we call this grouping of sea creatures who need water in order to live?"

After some discussion, group A is labeled "Creatures that breathe in the water"; group B is labeled "Creatures that breathe in the air."

Ms. Kovina then gives the students pieces of blue paper (for the sea) and green paper (for the land). Students also receive pictures of all the sea creatures because their task is to glue the different sea creatures on the appropriate color of paper based upon the labeled classifications. ∎

This lesson has a very different feel from the one found in most traditional classes. Traditional lessons emphasize "What is?" questions, where students identify the names of animals presented by the teacher. Students must think quickly. In many cases they provide incorrect responses in order to give the teacher some form of response. In concept formation, students have an opportunity to explore their own ideas. Teachers who use this approach will recognize that students are very skilled reasoners, even though they reason differently from the teacher. Some students who never raise their hands in response to "What is the definition of a natural resource?" will more quickly respond when asked "Which resources did you use this morning before you came to school?" or "Why do we need natural resources in order to live?"

The focus of concept formation is to enable students to construct their own understandings about phenomena. One especially positive aspect of concept formation is that both teachers and students become active participants in the teaching–learning process. Teachers must thoughtfully identify ways of helping students examine ideas; in other words, they must ask a variety of questions that help students form categories that can be justified. Students, on the other hand, must be able to see how different ideas (or terms) relate to one another. Student conceptual constructions enable teachers to view students as they put together the different ideas. Teachers can literally see the students' thinking!

The questioning strategies of teachers and the capacity to wait for student responses are critical to the success of this instructional model. Teachers cannot allow students to engage in concept formation on their own. Rather, the teacher must help students fully explore ideas, conceptual interrelationships, and broader understandings about how different ideas fit together. That is why some teachers use the closure phase of this model to have students develop a generalization about the different conceptual categories. In this way, the teacher can readily recognize how students are constructing larger understandings. With that knowledge, the teacher is then prepared to determine how to proceed with future lessons.

ⓟREVALENT ISSUES IN DIVERSE CLASSROOMS

Concept formation fosters student thinking, but it also makes some teachers feel as though they have lost control. Because students are more intimately involved in the data-analysis process, many teachers confront problems directly related to the structure, timing, and use of this instructional model. As indicated earlier, concept formation is not a pedagogically complicated strategy (that is, it does not have lots of steps), but problems do emerge when teachers use the technique.

Q: *Which is preferable, student- or teacher-generated data?*

A: It depends on the goals of the teacher. If the teacher wants the students to explore data relative to a traditional concept (for example, a sentence), then it makes sense for the teacher to provide the data. In such an instance, a teacher might limit the data set in order to limit the labels presented by the students (that is, the teacher wants students to specify a label that is conceptually congruent with one predetermined by the teacher). If, on the other hand, the teacher is reviewing information from a thematic unit, then student-generated data may make more sense. Students might be permitted to generate data as long as the momentum of the lesson is maintained.

Q: *Don't I waste time with the concept formation model?*

A: Whenever teachers relinquish some control, they will feel as though they are wasting time. One problem associated with the traditional school structure is the need to focus only upon basic skills, those skills that are easy to measure in a standardized fashion. As discussed earlier in Chapters 2 and 3, one of the most required skills in the global economy is a thinking, informed citizen. Thus, the need to help prepare future citizens with the thinking skills necessary should be a primary goal of schools. Teaching students to think is not a time-efficient process, but it does pay dividends in terms of what they learn. As Parker (1987) notes:

> Thinking takes time. Consequently, the amount of content to be learned needs to be reduced if thinking is to be infused into the curriculum and if, in turn, the curriculum is actually to be learned. The difficulty of this reduction makes it no less necessary. Too much content encourages superficial "coverage."… When content is merely covered, even if many important details are included, students have not necessarily been engaged in thinking about it; consequently, whatever measurable, so-called achievement may result from it is not to be taken too seriously (p. 50).

Q: *How can I use the cognitive style strengths of my students with the concept formation model?*

A: In utilizing the concept formation model, the teacher should be cognizant of the cognitive style strengths of the student population. Applying this model through cooperative learning techniques should be a must for those students who learn best through such collaborative approaches (Shade, 1989; Soldier, 1989; Vasquez, 1991). Using pairs and triads to generate terms, identifying and assessing alternative hypotheses and conclusions, and identifying groupings of terms will play to the strengths of the culturally diverse students described in Chapter 2. Further, the use of manipulatives (for example, in science and mathematics) will utilize the kinesthetic style strengths of African Americans and Hispanic Americans (Morgan, 1981; Soldier, 1989) but is important for all students regardless of their racial or ethnic backgrounds.

The use of both animate and inanimate pictures and objects to demonstrate concept groupings and terms helps in the development of concepts as described by the research of Prom (1982), Shade (1984), and Shade and Edwards (1987). Many of the teachers we have observed use objects or pictures and have students manipulate those within their groups. The hands-on nature of the learning really helps students *see* the groups emerge.

EVALUATION CRITERIA

The concept formation instructional model is an inductive approach to student learning. School districts often use evaluation methods that are essentially deductive in nature (for example, they expect teachers to proceed from big ideas to exemplars rather than from exemplars to big ideas). This reality complicates the evaluation process and makes it even more imperative that supplemental assessment strategies be used. The following evaluation criteria can be used by teachers to assess a concept formation lesson. Readers might practice using the criteria with the lesson presented by Ms. Kovina.

Phase I: Data Generation

1. What is the purpose of the concept formation activity? Is it used as a way of initiating a unit? Reviewing unit material? Other? Describe.

2. How are data generated by students or teachers categorized? Describe.

3. Is sufficient data generated before the teacher begins the categorization process? Explain.

4. Does the teacher clarify the meaning of all enumerated data to make certain students know the meanings of the various terms? In what ways?　　　　　○ Yes　○ No

Phase II: Data Grouping

1. Do students have a clear understanding of what they are expected to do in terms of categorizing the data?　　　　○ Yes　○ No

2. Does the teacher provide students with materials for creating the categories? (For example, sheets of paper with circles.) Evaluate the type of materials utilized.　　　　　　　　○ Yes　○ No

Phase III: Labeling

1. Does the teacher warrant all student groupings as valid? (That is, the teacher avoids using words such as "Right" or "You got it" that suggest there are correct categories.)　　　　　　○ Yes　○ No

2. Do the students have logical
labels for their groupings?　　○ Yes　○ No

3. Does the teacher require students to defend their categories
and explain the rationale for
each label grouping they have
created? Explain how the teacher
exhibits this behavior.　　○ Yes　○ No

Phase IV: Expanding the Category

1. Are students required to expand
the categories once the teacher
presents each grouping to the
class? In what ways does this
occur?　　○ Yes　○ No

2. Are students able to add data to
each category from different
sources (that is, they can even
add data that were not initially
enumerated in phase I)? Provide
examples.　　○ Yes　○ No

Phase V: Closure

1. Does the teacher offer a follow-
up activity that builds on student
understandings relative to the
categories they formed?
Describe and provide your
impression of the follow-up
activity.　　○ Yes　○ No

❺ AMPLE LESSONS　　

The following classroom episodes are intended to help readers further understand the concept formation model. The first scenario is another case study
example of a concept formation lesson. The second example is a lesson plan that
utilizes the concept formation model. Read each scenario and respond to the
questions that follow.

CASE STUDY

"Class, we have been studying the Middle Ages for several weeks. You now understand that *Middle Ages* and *Medieval Times* are two terms that represent the same time period. I want you now to write down several terms that best represent the Middle Ages to you.

"I am now going to ask that each of you go up to the board and write down at least three terms that you associate with that time period."

The students then begin to go to the board and list words such as *squire, serf, noble, knight, manor,* and so on.

After the students finish enumerating the data (approximately 50 terms), the teacher has the students get into groups (four students to a group) and create categories for the data.

"For all the data we have, class, see if you can group these terms together in a way that makes sense to you. Place items together that fit together. You can use any definition you want to create the fit."

The teacher gives the students sheets of paper with several large circles and has the students begin the categorization process. After 10 minutes, the students finish and the teacher requests that one group present its first set of data for the class to examine.

Shaneca's peer group provides the first set of data—*Sir Lancelot, King Arthur, King William*—and labels the group "People of the Middle Ages." The second group offers the group "Castle Parts." All the student groups provide their concept groupings until the board is literally full of terms.

At that point the teacher asks the students to review the work that they have put on the board and see if they can add anything to any of the concept groups that have been formed. She also reviews and refines the concept group names to determine if better language could be used to explore the meaning for a group of terms. ∎

Follow-up questions

1. In what ways would a teacher-generated set of data be more useful than a student-generated set of data for a unit?

2. How many terms should teachers allow students to generate (this teacher allowed 50) before proceeding to phase II?

3. What approaches should teachers use to help students form the categories? That is, should the teacher select one term and ask students to form a sample group around that term, or should students be free to create their own groups from the beginning of the lesson?

4. How can concept categories be expanded to explore student understandings of the ideas presented by the teacher?

5. What other types of closure activities could be used to help students use the categories they create?

The lesson plan provided below is for a teacher who is preparing to teach a concept formation lesson on the "Chemistry of Living Things" from the Prentice-Hall (1993) Integrated Science series book on "Cells." Read the lesson plan and answer the questions that follow.

Concept: Chemistry of Living Things

Objectives:
1. To ensure that students understand the meaning of the different terms associated with living things.
2. To determine how students organize concepts covered as part of the "Living Things" unit.

Methods:
1. Teacher will provide data to students by creating a worksheet with the following terms: *spontaneous generation, metabolism, ingestion, digestion, respiration, excretion, life, sperm, stimulus, response, element, compound, organic compound, carbohydrate, oil, protein, amino acid, enzyme, nucleic acid, DNA, RNA.*
2. Teacher will divide class into heterogenous student groups of three students. Each group will have one high-, one low-, and one average-ability science student.
3. Teacher will require each student group to review the definitions of all terms and then create three different concept groupings. A grouping can have no fewer than four terms.
4. Students will create concept groupings and add at least two of their own terms that fit within the category. All group members must be able to defend the grouping created.
5. Teacher will ask each peer group to label the various concept groupings and put their best grouping on a transparency, which will be shared with the entire class.
6. Class members will review the concept groupings as they are presented and will identify ways of expanding each concept grouping.

Closure: Students will write definitions for the terms presented to the class, and will be able to describe the relationship between and among the terms.

Follow-up questions

1. Is the review activity an appropriate one for the concepts associated with living things?
2. Should the teacher use a student-generated data set rather than a teacher-generated data set? Does it matter how the data are generated?
3. What other techniques might teachers use to review the concept groupings developed by the peer groups?

The concept formation strategy is a relatively easy, though intellectually rigorous, instructional model to use. In preparing to develop a concept formation lesson, the following materials and resources could be utilized or reviewed.

Suggested readings

Brown, R. 1973. "Taba Rediscovered." *Science Teacher* 40(8): 30–33.

Eggen, P. D., and D. P. Kauchak. 1988. *Strategies for Teachers* (2d ed.). Englewood Cliffs, NJ: Prentice-Hall. (See Chapter 4.)

Gunter, M. A., T. H. Estes, and J. H. Schwab. 1990. *Instruction: A Models Approach.* Boston: Allyn & Bacon. (See Chapter 7.)

Joyce, B., and M. Weil. 1992. *Models of Teaching* (4th ed.). Boston: Allyn & Bacon. (See Chapter 6.)

Neubert, G., and J. Binko. 1992. *Inductive Reasoning in the Secondary Classroom.* Washington, DC: National Education Association.

Peters, E., and R. Dixon. 1987. "Special Focus: Effective Instruction in Reading." *Teaching Exceptional Children* 19(2): 61–63.

Suggested videotapes

"Inductive Thinking in Cooperative Groups." Booksend Laboratories, 652 St. Andrews Drive, Rio Del Mar, Aptos, CA 95003.

Episode: "Synthesis: Concept Formation." Video Library of Teaching Episodes. Association for Supervision and Curriculum Development, 125 Northwest Street, Alexandria, VA 22314-2798.

Suggested lesson development

Teachers who are developing a concept formation lesson plan need to consider the following questions.

1. Will the reorganizing approach of concept formation be used to introduce or review a set of concepts?

2. What type of data-generation approach (student or teacher) makes the most sense given the students who will use the approach?

3. How many groupings will the students create and how many terms (at a minimum level) must be in each group?

4. How will the concept groupings be reviewed? Will students work individually or in groups?

5. What closure activity will be used to extend the students' understandings of the concepts?

SUMMARY

Concept formation is one of three different instructional strategies (or cognitive tasks) that Hilda Taba (1966) identified as useful in enhancing the thinking skills of students. The other two strategies are interpretation of data, which we allude to in Chapter 5, "Inquiry," and application of principle, which Taba suggests has a very specialized function:

> The essence of this task [application of principle] is using information already possessed to explain something new, to predict consequences of events, or to hypothesize about causes and effects. For example, if one knows what a desert is, the way of life a desert permits and how water affects agricultural production, one can predict what might happen to the desert way of life if water became available.... While interpreting and generalizing from raw data [concept formation] is an inductive process, applying known facts and generalizations is a deductive process (p. 41).

We emphasize the concept formation strategy because it fosters requisite inductive thinking skills and because teachers generally find it quite easy to learn and use. Concept formation is also motivational for students because it enables them to explore their own understandings about an idea or topic. Students pursue personal questions and create their own constructs; as a consequence, the teacher is able to see how students are "putting together" an idea. In Piagetian terms, the teacher actually views the schema of the students.

Teachers who use concept formation note that the type and level of student participation is very different from what is found in a traditional lesson. Because there are no necessarily correct responses, students are much freer to explore personal ideas and perspectives. Some "nonparticipation" students seem more willing to take a risk once they know that their constructed concept is just as valid as the ideas created by other students.

REFERENCES

Borich, G. 1988. *Effective Teaching Methods.* Columbus, OH: Merrill.

Brown, R. 1973. "Taba Rediscovered." *Science Teacher* 40(8): 30–33.

Eggen, P. D., and D. P. Kauchak. 1988. *Strategies for Teachers* (2d ed.). Englewood Cliffs, NJ: Prentice-Hall.

Gunter, M. A., T. H. Estes, and J. H. Schwab. 1990. *Instruction: A Models Approach.* Boston: Allyn & Bacon.

Haberman, M., and L. Post. 1995. "Multicultural Teaching in the Real World." Pp. 337–353 in A. C. Ornstein (ed.), *Teaching: Theory and Practice.* Boston: Allyn & Bacon.

Hale-Benson, J. 1982. *Black Children: Their Roots, Culture, and Learning Styles.* Baltimore, MD: Johns Hopkins University Press.

Hyerle, D. 1996. *Visual Tools.* Washington, DC: Association for Supervision and Curriculum Development.

Joyce, B., and M. Weil. 1992. *Models of Teaching* (4th ed.). Boston: Allyn & Bacon.

Maton, A. 1993. *Cells: Building Blocks of Life.* Chapter 1: Chemistry of Living Things. Englewood Cliffs, NJ: Prentice-Hall: 35–37.

Morgan, H. 1981. "Factors Concerning Cognitive Development and Learning

Differentiation Among Black Children." Pp. 14–22 in A. E. Harrison (ed.), *Conference on Empirical Research in Black Psychology* 6.

Neubert, G., and J. Binko. 1992. *Inductive Reasoning in the Secondary Classroom.* Washington, DC: National Education Association.

Newmann, F. M., and G. G. Wehlage. 1993. "Five Standards of Authentic Instruction." *Educational Leadership* 50(7): 8–12.

Parker, W. C. 1987. "Teaching Thinking: The Pervasive Approach." *Journal of Teacher Education* 38(3): 50–56.

Peters, E., and R. Dixon. 1987. "Special Focus: Effective Instruction in Reading." *Teaching Exceptional Children* 19(2): 61–63.

Prom, S. E. 1982. "Salient Content and Cognitive Performance of Person- and Thing-Oriented Low Income Afro-American Children in Kindergarten and Second Grade." Doctoral dissertation, Howard University, Washington, DC.

Shade, B. J. 1984. "Afro-American Patterns of Cognition: A Review of the Research." Paper presented at annual meeting of American Educational Research Association, New Orleans, LA.

———. 1989. "The Influence of Perceptual Development on Cognitive Style: Cross Ethnic Comparisons." *Early Child Development and Care* 51: 137–155.

———, and P. A. Edwards. 1987. "Ecological Correlates of the Educative Style of Afro-American Children." *Journal of Negro Education* 86: 88–99.

Soldier, L. 1989. "Cooperative Learning and the Native American Student." *Phi Delta Kappan* 71(2): 161–163.

Taba, H. 1966. *Teaching Strategies and Cognitive Functioning in Elementary School Children.* Cooperative Research Project 2404. San Francisco: San Francisco State College.

Vasquez, J. A. 1991. "Cognitive Style and Academic Attainment." Pp. 163–179 in J. Lynch, C. Modgil, and S. Modgil (eds.), *Cultural Diversity and the Schools: Consensus and Controversy.* London: Falconer Press.

Whimbey, A. 1977. "Teaching Sequential Thought: The Cognitive Skills Approach." *Phi Delta Kappan* 58: 255–259.

Wiederhold, C., and S. Kagan. 1992. "Cooperative Questioning and Critical Thinking." P. 203 in N. Davidson and T. Worsham (eds.), *Enhancing Thinking Through Cooperative Learning.* New York: Teacher's College Press.

Synectics

At the completion of this chapter, the reader will be able to:
1. *Identify the basic phases associated with the synectics model.*
2. *Identify the strengths and weaknesses of synectics.*
3. *Understand the theoretical and empirical grounding for the synectics model.*
4. *Evaluate lessons that use synectics strategies.*
5. *Create a lesson using synectics to help students creatively think through content material.*

❶ NTRODUCTION

No cultural group holds the patent on creativity. A quick perusal of eminent individuals who have evidenced excellence in their personal performance and who have been creative in their exploration of ideas illustrates that regardless of personal or cultural background, creative ideas are possible. In literature the names range from Toni Morrison (African American) to Amy Tan (Asian American) to Gerald Viznor (Native American) to Jose Antonio Villarreal (Hispanic American). With regard to mathematical reasoning the names include Benjamin Bannecker (African American), Yuan Lee (Asian American), Luis Alverez (Hispanic American), and Robert Whitman (Native American). In essence, cultural background neither advantages nor disadvantages the capacity for creative thought. Some individuals may be more creative than others, but a genetic cultural advantage cannot be claimed by any group.

Creative thinking is a by-product of how students learn to explore ideas. Although some argue that creative problem-solving cannot be taught (see Torrance, 1986), many others assert that students can learn how to think creatively if they use "disciplined" techniques for thinking through problems. Synectics is one such step-by-step technique. It is a technique that can be used by all students, not just those who claim the status of "gifted" or "talented." Indeed, one of the real advantages of synectics is that all students can participate in the creative process because creativity is more broadly defined as "everyday thinking that results in something new, either to the person doing the thing or to the world" (Weaver and Prince, 1990, p. 379). A definition such as this suggests that everyone has an ability to think about

Every human being has this creative urge as his or her birthright. It can be squelched and corrupted, but it cannot be completely extinguished.

MIHALY CSIKSZENTMIHALYI

old ideas in new ways. The essence of the creative process is for each individual to make new connections that make personal sense and enhance personal perspective.

Teachers tend to make conceptual connections for students. They create the conceptual structures; students are expected to memorize those structures and, on demand (through tests), give back what has previously been given to them by the teacher. The intellectual "cost" of this approach for many students is substantial. As Weaver and Prince (1990) argue, it tends to "foreclose on many promising lines of thought. [Students in these types of classrooms have]…a way of thinking that seems to be reinforced by an emphasis on precision, on right and wrong answers, and on punishment for mistakes" (p. 379).

As the following simulated 4th grade classroom example illustrates, creative problem-solving does not mean an absence of intellectual rigor. Rather, it is a way of enabling students to see the familiar in new and more intellectually demanding ways.

Ⓒase Study

"Class, we have been studying the earth for the past week, and you are developing some good understandings about the structure of our planet. Today I want you to look at the earth in a slightly different way. Specifically, I'm going to suggest that the earth is like a peach." At this point the teacher, Mr. Rodriguez, gives a peach to each of the student pairs (students are working in groups of two) and asks them to cut open the peach and look at its various parts.

"Before you explore my idea, my analogy, I want you to list all the things that you know about the earth on the left side of the paper I'm providing you, and all the things you know about peaches on the right side." The students fill in the chart (the final product of one student group looks like the one provided in Figure 7.1). Mr. Rodriguez then has students review their charts, and several additional items are added that students think make sense but that go beyond obvious ideas (see Figure 7.1 below the dashed lines).

Mr. Rodriguez then continues the lesson. "Excellent! You have really generated a tremendous number of good ideas. Now let's go back to my original idea. I asked you to consider that the earth is a lot like a peach. How is that true? In what ways is the earth like a peach? With your peer partner, identify three ways that the earth is like a peach." The students work together in pairs for a couple of minutes and then Mr. Rodriguez asks them to share their ideas.

"Roberto, why don't you share one of your ideas?"

"The earth is like a peach because they both have hard centers. The peach has a pit, and the earth has a solid core."

"Good," responds Mr. Rodriguez. "In fact, the core makes up about 15 percent of the earth's total volume, and the pit looks like it is about the same volume for the peach. Another idea, Portia?"

"The earth has a mantle, and the peach is made up of pulp. The mantle is very thick for the earth, and the pulp is most of the peach."

The Earth	The Peach
mantle	fuzz
outer (liquid) core	pit
inner (solid) core	juice
crust	pulp
Mohorovic boundary	bruise
faults	- - - - - - - - - - - -
rocks	stem
- - - - - - - - - - - -	
seismograph	
primary waves	
secondary waves	
epicenter	

FIGURE 7-1   Synectics Brainstorming Chart

"Do you recall what the mantle is made up of?"

"Yes, rocks," replies Portia.

The students continue to make several comparisons before Mr. Rodriguez stops them. He puts each comparison on the board as students suggest other ideas.

"You have really developed some terrific ideas. Now I want you all to close your eyes. Think with me for a few minutes about what it must be like to be the earth. Picture yourself as the earth, a living thing. People are drilling holes in you. They are building big buildings on you. They are polluting you with pesticides. Tell me now how you feel. And when you make your statement, be sure to start with the words, 'I feel.'... In other words, say something like 'I feel happy because people need my resources in order to live.' OK? (The teacher then pauses for a moment.) Ernesto, why don't you start us off."

Ernesto responds, "I feel hurt because the people keep drilling more and more holes in me. They take out my crude oil and then create pollution."

"Sarah?"

"I feel bruised because of the strip mining that occurs. They keep scraping away more and more of my surface. It's painful."

"Minda. What do you feel?"

"I feel used. People appear to have no concern for who I am."

Mr. Rodriguez allows the students to develop their ideas for almost 10 minutes and then says, "Now I want you to think what it must be like to be a peach. Share your ideas with me. Aurora?"

"I feel hurt when they pick me off the tree. It feels so good to grow on the tree and have the wind blow against me. Then some guy puts his big hand on me and pulls me off." (Several students laugh and poke fun at Aurora.)

"Luis."

"I feel...."

The lesson continues with the students articulating how they feel to be a peach.

"Now that you've shared how it feels to be a peach and the earth, I want you to think about the differences between a peach and the earth. In what ways are peaches and the earth different? We agreed that in some ways they are similar. Now consider ways in which they are different. Work with your partners to generate three differences."

The students work for several minutes, and the teacher then asks them to share their ideas.

The first student, Tara, suggests that the peach grows on a tree but that the earth doesn't grow on anything.

Another student, Javier, shares that a peach can be used in preparing meals, but the earth (the dirt) cannot be eaten.

The students share lots of ideas. On occasion, some students argue points—one student points out that the earth is part of the solar system and that's like the peach being part of the tree.

After much sharing, the teacher asks the students to think of other comparisons of the earth that they like better than a peach. Students work in their groups and generate an example that they like better, including an explanation of why their analogy is a good one. Many students use other fruits. Some, though, use other objects. One asserts that the earth is like a baseball because the surface is rough and has seams (like mountains), has an inner substance that is hard (like rocks in the mantle), and so on.

At the end of the lesson, the students are asked to read a section from the text on plate tectonics and to create a chart regarding the volume, density, and mass of the earth's different components. The students must also draw a diagram of the earth and of their analog. (See Figure 7.2 for an example.)

Finally they are asked to prepare a short essay that describes why they agree with or disagree with strip mining as a way of extracting valuable ores from the earth. ∎

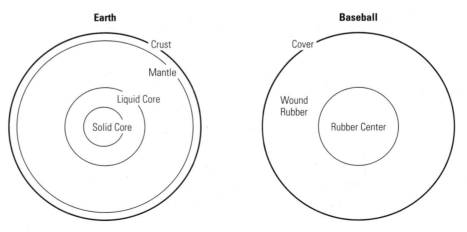

FIGURE 7-2 Cross-Sectional View of Earth and Baseball

Mr. Rodriguez uses synectics to help students understand the structure of the earth in a new and unique way. The teacher and students possess a substantial content knowledge base, but they are examining the concepts and facts in unique ways.

⊤HEORETICAL PERSPECTIVE

The basis of synectics is helping students see old ideas in new ways. Synectics creates within the students an excitement about concepts that are both familiar and unfamiliar. Students may not, and hopefully would not, be as excited as Archimedes was when he discovered the principle of fluid displacement (supposedly he jumped out of his bathtub and ran down the street, *naked*, yelling "Eureka!"), but they can begin to attach new meanings to familiar ideas. And those new meanings can foster a new enthusiasm for ideas.

The etymology of synectics traces to the Greek roots: *syn* means to bring together and *ectics* refers to diverse elements (Weaver and Prince, 1990). At the heart of a synectics lesson is the teacher's ability to use various forms of metaphoric thinking such as similes, metaphors, personification, and oxymorons. Metaphorical thinking causes students to look at reality in different ways—it shatters conventional views. This shattering process is perhaps the weakest aspect of the American educational system. American schools foster at least three different types of thinking: appositional, divergent, and generative. Unfortunately, too much emphasis is placed on the first type (appositional), and too little emphasis is placed on generative. *Appositional thinking* occurs, according to Weaver and Prince (1990), when students "limit their trial connections to material that is close to the problem" (p. 380). American students are seemingly preoccupied with relevance issues—How does this fact help me? When will I use this? It is not that appositional thinkers lack content understandings, they just censor their thinking in ways that limit their full exploration of ideas. They have, in essence, a very "low tolerance for anything that does not seem pertinent" (Weaver and Prince, 1990, p. 380).

Divergent thinking often creates instructional problems for teachers. When students think divergently, they develop a wide variety of ideas, but their intellectual leaps frequently fail to pay positive cognitive dividends because they do not see the conceptual connections between ideas. Of course, in some instances this is quite acceptable, especially when the teacher wants to involve all students in a lesson but is not particularly concerned that they reach a specific conclusion or analyze data in a distinctive manner.

Synectics fosters *generative thinking*. The generative thinker "is open to divergent beginnings but eagerly searches for connections to make ideas more workable" (Weaver and Prince, 1990, p. 380). Certainly synectics is not the only way to foster generative thinking, but because of its step-by-step nature (its linear, sequential process), it is *one* of the best ways to enable students to see how ideas connect.

Synectics was first introduced by William Gordon (1961). Gordon's notion was that creativity was and is a fundamental part of everyday activity. It is not a special ability, but if fostered properly by the teacher, it can be extremely useful in enhancing the problem-solving potential of students, indeed of all people regardless of their role. In addition, Gordon argued that "students" (or all learners) need to know that the creative process is not the exclusive domain of a "privileged" few. All students have an ability to be creative if they understand the process of creative thought and if they learn some strategies for engaging in creative problem-solving. Finally, because creative exploration is not necessarily the "right" of one student, it is possible for students to learn how to be creative both individually and cooperatively. Indeed, both individuals and groups can learn to create ideas in very similar ways if they understand how to make conceptual "excursions." An excursion is nothing more than a process of seeing problems in new ways. Weaver and Prince (1990) provide a more detailed description:

> There are three simple steps in using excursions. First, put the problem temporarily out of mind. This enables one to get distance from the problem he or she is working on. Second, deliberately focus on apparent irrelevancy. This can generate surprising or unusual connections. Third, force-fit the irrelevant material together with the problem and allow your mind to invent a way of connecting them. Force-fitting is a trick of the mind. Our mind automatically struggles to fit new connections into an existing pattern or, failing that, to create a new pattern. Being open to that new pattern or line of thought will enable us to produce ideas that are both useful and original (p. 384).

This description provides the reader with a general framework for creative excursions. The following description (Synectics I), which is structured similarly to that of Mr. Rodriguez's lesson on the earth's structure, is a simplification of the synectics process and also parallels the one proffered by the Association for Supervision and Curriculum Development ("Teaching Strategies Library: Part Two"). A second description (Synectics II) is also provided; it more closely matches a conceptualization of Gordon's (1961) work as represented by Joyce and Weil (1992) and Gunter et al. (1995).

ⓈYNECTICS I: TEACHING PHASES

Phase I: Identification of Topic Area

The synectics lesson begins once the teacher determines what concept the students should fully explore. Typically, the teacher will want students to develop a fuller, richer understanding of some big idea. If the class has been studying the respiratory system, the teacher might want students to focus on respiration and to understand in new ways how respiratory functions parallel what happens in other types of complex systems. In essence, the first step in synectics is to identify what concept, ideas, or knowledge structures require fuller exploration and development by the class.

How will the teacher know what ideas require such exploration? Through intuition and experience! Teachers who use synectics see it as a way of helping students see "*old*" ideas in new ways. The history of ideas is filled with examples of people who evidenced this ability for creative insight except they seemed to do it almost naturally: Copernicus thought about the earth's relationship to the sun in ways that contradicted other astronomers; Freud thought about dreams in ways quite different from those who preceded him (that is, he describes manifest dreams, the actual imagery of a dream, latent dreams, and the hidden meaning of the imagery). Students, in synectics, begin to think about the earth or cells or respiration in new ways, and their revelations represent new understandings.

Phase II: Direct Analogy

Once the teacher identifies what concept to extend and explore, the teacher then creates a direct analogy. A direct analogy is nothing more than a metaphoric comparison between two ideas (one the concept and the other an analog). For the respiratory system, a direct analogy might be "How are a train and train track like the respiratory system?" Recall that Mr. Rodriguez offered the direct analogy of "*The earth is like a peach.*"

Many teachers find it difficult to identify *perfect* direct analogies. That's because few, if any, *perfect* analogies exist. All objects differ in some ways; as a result, all efforts to create comparisons that reveal objects as identical in every way will fall short of the ideal. As Joyce and Weil (1992) note, the real purpose of a direct analogy is "to transpose the condition of the real topic or problem situation to another situation in order to present a new view of an idea or problem" (p. 222).

The teacher poses the direct analogy and asks students to think of 1) all the characteristics of the conceptual object, 2) all the characteristics of the analog, and 3) all the ways that they are analogous. A simple example follows for "An opera is like a football game" (see Table 7.1), which incidentally, is a direct anal-

TABLE 7-1 Analogical Comparison for Opera and Football Game

Characteristics of Opera	Characteristics of Football Game	Comparison
Costumes	Uniforms	An opera is like a football game because in an opera the performers wear costumes and in a football game the players wear uniforms.
Acts	Quarters	An opera is like a football game because in an opera there are acts and in a football game there are quarters.
Diva	Quarterback	An opera is like a football game because both have "stars"—in an opera the soprano who sings the lead role is called a diva; in a football game the star is called the quarterback.

ogy that one of the authors used while teaching a synectics lesson on opera to adults in Vienna, Austria—the goal was to enable the students to think about operas in a different way.

Students are expected to make a list of the characteristics of the object and the analog. Once exhaustive lists of individual characteristics are developed, they then make the comparisons. Some teachers find it useful to actually write out the comparisons; others rely on verbal representations.

Phase III: Personal Analogy

Once students have an understanding of the direct analogy, they then attempt to "lose themselves" in the concept. This is both an exciting and a challenging step for students—though much depends on how the teacher organizes and orchestrates the experience. The teacher needs to be able to sell this idea to the students by asking them to become the conceptual object and the analog. Recall that Mr. Rodriguez started this phase by stating, *"You have really developed some terrific ideas. Now I want you all to close your eyes. Think with me for a few minutes about what it must be like to be the earth. Picture yourself as the earth, a living thing...."* The students then go on to share their ideas. One student, Ernesto, responds that *"I feel hurt because the people keep drilling more and more holes in me."* Ernesto's response is a first-person description of an emotion—he feels hurt. But students can, according to Gordon (1961), describe other first-person sentiments as well. They may provide factual descriptions, like the student, Sarah, who felt bruised because of all the strip mining that occurs on her "surface." Or the student might have an empathic response similar to Minda's. Minda shared that she felt exploited and identified with the earth as an organic object. Personal analogies release the creative impulses and enhance the intellectual vitality of the individual. Gordon (1961) writes, "Personal identification with the elements of a problem releases the individual from viewing the problem in terms of its previously analyzed elements" (p. 37).

The teacher should encourage students to become both the analog and the object. As students express their ideas, the teacher lists the description, emotions, facts, or empathic feelings on poster board or on the chalkboard. This helps students see the commonalities associated with their feelings; it also is essential if teachers decide to use a compressed conflict strategy, which we will describe in the alternative model Synectics II section.

Phase IV: Analog Contrast

In the fourth phase, the student begins to contrast the analog and the conceptual object. As we shared earlier, no metaphoric comparison is perfect. All comparisons fall short in some ways! Thus, in the fourth phase, students begin to examine differences between the analog and the concept. Mr. Rodriguez offers the following as a transition to phase IV: *"Now that you've shared how it feels to be a peach and the earth, I want you to think about the differences between a peach and the earth. In what ways are peaches and the earth different? We agreed that in some ways*

they are similar. Now consider ways in which they are different. Work with your part-
ners to generate three differences."

One problematic statement that teachers use (and it is especially noticeable on the Association for Supervision and Curriculum Development Teaching Strategies tapes) is to say something similar to this: "Class, we have been studying how the earth is like a peach. But is the earth like a peach? No. I don't think so. Let's look at all the differences." Such a statement ("No. I don't think so.") implicitly says to the students: "I lied to you earlier. I said the earth was like a peach. Now I'm telling you that it's not." The teacher can create the contrast without being so pedagogically duplicitous. Teachers should simply share with students that conceptual objects and analogs are both alike and different. In the previous two phases the similarities are emphasized. In phase IV the students examine and list the differences. Encourage the students to write down statements that describe these differences and then have them share those with the class. Recall that Tara (from Mr. Rodriguez's class) noted that a peach grows on a tree, but that the earth does not grow on anything.

Phase V: New Analogy

Once students have examined both similarities (phases II and III) and differences (phase IV) between the conceptual objects and the analog, they are ready to create their own direct analogy, which is hopefully conceptually stronger than the original direct analogy. Most teachers who have conducted a synectics lesson observe that at some point during the implementation of a synectics lesson either they or the students think of metaphoric ideas that they like better than the one originally presented. Phase V provides an opportunity to explore new metaphoric possibilities. In phase V, the teacher asks the students to generate their own analogs. Mr. Rodriguez has the students work in groups in this phase as a way of stimulating more ideas. This is a good way to proceed, especially if students are using the model for the first time. As students develop more comfort with this instructional model, it will become more possible to have them work either independently or in cooperative learning groups to think of analogies that make sense.

Phase VI: Topic Refocus

Once students have finished the activity, the teacher should return to the original theme or conceptual topic and have students provide their reflections. Mr. Rodriguez had his students write a short essay that described their support for or opposition to strip mining. Synectics lessons should immeasurably enhance the type of language used by students to express their ideas and attitudes. Essay responses, of course, are not the only refocusing tasks a teacher might use (for example, the students might watch a movie on strip mining and orally discuss their reactions or go on a field trip to a rock quarry and take pictures of the effects of mining). The critical dimension is to make certain that students return to the original topic in order to "play with" the concept in a different way.

SYNECTICS II: TEACHING PHASES

The Synectics I lesson structure just outlined is a relatively simple form of the creative process encouraged by Gordon (1961). Many teachers find Synectics I a good one to start with when they first begin to use creative-thinking activities in the classroom. A second form of synectics, which some teachers we have worked with describe as more complex, requires the use of a compressed conflict. In this approach the teacher intentionally fosters contradictory ideas, but this is done in such a way that it enables students to formulate familiar ideas in new and creative ways. Many of the phases are similar to those outlined in Synectics I. However, some significant differences do exist and these, in particular, will be given a more detailed description. The case study in the sample lessons section at the end of this chapter is an example of the compressed conflict approach.

Phase I: The Topic

The teacher begins a compressed conflict synectics lesson in a similar fashion to that described in Synectics I. The students typically have spent some time prior to the synectics lesson trying to understand some specific content material. For example, they may have been studying a topic such as revolutions or cell structure or natural resources. Whatever the topic, the teacher begins by having students share descriptive words or phrases that they associate with the topic. The teacher then writes these terms on the chalkboard as they are being shared.

Phase II: Direct Analogy

Once all the terms are listed, the teacher begins to create a direct analogy. In the Synectics I lesson, Mr. Rodriguez provided the direct analogy. *In this instructional variation, the students are responsible for creating the metaphoric idea.*

The process begins when the teacher asks the students to look at the terms on the board and then think of a *game, plant,* or *machine* that they would associate with those terms. For example, for *opera* the students might begin by generating the descriptive terms in Table 7.2.

When one of the authors taught a lesson on opera, students were asked to think of a game that had the identified qualities (that is, was long, involved cos-

TABLE 7-2 Descriptive Terms for Opera

Long	*Treachery*
Several acts	*Expensive*
Costumes	*Hatred*
Music	*Lots of people*
Singing	

tumes, and so on). They generated a long list of potential analogical ideas that included things like:

Baseball because the games are long, the players wear uniforms, and so on.

Hockey because the players seem to hate one another and have to wear cumbersome, expensive uniforms.

Football because of the pageantry and large number of people who watch in the stadium.

Based on the many game options generated, the students were then asked to identify their favorite possibility among all those generated by the class—in the case of the lesson on opera, the author's class selected football: An opera is like a football game! This analogy was then written on the board and became the foundation for the next phase of the lesson. Incidentally, make certain all the students know the game. On a couple of occasions, teachers have selected a game (for example, chess) for the class to use only to discover that many students did not know how to play. That makes the next phase almost impossible to operationalize.

Phase III: Personal Analogy

This phase parallels what occurs in phase III of the Synectics I variation. Essentially, the students describe what it feels like to be the object and the analog. In the case of the opera and football game analogy, students would describe what it feels like to be a football game, and the teacher writes the terms down as students provide them. The terms in Table 7.3 are provided for the opera and football game analogy. Notice that the students provide a brief explanation justifying the term. The teacher should solicit student responses and require that students defend their responses with a "because" statement.

Phase IV: Compressed Conflict

Teachers who read about using compressed conflict often find the notion of combining words that are in dynamic tension with one another to be an overly complex process. But teachers who have enabled students to use compressed conflict find it to be very effective in fostering creative thought on the part of the students. With compressed conflict, the teacher has the students look at the descriptive terms used during the personal analogy phase (phase III) and then combine those terms that tend to be opposite one another. For example, beau-

TABLE 7-3   Personal Analogy Statements

Tired because the game is so long.	***Dirty*** because I'm muddy after the game.
Beautiful because my costume or uniform is so expensive.	***Protected*** because of my equipment.
	Energized because of the cheering audience.

tiful and dirty or tired and energized. That is, things are not normally thought of as being both beautiful and dirty, but a football coach would perceive a lineman as "beautiful" if his uniform is dirty at the end of a game.

The students combine words that conceptually (and dynamically) fit together (for example, beautiful and dirty are adjectives describing how one looks), yet are contradictory when found in nature (that is, how can one be both beautiful and dirty?). The teacher has the students generate as many compressed conflicts as they can identify. The students should then vote about which of the compressed conflicts they like the best. In this instance, let us assume that beautiful and dirty are selected.

Phase V: New Analogy

The teacher next asks the students to create a new direct analogy. The teacher takes the compressed conflict (beautiful and dirty) and has students identify some object (animal or machine or food) that has these compressed conflict qualities. The object (animal or machine or food) does nothing more than provide a focus for the students' ideas—it keeps their ideas somewhat together in the pattern of their thinking. The options developed in this case might be:

- An engine in a car (the engine is dirty, but the car is beautiful)
- A "dirt" cake as a dessert (the cake looks messy once eaten, but it is beautiful just before the dessert is cut and distributed)

After students generate a number of new possibilities, the teacher then asks them to select the one they like the best. (Usually students reach some sort of consensus, but the teacher may need to do some modest "directing" to make certain all students understand the selected new analogy.) In this case, the students select "an engine in a car."

Phase VI: Topic Refocus

In this phase, the teacher begins to revisit the original topic. If the original topic was the student's perceptions of the opera, then the teacher asks the student to consider how the opera (the topic) is like an engine in a car (the new analog). The students then generate as many ideas as possible—actually this process usually starts slowly, and then as some students see possibilities (that is, other students create ideas) the rest of the students in the class become more generative in their thinking. For instance,

An opera needs music, and a car requires gasoline.

An opera needs a conductor, and a car requires a driver.

Phase VII: Extension

After students have generated a substantial list of new ideas concerning the concept, the teacher should begin to critically extend some of the students' ideas. The teacher might, for example, have students write a description of what it means to "run" an opera, or to develop a report on all the different elements that need to be in place if an opera is to be "run" effectively.

Some teachers get to phase VI and let the lesson drop. This significantly mitigates the power of this instructional model. The model is intended to stimulate student thinking about a topic, and unless the teacher intentionally extends the students' thoughts about the topic and forces them to reexamine that topic, the full impact of the lesson will not be achieved. Remember synectics is not a gimmick or game. It is, instead, a pedagogical vehicle for enhancing the quality of student thought.

APPLICATIONS TO DIVERSE CLASSROOMS

Synectics embraces the fundamental notion that not all learners are the same, but that all learners are able to think creatively. Students make sense out of their environment in different ways; they construct meaning based on their experiences and their individual, unique interactions with the ideas presented by the teacher. A number of professional organizations (for example, National Science Teacher's Association, National Council for the Social Studies) have presented the notion that schools should espouse and implement a "less is more" philosophy. They implicitly suggest that schools are endeavoring to cover too much material too quickly. The issue for teachers becomes one of understanding how to develop lessons that extend learning opportunities for students. Teachers tacitly ask: How can I extend my lesson once students seem to understand the ideas that I think are important? How can I enable students to "play with" the ideas? Synectics is one way of substantively extending the way in which students experiment with ideas, and it does so in a way that uses the background experiences of each child.

The students in synectics use their own images and ideas to make sense out of the world. This is what is proposed by Foster (1993), Henry (1990), and Ladson-Billings (1994), to name a few, when they suggest that the culture of the school should utilize the ideas, resources, and experiences of the local community. The relationship between the culture of the community and the culture of the school has many powerful positive effects upon learning. This instructional model is one strategy that facilitates such a dynamic relationship. The teacher may begin with a direct analogy, which reflects the teacher's schema, but the students subsequently create their own analogs that evolve out of their own experiences (the students' schema). Metaphoric thinking is intensely personal because students have to transcend impersonal concepts in ways that have personal meaning: How does it feel to be the earth? Gardner (1995) talks about the "personalization of education"; it is education based on such propositions as "we are not all the same; we do not all have the same kind of minds; education works most effectively for most individuals if…differences in mentation and strengths are taken into account…" (p. 208). Synectics takes such differences into account. Indeed, the model encourages divergent and generative thinking in ways that warrant the uniqueness of each child. Synectics fosters many different types of relational thinking (see Table 7.4). It also engenders analytical thought because students have to think in terms of the specific properties of objects or ideas—how an opera is like a football game. In synectics, students are expected to be creative, to think divergently, and to express their own ideas. During the past

TABLE 7-4   Relationship of Synectics Model to Cognitive Skills

Model	Relational Skills	Analytical Skills
■ Synectics	■ Creativity	■ Object-oriented (observes formal properties and attributes)
	■ Global views	
	■ Divergent thinking	
	■ Expressive	
	■ Holistic	
	■ Inductive	
	■ Evolving definitions	
	■ People-oriented	

decade, there has been a real movement toward conceptual reductionism. School policymakers attempt to assuage public demands for accountability by focusing on more and more definable and discrete pieces of information (that is, assessing basic skills). Such a circumstance is regrettable because it places students in the vulnerable position of robotically responding to stimuli rather than personally creating meaning and experiencing enjoyment out of what they have learned. The intent of synectics is to create personal meaning. The cultural background of the student becomes an asset in such a setting. The goal of the student is not to think like the teacher. Rather, the goal is to look at ideas, whether in relationship to cell structure or revolutions or plate tectonics, in new and different ways; to momentarily suspend the reality of the known with the possibilities of the imagination. When that happens, students see old ideas in new ways and are able to explore the inherent complexity of ideas in ways that reveal more personal meaning. To use Gordon's (1961) terms, they can make either the strange familiar or the familiar strange.

ⓟREVALENT ISSUES IN DIVERSE CLASSROOMS

Teachers who use synectics for the first time are often perplexed by the model—they argue that the steps are difficult to keep track of. Indeed, many teachers we have worked with describe the model as too complicated for students to understand. It is true that synectics can be somewhat complicated; but once teachers have used the model and understand the inherent structure of the model, they usually feel much more comfortable and confident. The only way to overcome pedagogical discomfort is to practice the model on more than one occasion. Still, even with experience, some problems will emerge. Those problems require that the teacher more fully challenge students by showing them that creativity is an important part of school life.

Q: *How do I deal with students who think that the personal analogy stage is ludicrous?*

A: In our observations of and conversations with teachers, those who have had the most difficulty with the personal analogy stage are teachers who do not see the value in this stage themselves. In essence, it seems that their students embrace the feelings that the teacher projects. Young children and even those in the middle grades seem to have no difficulty with using personal analogies—with becoming the analog and the concept themselves; they can suspend reality and pretend they are something else. Older students, especially those who are very analytical, are often the toughest "sell" because they do not see that using personal analogies represents real learning. For these students, real learning is assimilating new content material, not exploring ideas. Indeed, some "bright" students may not like the model because the teacher is not really "teaching"—telling them facts.

Teachers who work with older students frequently find it useful to have students close their eyes and visualize the metaphoric ideas. Other teachers use concrete objects to facilitate the students' thinking. For example, one teacher who was using the novel *The Pinballs* by Betsy Byars to help students explore their emotions described that emotions are like pinballs. She brought in some handheld pinball machines and then had students engage in personal analogy projections. Concrete objects help students more vitally "feel" the analog and, hopefully, the concept as well.

Much of Gordon's (1961) original work was with older students (that is, adults). Indeed, his book is filled with examples of how individuals in professional roles use personal analogies to explore some old problem in a new way. Gordon writes:

> A chemist makes a problem familiar to himself through equations combining molecules and the mathematics of phenomenological order. On the other hand, to make a problem strange the chemist may personally identify with the molecules in action. Faraday "looked…into the very heart of the electrolyte endeavoring to render the play of its atom visible to his mental eyes." The creative technical person can think himself to be a dancing molecule, discarding the detachment of the expert and throwing himself into the activity of the elements involved. He becomes one of the molecules. He permits himself to be pushed and pulled by the molecular forces. He remains a human being but acts as though he were a molecule. For the moment the rigid formulae don't govern, and he feels what happens to a molecule (p. 37).

Q: *How does the teacher effectively teach a synectics lesson in a standard class lesson period?*

A: The problem in this instance is the teacher's assumption that a lesson should cover one discrete time period of 45 minutes. The reason some schools are embracing block scheduling is because of a need to move beyond the confines of a 45-to-55-minute class period. Longer time periods liberate teachers to use models such as synectics. O'Neil (1995) writes about the block schedule approach:

The longer class periods liberate teachers whose innovative methods don't fit the traditional schedule.... "You cannot just lecture" when classes run past one hour in length...." [As one principal who observed block scheduled teachers noted] "I definitely see a wider variety of cooperative learning, hands-on projects, and other strategies [such as synectics!] aimed at encouraging student involvement [being used by teachers]...") (pp. 12–13).

Of course, not every school embraces block scheduling. High school teachers, as a consequence, may need to use two class periods on some occasions. Elementary school teachers have more flexibility in scheduling and may need to examine how synectics can be used in an interdisciplinary sense—combining language arts with other disciplinary areas. Even in elementary schools, though, more innovative scheduling procedures are being adopted (see Canady and Rettig, 1995). Those procedures are providing teachers with the blocks of time needed to explore ideas in depth and to extend students' thinking.

ⒺVALUATION CRITERIA

The teachers who use synectics for the first time will find that they have to pay close attention to all the steps in the process—many teachers keep a set of notes detailing the phases of the process so that they know what instructional sequence to follow. Although synectics lessons are not necessarily complicated, they are also not easy to conduct unless the teacher has a clear sense of how all the pieces of the lesson fit together. Teachers, therefore, should evaluate their performance using the following questions; but they should be less concerned with whether each step is followed than they are with whether the students are creatively thinking through the ideas by the time a lesson is completed.

Phase I: The Topic

1. Is the concept or "big idea" to be focused on during the synectics lesson sufficiently significant to warrant creative extension?   ◯ Yes   ◯ No

Phase II: Direct Analogy

Determine whether Synectics I or II will be used. If Synectics I:

1. Does the teacher's direct analogy stimulate student thought?   ◯ Yes   ◯ No
2. Do the students generate all the characteristics of the object and of the analog?   ◯ Yes   ◯ No

If Synectics II:

1. Do the students generate an inclusive list of descriptive terms for the concept being taught? ○ Yes ○ No

2. What analog category does the teacher use? ____ game ____ plant ____ machine

3. Do the students offer and defend analogical ideas? (For example, are the students required to use "because" statements?) ○ Yes ○ No

4. Does the class identify one analogy for use in the third phase of the lesson? ○ Yes ○ No

Phase III: Personal Analogy

The phase III processes are essentially the same regardless of whether the teacher uses Synectics I or Synectics II.

1. Does the teacher require the students to become both the analog and the concept? ○ Yes ○ No

2. Are students required to use "I feel" statements as they express their feelings about being the analog and the concept? ○ Yes ○ No

3. Does the teacher write the terms on the board as the students express their feelings? ○ Yes ○ No

Phase IV: Compressed Conflict

If Synectics I (Contrast):

1. Does the teacher ask students to think of ways in which the analog and the concept are different? ○ Yes ○ No

2. Does the teacher accomplish the contrast between analog and concept in a way that does not diminish the power of the original analogy? ○ Yes ○ No

If Synectics II (Compressed Conflict):

1. Does the teacher ask students to combine words that are in dynamic tension with one another?   ○ Yes   ○ No

2. Do the students select a compressed conflict that makes a lot of sense to them, and can they defend why they like it?   ○ Yes   ○ No

Phase V: New Analogy

If Synectics I:

1. Are students able to generate their own new analogies?   ○ Yes   ○ No

2. Describe how the teacher has students create the new analogies (for example, work in groups, and so on).   ○ Yes   ○ No

If Synectics II:

1. Are students able to take the compressed conflict and identify an object that exhibits these qualities?   ○ Yes   ○ No

2. What object does the teacher use as a focus for the new analogy?   ___ animal ___ machine ___ food

Phase VI: Topic Refocus

1. Describe what the students were expected to do after they developed the new analogy and were asked to reexamine the original topic (for example, write an essay, discuss as a class new insights about the topic, and so on).   _____ _____ _____

SAMPLE LESSONS

The case provided at the beginning of the chapter was illustrative of Synectics I. The simulated classroom example provided below is prototypic of Synectics

II. As the reader will note in this lesson, the students are expected to use compressed conflict as part of the analysis and creation of direct analogies.

CASE STUDY

Ms. Ruth Yellowhawk is preparing to teach her 9th graders a unit on poetry. The students represent a range of abilities and are heterogeneously grouped for English class. She knows some of the students enjoy poetry because of previous work with song lyrics. Still, she wants to get all the students excited about how poetry can shed new light on their lives and their relationships with others. She begins by describing how poetry surrounds the students—it's on television, in songs, on the playground, and in the religious experiences of the various students. She then asks the students to share all the terms they can associate with poetry. The students generate the following terms: long, confusing, boring, pretty, interesting, thoughtful, imaginative, complex, and colorful.

After the students list all the terms, Ms. Yellowhawk asks them to think of a game that has many of the qualities they just listed. One student, Rayford, suggests chess; another, Kalhis, offers the game Jingo; and a third, Jacy, thinks that a jigsaw puzzle is the most logical.

"Why, Jacy?" asks Ms. Yellowhawk.

"Because jigsaw puzzles take a long time to put together. They can be boring, especially if you do them alone; but they are pretty and interesting to look at once they are completed."

The students suggest several other games and describe why they fit with the terms for poetry. But when they are asked to vote for the game they like the best, the jigsaw puzzle is the class favorite.

"Excellent," responds Ms. Yellowhawk. "Today we are going to look at how poetry is like a jigsaw puzzle. As we consider this, I want you to close your eyes. For a few seconds, pretend that you are a jigsaw puzzle. What does it feel like?" (The teacher lets the students sit quietly for several seconds and then continues the lesson.)

"Share with me all the feelings that are going through your mind. Joe, what do you feel like?"

"I feel broken up. There are pieces of me all over the place."

"Great thought. Mindy, how do you feel?"

"I feel hurt because some parts of me are on the floor. The people walk on me and the dog is now sticking part of me in his mouth."

After the students generate a number of feelings and the reasons for the feelings (see Table 7.5), Ms. Yellowhawk asks the students to select the words that go together yet "argue with one another."

One student suggests "unwanted" and "important." Another offers "tired" and "pretty." A third indicates scattered and connected.

Ms. Yellowhawk then asks the students to identify which of the conflicts they like the best. Which one "argues" or conflicts in a way that they really like the tension between the terms?

The students discuss which ones they like the best and then vote to select the conflict: unwanted and important.

"What we now need to do," remarks Ms. Yellowhawk, "is to create a new analogy. Except, in this instance, I want to use your terms, *unwanted* and *important*, as the descriptors for the new direct analogy. Can you think of an animal that is both unwanted and important? Stephen?"

"The snake."

"Why, Stephen?" asks Ms. Yellowhawk.

"Well, a snake is not something most people want around, but snakes do eat some rodents and they are part of the food chain."

"Shaneca, what do you think?"

"Bees. Bees are a real nuisance, but they pollinate plants and they make honey."

The students go on to identify several other unwanted but very important animals: lion, pigeon, bear, and so on. After several minutes of enumeration, the students are asked to select the one they like the best. They decide on bees. Bees can cause pain and they can be a problem, but their benefits are readily apparent.

"So, students, you have selected bees. Consider bees for a few moments then tell me all that you know about bees." The students list the following:

- They are social (live in colonies).
- They have enemies (bears eat honey).
- They divide the labor (queen bees only lay eggs).
- They make wax.
- They make honey.
- The queen mates with males in flight.
- They are a hobby for some people (beekeepers).

TABLE 7-5 Feelings About Being a Jigsaw Puzzle

Broken up because I'm all over the place.

Hurt because I'm on the floor and being stepped on.

Tired because it's taking so long to put me together.

Scattered because I'm not together.

Unwanted because as soon as they have me together they take me apart and put me in a box.

Sticky because people have food on their hands and then touch me.

Pretty because when I'm together, I know I look good.

Important because I'm often given as a gift.

Connected because when all my pieces fit together I feel secure.

"How can this information about bees help us better understand poetry?" asks Ms. Yellowhawk. "I want you to think of how information about bees can shed more light on poetry. For instance, you said that bees are a hobby for some people. Is it not true that some people make a hobby out of poetry? Some people write it for fun; others read it for enjoyment."

The students share their ideas for several minutes. (For example: Poetry can be like food [honey] because it nourishes your soul. Poetry can be a social experience, especially during poetry readings.)

Ms. Yellowhawk then distributes a set of 10 poems. The students are asked to identify which one "nourishes" them the most and to write a short essay on why that is the case. ■

Follow-up questions

1. What other ways might a teacher introduce poetry to students?

2. What other mechanisms might a teacher use to help students think of what it must be like to be a jigsaw puzzle? (This teacher had students close their eyes and visualize themselves as a puzzle. Identify other ways to do this.)

3. What other phrases could be used to describe the compressed conflict? This teacher asked students to select terms that "go together yet argue with one another." Is there a clearer way to describe this to the class?

❶ESSON PLAN: A CRITICAL PERSPECTIVE

Assume that you are a 6th grade social studies teacher preparing to teach different types of political revolutions. You are planning to spend most of your time on the American Revolution (1775–1783) and the French Revolution (1789). Design either a Synectics I or Synectics II lesson for the concept of *revolution*.

Concepts: Political Movement, Revolution, Social Revolution.

Definition: A *revolution* involves a fundamental change in the character of a country's governmental system. Although there are different types of revolutions (social, cultural, political), the emphasis for your unit will be on political revolutions.

Considerations:
1. Determine which instructional approach you will use: Synectics I or Synectics II.

2. Determine at what points in the lesson you will write the students' ideas on the chalkboard or on poster paper.

3. Determine at what points in the lesson students will work individually or in a group to generate ideas.

4. Identify two different ways to enhance the students' abilities to participate in the personal analogy phase. Some teachers have students close their eyes and visualize possibilities. Identify other strategies for enhancing student participation in becoming the analog and/or the concept.

5. Determine a specific strategy for refocusing students' attention once they have generated their own *new* direct analogies. Remember, one of the most important steps in the process is enabling students to critically reexamine the topic—to see old ideas in new ways. Careful attention must be given to the technique the teacher will use to refocus the students' attention on the idea of what a revolution is.

ⓛ ESSON PREPARATION

Synectics is not an instructional model teachers will use more than three or four times a year. The underlying intention of the model's usage is to teach students a process for learning how to think creatively. The use of metaphors and oxymorons is one strategy that students can use to explore familiar topics in ways that reveal potentially unfamiliar meanings. In preparing synectics lessons, teachers might find it useful to utilize the following written and media resources.

Suggested readings

Gardner, H. 1995. "Reflections on Multiple Intelligences: Myths and Messages." *Phi Delta Kappan* 77(3): 200–209.

Gordon, W. 1961. *Synectics: The Development of Creative Capacity.* New York: Harper & Row.

Weaver, W. T., and G. M. Prince. 1990. "Synectics: Its Potential for Education." *Phi Delta Kappan* 71(5): 378–388.

Suggested videotapes

"Teaching Strategies Library: Part Two. Synectics." Washington, DC: Association for Supervision and Curriculum Development. (This tape is useful primarily for reinforcing the process outlined in Synectics I.)

"Synectics." Booksend Laboratories, 652 St. Andrews Drive, Rio Del Mar, Aptos, California 95003. (This tape is especially useful for understanding the processes outlined in Synectics II.)

Suggested lesson development

The best strategy for really understanding synectics is to try the model out with a group of students. In preparation for teaching a synectics lesson to a class, the teacher should be attentive to the following steps:

1. Make certain that the concept or focus for a synectics lesson is significant. Synectics lessons take time, and teachers need to make certain that the focus of their efforts is worth the time invested.

2. Determine which synectics approach will be used. (Most teachers we have worked with find Synectics I easier to use than Synectics II, but they find that Synectics II fosters more creative student thinking than Synectics I.)

3. Identify some specific ways of enhancing students' participation in the personal analogy phase.

4. Determine the specific times in the lesson when the teacher will write student responses down on the chalkboard or poster paper.

5. Identify specifically how the students' attention will be refocused on the topic during the final phase of the synectics lesson. What will students be expected to do immediately after they have generated their own new direct analogies?

ⓈUMMARY

Synectics is more generative than reactive in character. That is, teachers who structure thoughtful synectics lessons are not trying to elicit a set of student responses to a defined set of teacher questions (reactive instruction). Though reactive instruction is common in schools, it has the most limited potential for eliciting from students the type of generative thinking needed to explore ideas in novel or unique ways, which Ornstein (1995), drawing on the work of Carl Rogers, has described as the very essence of the creative endeavor.

The synectics instructional model fosters generative thinking. Students are not simply reacting to teacher ideas; they are, instead, creating ideas of their own. True, the teacher sets the "stage," but the students determine the direction of the "play." Their ideas and past experiences, not the teacher's, shape how the metaphoric process evolves and how the original topic is examined. This generative process leads to more "ahas" during the instructional sequence. For many veteran teachers, the "aha" feeling has long since been lost! Most teachers experience pedagogical epiphanies at the beginning of their careers because they are teaching content for the first time—and for some, they possess only inchoate understandings of that content themselves. But once planets or revolutions or cell structure have been taught a few times, teachers fall into a pattern of knowing what to teach and how to teach it. The consequence: The "aha" feeling is lost and, concomitantly, some of the excitement of teaching is mitigated. One way to "reconnect" with content is to find new ways of exploring old ideas. The reconnection process does not ensure student achievement gains, but it does increase the excitement of teachers for ideas and enhance the possible enthusiastic response of students to those ideas. That enthusiasm not only will pay educational dividends in the classroom (some researchers argue that students will achieve more), but it will also be personally beneficial for students because they will have learned a process for creatively exploring ideas and discovering hidden meanings.

ⓇEFERENCES

Canady, R. L., and M. D. Rettig. 1995. "The Power of Innovative Scheduling." *Educational Leadership* 54(3): 4–10.

Foster, M. 1993. "Constancy, Change, and Constraints in the Lives of Black Women Teachers: Some Things Change, Most Stay the Same." *NWSA Journal* 3(2): 233–261.

Gardner, H. 1995. "Reflections on Multiple Intelligences: Myths and Messages." *Phi Delta Kappan* 77(3): 200–209.

Gordon, W. 1961. *Synectics: The Development of Creative Capacity.* New York: Harper & Row.

Gunter, M. A., T. H. Estes, and J. H. Schwab. 1995. *Instruction: A Models Approach* (2d ed.). Boston: Allyn & Bacon.

Henry, A. 1990. "Black Women, Black Pedagogies: An African-Canadian Context."

Paper presented at the American Educational Research Association, Boston.

Joyce, B., and M. Weil. 1992. *Models of Teaching* (4th ed.). Boston: Allyn & Bacon.

Ladson-Billings, G. 1994. *The Dreamkeepers.* San Francisco: Jossey-Bass.

O'Neil, J. 1995. "Finding Time to Learn." *Educational Leadership* 53(3): 11–15.

Ornstein, A. C. 1995. *Strategies for Effective Teaching* (2d ed). Madison, WI: Brown and Benchmark.

Torrance, E. P. 1986. "Teaching Creative and Gifted Learners." Pp. 630–647 in M. C. Wittrock (ed.), *Handbook of Research on Teaching.* New York: Macmillan.

Weaver, W. T., and G. M. Prince. 1990. "Synectics: Its Potential for Education." *Phi Delta Kappan* 71(5): 378–388.

What content should every student know? And what is the most efficient and effective way to teach that content? With the increased emphasis on student achievement by state education departments and school districts, it is becoming more important for teachers and policymakers to specifically determine what facts, skills, and concepts to teach all students.

Other units in this text emphasize ways in which teachers can foster critical-thinking skills. The two chapters that comprise this unit do not have that as a primary focus. Mnemonics and direct instruction models are efficient means for teaching discrete knowledge, and they are not oriented toward engendering critical perspectives on content. If the teacher is teaching students how to multiply fractions, one strategy for solving $1/4 \times 3/5$ is for the teacher to delineate in a step-by-step fashion the process for deriving the answer of $3/20$. Such a process should not be used when teaching all facts, skills, and concepts, but it most definitely should be a part of the instructional repertoire of every teacher. Teachers who rely too heavily on mnemonics and direct instruction limit the full intellectual potential of students. Those who disdain these instructional models fail to understand that good teachers determine the instructional model based on their instructional goals. Learning to fly an airplane is not something one should learn inductively. And learning to write poetry is not something one assimilates through exclusive reliance on deductive, step-by-step processes. ■

Models that Foster Remembering Skills

3

EIGHT

• *Mnemonics*

At the completion of this chapter, the reader will be able to:

1. *Identify the essential phases for the effective use of the mnemonic model.*
2. *Identify the strengths and weaknesses of mnemonics.*
3. *Understand the theoretical and empirical grounding for the mnemonic model.*
4. *Evaluate lessons that use mnemonic strategies.*
5. *Create a lesson using the mnemonic instructional model.*

❶NTRODUCTION

The model presented in this chapter is useful for helping students learn and memorize new information. In ancient times, the memory capacity of individuals was essential to the educational process because books and other printed materials did not exist. Oral traditions were dominant. Salient ideas and stories were remembered and passed down from one generation to the next by those who possessed the gift of imagination and the capacity for memory. Modern American educators still place substantial emphasis on remembering facts, concepts, and generalizations, but they spend very little time showing students *how* to remember information. Some might argue that memorizing information is antithetical to educational enlightenment. Indeed, many of the recent reform initiatives focus on enabling students to become better problem-solvers and processors of information; students need to know how to access information, but they do not necessarily need to memorize facts. Others view the acquisition of certain facts as essential, if not necessary, to being an educated citizen (Hirsch, 1988). Our view is that either extreme position represents a potentially negative circumstance. To disdain any need for memorization (why learn any facts when you can always look them up?) would be foolhardy. Although it is true that much information can be looked up, imagine the complications of daily life for someone who is so information deficient that the individual could not make change or did not know basic information about how to access necessary services in a community. On the other hand, imagine how ludicrous it would be to memorize mountains of data, some of it remote in relevance, when computer access makes the information instantly retrievable.

All memory, whether trained or untrained, is based on association.

HARRY LORAYNE AND JERRY LUCAS

Sizer (1992) suggests that a balance between the extreme positions can be attained if teachers selectively engage students in what he describes as "exhibitions." In essence, the student in some way must "exhibit the products of his or her learning" (p. 25). Sizer identifies several different types of exhibitions that might be illustrative of the expectations schools have for students to memorize information. Examples include reciting an important speech from history (for example, the Gettysburg Address), drawing a freehand map of the United States, or reciting an important poem (for example, "The Mending Wall").

The student memorizes information not just for mental discipline, but also to acquire the intellectual habits necessary for leading the good life. One of the essential intellectual habits, argues Sizer (1992), relates to the pleasure "of knowing some things well enough to commit them to memory, and [to] the joy of reciting them" (p. 66).

Teachers need to make conscious decisions about what "exhibits" students need to have in their long-term memory. Such decisions require substantial dialogue about what ideas are so important that they warrant student memorization or, as the following case illustrates, what content knowledge is of sufficient significance that, by memorizing it, students are able to more effectively process other types of relevant data.

❸ASE STUDY

Susan Sternberg is preparing to teach a unit on Canada to her 6th grade students. In preparation for the unit activities, Susan expects all the students to know the location of the 11 provinces of Canada and to be able to identify the capitals of each province. Her first lesson today will focus only on the province locations.

"Class, today, in preparation for our unit on Canada, I am going to teach you the locations of each Canadian province. That will be important information for you to know as we work our way through this unit. We will be having discussions that require you to memorize the locations of all Canadian provinces. By the end of our class period, each of you will be able to correctly label the Canadian map I have on the board [see Figure 8.1]. To begin this unit I want you to look at the map of Canada and read each province name silently to yourself. [A couple of minutes pass as the students silently read the province names.]

"Now to help you learn the province names, I am going to tell you a story using another map of Canada with linkwords labeled for each province [see Figure 8.2]. The story is about my favorite cartoon character *BC* and his best buddy *Al*. You all know Al! He is the workshop assistant on the television show, 'Home Improvement.'

"One day, BC [the teacher points to the location of British Columbia] and his best buddy Al [the teacher points to Alberta] decide to take a trip. The trip is going to be a long one and many supplies will be required, so they will need a strong helper to carry the supplies. To assist them, they pick up *Saskatch* or Big Foot [Ms. Sternberg points to Saskatchewan].

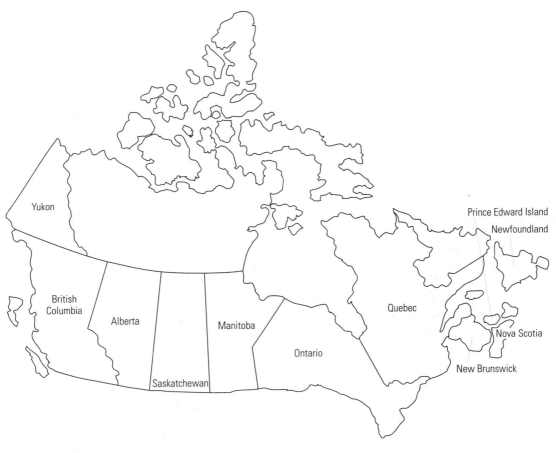

FIGURE 8-1 The Provinces of Canada

"BC, Al, and Saskatch journey for several days then stumble onto something very unusual—a *tuba man* [or gigantic man sitting in a very tiny tuba—she points to Manitoba]. Can you imagine what this must have looked like? What a strange thing to see! Even weirder to look at is the fact that this tiny tuba is sitting on miles and miles of *tar* [she points to Ontario].

"Let's review what's happened so far: BC and his best friend Al...." Ms. Sternberg carefully reviews the first five steps of the story.

"Now, class, something really amazing happens as BC, Al, and Saskatch are watching tuba man on the tar: they are distracted by a *Queen* who is *beckoning* them [she points to Quebec]. Jacob, what does it mean to be beckoned?"

"It's when someone motions for you to join them, like this [Jacob then uses a forefinger to beckon the teacher]."

"Great, Jacob. You're right! What's strange in this instance, though, is that BC, Al, and Saskatch can't figure out what the Queen is using to do the beck-

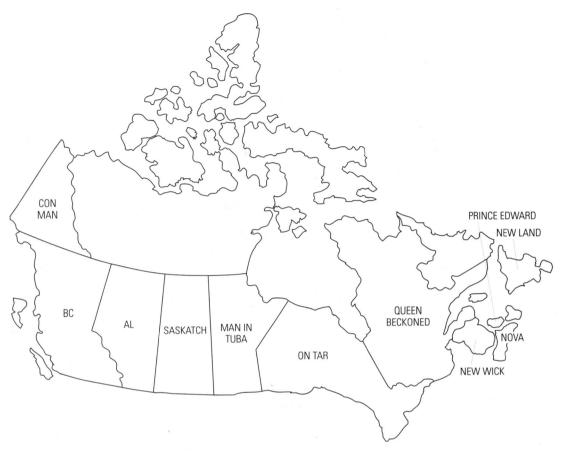

On the map, the following labels appear:

CON MAN

BC

AL

SASKATCH

MAN IN TUBA

ON TAR

QUEEN BECKONED

PRINCE EDWARD

NEW LAND

NOVA

NEW WICK

FIGURE 8-2 Linkword Story About the Provinces of Canada

oning. Then as they get closer to the Queen, it becomes very clear—the Queen is using a huge new *candlewick* to beckon them [Ms. Sternberg points to New Brunswick]. Wouldn't that be strange to see? A queen using a new candlewick to beckon these three people!

"Well, even stranger is the fact that standing next to the Queen with this candlewick was the candle's owner, *Prince Edward.* [Ms. Sternberg points to Prince Edward Island.] Unfortunately, though, the Prince is not a wealthy prince—he's poor. Very, very poor! That's why he has given the Queen only one candle. Because of that fact, the Prince is forced to drive a rather modest car, a *Nova.*" [Ms. Sternberg points to Nova Scotia.]

Ms. Sternberg continues, "At about this same time, the Prince gets tired of standing next to the wick and decides to strike out on his own sightseeing trip. On the way he discovers a brand new land, which he names his *New Found Land.* [The teacher points to Newfoundland.] Wow! Can you imagine his excitement? What a great thing to have happen. Well, the Prince proceeds on his journey and keeps looking for other new places and interesting people [Ms. Sternberg moves her hand across northern Canada], but all the Prince can find are con men [she points to the Yukon].

"Isabelle, what's a *con man*?"

"It's someone who pretends to be something he isn't—a fake."

"Right! Class, let's review our whole story." And with that, Ms. Sternberg has the students break up into pairs. They review the substitute words and then review the linkword story. One student tells the story to a student partner and then the peer pair roles are reversed.

Once all the students have the story memorized, Ms. Sternberg carefully describes the substitute term for each province in the story. That is, *BC* stands for *British Columbia*, and so on.

At the completion of the lesson, she provides the students a blank Canadian map. They fill in the names of each province. Several students have trouble remembering the province of New Brunswick.

"Class, several of you forgot New Brunswick. Can you think of a better image than the one I used, which was *candlewick*?" The students decide on two good possibilities.

Two days later Ms. Sternberg reviews the story again and uses a keyword technique to teach the students the capitals of each Canadian province. ■

The case study from Ms. Sternberg's class is an example of a teacher-directed mnemonics lesson. The teacher is teaching the students content material they will need for their unit activities. In this chapter, we will more fully explore the mnemonic instructional model and its uses in teaching.

❶HEORETICAL PERSPECTIVE

As described previously in this chapter, memory systems are not new as learning aids; they date to ancient times. The Greek poet Simonides (circa B.C. 500) is often considered the originator of the use of trained memory systems (Lorayne and Lucas, 1974). He developed the memory technique because of a rather unusual circumstance. It seems that a banquet hall where Simonides had just eaten collapsed and Simonides was asked to assist with the identification process of the bodies—many were so damaged by the catastrophe that Simonides had to *recall* where each guest had eaten (Rose, 1985). Rose writes that "in clarifying [Simonides's]…method, Cicero explained that you would first visualize a series of places about the house. (The Latin for place is locus, from which we get our word location.)" (p. 57). The Greeks and Romans used memory systems to help as part of their orations. Oratory was a craft of considerable importance in the days of antiquity, and individuals skilled in its use were expected to deliver long speeches from memory. *Mnemonics* is a term derived from the Greek word *Mnemosyne*, who was the Greek goddess of memory (Higbee, 1996). Lorayne and Lucas (1974) describe how the Greeks associated thoughts with visual images of specific objects:

What they [the Greeks] did, basically, was associate each thought of a speech to a part of their own homes. These were called "loci," or "places." The opening thought of a speech would, perhaps, be associated to the front door, the second thought to the foyer, the third to a piece of furniture in the foyer, and so on. When the orator wanted to remember his speech, thought for thought, he actually took a mental tour through his own home. Thinking of the front door reminded him of the first thought of his speech. The second "place," the foyer, reminded him of the next thought; and so on to the end of the speech. It is from this "place" or "loci" memory technique that we get the time-worn phrase "in the first place" (pp. 1–2).

Throughout the Middle Ages, the great thinkers (Cicero, St. Thomas Aquinas, and others) used memory aids to help them recall information that would assist them in their quest to master religious and philosophical ideas. Indeed, in the seventeenth century, philosophers (for example, Francis Bacon) explicitly taught memory systems to their students.

The interest in memory systems continues today. Some researchers have been fascinated by the mnemonic abilities of certain individuals. The Russian psychologist Luria (1968), for example, studied a now-famous subject "S," who as a journalist exhibited incredible powers of recall:

The simplest structure was one S used to recall tables of numbers written on a blackboard. S would study the material on the board, close his eyes, open them again for a moment, turn aside, and, at a signal, reproduce one series from the board. Then he would fill in the empty squares of the next table, rapidly calling off the numbers. It was a simple matter for him to fill in the numbers for the empty squares of the table either when asked to do this for certain squares I chose at random, or when asked to fill in a series of numbers successively in reverse order. S could easily tell me which numbers formed one or another of the vertical columns in the table and could "read off" to me numbers that formed the diagonals; finally, he was able to compose a multi-digit number out of the one-digit numbers in the entire table (p. 16).

Jerry Lucas, Harry Lorayne, and others regularly conduct workshops in which they demonstrate (and help others develop) their powers in memorizing huge amounts of material in short periods of time. These "mnemonists" often appear on talk shows and demonstrate their memory powers by identifying the names of each member of the audience after having met them just prior to the show.

The educational research on the use of mnemonics is increasing, especially with the new emphasis on developing the content knowledge of students (Levin, 1993; Mastropieri, Scruggs, and Levin, 1987; Pressley, Levin, and Delaney, 1982). That research base suggests that mnemonic strategies (or aids to memory) can be useful in developing a student's recall of factual information.

However, the results of studies on the topic vary considerably in terms of which methods are most efficacious in fostering student learning. Levin (1993) notes that the best mnemonic strategies are those designed to learn specific content material (for example, a keyword mnemonic for an English vocabulary term), and those that are used with educationally handicapped students. Levin notes that it "is particularly noteworthy…[that the keyword and pegword techniques are powerful learning devices with] students with documented learning problems" (p. 238).

Clearly there are variations in how much information different people can remember. Some persons are able to create and use mnemonic devices much better than others—though it does appear that within reasonable limits everyone is at least somewhat capable of enhancing their memory capacities. Described below are three such memory-enhancing strategies that researchers suggest have real instructional efficacy.

The *keyword* strategy is a two-stage process of mnemonically transforming an unfamiliar word to something that is familiar. Levin (1993) describes the keyword approach in learning new vocabulary terms:

> Consider a fourth grader challenged to learn the definitions of 20 new vocabulary words by next Monday—words such as *accolades, equestrian, diversion, flatware, persuade,* and *gesture.* Rather than attempting to memorize the vocabulary list through either repeated rote rehearsal or—in the words of one student we tested—"brute force," a student applying [the]…*keyword method* would mnemonically transform the unfamiliar vocabulary items into something more meaningful and memorable. Part of the unfamiliar word *accolades,* for example, sounds like the more familiar beverage *Kool Aid* and, thus, the former could be recoded as the latter. Once transformed, the recoded word (or keyword) *Kool Aid* can be meaningfully related to the to-be-remembered definition of accolades (praise for something well done). In this case, one could imagine a group of people raising their glasses of *Kool Aid to toast an accomplished guest of honor* (p. 236).

Keywords are not difficult to learn and have proven useful for enhanced student learning at all levels (Levin, 1993). The keyword strategy may be especially powerful when it is combined with a second mnemonic strategy, the pegword.

Pegwords consist of taking the numbers 1 through 10 and correlating the numbers with rhyming words that the students already know well. Mastropieri, Scruggs, and Levin (1987) write that the "mnemonic 'pegword method'…capitalizes on the childhood rhyme, 'one is a bun, two is a shoe, three is a tree…ten is a hen'" (pp. 506–507). Hence, if a student is learning the three primary reasons for the War of 1812 or the five animal kingdoms, the teacher would create a picture that illustrates the item's number and the pegword. Mastropieri, Scruggs, and Levin (1987) describe how students would learn that the third most plausible reason for the extinction of dinosaurs is the exploding star theory. Figure 8.3 is the pegword illustration for the plausibility of the exploding star theory—notice the tree (three), the star (exploding), and the dinosaur. The third most logical and plausible explanation for the extinction of the dinosaur is the energy created from the explosion of stars—the energy that killed substantial

This is incorrect! There are 3 kingdoms of living things

portions of plant life on earth was detrimental to dinosaurs, who needed plant life to sustain their existence. The pegword strategy is not at all new. The strategy can be traced to the mid-1600s and was created to enable people to remember large sets of information (Higbee, 1996).

The *link* strategy is used as a means of remembering things in sequence. Recall that Ms. Sternberg wanted the students to learn the precise location of each Canadian province as part of her geography lesson. In using the link system, the learner does nothing more than link one item to another—ideally with images that directly interact. To understand the importance of interaction in terms of memory, consider the following observation of Rose (1985):

> We know visual images to be strong. But imagery can itself be strengthened if it is made to be interactive. Psychologist Gordon Bower reported on a test in which subjects were given 12 pairs of words and eight seconds in which to learn them. Only 33 percent of the repeated pairs were remembered, but when the subject was told to create a visual association between the pairs, the correct recall of the pairs shot up to 80 percent.

THREE (TREE)   EXPLODING STAR

FIGURE 8-3   Example of a Mnemonic Illustration: Pegword

Source: M. A. Mastropieri, T. E. Scruggs, and J. R. Levin. 1987. "Learning Disabled Students' Memory for Expository Prose: Mnemonic Versus Nonmnemonic Pictures." *American Educational Research Journal* 24(4): 508.

When the association specifically involved a direct interaction between the images, then the recall went up even further. Thus suppose the pair of words were *dolphin* and *flower*. An acceptable visual image would be a giant daisy floating beside the dolphin. But that brings in no *direct* connection. A better image would be a smiling dolphin blowing a stream of highly colored flowers out of the blowhole on its head. This image has got interaction and movement and color. The more detailed and developed the image, the better (p. 62).

In the case study, the provinces of British Columbia (BC) and Alberta (Al) were linked as two friends embarking on a trip. To enable the students to remember the location (or the order) of the provinces, Ms. Sternberg created a story that linked the ideas together using substitute words (*BC* for *British Columbia*, and *Al* for *Alberta*). She accomplished these linkages by using a number of ridiculous associations to help get the students' attention, and to retain their interest and help them acquire the knowledge of the Canadian provinces. For each association the teacher expected students to create visual images and to link one visual image with the next one. Those associations were based on a relatively simple set of rules (Higbee, 1996; Joyce and Weil, 1992; Lorayne and Lucas, 1974). Specifically, Ms. Sternberg was able to:

Rule #1: *Create substitutions.* Essentially, the teacher substitutes or replaces one item that is familiar with another that is unfamiliar. Ms. Sternberg substituted a "*tuba man,*" something concrete that students could picture to represent Manitoba, for something that was more abstract (the province's name).

Rule #2: *Create objects that are out of proportion.* The out-of-proportion rule occurs in Ms. Sternberg's lesson by *creating a gigantic man and a tiny tuba.* Part of the effectiveness of good linkages is the use of ridiculous visual images. A gigantic man in a tiny tuba is easier to remember than an average-size man in a normal-size tuba.

Rule #3: *Create exaggeration.* With exaggeration, the teacher literally expands the idea to proportions that extend beyond anything people would normally consider. Notice that for Ontario (*on miles and miles of tar*), the teacher creates an *image of tremendous amounts of tar,* not a more ordinary image that one would normally expect such as the tuba just sitting on the ground. If you doubt the power of this notion, just consider the fact that what you tend to recall most readily about a day's events are the ridiculous occurrences, not the normal ones.

Rule #4: *Create action.* The characters and images in the link story about Canada are creating action—they all do something: *BC and AL are taking a trip. Quebec is beckoning with the new [Bruns]wick. The Prince is forced to drive a rather modest car, a Nova.* The action helps the learner create stronger linkages.

Using the link strategy takes time and effort on the part of a teacher. The teacher also needs to understand the teaching phases required to help students fully learn the ideas presented as part of the mnemonic model. Those phases are outlined in the next section (see also Joyce and Weil, 1992).

Ⓜ NEMONICS: TEACHING PHASES

Phase I: Focus Attention

For students to remember anything, they must pay attention to what is important. Anyone who has ever read a book in preparation for a test understands this phenomenon. That individual often takes some type of highlighter and marks passages or ideas that need to be retained for long-term memory. Other devices for recalling information are also used. For example, one of the authors of this book has a daughter in high school. When she prepares for tests, she makes lists of those ideas she needs to remember. Recall that Ms. Sternberg used "focusing" when she said, "*I want you to look at the map of Canada and read each province name silently to yourself.*"

There is no right way to focus students' attention. The key is to make certain that students are really paying attention to what is being taught. Using the author's daughter as an example again, her science grades for one term in middle school were very low. Test after test she received grades lower than her father expected. Then, one day, she showed up at home with a high grade. Her father asked, "Wow, what did you do differently?" She responded somewhat nonplussed, "I paid attention!"

Phase II: Create Connections

Most mnemonic strategies are nothing more than visual or conceptual connections of familiar material with the unfamiliar. Four such connecting strategies can be used in classrooms and have been highlighted directly or indirectly earlier: first-letter mnemonic, keyword, linkword, and pegword.

First-letter mnemonics entail using a series of letters or lines in which certain letters form a name or message when sequenced appropriately. Acronyms are the simplest of these mnemonic strategies. When students take art they learn ROY G BIV, which represents the colors of the spectrum (red, orange, yellow…indigo, violet) and HOMES, which represents the five Great Lakes (Huron…Superior). A student in one of the authors' classes required her students in English class to memorize the eight parts of speech and used the acronym NAVACIPP (noun, adjective, verb…preposition). Acronyms are useful, especially when the number of items to be recalled is relatively limited in number and the word formed by the first letter makes sense. They have less utility when a large volume of factual material must be remembered or when a meaningful acronym cannot be formed. It is, however, a technique that can be used quickly and efficiently. Acrostics entail using the first letter of words to be remembered, and connecting (or linking) those letters by creating some type of meaningful phrase (Higbee, 1996). For example, after students learn the five kingdoms in biology, the teacher might ask, "*Class, let's think of an acrostic we can use to recall this information. One might be: All (Animal) My (Monera) Pretty (Protista) Ponies (Plants) Fly (Fungi).*" One of the most famous acrostics is the one many people learn relative to the positions of the nine planets: <u>M</u>y (Mercury) <u>V</u>ery (Venus) <u>E</u>ducated (Earth) <u>M</u>other (Mars) <u>J</u>ust (Jupiter) <u>S</u>erved (Saturn) <u>U</u>s (Uranus) <u>N</u>ine (Neptune) <u>P</u>izzas (Pluto). Even some textbooks now use acrostic-like mnemonic devices to help students remember information. The Harcourt Brace Jovanovich (1992) *Mathematics Plus* text encourages students to remember the order of mathematical operations by using <u>P</u>lease (Parentheses), <u>E</u>xcuse (Exponents) <u>M</u>y (Multiplication) <u>D</u>ear (Division) <u>A</u>unt (Addition) <u>S</u>ally (Subtraction).

Keyword strategies are useful for memorizing social science data (for example, state capitals), scientific data (for example, information about the periodic table), information in the language arts area (for example, the parts of speech), and foreign languages. In fact, the strategy was originally created in the mid-1970s to assist individuals in learning foreign languages (Higbee, 1996). Keywords are useful for recalling facts that need not be remembered in any particular order. With the keyword approach, a familiar term is used to remember an unfamiliar term. Higbee (1996) observes that the keyword mnemonic entails the use of "substitute words and visual associations" (p. 101). The visual associations enhance the memory capacity. For example, when Ms. Sternberg taught the students the province capitals of Canada, she could have created a picture similar to the one in Figure 8.4, where for Winnipeg, Manitoba, you see tuba man (the substitute word for Manitoba), or a giant man in a tiny tuba, holding a Winnie the Pooh bear (or Winnipeg). The substitute words are "Winnie-the-pooh" and "tuba man," and the visual image is similar to the one in Figure 8.4. In the Bornstein (1983) mnemonic cards for state capitals, the Topeka, Kansas, substitute words are *tapioca* and *can* and the visual association is tapioca in a can. Higbee (1996) observes that keyword mnemonics can be used for learning either abstract or concrete terms:

> The procedure for using imagery to help remember abstract terms is the same as for concrete terms except that you add a step using "substitute words." You substitute a concrete word to represent the abstract word. One way of doing this is to use objects that typify the abstract term: for *liberty*, you might picture the Liberty Bell; for *justice*, a judge; for *happiness*, a smiling face; for *education*, a schoolhouse; for *fashion*, a model; for *depth*, a hole; for *agree*, a nodding head; for *salary*, a paycheck. A second way of substituting a concrete word for an abstract one is to use objects whose names sound like the abstract term: celery for *salary*; fried ham for *freedom*; happy nest for *happiness*. You can even use this technique to remember nonsense syllables: Cage for KAJ; rocks for ROX; seal for ZYL; sack for XAC.... Research on the Keyword mnemonic has found that people are quite adept at using the above two approaches to "concretize" abstract materials for effective visual images. However, one study found that for college students who had no experience with substitute words, the first approach (based on meaning) was more effective than the second approach (based on sound-alikes) but was also more difficult to use (p. 109).

Link strategies are used to remember sequences—the order of items. For example, the teacher may want students to remember the names of the original 13 colonies or the sequencing of the different geologic ages of the world. By

FIGURE 8-4   Example of a Mnemonic Illustration: Winnipeg, Manitoba

Source: Illustrated by Janet Olney Lasley.

recalling one link in a sequence, the student is able to create a connection with (and remember) the items (using the substitute words) that are linked with the identified term. If the student recalls the substitute word *tuba man*, then the student will link that with where the tuba sits (on tar, or *Ontario*), and who observed the tuba man sitting on tar, *Saskatch* (or *Saskatchewan*). The "story link" is also a relatively easy mnemonic for teachers to use. We have heard story links used to help students learn the position of colonies, countries, and parts of machinery.

Pegwords are used when the teacher wants students to recall not only the sequence of ideas, but also the specific position of an item. If someone asks who the 16th President of the United States was, the learner should not have to count the "links" to 16, though that is one possibility. Rather, a peg strategy can be used to identify a president quickly.

The pegword strategy is based on the connection of the numbers to rhyming sounds (one is bun, two is shoe, three is tree...ten is hen). Each noun (for example, *bun*) rhymes with a corresponding number (for example, one). Once students have learned the pegs, they are ready to peg the word to a specific idea within a sequence. Recall that in Figure 8.3 the major reason that *three* (*tree*) was used for the dinosaur's extinction was the exploding star theory. Once the student learns the pegword system, that student will visually picture a tree (three) with an exploding star. More elaborate pegword strategies even allow students to recall the specific position of numbers in a sequence (for example, 578, 3314). For the purposes of this chapter, only sequences of word information (not number sequences) will be emphasized. The pegwords we suggest (and that the students must memorize) are the same as those recommended by Levin (1993):

one—bun	six—bricks
two—shoe	seven—heaven
three—tree	eight—rake
four—door	nine—pine
five—(bee)hive	ten—hen

Essentially, the pegs are all concrete images, and these concrete images are used for remembering the order of information. The peg system can also be expanded to remember more than 10 objects by simply taking sets of 10 and connecting them to specific seasonal locations (the *loci* system). Hence, 1–10 would be near a house in the spring, 11–20 would be near a lake in the summer, and so on. For example, item 16 (the 16th U.S. President, Abraham Lincoln) could show a Lincoln car with bricks (the peg for six) on its top sitting near a lake in the summer (see Figure 8.5). If the teacher wants to have students also remember certain facts about each president, images can be added to the picture. For example, if the teacher wanted students to remember that Lincoln signed the Emancipation Proclamation and was president during the Civil War, then on one side of the car the teacher could place a man reading a proclamation and on the other side show two men fighting.

Higbee (1996) writes about the effectiveness of the combined peg and *loci* strategies:

> Eighth-grade students used the Peg and Loci systems to learn the names of the U.S. presidents. They used the pegwords for the numbers from 1 to 10. Seasonal loci represented decades of numbers; 1–10 was a spring garden scene, 11–20 a summer beach scene, 21–30 a fall football scene, and 31–40 a winter snow scene. Presidents' names were represented by substitute words, and the associations were presented in pictures. Two sample associations are: Tyler (tie)...10 (hen)...garden [spring], and Garfield (guard)...20 (hen)...beach [summer]. The students also learned biographical information on the presidents. This combined Keyword-Loci-Peg system has been expanded for extreme cases to learn up to 260 items, using alphabet scenes from an *airplane* scene to a *zoo* scene (10 pegwords × 26 alphabet loci = 260 items of ordered information).
>
> Sixth-grade students who were trained over several days in the use of the Peg system used it to learn a list of names and recipe ingredients. In another study, learning-disabled students in the sixth to eighth grades used the Keyword mnemonic (substitute words) and the Peg system to learn information on dinosaurs. In both studies, students who used the Peg system remembered the information better than those who did not use it (p. 165).

Use of any of the strategies—first-letter mnemonics, keywords, linkwords, and pegwords—takes practice and requires student attention, as we will discuss more fully in phases III and IV.

Phase III: Create Associations

To remember anything requires effort—learners must pay attention to what they want to learn. Memory capacity is enhanced when the associations that are formed are ridiculous—the more ridiculous, the better! Four rules for creating ridiculous associations were described earlier in this chapter. Those rules, as Joyce and Weil (1992), Lorayne and Lucas (1974), and Higbee (1996) describe them, are the rule of substitution, the rule of exaggeration, the rule of out-of-proportion, and the rule of action.

These four rules are essential for enabling students to fully recall ideas. But even after the students have the visual images clearly in mind, the teacher must create conditions for practice to enable students to recall ideas or facts once they are learned.

Phase IV: Foster Recall

The only way to remember ideas for a long period of time is to periodically practice or think through what was once learned. Teachers all too often have an implicit philosophy of "once learned, always learned." The spurious nature of this assumption is quickly highlighted once the reader tries to recall the capital of any state not recently visited. If one lives in Maine, try to recall the capital of South Dakota; if South Dakota, try Maine.

The way to enhance recall is to create conditions in which students are forced to think through the ideas several times just after they learn the information (immediate review) and then periodically throughout the schooling experience (delayed review). Both immediate and delayed reviews are essential. Ms. Sternberg used immediate review when she had the students break up into pairs and review the story (on the provinces) with a peer partner. She also used delayed review. As you will recall, two days after she presented the lesson on Canadian provinces, she asked the students to review the story in preparation for learning the names of the province capitals.

Ⓐ PPLICATIONS TO DIVERSE CLASSROOMS

Twenty to forty years ago, many teachers held higher expectations for students regarding the need to memorize poems, stories, and mathematical facts. A tremendous emphasis was placed on declarative knowledge, or knowledge that focused on "what" questions. Although teachers are now being encouraged to emphasize more procedural knowledge in their classes, some focus on facts and specific content will always be present. Students still memorize their multiplication tables even though the increased use of computers and other quick data-retrieval devices has limited the degree to which teachers feel a need to require students to memorize information.

Some recent educational theories (such as constructivism) implicitly diminish student need for memorization. Constructivist teachers place an emphasis on students' ability to classify, analyze, predict, and create. As a consequence, some teachers (clearly not all!) may suggest that memorizing facts is antithetical to constructivist thinking. Such an assertion is conceptually erroneous! Students who explore concepts must know certain facts in order to engage in the analysis that is required. The difference is that the facts they use have personal relevance and meaning, rather than having the teacher use a mimetic approach in which students commit to short-term memory information that they subsequently give back to the teacher. The students draw on their own experiences and ideas—they think for themselves. Teachers who attempt to mediate student thinking must possess certain facts in order to effectively help students shape their thoughts. Constructivist teachers ask a lot of questions, but they rely on a tremendous amount of information that will allow them to ask questions that move the students' thinking forward (Brooks and Brooks, 1993). In essence, all students, regardless of their cultural background, and all teachers, regardless of their educational philosophy, need to possess certain facts in order to learn and teach new material.

Students from some cultural backgrounds readily adjust to the expectation to memorize material. Part of the substantial success of the so-called "model minority" Asian American students is that they are extremely hardworking and high-achieving (Bennett, 1995). (As an aside, it is interesting to note that there is emerging evidence to suggest that the more assimilated the group, even for Asian Americans, the more the performance of that group mirrors the achievement levels of other mainstream groups.) Hard work requires that students pay close attention to what the teacher is teaching—the content of the lesson. Recall that the very first requirement for successful memorization is that a student attend to what the teacher expects the student to learn. Without some level of attentiveness, essential facts and concepts cannot be learned.

The beauty of using a variety of instructional strategies is that teachers are more likely to capture students' interests. A teacher who occasionally uses the mnemonic instructional model, and who helps the students create visual images of the content material, taps the strengths of those students who have high spatial intelligence or who have cultural or personal learning dispositions that favor the visualization process. The teacher does not use this model simply because certain ethnic or racial groups tend to favor visual processes for learning. Rather, the teacher uses a visual strategy because it builds on the strengths of all students (regardless of their cultural background) who learn best by creating visual images, and it enhances the cognitive repertoire of those students who do not rely on visual strategies as a learning device.

Mnemonic strategies are not effortless endeavors. They necessitate work—but they foster a type of work that can be potentially very rewarding. Cajete (1994), in describing the saliency of indigenous educational practice with Native Americans, poignantly points out that "Indigenous teaching revolves around some form of work. Indigenous teachers recognize that work invites concentration and facilitates a quietness of mind" (p. 225). That quietness translates into a capacity of the student to assimilate and construct meaningful learning experiences, and it transcends the learning propensities of any particular cultural group—all students can benefit from such experiences. But for mnemonics to be effective, teachers need to know the cultural backgrounds of their students. Levin (1993) asks and answers a powerful question relative to mnemonic usage with ethnically diverse students:

> To maximize mnemonic benefits, must materials incorporating ethnically relevant content be developed by teachers and students from the target populations? Concerning...[that] question, it may be assumed that if the specific mnemonic content is not meaningful to a student, then the strategy will not function as intended. In fact, it is bound to complicate the learning process including additional unfamiliar or arbitrary information (e.g., "kool aid" for someone who does not know what that is). In a real mnemonic sense, then, one student's "cool aid" may be another's poison (p. 241).

Mnemonics fosters both relational and analytical thinking skills. As Table 8.1 illustrates, the teacher creates opportunities for students to learn specific facts. The teacher identifies what information (or facts) students need to attend to in a picture or word phrase and then carefully directs them in ways to remember that information. Creativity emerges as students create their own mnemonic associations or when they re-create mnemonic strategies that the teacher offers. That is, if students are taught material using mnemonic strategies and then forget some of the material, they need to know how to revise their mental images to make them more ridiculous or vivid so that they will be remembered. Finally, the teacher can foster, through the use of mnemonics, both convergent and divergent thinking. *Convergence* occurs as the teacher focuses the students' attention on particular ideas (to memorize and attend to). *Divergence* occurs when students begin to create their own images to replace those of the teacher that "don't work."

TABLE 8-1   Relationship of Mnemonics Model to Cognitive Skills

Model	Relational Skills	Analytical Skills
■ Mnemonics	■ Creativity	■ Memory for specific facts
	■ Divergent thinking	■ Convergent thinking
		■ Linear
		■ Object-oriented

Ⓟrevalent Issues in Diverse Classrooms

The mnemonics instructional model and its variations were created to help students memorize and acquire factual information. Memorization was once used often by America's teachers. However, with the emphases upon developing thinking skills and applying knowledge and skills to new and complex situations, teachers rarely draw upon this model. This may be due to a shift in instructional goals and priorities or to a lack of training in teacher-preparation institutions. At any rate, the following represent questions that teachers have asked us in our staff development efforts with them:

Q: *How can I create all the required mnemonic devices?*

A: Many teachers look at mnemonics as a difficult pedagogical strategy because of the vast array of pictures and illustrations that are required. Whether students are learning the names and order of the presidents or the location and capitals of the states, teachers perceive the task of creating all the mnemonic strategies as overwhelming. There are a couple of ways in which this problem can be solved. First, some teachers use commercially produced mnemonic materials— see the end of the chapter for citations and addresses. The authors have worked with teachers who have used both the materials created by Rodriguez and Rodriguez (1994) and the Bornstein (1983) illustrations. Bornstein, for example, provides an array of mnemonic aids for learning facts (state capitals, multiplication tables, and so on), remembering names and faces, retaining vocabulary, and recalling numerical data. Illustrations are available for teachers to purchase and use in each of these areas. For learning state capitals, for example, Bornstein provides 50 picture illustrations: Harrisburg, Pennsylvania, is a bird carrying a pencil (in its claws) and preparing to drop it (the pencil) to a man with "Harvey" typed on his chest. For Bornstein's mathematical facts, an illustration, such as 9×5, might show Team 9 playing Team 5 on a football field with the ball on the 45-yard line. We are not suggesting that all commercial materials are excellent, just that they represent an option.

Second, classroom teachers can work with specialization teachers (in art, for example) to create their own mnemonic devices. Decide with students what visual pictures represent the best illustration of a fact. Teachers may want to work with students to accomplish this because the students' ideas may make more sense than illustrations conceived of by teachers or commercial publishers. Then have the students in art classes (or during enrichment times) create the illustrations for classroom use. With younger children, teachers may want to solicit the assistance of older students who can help create and design the illustrations.

Third, students can create their own mnemonics for a lesson. One of the ways we have used this is by having either students or teacher groups develop their own mnemonics as a review activity for a lesson. The excitement and enthusiasm this has generated among the groups has been amazing! Students who create their own mnemonics build connections that are more personally meaningful. A teacher's substitute word may not make as much sense to a student as one generated by the student. Higbee (1996) writes:

> There are several possible reasons why you are likely to remember your own mnemonics better. You may put more thought and effort into them than into mnemonics that someone else gives you. Your own mnemonics are likely to be the first associations to come to you at recall time. Another possible reason is that because other people suggest mnemonics different from the ones you would think of yourself, they are not as meaningful to you (p. 110).

Q: *What facts should the students be expected to learn?*

A: This question will most likely persist as long as America does not adopt a nationalized curriculum. As long as each state and, in many cases, each school district creates its own curriculum, debate will rage regarding what facts are of the most worth. Several years ago, Hirsch (1988) argued that:

> Cafeteria-type education, combined with the unwillingness of our schools to place demands on students, has resulted in a steady diminishment of commonly shared information between generations and between young people themselves. Those who graduate from the same school have often studied different subjects, and those who graduate from different schools have often studied different material even when their courses have carried the same titles. The inevitable consequence of the shopping mall high school is a lack of shared knowledge across and within schools (pp. 20–21).

Hirsch, of course, offers in his text's appendix a list of terms, dates, and names that every literate person should know (see Figure 8.6). Whether one agrees or disagrees with Hirsch's essentialist philosophy, and he clearly evidences a Western bias in what he deems to be important information, his basic premise holds some merit: Society needs to decide what students need to know and then ensure that a curriculum exists that helps students acquire or learn those ideas. Educators can take a first step toward achieving this if they work together to decide what they perceive as essential ideas—terms, facts, names—that all students should know. Even within particular schools some measure of consensus can be achieved regarding the essential ideas. Recall that Sizer (1992) suggested that teachers identify those "exhibits" that all students should memorize. The teachers in that fictional school were not endeavoring to decide what all students everywhere should know (the Hirsch claim); rather, they were seeking to define in very particularized (school-specific) ways what made sense for their students.

1066	H$_2$O
1492	ice age
abolitionism	Iron Curtain
Achilles	Joan of Arc
alienation	Kill two birds with one stone.
baptism	Lennon, John
Bell, Alexander Graham	lesbian
Berkeley, CA	mania
Caesar, Julius	naturalism
capitalism	Practice what you preach.
chivalry	satire
cholesterol	Seuss, Dr.
cross to bear	South Africa
Dark Ages	touché
democracy	visual aid
Dr. Jekyll and Mr. Hyde	Watergate
Every cloud has a silver lining.	*War and Peace*
Fahrenheit	X-ray
feminism	Yugoslavia
Galileo	zodiac
Golden Rule	

FIGURE 8-6 Examples of Hirsch's Essential Names, Phrases, Dates, and Concepts

Source: E. D. Hirsch. 1988. *Cultural Literacy.* New York: Vantage Books: Appendix.

Q: *Are there culturally relevant experiences or techniques that could be used in implementing the mnemonics model?*

A: Certainly! To be responsive, teachers should provide opportunities for students to work with factual information from their personal and cultural frames of reference. The benefits of cultural sources come through sharing of cultures within the group and by conveying to students that teachers are aware of and sensitive to student experiences. Teachers using the mnemonic model might use a choral approach (Gilbert and Gay, 1985) so often found in African American churches. In addition, a very modern technique could involve the use of rap and hip-hop rhymes and rhythms (for example, "Gangsta's Paradise") to teach factual information deemed important for the students to remember. One chemistry teacher, for example, uses songs as a way of teaching chemical formulas. A student who had this teacher recalled that the technique was really great except during exams—it seems that periodically you could hear students humming to themselves as a way of recalling the needed information.

Efforts to evaluate mnemonics lessons require that the assessor first clearly determine the importance of the memorized material. From E. D. Hirsch's (1988) *Cultural Literacy* to Ravitch and Finn's (1987) *What Do Our 17-Year Olds Know?*, arguments exist regarding the essential facts and concepts that all students should be able to recite. An important precondition for evaluating any mnemonics lesson is, therefore, what facts or information should students learn, and how essential is that information to the students' overall cognitive development. Considerable debate is occurring in the 1990s regarding whether a national curriculum should be in place. Some claim that the academic advantage of countries such as Japan and Germany is because of the existence of nationalized curricula. While we have some modest concerns with the notion of nationalizing a curriculum, we have no problems with a determination concerning what curriculum concepts (or big ideas) should be taught. Students should not memorize just to memorize! They should purposefully memorize important information from the academic disciplines. Hence, before initiating an evaluation of a lesson, it is important to respond to the following three questions:

1. What are the specific facts and concepts that students need to learn?

2. Is the teacher expecting students to memorize specific isolated facts (for example, capitals) or a specific sequence of facts (for example, the order of the planets)? What are they? List below.

   Specific isolated facts _____

   Specific sequence of facts _____

3. Do these facts or concepts fit within the total curriculum to be implemented?

Phase I: Focus Attention

1. Does the teacher specifically draw the students' attention to the material that they will memorize?

   ◯ Yes ◯ No

2. What mnemonic strategy does the teacher use to draw the students' attention to the facts and concepts that they will learn?

   First-letter mnemonic ____
   Keyword ____
   Linkword ____
   Pegword ___

Phase II: Create Connections

1. Which of the four mnemonic strategies does the teacher use? _____

2. If acronym or acrostic, is the word or phrase clear and understandable? ○ Yes ○ No

3. If keyword, is the teacher using substitute words that make sense and that are vivid in nature? ○ Yes ○ No

4. If linkword, does the teacher have students learn the sequence of facts in ways that are logically interconnected? ○ Yes ○ No

5. If pegword, do the students know the pegs? Are the pegs appropriately connected with the information to be remembered? ○ Yes ○ No

Phase III: Create Associations

1. Which of the four rules does the teacher use to help students expand their senses through the creation of ridiculous associations?

   Substitution _____
   Exaggeration _____
   Out of proportion _____
   Action _____

2. Explain how one or more of these strategies is used by the teacher.

   Peer teaching _____
   Teacher review _____
   Other (explain) _____
   _____

Phase IV: Foster Recall

The final phase requires that the teacher systematically review with students the facts and concepts they have learned.

1. Identify which review strategies the teacher uses, and describe whether those approaches are effective.

   _____
   _____
   _____
   _____

❂ SAMPLE LESSONS

Mnemonic lessons are difficult to structure unless teachers have a very clear sense of the precise information that they want students to understand. Elementary school teachers often find mnemonic lessons easier to develop than secondary school teachers because of the basic nature of many of the facts emphasized in elementary school. The following case study is for high school students and builds on a research study published by Mastropieri, Scruggs, and Levin (1987).

CASE **S**TUDY

Ms. Ebony Foxx's 10th graders in advanced-placement (AP) biology are preparing to learn about vascular plants. She wants her students to know the subdivisions of angiosperm and gymnosperm and to know the four classes associated with the two subdivisions (see Figure 8.7). Further, her AP students are expected to memorize the order names as well.

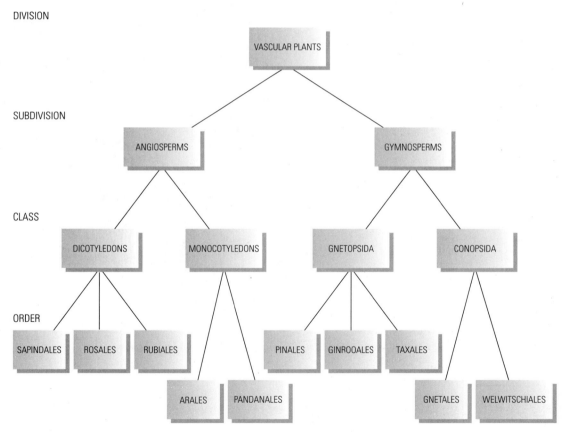

FIGURE 8-7 Plant Classification System

Adapted from M. E. Levin and J. R. Levin. 1990. "Scientific Mnemonomies: Methods for Maximizing More Than Memory." *American Educational Research Journal* 27(2): 304.

Ms. Foxx has already spent considerable time working with the students to know the definitions of the different terms. The students have learned the division, subdivision, and class labels. What they are having difficulty learning are the order names.

"Class, I know that some of you now have good basic definitions of vascular plants. You understand the differences between angiosperms, or flowering plants, and gymnosperms, which we described as 'naked seed plants.' As you make progress in your coursework, you need to be able to quickly recognize the various class and order designations. That's where many of you are having difficulty. To assist you in this learning process—to memorize the classes and orders of all the names in the plant classifications—I will show you how to use some mnemonic devices to assist you in learning the names.

"The first mnemonic [see Figure 8.8] is for angiosperms. For you to recall that angiosperms include dicotyledons, look carefully at the picture. Notice that the angel (angiosperm) has a pet dinosaur (dicotyledons). That image should help you connect angiosperm with dicotyledon. Now to remember three of the orders—rubiales, sapindales, and rosales—picture the dinosaur

FIGURE 8-8 Example of a Mnemonic Illustration: Angiosperm

Illustrated by Janet Olney Lasley. Based on illustration by M. E. Levin and J. R. Levin. 1990. "Scientific Mnemonomies: Methods for Maximizing More Than Memory." *American Educational Research Journal* 27(2): 305.

climbing up Rubik's cubes and preparing to lick sap that covers the leaves of a huge rose plant. One thing, students, with the advent of molecular biology and the ability to study DNA, the classification of plants is undergoing tremendous revision. As a consequence, many disagreements exist about the specific relationships in the classification system that I am having you memorize.

"Look carefully at the picture and then describe it to your peer partner."

The students all take a moment to look at the picture, then each person in the pair describes the picture verbally to their partner.

Ms. Foxx continues the lesson. "Let's look now at the other class and order terms for angiosperm. Angiosperms also include monocotyledons, or monocots. Remember that the monocots include such things as wheat, corn, and lilies. Picture an angel—the same one, in fact, that we described earlier—with a pet monkey. And that monkey is very talented, so talented that the monkey can shoot arrows at tiny pans and successfully hit them [see Figure 8.9]. With this image in mind, you can now remember that angiosperms (angel) includes monocots (monkeys) who shoot arrows at pans. Once again, class, take a minute to describe the picture to your partner."

FIGURE 8-9 Example of a Mnemonic Illustration: Angiosperm

Based on illustration by M. E. Levin and J. R. Levin. 1990. Scientific Mnemonomies: Methods for Maximizing More Than Memory. *American Educational Research Journal* 27(2): 305.

After a minute or so, Ms. Foxx continues her lesson by reviewing gymnosperms using pictures similar to those for angiosperms, though she shares with the students that the gymnosperm categorical relationships are changing and that the "old" form she is having them memorize may differ from some new forms they will see in college. At the end of the class, Ms. Foxx distributes a blank schematic of vascular plants and asks that the students attempt to complete it keeping in mind the mnemonics she used. The students finish and grade the task. Students who couldn't remember one of the terms (for example, the order names for monocots) are asked to revise their images to make them even more ridiculous. ■

Follow-up questions

1. Are the mnemonics that the teacher uses appropriate for teaching the major concepts in this lesson?

2. What other mnemonics might you use to teach the various class and order designations?

3. Identify three alternative strategies teachers might use to help students practice learning the class and order names (for example, peer teaching). Be specific regarding what steps you would have the students follow.

4. What other strategies might Ms. Foxx use for rehearsal and feedback if students are unable to recall one of the terms?

5. Is it appropriate to have students memorize information for which disagreement exists about the specifics of the conceptual relationships? Should dynamic knowledge be committed to memory?

❶ESSON PLAN

Concept: Solar System

Objectives:
1. To develop in students an understanding of the order of the planets.
2. To enable students to learn some basic facts about the planets.

Methods:
- Teacher will ask students to generate the names of the planets in the solar system without identifying the location of each planet and list these on the chalkboard.
- Teacher will teach students the acrostic phrase "My Very Energetic Mom Just Served Us Nine Pizzas." She will write the words on the board as follows:

My

Very

Energetic

Mom

Just

Served

Us

Nine

Pizzas

Teacher will note that two of the planets begin with the letter *m*. She will ask them to note that Mercury begins with *m* and ends with *y*, which corresponds to the first and last letters of the pronoun *my*.

Teacher will write the names of each planet next to the word in the phrase to which it corresponds.

Mercury	My
Venus	Very
Earth	Energetic
Mars	Mom
Jupiter	Just
Saturn	Served
Uranus	Us
Neptune	Nine
Pluto	Pizzas

Teacher will have students form three groups—each with 10 students. The students are each given a planet's name; one student is given a card for the sun. They are asked to order themselves in front of the class in the same position as the planets appear in the solar system.

Closure: Students will be given a worksheet that requires them to position the planets as they appear in the solar system and to identify four facts about each planet.

Follow-up questions

1. Is it appropriate for elementary-age students to learn the order of the planets?

2. Is the acrostic phrase the teacher uses clear? What other phrases could have been used?

3. How else could students learn to remember the names of the two *m* (Mercury and Mars) planets?

4. Could you design this lesson using either the linkword or pegword strategy? Describe how you would do this.

5. What other activities would you suggest for closing the lesson? What homework might you require?

The creation of good mnemonic strategies takes time, effort, and thought. The following readings and media resources may be useful as teachers consider the process of structuring a mnemonics lesson.

Suggested readings

Carney, R. N., M. E. Levin, and J. R. Levin. 1993. "Mnemonic Strategies: Instructional Techniques Worth Remembering." *Teaching Exceptional Children* 25(4): 24–30.

Levin, J. R. 1993. "Mnemonic Strategies and Classroom Learning: A Twenty Year Report Card." *Elementary School Journal* 94(2): 235–244.

Pressley, M., J. R. Levin, and G. E. Miller. 1981. "How Does the Keyword Method Affect Vocabulary Comprehension and Usage?" *Reading Research Quarterly* 16: 213–226.

Suggested audiotapes and videotapes

"Memory Assists." Booksend Laboratories, 652 Andrews Drive, Rio Del Mar, Aptos, CA 95003.

Tapes and mnemonic cards are available on the following subjects from the Bornstein School of Memory Training, 11693 San Vincente Boulevard, West Los Angeles, CA 90049:

- How to Retain Facts and Ideas for School and Business
- How to Develop Concentration and Visualization Techniques
- How to Remember Names and Faces
- How to Develop and Retain Your Vocabulary
- How to Retain and Master a Foreign Language
- How to Remember Numerical Data

Suggested lesson development

The use of mnemonics may not be appropriate for all classroom lessons. Teachers need to think carefully about how and when to use mnemonics with students. Specific steps to follow are:

1. Determine what facts or concepts students should retain in their long-term memories.
2. Identify specific ways to draw attention to those facts and concepts.
3. Determine what mnemonic strategy (first-letter mnemonics, keyword, peg-word, linkword) is best suited to help students retain the information.
4. Develop strategies to help students practice the use of mnemonics.
5. Identify methods students can use to reinforce their understanding of the memorized information.

SUMMARY

Students are confronted with an abundance of new information each day in schools. Teachers frequently assume that students inherently know how to remember all the information that is imparted during a school day. They also forget how much new vocabulary is part of the everyday experience of most students. For example, the amount of new vocabulary introduced in science lessons is often equivalent to that evidenced in foreign language instruction—anyone who has had a son or daughter in a high school biology class of a traditional teacher need look no further than their last chapter quiz to verify this observation.

Mnemonics are a user-friendly way of taking factual information that students need to know and showing them a way that will enable them to remember that information. The technique also draws on the more creative dimensions of a student's intelligence. Because so many mnemonics require visualization (imagination), students can draw on spatial or musical intelligences—they can create pictures or use songs as mnemonic devices.

The critical question, of course, is: Do mnemonics work? Drawing on the data of a wide variety of researchers, Carney, Levin, and Levin (1993) noted the following:

1. *Content generality*. Mnemonic strategies have been found to improve students' memory for terminology and factual information in a variety of curricular domains, including language arts (English and foreign vocabulary, reading comprehension), social studies, science, mathematics, and art....

2. *Student characteristics*. Mnemonic strategies have been used profitably by all types of students, ranging from young children to college-age adults and the elderly, from those with mental disabilities to those with academic gifts, and across a variety of social class groups....

3. *Remembering new information*. With particular regard to remembering new vocabulary and technical terminology, of all instructional strategies in current use or under current scrutiny, mnemonic strategies have proved to be the most effective....

4. *Improved retention*. The learning gains associated with mnemonic strategies have been found to last for long periods of time, namely, several weeks and, in some cases, months....

5. *Strategy transfer*. Students can be instructed in the effective application of mnemonic strategies so that they are later able to use such strategies on their own in other learning contexts....

6. *Strategy flexibility*. Mnemonic strategies can be successfully combined or integrated with alternative instructional strategies as seen fit by either teachers or students....

7. *Higher-order thinking*. Critically, and contrary to popular belief, mnemonic strategies do not foster simple rote memory at the expense of comprehension, usage, and problem solving. In fact, the available research evidence sug-

gests that acquiring factual information via mnemonic strategies can often improve students' ability to apply that information....

8. *Motivation.* Apart from these performance-based conclusions, feedback received from students indicates that using mnemonic strategies is more enjoyable than traditional methods of study, which in turn increases students' task engagement and persistence... (pp. 26–27).

Clearly, mnemonic strategies have more potential than just helping students retain facts. Used correctly, they motivate some students who within traditional classrooms are permitted only to explore narrow dimensions of their intellectual potential. Lorayne and Lucas (1974) observe that in the "ancient world, a trained memory was of vital importance" (p. 1). In this modern information age, it is even more important! Unfortunately, with the abundance of information access systems now available to students, the expectations for memorizing information are not what they once were. That circumstance is unfortunate! Certainly, an educated person needs to know how to access information, but that person must also know how to retain some of that necessary information once it is accessed.

ⓡ EFERENCES

Bennett, C. I. 1995. *Comprehensive Multicultural Education: Theory and Practice* (3d ed.). Boston: Allyn & Bacon.

Bornstein, A. 1983. *Bornstein School of Memory Training.* Los Angeles: Bornstein School of Memory Training.

Brooks, J. G., and M. G. Brooks. 1993. *The Case for Constructivist Classrooms.* Washington, DC: Association for Supervision and Curriculum Development.

Cajete, G. 1994. *Look to the Mountain: An Ecology of Indigenous Education.* Durango, CO: Kivaki Press.

Carney, R. N., M. E. Levin, and J. R. Levin. 1993. "Mnemonic Strategies: Instructional Techniques Worth Remembering." *Teaching Exceptional Children* 25(4): 24–30.

Gilbert, S., and G. Gay. 1985. "Improving the Success in School of Poor Black Children." *Phi Delta Kappan* 67(2): 133–137.

Higbee, K. L. 1996. *Your Memory* (2d ed.). New York: Marlowe.

Hirsch, E. D. 1988. *Cultural Literacy.* New York: Vintage Books.

Joyce, B., and M. Weil. 1992. *Models of Teaching* (4th ed.). Boston: Allyn & Bacon.

Levin, J. R. 1993. "Mnemonic Strategies and Classroom Learning: A Twenty Year Report Card." *Elementary School Journal* 94(2): 235–244.

Levin, M. E., and J. R. Levin. 1990. "Scientific Mnemonomies: Methods for Maximizing More than Memory." *American Educational Research Journal* 27(2): 301–321.

Lorayne, H., and J. Lucas. 1974. *The Memory Book.* New York: Ballantine.

Luria, A. R. 1968. *The Mind of a Mnemonist.* Chicago: Henry Regnery.

Mastropieri, M. A., T. E. Scruggs, and J. R. Levin. 1987. "Learning Disabled Students' Memory for Expository Prose: Mnemonic Versus Nonmnemonic Pictures." *American Educational Research Journal* 24(4): 505–519.

Mathematics Plus. 1992. Orlando, FL: Harcourt Brace Jovanovich. (See Grade 7 text, p. 169.)

Pressley, M., J. R. Levin, and H. D. Delaney. 1982. "The Mnemonic Keyword Method." *Review of Educational Research* 52: 61–91.

Pressley, M., J. R. Levin, and G. E. Miller. 1981. "How Does the Keyword

Method Affect Vocabulary Comprehension and Usage?" *Reading Research Quarterly* 16: 213–226.

Ravitch, D., and C. E. Finn, Jr. 1987. *What Do Our 17-Year Olds Know?* New York: Harper & Row.

Rodriguez, D., and J. Rodriguez. 1994. *Times Tables the Fun Way.* Sandy, UT: Key.

Rose, C. 1985. *Accelerated Learning.* New York: Dell.

Sizer, T. R. 1992. *Horace's School: Redesigning the American High School.* Boston: Houghton Mifflin.

• *Direct Instruction*

At the completion of this chapter, the reader will be able to:
1. *Describe the theoretical basis for the direct instruction model.*
2. *Identify the essential phases of the direct instruction model.*
3. *Identify the strengths and weaknesses of the direct instruction model.*
4. *Describe ways in which direct instruction can be used with diverse student populations.*
5. *Create a direct instruction lesson for personal use in a classroom.*

❶NTRODUCTION

One of the most misused and least understood models is direct instruction. For as long as schools have existed, "teacher talk" has dominated the way in which students learn information and teachers communicate facts. Indeed, many teachers believe that once they utter the words in the classroom, the students have learned the information. Teacher talk for many teachers has been considered synonymous with student learning. Such a circumstance is regrettable! For although direct instruction does require that teachers make a number of preinstructional decisions, it does not suggest that students are unimportant, passive observers in the teaching–learning process. Direct instruction requires that teachers make explicit instructional decisions, but it also demands that teachers know what they are going to assess and whether students adequately acquire the requisite skills taught by the teacher.

Not all concepts taught by teachers are amenable to direct instruction. Several years ago, the then Secretary of Education, William Bennett, was asked to teach a lesson to high school students on James Madison's *Federalist Paper 10*. Mr. Bennett exhibited substantial content knowledge of the James Madison treatise regarding why the Constitution should be ratified. The lesson was taped and a transcript sent to several evaluation experts in the field of education, one of whom had considerable expertise in direct instruction as an instructional model. The expert, Barak Rosenshine, reviewed the tape for instructional effectiveness and suggested that it was difficult to assess the lesson because Mr. Bennett was teaching content concepts, not specific, concrete

> *It would be a mistake to say that this systematic, small-step approach applies to all students or all situations. It is most important for young learners, slow learners, and all learners when the material is new, difficult, or hierarchical.*
>
> BARAK ROSENSHINE

skills. What that expert observed is fundamental to understanding how and when to use direct instruction: The model is best used when teachers are teaching skills, not when communicating conceptually complex content ideas. To illustrate this, Rosenshine (1986) describes the difficulty of using some steps of the direct instruction model when teaching content material.

> My main point is that it is difficult to apply some of the major findings we have learnt from studying the teaching of skills to lessons which teach content. Some of these findings include checking for student understanding, providing for active student participation, providing for a high success rate, correcting errors, and providing for guided practice and independent practice. But such findings do not, and will not, transfer easily to the teaching of content....
>
> In this [Bennett's] lesson, the students need practice in explaining the problems and solutions developed in Federalist 10, their relevance for our time, and the view of human nature and human rights embodied in the thought of these founders. The teacher needs to hear how well the students are doing, and the students need feedback on their efforts. All these would occur easily when teaching a skill. Unfortunately, we do not have mechanisms for doing this when teaching content (p. 306).

In essence, the instructional model a teacher uses is necessarily influenced by the instructional goals the teacher establishes. A teacher who wants to teach a specific skill (for example, how to divide fractions, how to diagram a sentence, or how to construct an origami butterfly) is best served by using the direct instruction model. On the other hand, a teacher who wants students to understand social issues or appreciate poetry will be far less pleased, as will the students, with the results of a direct instruction lesson. Rosenshine (1987) writes:

> These findings [about direct instruction] are less applicable for teaching in areas that are less well structured—that is, those in which skills do not follow explicit steps or where concepts are less identifiable and distinct....
> Thus the results of this research are less relevant for teaching composition writing of term papers, reading comprehension, analysis of literature or historical trends, or discussion of social issues or concepts such as liberalism or modernity (p. 75).

Teachers make decisions about what to teach. If what they plan to teach is a concrete skill, then direct instruction is the most appropriate strategy to ensure maximal student achievement. If the teacher is planning to teach content concepts, then direct instruction still has applicability, though the teacher will need to rely a bit more on the literature regarding lecturing and explaining (see Rosenshine, 1986). That is, for presenting content material the teacher needs to do such things as use questions to maintain student attention, signal transitions between sections, signal those points that are most important, use humor to hold student attention, summarize material within the context of the lecture, give or ask students for relevant examples, and review relevant background knowledge.

Direct instruction requires that teachers proceed in a way that limits information flow but enhances information transfer. The human brain can process only so much information at one time. Some teachers present too much information, and what they do present is covered in a very disjointed fashion. The teacher's obligation is to find ways of clustering and connecting ideas, facts, and information so that students can effectively process what the teacher presents. That means that the teacher must be clear about specifying the goals of a lesson, systematic in identifying how students are to learn material, and vigilant in checking on whether students are actually learning the content. In essence, the teacher must determine what skill to teach and then teach that skill in a step-by-step process. Finally, the teacher must check to see whether students have learned what has been taught. Let us see what this looks like in one 6th grade classroom.

❻ASE STUDY

Mr. Dale Carthridge begins his mathematics unit with the following statements:

"During the past several weeks we have been studying how to add and subtract fractions. Last week we investigated how to multiply fractions. Let's take a couple of minutes to review the process that we followed in multiplying $3/4 \times 1/2$." At this point Mr. Carthridge reviews the steps the students should follow in multiplying fractions. Once the class completes the review, Mr. Carthridge begins a new segment of the unit.

"Today, class, we are going to learn how to divide fractions. There will be two purposes for our lesson. First, you will list the specific steps that must be followed in dividing fractions; and second, you will describe why you follow the steps used in the division process.

"Let's begin. First, I want you all to get your slates out and put them on your desks." (Mr. Carthridge has slates and chalk that the students use during math drill and practice exercises.)

"I am going to work three problems on the board. You will see each step labeled clearly, but I want you to perform the work on your slates as I perform the work on the board. The problem we will start with is $1/2 \div 3/8 = ?$"

The teacher then puts the acronym PIRMS on the board: Problem Invert Reduce Multiply Solve. "Let's look at what each of these letters in the acronym mean for $1/2 \div 3/8$. I call this the PIRMS process."

Mr. Carthridge works the first problem slowly, and next to each of the words he identifies the step the students must follow. When he is finished, the problem on the board looks similar to the one in Table 9.1.

The students have the same problem worked out on their slates. As Mr. Carthridge presents each step, he carefully talks them through the process: "First, class, you state the problem, which in this case is $1/2 \div 3/8$. Next, class, Step 2: You invert the fraction on the right side. To remember this, just think that it's right to invert on the right. Sharonda, what does invert mean?" (Sharonda correctly describes how to invert.)

TABLE 9-1 Sequential Organizer for Solving Division Problem

STEP 1: Problem	$1/2 \div 3/8 = ?$
STEP 2: Invert	$1/2 \times 8/3 = ?$
STEP 3: Reduce	$1/2 \times 8/3 = 1/1 \times 4/3$
STEP 4: Multiply	$1/1 \times 4/3 = 4/3$
STEP 5: Solve	$4/3 = 1 1/3$

Mr. Carthridge meticulously describes the first problem and then erases, at the end, all of the numbers on the right side of Table 9.1 and puts a new problem on the board: $3/4 \div 1/3 = ?$ Once again he very carefully describes the mathematical processes step-by-step. The students follow each step by performing the steps on their personal slates. At the end, Mr. Carthridge erases the problem and all the steps.

"Now, class, I'm going to give you a third problem. But in this case, you will be helping me. Let's begin. I'll start by giving you a problem: $3/5 \div 1/2 = ?$ Joshua, what's the second step that we use?"

"You invert the numbers and multiply."

"Which numbers?"

"The $1/2$."

"Why?" responds Mr. Carthridge.

"Because it's on the right side," says Joshua.

"Yes, and a little later you'll also know the more technical reason for inverting the $1/2$. What's the next step after we have $3/5 \times 2/1$? Jasmine?"

"You simplify."

"And what do you mean by simplify, Jasmine?"

"You see if any of the numbers are factors of the other numbers."

"Excellent. I like how you explained that. Well, are any of the numbers factors and can you simplify? Lanita?"

"No."

"Good. So what's the next step?"

"You multiply."

"Yes. First you multiply the numerators, and then you multiply the denominators. What would you get if you do that? Troy?"

"$6/5$."

"Correct. So $3/5 \times 2/1 = 6/5$. Now the last step is to solve the problem. Remember last week I indicated that this means putting the improper fraction $6/5$ into its lowest terms. And what would that be? Nathan?"

"$1 1/5$."

"Yes. So $3/5 \div 1/2 = 1 1/5$.

"Now I want you to do one on your slate. When you finish, please show all your work, and hold your slate up so I can see your work. Now, try $3/7 \div 2/3 = ?$"

The students work the problem and hold up their slates. Mr. Carthridge moves around the room and checks the students' progress. He then gives them three more problems: $1/5 \div 1/3 = ?$; $2/9 \div 4/5 = ?$; and $1/4 \div 1/2 = ?$ After the students complete each problem, Mr. Carthridge reviews each step with the students to make certain everyone understands.

"Tomorrow, class, we are going to look at why you invert to get the answer. Once you know that, you will have an even better sense of why you follow these steps. For homework I want you to do the 20 problems on the worksheet...." ∎

Mr. Carthridge is teaching a concrete skill—dividing fractions—using the direct instruction model. The step-by-step process coupled with constant efforts to check for understanding are the foundation upon which this instructional model is grounded.

❶ HEORETICAL PERSPECTIVE

Direct instruction is grounded on the fundamental assumption that unless the teacher knows where a lesson is headed, it will be impossible to know whether a goal has been reached. Far too many teachers have an unclear sense of what they want to accomplish during an instructional lesson. They know that they want students to be busy (to work), but they are often less certain of the specific, academic goals they wish to achieve.

Direct instruction is not new! In the 1800s a form of direct instruction was used to teach students how to read. McGuffey (in the 1860s) instituted a system of reading that demanded that teachers repeat and pronounce words in particular ways in order to assist the beginning reader (see Finkelstein, 1989). In fact, M. C. Hippean, who observed American teachers in the 1850s, noted that "teachers were particularly exacting about sounds that were difficult.... Teachers explained to the students the position of the teeth and lips, the location of the tongue...and then watched carefully to see if students reproduced the sounds properly" (Finkelstein, 1989, pp. 54–55). Reading has always been a focus for direct instruction strategies because reading skills are so fundamental to school success. Bereiter and Engelmann (1966) created the modern model as part of the direct instruction program for preschool children to help them acquire basic skills in arithmetic and language. Gagne (1977) conceptualized the basic model (anticipatory set, statement of objectives, lesson preparation with checks for student understanding, guided practice, and closure) and made it a part of the educational psychology literature. Rosenshine (1983) slightly redefined the technique (see Table 9.2) to a six-step instructional functions model (offer daily review, present new content, initial student practice, provide feedback and corrective assessment, provide independent practice, and offer weekly reviews). Hunter (1976), though, is most notable in popularizing the model. Her model includes a seven-step process that is quite similar to Rosenshine's approach, but clearly it was Hunter's ability to articulate ideas (she was a gifted presenter) that brought life to an otherwise staid model. To Hunter's credit, she never argued that alternative instructional models could not be utilized in her presentation

TABLE 9-2 Instructional Functions

1. *Daily review:*
   Checking homework
   Reteaching areas where there were student errors

2. *Presenting new content/skills:*
   Provide overview
   Proceed in small steps (if necessary), but at a rapid pace
   If necessary, give detailed or redundant instructions and explanations
   New skills are phased in while old skills are being mastered

3. *Initial student practice:*
   High frequency of questions and overt student practice (from teacher and materials)
   Prompts are provided during initial learning (when appropriate)
   All students have a chance to respond and receive feedback
   Teacher checks for understanding *by evaluating student responses*
   Continue practice until students are firm
   Success rate of 80 percent or higher during initial learning

4. *Feedback and correctives* (and recycling of instruction, if necessary):
   Feedback to students, particularly when they are correct but hesitant
   Student errors provide feedback to the teacher that corrections and/or reteaching is necessary
   Corrections by simplifying question, giving clues, explaining or reviewing steps, or reteaching last steps

5. *Independent practice* so that students are firm and automatic:
   Seatwork
   Unitization and automaticity (practice to overlearning)
   Need for procedure to ensure student engagement during seatwork (that is, teacher or aide monitoring)
   95 percent correct or higher

6. *Weekly and monthly reviews:*
   Reteaching, if necessary

Source: B. Rosenshine. 1983. "Teaching Functions in Instructional Programs." *Elementary School Journal* 83(4): 338.

phase, but many teachers who have learned her model use the structure of the lesson in an almost legalistic, linear, sequential fashion. The result has been stilted, uninteresting instruction for many youngsters!

The research on direct instruction suggests that the model has the most power in teaching basic skills. As a consequence, teachers in any academic discipline that has a heavy skill base (for example, mathematics) will find the direct instruction model powerful and useful. Rosenshine (1983) reported a series of studies that investigated whether teacher use of direct instruction enhances student academic performance. In several different studies, he found enhanced student academic achievement as a consequence of teacher use of the direct instruction model (Rosenshine also identifies it as "explicit teaching").

Not all studies on direct instruction, however, suggest the "marked" growth described by Rosenshine. In the now-famous Napa Valley studies, researchers collected longitudinal data on the academic growth of students whose teachers were trained using the Hunter model. Stallings and Krasavage (1986) describe the Hunter model as follows:

> Basic to the model are five elements of a lesson design. When a new lesson is started, the teacher presents a set activity that involves all of the students. A good set links the students' experience and prior knowledge to the new material to be learned. The set includes a statement of the lesson's purpose and clear, observable objectives. The objectives are stated behaviorally, for example, at the end of the lesson the learner will be able to count by fives to 100. The next element is presenting the new information in small segments. Instruction often takes the form of modeling or demonstration. After each segment of the lesson, all students are checked for understanding. Based on the students' responses, the teacher monitors and adjusts the level of the lesson, reteaching as necessary. The element following instruction is guided practice. Here the teacher provides opportunities for the students to practice the new learning. They are given feedback and assistance until they have mastered the new lesson. When the teacher is assured the students can work independently without errors, a closure activity provides one more practice item. Following closure, students do independent practice to overlearn the material (p. 118).

The results from the Napa Valley students were disappointing, especially when the long-term effects were measured. Initial gains by students in trained teachers' classrooms were evident, but those gains diminished the longer teachers utilized the direct instruction model. Although a number of researchers offer insights into why that circumstance occurred (see Porter, 1986; Robbins, 1986; Stallings and Krasavage, 1986), their observations do not completely obviate the potential power of the model. One significant observation they made has to do with how teachers use time. For a number of years educators have known that allocated time and student-engaged time were important dynamics for learning success. One of the most important by-products of direct instruction may be how teachers choose to use time and how they work with students to ensure success during the instructional sequence. For teachers who already have high student-engagement rates, the payoffs for direct instruction may be limited; but for those teachers who struggle to maximize student engagement during class lessons, the didactic structure of direct instruction may be efficacious, especially in teaching discrete skills. Porter (1986) confirms this observation based on his investigation of the Napa Valley schools. He writes:

> It is interesting to note that the effects of the ITIP [Instructional Theory into Practice] program on student achievement were small, even though

fairly substantial changes were produced in engaged time. Even in the disastrous third year, time-off-task was less than half what it had been at the start of the study. Two similar Follow-Through studies conducted at the same time as the Napa project both apparently found that training in classroom management increased time-on-task but did not increase student achievement.... A problem cited in...[some] studies is that most classes began so high in time-on-task that there was little to be gained. In Napa, six of the 13 classes began above 80% on-task, and 10 were above 70%.

Pushing time-on-task above, say, 80% may be of limited value in increasing student achievement (p. 170).

A couple of cautions are in order before we present the model. First, most of the research conducted on direct instruction has been with elementary-age students. That fact does not suggest that the model is inappropriate for older students, but it does indicate the limited scope of research to determine the power of the technique with different student populations. Second, direct instruction does suggest specific sequencing of instruction and it does demand that teachers clearly know what skill or content objectives they want to achieve. In essence, teachers provide the conceptual structuring for this model. They create and present the schema that students are expected to learn and assimilate. Teachers who want students to engage in critical thinking will find the model less useful. Direct instruction is a time-efficient way to communicate content, but it does not treat the disciplinary content as problematic—why does one invert and multiply? Direct instruction removes some of the mystery, but it can also help ensure that all students know a particular process.

ⓓ IRECT INSTRUCTION: TEACHING PHASES

Phase I: Review

The first step in the direct instruction model is to review what students already know about the topic to be covered. Although the review process appears self-evident (wouldn't any good teacher conduct a review?), the reality is that many teachers fail to make the conceptual connections necessary for students to see how what is taught one day fits with what was taught on another. Borich (1988) describes several ways that teachers can create meaningful review processes:

1. Students might correct each other's homework at the beginning of a class.
2. Students who represent a range of abilities can be called upon to assess their level of understanding.
3. Teachers can specifically review the material that has been previously taught.

Notice that Mr. Carthridge used the third strategy. He wanted to assess the students' understanding of multiplying fractions so, in a step-by-step fashion, he reviews the steps students must follow when solving a multiplication problem. The second strategy (calling on a range of students) can also be effective. All too often teachers call on top-performing students and exclude input from lower-performing students. The reasons for this circumstance are obvious, but the educational costs are equally evident. For direct instruction to work, students must experience a high degree of success. That success is jeopardized if the teacher ignores an important segment of the student population.

Phase II: Presenting New Material

In the second phase, the teacher begins to frame the ideas and present the new content material. The teacher begins this phase by stating the purpose of the lesson. Some teachers do this in a very explicit way, similar to Mr. Carthridge's approach. Recall that Mr. Carthridge quite specifically noted that there were two purposes for the lesson, and he then discussed those with the class. Some teachers even write TLW (The Learner Will) statements on the board that explicitly describe what students will be able to perform by the end of the class: "*The Learner Will* be able to subtract two-digit numbers" or "*The Learner Will* be able to define what a noun is and correctly identify nouns in a sentence." (Recall, in this regard, our discussion of performance objectives in Chapter 3.) Teachers who work with older students often resist writing specific performance objectives. Although this is understandable for some types of lessons that involve substantial brainstorming, we would argue against the practice when teaching students a discrete skill. If you want students to know RNA/DNA translation and transcription, then specifically state that expectation in the form of performance objectives at the beginning of the lesson.

In stating performance objectives and describing how various ideas fit (today's lesson with yesterday's), many teachers use advance organizers. An advance organizer, according to Ausubel (1960), is nothing more than a conceptual focus for understanding the context for and meaning of new material (in relationship to old material). Teachers use three types of organizers in presenting content material to students: expository, comparative, and sequential.

Expository organizers are used when a teacher creates a vertical conceptual organization of ideas. That is, the teacher works from a broad conceptual construct and then begins to break down one concept into a number of different subordinate concepts. (Refer also to this discussion in Chapter 4, "Concept Attainment.") The teacher progressively differentiates the disciplinary concepts with students learning more and more conceptual detail (Joyce and Weil, 1992). If, for example, a teacher has been teaching the parts of speech and plans on covering common nouns, the expository organizer might look something like:

"*We have been covering the parts of speech. Recall that all sentences are composed of words and each of those words has a function. Some are nouns: a person, place, or thing. Other words are verbs: they act on the noun. We have also talked about adjectives and adverbs. Today, we are going to begin taking some of these parts of speech and showing how they can be of different types. Today and tomorrow we will be studying common and proper nouns....*"

Figure 9.1 shows how the parts of speech would be structured using expository and comparative organizers.

Comparative organizers are used when the teacher utilizes what is known at one level of conceptual thought to make a comparison at the same level (that is, nouns to verbs). Mr. Carthridge uses a comparative organizer when he uses mul-

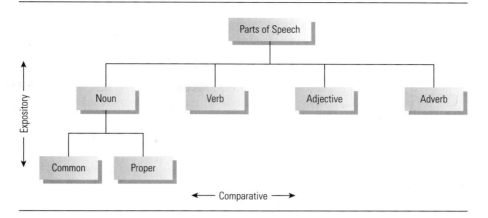

FIGURE 9-1 Advanced Organizers

tiplication of fractions to introduce students to division of fractions. Mr. Carthridge uses what the students know about multiplying fractions to help them understand the steps for dividing fractions. Joyce and Weil (1992) observe that comparative organizers "are used with relatively familiar material. They are designed to discriminate between the old and new concepts in order to prevent confusion caused by their similarity" (p. 188).

Sequential organizers are used, particularly in mathematics, to show students the steps that will be followed in performing a skill (Borich, 1988). Mr. Carthridge uses a comparative organizer to help students see the division of fractions in relationship to the multiplication of fractions. But he uses a sequential organizer when he lists the steps on the board for students to follow (see Table 9.1).

Although teachers most frequently use advance organizers in deductive (direct instruction) lessons, there is nothing that precludes the use of organizers in other types of lessons. Indeed, teachers who use concept attainment lessons rely on organizers as they decide how to present concepts and identify concept attributes.

Once the students know the purpose of the lesson and understand the conceptual context, the teacher then presents the information. Teachers need to present academic material in a step-by-step fashion by using an abundant number of examples at each step. One of the major weaknesses of many teachers is that they assume too much about what students know. This is especially true of high school teachers, but it is equally true of teachers in general. Japanese teachers tend to teach for overlearning by meticulously taking students through class routines or lessons in a step-by-step fashion (Stevenson and Stigler, 1992). American teachers practice an opposite instructional approach. Because American schools tend to be more focused on keeping students busy, teachers seem less concerned with making certain that everyone understands content material before they initiate independent practice. American teachers assume that if they presented the material, students learned it. But they fail to sequence the learning with a sufficient number of step-by-step demonstrations. Rosenshine (1983) notes:

> [R]ecent research in Grades 4–8 has shown that effective teachers of mathematics spend *more time* in demonstration than do less effective teachers.... For example, [one researcher]...found that the most effective mathematics teachers spent about 23 minutes per day in lecture, demonstration, and discussion, compared with 11 minutes for the least effective teachers. The effective teachers are using this additional presentation time to provide redundant explanations, use many examples, provide sufficient instruction so that the students can do the seatwork with minimal difficulty, check for student understanding, and reteach when necessary (p. 339).

Notice that the use of repeated explanations and numerous examples is essential for student understanding. Educators have long understood that clarity is an important characteristic of good teachers. Clear teachers use different explanations and myriad examples to ensure student understanding. Unclear teachers explain ideas a second time, *in the same way*, but *louder.*

Phase III: Guided Practice

Once students have been introduced to the skill or content material, teachers proceed by enabling students to practice what they have learned. They can do this by asking a variety of questions, by striving to ensure high levels of student success in answering questions, and by checking for understanding.

The use of questions to assess student understanding is critical to the success of direct instruction. Some questions will be highly specific and demand immediate student recall of a step, process, or piece of information. A quick review of Mr. Carthridge's lesson at the beginning of this chapter illustrates this point. Mr. Carthridge, however, not only asked for informational recall, he also demanded that students think through why they did what they did. One segment of his lesson illustrates this point:

"Now, class, I'm going to give you a third problem. But in this case, you will be helping me. Let's begin. I'll start by giving you a problem: $3/5 \div 1/2 = ?$ Joshua, what's the second step that we use?"

"You invert the numbers and multiply."

"Which numbers?"

"The $1/2$."

"Why?" responds Mr. Carthridge.

"Because it's on the right side," says Joshua.

"Yes, and a little later you'll also know the more technical reason for inverting the $1/2$."

One of the most underutilized and misunderstood elements of a direct instruction lesson is guided practice. Most teachers assume that once they have taught material (phase II), they are ready to allow students to engage in independent practice (phase V). This spurious reasoning explains why so many students exit schools with an inadequate understanding of salient skills and content. Rosenshine (1983) observed that the most effective teachers (those who taught students to retain skills or concepts) were those who "spent more time in guided practice, more time asking questions, more time correcting errors, more time repeating the new material that was being taught, and more time working problems under teacher guidance and help" (p. 341).

Asking a lot of questions, though, is only part of the equation for teacher success. Another extremely important ingredient is for students to be able to answer questions correctly—not necessarily 100 percent of the time, but at least at an 80 percent rate. Effective teachers work toward high success rates, and they involve a wide variety of students in the guided practice phase. Anyone who has ever taught knows that it is quite possible to obtain high levels of student success if only certain students are involved. If the teacher calls on only the high-ability students, success rates can be inflated. Effective guided practice requires that the teacher call on a wide range of students, and this can best be accomplished by calling on both volunteers and nonvolunteers. We suggest that guided practice start with involvement by volunteers, and then as the lesson progresses the teacher should call on students who do not have their hands raised (nonvolunteers). Mr. Carthridge used both volunteers and nonvolunteers, but he also relied on a form of group responding—the use of slates on which all students could write their answers. That technique is supported in the research (see W. C. Becker, 1977) and is an excellent way for the teacher to monitor whether students are understanding the content material.

Regardless of what strategy the teacher uses to check for understanding (for example, calling on students to summarize points, calling on students who raise their hands, or students' raising or lowering their thumbs to show agreement or disagreement with the teacher), the important factor is that the teacher assess whether students have really learned the material. As the reader will note in the next section, student success must also be "read" by the teacher to determine if students really understand ideas in depth.

Phase IV: Feedback and Correctives

Once a student responds to a teacher, the teacher is positioned to see how the student understands the material presented in phase II. A correct response on the part of a student is most desirable, but an incorrect response also communicates important information to a teacher. Incorrect responses reveal something of the conceptual schema of students. Therefore, when students respond to teacher questions, teachers need to assess both the correctness of the response and the nature of their own reaction to students so as to maximize student learning.

If a student responds to a teacher question with a correct, certain answer, *then* the teacher acknowledges the answer ("Yes," "Good," or "Correct") and asks the next question.

If a student responds with hesitancy, *then* the teacher acknowledges the response ("Yes," "Good," or "Correct") and also provides, according to Rosenshine (1983), some type of "process" feedback. Process feedback is nothing more than a reexplanation of how a student obtained an answer. It might sound something like this:

Teacher: *"What do you do after you invert in dividing fractions? Jerrod?"*
Jerrod: *"You...ah...you...I think you see if it's possible to reduce anything."*
Teacher: *"Right. Remember that the next step is to see if any of the opposite numera-*

tors and denominators are factors. So in $^1/2 \times ^8/3$, the 2 is a factor of 8. Thus the 2 is reduced to 1. The 2 divides into 2 one time and the 2 divides into the 8 four times.

If the answer is incorrect, *then* the teacher has three choices:

Choice 1: Match the student's incorrect response with a statement that makes the incorrect response correct. Example:

Teacher: *"What do you do after you invert in dividing fractions? Jerrod?"*
Jerrod: *"You solve the problem."*
Teacher: *"No, you solve the problem after you reduce all numerators and denominators. I asked what you do after you invert."*
Jerrod: *"You reduce."*
Teacher: *"Correct."*

This approach enables students to understand how the relationship of what they say fits with what the teacher expects (this student did know to solve the problem!). It cannot (and should not) be used in every instance, but it does represent an option for the teacher to use.

Choice 2: Reteach the material so that the students see the steps once again. This approach may be especially useful at the beginning of the phase IV process, when students may still have an unclear understanding of the skill or content that is presented by the teacher.

Choice 3: Provide hints or ask an even simpler question. Rosenshine (1983) and Stallings and Kaskowitz (1974) argue for using this technique, but teachers need to be careful when the students do not understand the material well. In essence, hints may be useful when students have a reasonably good grasp of the material just presented by the teacher. But teachers will be ineffectual if students are not able to quickly use the hint to answer a question correctly. We have observed teachers provide so many hints that they both frustrate students and destroy the momentum of a lesson.

Regardless of what strategy the teacher uses, the most important thing to remember is that an incorrect response must not go unrecognized. Further, when a student provides an incorrect answer, the teacher should stay with that student to help elicit a correct response. Such an approach helps teachers see the "process" of how students reason: How did they derive an answer? Most teachers simply call on another student, who provides the correct response. Such a strategy does little to help the first student who responded incorrectly, and it does little to help the teacher understand how a class presentation might have created the incorrect response given by the student.

Phase V: Independent Practice

Perhaps one of the most problematic aspects of direct instruction is independent practice, especially if students do not fully understand a skill or concept. Rosenshine (1983) argues that it is during this time that students go through *unitization* and *automaticity*:

During unitization the students are putting the skills together. The students make few errors, but they are also slow and expend a good deal of energy toward accomplishing the task. After much practice the students achieve the "automatic" stage where they respond successfully and rapidly and no longer have to "think through" each step (p. 345).

Independent practice within American schools occurs either during independent seatwork or through homework that is specifically assigned by the teacher. For independent seatwork to be successful, teachers need to spend more time in the guided practice phase to make certain students *know* the skills they are going to practice. American teachers are inclined either to start independent practice before students really know the skills, or fail to review and evaluate the work of students once students spend time working independently (Stevenson and Stigler, 1992). To ensure the maximum impact of independent practice, teachers must make certain students have a reasonable understanding of the skills the teacher has taught.

Work that is assigned to be completed at home requires that students strive for automaticity. Too many teachers assign students skills to practice (for homework) that students simply do not fully understand. Such a circumstance leads to mislearning—students practice skills incorrectly and mislearn how to use a skill. Not only do American children often practice skills at home that they do not fully understand, but when they do have reasonable skill understanding, teachers fail to assign enough practice to ensure automaticity.

Stevenson and Stigler (1992) observed in their cross-cultural study that Asian teachers assign significantly more homework than American teachers; in some cases the rates of assignments were up to seven times as high (these comparisons were for Taipei schools as compared with Minneapolis schools). Homework is not busywork! Homework is intended to ensure that students truly understand the content material presented by the teacher. Some do's and don'ts of assigning homework are provided in Table 9.3.

TABLE 9-3   Some Do's and Don'ts of Homework

. . . .

1. Do not *ever give homework as punishment.*

2. Do not *make up spur-of-the-moment homework assignments.*

3. Do not *assume that because there are no questions asked about a homework assignment students have no questions about the assignment.*

4. Do not *expect students (even your best students) always to have their homework assignments completed.*

5. Do *understand that not all types of homework assignments are equally valuable for all types of students.*

6. Do *explain the specific purpose of every homework assignment.*

7. Do *listen to what students say about their experiences in completing your homework assignments.*

8. Do *acknowledge and be thankful for efforts students make to complete their homework.*

. . . .

Source: D. A. England and J. K. Flatley. 1985. *Homework—and Why.* Bloomington, IN: Phi Delta Kappa: 36–37.

In essence, for independent practice to be useful, teachers need to 1) be certain that they have adequately taught material before allowing students to engage in practice, 2) be able to check the students' progress and success in using the skill (by circulating around the room while students work), and 3) be able to provide immediate feedback to students who are having difficulty. That feedback, incidentally, should be of relatively short duration (a quick correction). If a teacher finds that long periods of time are spent explaining material to students, then it is quite likely that the guided practice phase was not sufficient (did not take hold) to ensure full student comprehension of the skill.

APPLICATIONS TO DIVERSE CLASSROOMS

Direct instruction fosters heated debate among educators. Because many teachers equate direct instruction with lecture, there are substantial misunderstandings about the efficacy of this instructional model for culturally diverse students. Direct instruction and lecture are not the same! They have structural similarities, but they are, in fact, different. Direct instruction is skill focused! The goal of the teacher is to teach a specific skill in a sequenced, segmented way. Lectures have specific academic content objectives, but the teacher may or may not be interested in teaching specific skills. More importantly, direct instruction requires active student involvement (during guided and independent practice); lecture places students in a more passive role.

Losey (1995), in an analysis of the learning dispositions of Mexican American students, observed that successful classroom environments were those that were designed around student interests and that fostered a level of belongingness for students. Direct instruction, when properly implemented, enables both of these circumstances to be evidenced, but to do so requires that the teacher make certain that students recognize the relationship of the skills they are learning to the real-world problems they will face. Relevancy becomes important. Students need to recognize how a skill is relevant for them, and teachers must be able to move beyond the teaching of skills by rote memorization, to the teaching of skills or content material within a substantive context. An example of how a teacher contextualized content material will illustrate our point.

A teacher of American government in an urban high school was preparing to teach the amendments of the U.S. Constitution. Such academic material in and of itself is not typically interesting for students. After spending some time discussing the nature of "rights," the teacher shared that the goal for students on this particular day would be to understand which amendment empowered the students to become full participants in the democratic process. The teacher asked all of the students to stand and then told them to listen carefully to the following instructions, and to either sit down or remain standing depending on the way an instruction was worded. The instructions given included:

1. If you are not white, sit down.
2. If you are not male, sit down.
3. If you do not have $2.00 in your pocket, sit down.

After the teacher asked six such questions, one white male student (Josh) remained standing. The teacher then commented something like, "Class, without the amendments to the U.S. Constitution, only Josh would have the right to vote. By the end of today's class you will know which amendments enable you to remain standing."

This teacher made relevant something that is often perceived by students as arcane. A similar form of relevancy is needed whenever skills or discrete content concepts are taught to all students in general, but to culturally diverse students in particular. That relevancy will impact the teacher's expectations about what students can learn and the students' expectations for their own learning. Relevancy connects the students to the ideas being presented by the teacher. Trueba, Jacobs, and Kirton (1990) observed among the Hmong refugee children that when American teachers refused to adjust their instruction (that is, they would teach skills in isolation, for example), the "children...showed deep frustration and an attitude of hopelessness as they failed to engage meaningfully in learning activities" (pp. 75–76). Rothman (1995) is even more pointed in his emphasis on relevancy. He writes:

> Thus teaching abstract concepts, in isolation from the real world, does not help children learn and may in fact keep them from learning. But that is what schools do. Researchers have found, for example, that children in all parts of the world have a highly developed sense of mathematical concepts such as "number." They know, from observing the world, that if they add something to something else, they will have more of it (pp. 66–67).

Direct instruction fosters boredom and hopelessness when students cannot connect what they are learning with what they perceive they need to know to be successful in the real world. Hunter (1976) argued for using an anticipatory set—establishing a context for the learning that would occur. Direct instruction is also problematic if the reason for using the technique by the teacher is an assumption that students cannot learn in any other way. Haberman and Post (1995) describe this as a "pedagogy of poverty." Teachers reduce the teaching act to providing information and asking questions, but fail to embrace a personal philosophy that suggests that all students can learn and that requires instructional methods to be adjusted based on what students are expected to learn.

Direct instruction contains both analytical and relational elements. The degree of emphasis (toward analytical or toward relational) relates primarily to the way in which a teacher structures the lesson. Escalante (see Mathews, 1988), in the classroom scenario that follows, uses a form of direct instruction. However, the way in which his lesson develops requires many relational elements (for example, an emphasis on creativity and memory). Most educators do not believe that direct instruction fosters the development of creativity and, indeed, in most instances the way in which the model is used mitigates such opportunities. Still, the model in and of itself does not preclude many relational elements from being introduced into the lesson. Table 9.4 does not include creativity as a relational skill because in most instances the *teacher's focus* in direct instruction is not on creativity. Table 9.4 includes the categorizations based on the primary focus of a teacher during a direct instruction lesson.

Escalante, now famous for the movie *Stand and Deliver*, is known for making ideas relevant that appear on the surface as esoteric or remote. Escalante enabled his students to apply mathematical skills through their own real-life experiences. Notice in particular how Escalante uses relevancy, repetition, and feedback to teach the concept of absolute value.

"You guys play basketball? You know the give and go?" He bounced an imaginary ball in front of him. He crouched with his back to an imaginary basket, passing the ball to an imaginary guard crossing on his right. He repeated the routine, this time passing to the left.

"The absolute value function is the give and go. I have two possibilities. If this fellow on this side is open, it is going to be from the left." He wrote $x < 0$ on the board. "If it is from the right, then $x > 0$."

"So my little ball is going to be the absolute value. I don't know which ball I'm going to use. This guy has two options, come from the left, he's gonna make it, or come from the right. Every time you see a number between two bars"—he wrote $|x|$ on the board— "you have to, you have to, you have to say, well, all right, it's coming from the left or from the right. You have to break it down into two parts. I can do that."

He wrote:

$$|a| = a \text{ if } a > 0$$
$$|a| = -a \text{ if } a < 0$$

"But you must take into consideration three positions, I call, the three-second violation. Now, I don't really understand what is the three-second violation. Can somebody explain to me?"

"I use the three-second violation my own way. The three-second violation is, this is one ball: $|x| < a$; this is the second ball: $|x| = a$; and the third ball $|x| > a$. That right?"

"Yeah, right."

TABLE 9-4   Relationships of Direct Instruction Model to Cognitive Skills

Model	Relational Skills	Analytical Skills
■ Direct Instruction	■ Global views (especially when used with effective conceptual connectors such as an anticipatory set)	■ Conformity ■ Memory for specific facts ■ Convergent thinking ■ Controlled ■ Linear ■ Deductive ■ Object-oriented

"How many you see?"

"Three."

"You know, you gonna be in bad shape if you don't know how to solve these three things." He thumped the board next to each expression. "When the *absolute value* is greater than *a*, when the *absolute value* is equal to it, when the *absolute value* is less than *a*. You have to *know* this three-second violation. Look."

He wrote, with sweeping gestures, the meaning of each expression in turn:

$$-a < x < a \qquad x = a \qquad x < --- \text{ or } x > a$$
$$x = -a$$

"As soon as you see that, absolute value of *x* is more than *a*, be able to say, immediately, minus *a* is more than *x*, or *x* is more than *a*."

He assigned homework to underscore the point. Absolute value would be vital to understanding calculus. They had to get it down now. He had glossed over some mathematical niceties, but it was important first to help his audience find the theater before he directed them to their seats (Mathews, 1988, pp. 118–120).

Prevalent Issues in Diverse Classrooms

The direct instruction model is an instructional model that helps students acquire academic skills through practice and drill. The model uses a step-by-step sequence of teacher phases to help students recall and recognize what teachers deem important for students to learn. The model has elicited controversial criticisms from some educational circles. The following questions help address some of these concerns:

Q: *Is it possible to use direct instruction when trying to move students toward analysis or synthesis objectives?*

A: No. One of the reasons so many educators have frustration with direct instruction (in fact, many denigrate the technique) is that it is used inappropriately. A teacher should use direct instruction to teach particular skills or a sequence of actions, not to teach the type of critical thinking required of students through analysis and synthesis activities. One of the recurring themes of this book is that teachers need to know *how* and *when* to use different instructional models to achieve particular purposes. Borich (1988) writes:

> Various expressions have been used by different learning theorists to describe these two types of learning [learning to recognize patterns versus learning to carry out a sequence of action], but facts, rules and action sequences are most commonly taught using instructional strategies that emphasize knowledge acquisition, and concepts, patterns, and abstractions are most commonly taught using instructional strategies that emphasize inquiry or problem solving (p. 143).

Elementary school teachers may well find that they use direct instruction more than teachers at the more advanced grade levels. Especially in the primary grades, teachers are attempting to teach a large number of facts and skills—they are establishing the groundwork for later learning that students will experience. Direct instruction is not inherently good or bad, and teacher-centered instruction is not necessarily positive or negative. If used properly and purposefully (for teaching of basic skills), direct instruction can have a positive and powerful impact on student growth and development.

Q: *What happens when some students refuse to respond or are afraid to respond to the myriad questions asked by the teacher during guided practice?*

A: There are several ways in which feedback from students can be obtained by the teacher. Much of the original direct instruction work was with young children (Grades K–3) who were from lower-income families. The original direct instruction processes (known as the Follow Through program) required choral (collective) responses from the students. That is, the teacher would present a small bit of information, the children would repeat the information, and then the teacher would ask a question focused on that piece of information that required the students to respond as a group (similar to elements of the mnemonic model). The teacher would observe and listen carefully to determine who was and who was not responding to the teacher-directed question.

Recall that Mr. Carthridge required his students to use slates on which to record their answers and show their work. The slates enable the teacher to look around the room and do a quick assessment of whether each student really understands the work.

With older students, some teachers use more peer teaching. With peer teaching the teacher creates pairs and assigns all students as "1s" or "2s." The teacher then teaches the information and when finished asks the "1s" to teach the "2s" the information the teacher just taught the whole class. The teacher listens to the paired explanations, and reteaches material that the students do not fully understand. Once the reteaching is completed, the teacher then asks the "2s" to teach the "1s."

A third strategy that was used by one high school teacher reflects the teacher's need for sensitivity in order to save face for students who do not understand material but who need to know the information being taught to the class. This particular urban high school mathematics teacher asked the students to signal when they were not understanding a step in a mathematical equation by quickly blinking their eyes twice. This enabled a student to say to the teacher, "I don't understand," without having to either utter the words or be called upon and fail to respond. The teacher reported that the students were extremely good at using the nonverbal device to communicate information to the teacher.

Regardless of what technique a teacher uses, it is imperative that the teacher understand that direct instruction will not work unless information is taught sequentially, in a step-by-step manner, and with vigilant analysis of the students' comprehension of the material. Teachers in the early grades may use "choral" guided practice, while teachers in high school may call on volunteers/nonvolunteers or use peer teaching. All teachers who use this instructional model must constantly assess whether students understand what is being taught.

ⓔVALUATION CRITERIA

The step-by-step nature of the direct instruction model makes it one of the easier models to assess. Because the information presented is sequenced in such a linear, defined way, observers of direct instruction lessons can typically see the lesson more clearly unfold. Two cautionary notes, though, are needed. First, not every direct instruction lesson requires that every step of the process be followed. Good teachers make decisions about when and how to use an instructional model. Of paramount importance is whether students are learning the material. Of secondary importance is whether the model steps are followed with legalistic precision. Second, direct instruction does not need to be boring. Good demonstrations that excite the students can still be used during phase II of the model to ensure that students understand the content material. It is true that direct instruction is highly structured. It is not true that direct instruction requires teachers to boringly present discrete bits of information in an unenthusiastic manner.

Phase I: Review

1. Does the teacher review ideas
from the previous day's lesson?   ○ Yes   ○ No

2. Does the teacher reteach content
material that students had difficulty understanding?   ○ Yes   ○ No

Phase II: Presenting New Material

1. Does the teacher clearly state
the objectives for the lesson?   ○ Yes   ○ No

2. Does the teacher teach the skill
or action sequence in a step-by-step fashion?   ○ Yes   ○ No

Phase III: Guided Practice

1. Does the teacher frequently ask
questions to assess student
understanding?   ○ Yes   ○ No

2. Does the teacher call on both
    volunteers and nonvolunteers?   ○ Yes   ○ No
3. Do all students have an opportu-
    nity to respond to the teacher's
    questions?   ○ Yes   ○ No
4. Are students successfully
    responding to most of the
    teacher's questions (at approxi-
    mately an 80 percent rate of
    success)?   ○ Yes   ○ No
5. Does the teacher continue to
    practice the skill until student
    understanding appears firm?   ○ Yes   ○ No

Phase IV: Feedback and Correctives

1. Does the teacher provide specific
    feedback to students when their
    responses are hesitant?   ○ Yes   ○ No
2. Does the teacher reteach mate-
    rial when student responses are
    incorrect?   ○ Yes   ○ No

Phase V: Independent Practice

1. Does the teacher provide an
    appropriate number of problems
    for independent practice?   ○ Yes   ○ No
2. Are students assigned homework
    that is meaningful and appropri-
    ate?   ○ Yes   ○ No
3. Do students appear to know how
    to do the homework success-
    fully?   ○ Yes   ○ No

SAMPLE LESSONS

Two sample lessons are now provided to illustrate the direct instruction model.
In the case study, the teacher seeks to have junior high school students understand the difference between common and proper nouns. As you read the case
study, identify for yourself when the teacher moves from one phase to the next
in her lesson. The second example is a lesson plan on different types of triangles. The first lesson focuses on content concepts and is less skill oriented; the

second lesson has more skill elements to it—you may want to try teaching this lesson to a group of students to practice your understanding of the direct instruction model.

CASE **S**TUDY

Susan Sparks begins her 4th period English class with a brief discussion concerning nouns. The students have already learned that a noun is a person, place, or thing. In today's lesson, Susan wants the 7th graders to describe the difference between common and proper nouns.

"The objective for today's lesson," begins Ms. Sparks, "is to be able to define and identify common and proper nouns. I know some of you have a general idea of the differences, but by the end of our class session today, I want to make certain that each of you can specifically state what a common and proper noun is. John, why don't you help get us started by identifying the nouns in this sentence." (Ms. Sparks points at the following sentence, which she has on the board. "The wealthy brothers were preparing the plantation for the fall harvest when Abraham Lincoln signed the Emancipation Proclamation.")

John responds by listing all the nouns: "I think the nouns are *brothers, plantation, harvest, Abraham Lincoln*, and *Emancipation Proclamation*."

"Excellent, John. Now what I want us to be able to do is identify the difference between the common nouns and the proper nouns that John has listed. Does anyone know which ones are common and which ones are proper?" Several students offer ideas. Some guess that the capital letters are important in deciding which terms are proper.

"You have some good ideas, class. Now, let's make certain we all understand. A common noun is the general name for a person, place, or thing. So *brothers, plantation*, and *harvest* would be, as some of you suggested, common nouns. A proper noun is the name of a particular person, place or thing. *Abraham Lincoln* is a particular or specific person. The *Emancipation Proclamation* is a particular and very important document."

"I now want to give you some examples of each of these nouns." (Ms. Sparks writes *common noun* and *proper noun* on the board.) "I will provide you with two examples for each, and then I'll ask you to label the rest." Ms. Sparks begins with the following information:

Common Nouns	Proper Nouns
cars	Buick
cities	New York

"Class, as you can see, *cars* and *cities* are general terms for things and places. But *Buick* and *New York* represent a particular thing and a particular place. As I provide you with additional examples, you tell me where to place the terms. All right, where would I place *landmark*? Josiah?"

"It's a common noun."

"Right!"

"And, how about *musician*? Ophelia?"

"Common noun."

"Yes."

"What about Martin Luther King? Sarina?"

"Proper noun."

"Great!"

"And, Marcus, what about this object (teacher holds up a baseball)?"

"*Baseball* is a proper noun."

"Why do you think so?"

"Because it's a particular kind of ball."

"True. But *baseball* is a name for a group of objects. There are lots of baseballs. Some have specific names such as *Rawlings* or *Spaulding*, but when you refer to *ball* as part of a group it is a common noun. So in this case *baseball* is a common noun."

The class continues until the chart contains the following examples:

Common Nouns	Proper Nouns
cars	Buick
cities	New York
landmark	Statue of Liberty
musician	Michael Jackson
building	Pentagon
street	Main Street
picture	Mona Lisa
pencil	Bic
railroad	Amtrak
baseball	Spaulding

The students accurately label all the terms. Ms. Sparks calls on several nonvolunteers. She also matches the examples so that the distinctions are even clearer between common and proper nouns. That is, she matches *cars*, a common noun, with *Buick* (a specific car), a proper noun, *cities* with *New York*, and so on. (In this regard the lesson actually has the "feel" of a concept attainment lesson—see Chapter 4.)

"Class, I now want you to identify with a partner all the proper and common nouns in the following three sentences. Put a line under each common noun and two lines under each proper noun."

The students work in pairs and identify all the appropriate terms. Ms. Sparks checks the students' work as she moves around the room.

"Now, I want you to complete the next three sentences on your own and then show your work to your partner." This time the students work independently, and after completing the three sentences they show their answers to their partners. Ms. Sparks moves around the room and observes the students as they work. She helps a couple of students, but almost everyone seems to understand.

"You can now get your grammar books out and turn to page 73. Do the 10 sentences listed there. Put one line under the common noun and two lines under the proper noun. Please write out the sentences. You can begin." ∎

Follow-up questions

1. Describe three other ways this teacher could have introduced the concept of common nouns and proper nouns to the students in the class.

2. Identify other concepts or skills that you might teach that would be appropriate for use with direct instruction.

3. Identify the strategies a teacher can use to deal with an incorrect student response. Which one does Ms. Sparks use? How else might she have responded?

The above lesson focuses on disciplinary content in English—parts of speech. Table 9.5 provides additional information, based on extensive research (see Rosenshine, 1986), that should prove useful to readers who are teaching content concepts rather than skills.

TABLE 9-5   Suggestions for Enhancing Student Achievement of Content Material

- *State the purposes of the lesson.*
- *Provide relevant background knowledge for the lesson.*
- *Signal transitions between sections of the lesson.*
- *Use questions to maintain student attention.*
- *Make explicit the internal structure of the content material to be learned.*
- *Identify the most important points.*
- *Use humor to maintain student attention.*
- *Summarize material within the lecture or presentation.*
- *Give or ask for examples to illustrate major concepts.*
- *Avoid vague terms such as "kinda" or "and so forth and so on."*

Adapted from B. Rosenshine. 1986. "Unsolved Issues in Teaching Content: A Critique of a Lesson on Federalist Paper No. 10." *Teaching and Teacher Education* 2(4): 307.

The teacher who presented the following lesson was interested in teaching students how to name the three types of triangles based on sides; they already know how to name triangles based on angles (for example, obtuse, right). Look at the objectives and then develop a direct instruction lesson plan for the concepts.

Concepts: Figure, Polygon, Triangle, Isosceles, Scalene, Equilateral

Objectives:
1. Students will be able to define the three types of triangles.
2. Students will be able to identify and to create isosceles, scalene, and equilateral triangles.

Definitions: Scalene: A triangle that has no sides of the same length.

Isosceles: A triangle that has two sides of equal length.

Equilateral: A triangle with all equal sides.

Activity: For phases II and III, three different ways will be used to present the concepts to students. For example, the teacher might begin by presenting the following schematic (or concept family tree) to the students and then the teacher will define each type and provide three examples.

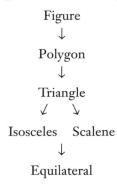

Closure: Students will be asked to draw their own examples with a partner.

Follow-up questions

1. What anticipatory set might a teacher use to prepare students for a lesson on the different types of triangles?

2. Should a teacher use nonexamples of the different types of triangles in order to teach the concept during the presenting new material phase? In other words, for equilateral triangles, should the teacher provide four different equilateral triangles: one with 4" sides, one with 5" sides, one with 6" sides,

and one with 7" sides? Or should the teacher create three positive examples and then ask whether the fourth example (a triangle with two sides of 7" and one of 5") fits the definition? Think of different ways to present the content.

❶ LESSON PREPARATION

Direct instruction is a very important model for all teachers to know and use. If used properly, the technique can help students learn content material efficiently and effectively. If overused, it diminishes the natural curiosity of students to explore ideas. In preparing lessons that require direct instruction strategies, teachers could consult the following resources:

Suggested readings

Gage, N. L., and M. C. Needels. 1989. "Process-Product Research on Teaching: A Review of Criticisms." *Elementary School Journal* 89(3): 253–300.

Hunter, M. 1976. *Prescription for Improved Instruction.* El Segundo, CA: TIP.

———. 1986. "Comments on the Napa County, California, Follow Through Project." *Elementary School Journal* 87(2): 173–179.

Rosenshine, B. 1983. "Teaching Functions in Instructional Programs." *Elementary School Journal* 83(4): 335–352.

Suggested videotapes

Episode #7, "Eighth Grade Social Studies." Alexandria, VA: Association for Supervision and Curriculum Development.

Episode #30, "Tenth–Twelfth Grade Mathematics." Alexandria, VA: Association for Supervision and Curriculum Development.

ABC News. *20/20.* "Philosophy of Teaching." New York, New York.

Suggested lesson development

Once teachers understand the basic elements of the model, they need to carefully design a direct instruction lesson for the students they teach. The steps to follow include:

1. Identify the specific skill or concept that will be taught.
2. Determine the way in which the objective for the lesson will be shared with students (for example, written on the board or verbally presented).
3. Identify the examples that will be used during the presenting new material phase to help students learn the skill or concept.
4. Determine *two* different ways to check for understanding.
5. Identify the problems that will be given to students for independent practice.

ⓈUMMARY

The direct instruction model is predicated on the fundamental assumption that teachers are responsible for enabling student learning, that all students are capable of learning what teachers present, and that student success requires thoughtful, explicit teacher practice. These assumptions, based on research, are neither new nor revelatory. The now-famous Project Follow Through studies established the initial research base for the technique, and subsequent research by a variety of scholars has confirmed the efficacy of the direct instruction model.

Direct instruction is not a flashy, innovative strategy, but it is effective, especially when used appropriately in teaching skills or discrete concepts. Many educators disdain the model because they view it as simplistic and reductionistic; it does not problematize disciplinary concepts or cause students to consider why something exists as it does. Those educators argue that it places the students in a role that is too passive and intellectually disengaging. Nothing can be further from the truth. Direct instruction is a powerful teaching strategy when used appropriately. Its disfavor has occurred largely because it has been either misused or overused. Some teachers have perceived that direct instruction means boring instruction. The teaching phase of presenting new material, however, enables teachers to be creative (that is, to use demonstrations). Direct instruction becomes boring when teachers present information in the same way every time they teach—when teacher talk is considered synonymous with student learning. Direct instruction requires that teachers be active in the classroom. As Brophy (1982) argued over a decade ago, "Effective teachers of inner city students...actively teach their students in large and small groups—demonstrating skills, explaining concepts, conducting participatory and practice activities, and reviewing when necessary" (p. 528). Direct instruction is neither a simple nor an easy model to implement; it is a demanding one, largely because it requires teachers to clearly think through how to teach an idea, skill, or fact and then to thoughtfully assess whether students learned what was just taught.

ⓇEFERENCES

Ausubel, D. P. 1960. "The Use of Advance Organizers in the Learning and Retention of Meaningful Verbal Material." *Journal of Educational Psychology* 17(3): 400–404.

Becker, W. C. 1977. "Teaching Reading and Language to the Disadvantaged—What We Have Learned from Field Research." *Harvard Educational Review* 47: 518–543.

Bereiter, C., and S. Engelmann. 1966. *Teaching Disadvantaged Children in the Preschool.* Englewood Cliffs, NJ: Prentice-Hall.

Borich, G. 1988. *Effective Teaching Methods.* Columbus, OH: Merrill.

Brophy, J. 1982. "Successful Teaching Strategies for the Inner-City Child." *Phi Delta Kappan* 63: 527–530.

England, D. A., and J. K. Flatley. 1985. *Homework—and Why.* Bloomington, IN: Phi Delta Kappa.

Finkelstein, B. 1989. *Governing the Young.* New York: Falmer Press.

Gage, N. L., and M. C. Needels. 1989. "Process-Product Research on Teaching: A Review of Criticisms." *Elementary School Journal* 89(3): 253–300.

Gagne, R. M. 1977. *The Conditions of Learning* (3d ed.). New York: Holt, Rinehart and Winston.

Haberman, M., and L. Post. 1995. "Multicultural Teaching in the Real World." Pp. 337–353 in A. C. Ornstein (ed.), *Teaching: Theory and Practice*. Boston: Allyn & Bacon.

Hunter, M. 1976. *Prescription for Improved Instruction*. El Segundo, CA: TIP.

———. 1986. "Comments on the Napa County, California, Follow Through Project." *Elementary School Journal* 87(2): 173–179.

Joyce, B., and M. Weil. 1992. *Models of Teaching* (4th ed.). Boston: Allyn & Bacon.

Losey, K. M. 1995. "Mexican American Students and Classroom Interaction: An Overview and Critique." *American Educational Research Journal* 65(3): 283–318.

Mathews, J. 1988. *Escalante*. New York: Holt.

Porter, A. C. 1986. "From Research on Teaching to Staff Development: A Difficult Step." *Elementary School Journal* 87(2): 159–164.

Robbins, P. 1986. "The Napa-Vacaville Follow-Through Project: Qualitative Outcomes, Related Procedures, and Implications for Practice." *Elementary School Journal* 87(2): 139–158.

Rosenshine, B. 1983. "Teaching Functions in Instructional Programs." *Elementary School Journal* 83(4): 335–352.

———. 1986. "Unsolved Issues in Teaching Content: A Critique of a Lesson on Federalist Paper No. 10." *Teaching and Teacher Education* 2(4): 301–308.

———. 1987. "Explicit Teaching." Pp. 75–92 in D. C. Berliner and B. Rosenshine (eds.), *Talks to Teachers*. New York: Random House.

Rothman, R. 1995. *Measuring Up*. San Francisco: Jossey-Bass.

Stallings, J., and P. Kaskowitz. 1974. *Follow Through Classroom Observation Evaluation, 1972–73*. Menlo Park, CA: Stanford Research Institute.

Stallings, J., and E. M. Krasavage. 1986. "Program Implementation and Student Achievement in a Four-Year Madeline Hunter Follow-Through Project." *Elementary School Journal* 87(2): 117–138.

Stevenson, H. W., and J. W. Stigler. 1992. *The Learning Gap*. New York: Summit.

Trueba, H. J., L. Jacobs, and E. Kirton. 1990. *Cultural Conflict and Adaptation: The Case of Hmong Children in American Society*. New York: Falmer Press.

American students understand competition. Indeed, many young people are so thoroughly schooled in competition that they believe that helping those around them is inappropriate. Students feel a sense of responsibility for themselves, not for others. School policies and practices consistently reinforce the competitive ethos. High schools rank order students from the top (valedictorian) to the bottom—someone has the distinction of graduating last in the class. Within classrooms, the hand-raising behavior of students reinforces this competitive ethos. Anyone who doubts this should observe what happens when young people are asked a factual question and a student provides the wrong answer—a myriad of other students raise their hands with the correct answer.

Cooperative learning and oral discussion are two strategies that focus on enabling students to connect with one another. These strategies engender a group consciousness and diminish, as a consequence, self-consciousness. Students do not gain an appreciation for the group by chance; they develop such consciousness through experience. And it is the teacher's responsibility to structure such experiences for youngsters.

The two instructional strategies in this unit enable teachers to achieve both cognitive and affective outcomes. Students who learn to work with others not only learn more but also understand more about themselves in relation to others. Developing positive self-esteem, deriving satisfaction from learning, reducing prejudice and bias, and enhancing interpersonal skills are best achieved in learning situations where students work together (and talk together) to achieve a common goal. ■

Models that Foster Relating Skills

• *Cooperative Learning*

At the completion of this chapter, the reader will be able to:

1. *Describe the theoretical basis of the cooperative learning model.*
2. *Identify the essential characteristics of cooperative learning.*
3. *Identify several different types of cooperative learning strategies that can be used for team building, content mastery, and concept development.*
4. *Identify the strengths and weaknesses of the model.*
5. *Describe ways in which cooperative learning enhances the learning opportunities for culturally diverse populations.*
6. *Create a cooperative learning lesson for personal use in the classroom.*

❶NTRODUCTION

In many American classrooms, the primary learner is the teacher. The teacher decides what content to teach (usually after consulting a district course of study); the teacher determines how to teach the material; and the teacher even creates a conceptual structure for students to follow in learning the material (that is, something quite similar to the discussion on the planning process found in Chapter 3). In essence, the intellectual burden appears to be on the shoulders of the teacher more than it is on students. Some teachers are quite satisfied with this circumstance. They see no reason to instigate change. Others, however, advocate a new direction—one that places more intellectual burden on the student. Roy Smith (1987), a junior high school English teacher, embraces cooperative learning because "it places the responsibility for learning where it belongs: on the students" (p. 663).

Many teachers experience real discomfort when they do not have complete control over how students process content. Such teachers believe that they have somehow lost control of the teaching–learning process. The irony is that even within the most didactic and structured pedagogical circumstances, the teacher really does not have total control. Teachers cannot make students learn; they cannot force students to assimilate ideas. Teachers experience a false sense of control over what is occurring in the classroom. In essence, they create the environment for learning, but they cannot force students to learn.

> *The problem with the competitive nature of grading is that it creates a situation in which students hope their classmates will fail.*
>
> ROBERT SLAVIN

The question becomes, then: Under what pedagogical conditions do students learn best? The answer is both simple and complex: They learn best when they have a positive attitude (toward themselves and their classmates) and when they enjoy what they are learning and how they are learning it! These conditions for learning are not easily met, but increasingly one strategy stands out as an effective vehicle for enabling students to experience enhanced achievement and an improved attitude toward learning. That strategy is cooperative learning! As the reader will recall from the first few chapters of this book, culturally diverse youngsters have demonstrated affective tendencies toward building and maintaining relationships with others. These interactional activities of collaboration and communication by diverse learners are strengths that schools need to capitalize upon in developing the skills of all youngsters. As the following example illustrates, cooperative learning not only focuses on the content knowledge that students need to learn, but also on the social interactions between and among students as they begin to explore ideas together.

CASE STUDY

The students in Ms. Bernardo's 7th grade class have just begun to discuss geologic time. A couple of students share that they watched *Jurassic Park*, and Ms. Bernardo spends a few moments talking about the types of animals the students recalled seeing in the movie—Velociraptors, Tyrannosaurus Rex, and Apatosaurus.

"I'm pleased several of you watched *Jurassic Park*. It's a fun movie, though some of it was a bit too violent for my personal taste."

"No, it wasn't," responds Theo. "I loved how those Velociraptors chased after the kids. Those dinosaurs were mean!"

"Well, that's quite true—they were mean! They were, in fact, carnivores. Some believe they were among the fastest and meanest of the meat-eating predators that existed in that time period. But recall that *Jurassic Park* occurred in the present. The animals were just depicted from the past. What I want you to understand is when, in terms of geologic time, the dinosaurs existed in relation to the present. Scientists believe that the earth may be as much as 4.6 billion years old, even though rocks have only been dated to 3.9 billion years. Yesterday I shared with you that there were four major time divisions in geologic time: Precambrian, Paleozoic, Mesozoic, and Cenozoic. I also indicated that I want you to memorize the order of those divisions, and you used the mnemonic device of Please (Precambrian) pay (Paleozoic) me (Mesozoic) cash (Cenozoic). I hope the device helps.

"Today we are going to look at what animals appeared during the time periods that make up the major geologic time divisions. On the sheet I have provided for you, you will see that I have a brief description of each time period [see Figure 10.1]. What I am going to do today is to use our numbered heads together strategy to enable you to see if you can correctly place each animal in the right time period based on the limited descriptive information I have provided. By the end of the class, I want you to be able to identify when

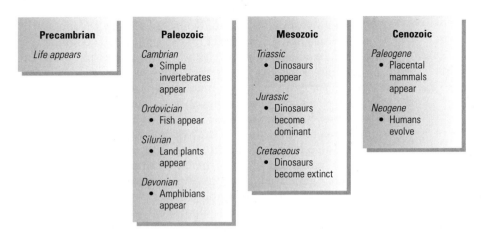

| Precambrian | Paleozoic | Mesozoic | Cenozoic |

Precambrian

Life appears

Paleozoic

Cambrian
- Simple invertebrates appear

Ordovician
- Fish appear

Silurian
- Land plants appear

Devonian
- Amphibians appear

Mesozoic

Triassic
- Dinosaurs appear

Jurassic
- Dinosaurs become dominant

Cretaceous
- Dinosaurs become extinct

Cenozoic

Paleogene
- Placental mammals appear

Neogene
- Humans evolve

FIGURE 10-1 Geologic Time Descriptor Sheet (Selected Time Periods)

various life forms appeared and to describe how the complexity of life became more noticeable as geologic time progressed. Let's start by having you get into groups of three. Once you're in your group, number off with 1, 2, 3."

Ms. Bernardo places the students in groups with one high, one middle, and one low-ability science student. She predetermined the groupings based on the students' previous test scores in science. The students then get into their groups, number off (1, 2, 3), and prepare for Ms. Bernardo's first example.

"Class, my first example is a rather famous one [she shows the students a picture of a trilobite]. It's the trilobite, the state fossil of Ohio. Discuss among yourselves the time period in which you would place the trilobite."

The students look at the example and begin discussing its characteristics. They share ideas for several minutes, then Ms. Bernardo asks the number 2s in the class to raise their hands. All the 2s put their hands up, and Ms. Bernardo calls on Sonya (a low-ability student).

"Sonya, where would you place the trilobite and why?"

"I would place it in the Precambrian period. Our group thought that these types of animals were common then."

"Good," responds Ms. Bernardo. "Does anyone in that group want to add anything? Kareem [a high-ability student in the same group]?"

"We talked about the fact that the trilobite was an invertebrate and that it lived when marine life was really abundant. I also read stuff about the trilobite, and I know it goes in that time period."

"Excellent! Well, does anyone want to disagree with Sonya's group classification? Have any of you read something different from what Kareem shared?" No students respond.

"You're right, Sonya. It goes in the Precambrian period. Let's look at another animal, the Brontosaurus." Once again an example is shown to the students. This time the excitement is palpable. The students share a few ideas and then look at the teacher, waiting for her to call on someone.

"OK. It looks like you think you know this one. All 3s need to raise their hands." All the 3s raise their hands, and Ms. Bernardo calls on Javier (an average-ability science student).

Javier responds, "That's easy. The Jurassic."

"Why are you so certain, Javier?"

"Because the dinosaurs lived during the Jurassic."

"Does everyone agree? Ana?"

"Javier's right about the Jurassic, but they also lived in the Cretaceous period. They became extinct during the Cretaceous. They were abundant during the Jurassic." The students then argue over when the dinosaurs first appeared. The chart says Triassic, but some students disagree.

The class continues to identify classifications, with the groups sharing with one another their ideas, and then responding to teacher questions when Ms. Bernardo asks for a "numbered head" response.

Ms. Bernardo is using one type of cooperative learning approach (numbered heads together) to facilitate enhanced student academic and social achievement. This strategy is one of several relatively simple cooperative learning strategies that teachers can use to foster enhanced student learning and interpersonal cooperation. ■

❶HEORETICAL PERSPECTIVE

Competitive people enjoy competitive situations only when they believe they can *win*. Those persons who love to play "Trivial Pursuit," because they know a lot of trivia, may be the same individuals who do not want to play charades because they are not good at acting out famous phrases, movies, or song titles.

Schools, as presently structured, are competitive places! Students are constantly ranked and compared. They are grouped, sorted, and classified each day, and by the end of every school year all youngsters have a pretty good sense of where they belong. In the early grades, reading achievement appears to be the sorting mechanism. Students who read well have high status; those who read poorly have low status. Cohen (1986) poignantly describes this reality when she observes:

> Rank in reading ability is evidently public knowledge in many elementary classrooms. In most classrooms…the students were able to rank each other on reading ability with a high level of agreement. Furthermore, the teacher's ranking was in agreement with the students' ranking. This means that if you are [a] poor reader, it is not only you who expect to do poorly— all your classmates expect you to do poorly as well! (p. 26)

The move toward heterogeneous grouping has mitigated the effects of some of what Cohen noted; but as students mature, other school practices emerge that replace reading as the salient sorting device. One of those is described by Kagan (1989/1990) as the Whole-Class-Question-Answer:

In this arrangement students vie for the teacher's attention and praise, creating negative interdependence among them. That is, when the teacher calls on one student, the others lose their chance to answer: a failure by one student to give a correct response increases the chances for other students to receive attention and praise. Thus, students are set against each other, creating poor social relations and peer norms against achievement (pp. 12–13).

In essence, every time a teacher organizes a classroom to achieve some learning goal, students are engaged in more than one type of learning. They learn not only content, but also important information about themselves in relationship to their peers. Certainly some such information can be positive, especially when a student is reasonably secure vis-à-vis varied intellectual abilities. But it is negative when students are uncertain about themselves (and most are!), because it diminishes the students' sense of what they can be.

Johnson and Johnson (1987) would describe the Whole-Class-Question-Answer Strategy as an example of a competitive goal structure. A *goal structure*, simply defined, is how the teacher has students work together to achieve a learning goal. According to the Johnsons, three different types of goal structures exist in classrooms: competitive, cooperative, and individualistic. When students work against one another to achieve a learning goal (Whole-Class-Question-Answer), they are functioning within a *competitive goal structure*. When they work on their own (that is, their peers' performances are of no importance), the goal structure is *individualistic*. And, when they work together to achieve a learning goal, the lesson structure is *cooperative*.

It is important to note that not all lessons need to follow a cooperative structure. There are, indeed, times when competitive and individual goal structures can be used to achieve specific cognitive outcomes (see Table 10.1). In America's classrooms of the past, the teaching strategy of choice has been essentially competitive. For those students who have high mathematical and linguistic abilities (the two skill areas most emphasized in schools), or those students who come from cultural backgrounds that reward competitive abilities, the school's historical tendencies have been unduly advantageous. Many other students, however, have been disadvantaged by this competitive ethos. For these students (for example, Native American students), to "beat" a friend is the functional equivalent of an act of cultural sabotage!

The pedagogical goal for the teacher should be to achieve an understanding of when and how to use the different goal structures in ways that advantage all students. The focus of this chapter is on cooperative learning, but for those interested in how to utilize competitive and individual goal structures appropriately, we suggest the Johnsons' text *Learning Together and Alone* (second edition).

As Table 10.2 suggests, cooperative learning is useful when 1) the teacher has a defined learning goal that is perceived to be important, 2) the nature of the task is both conceptual and complex (two heads generally do a better job of solving problems), and 3) students can work together in ways that enable all students to be successful—not just the top students. More specifically, there are five components to successful cooperative learning. Using the mnemonic PIGSS, these components can be readily recalled as: positive interdependence (students need

TABLE 10-1 Goal Structures and Cognitive Outcomes

Cognitive Outcome	Cooperative	Competitive	Individualistic
Mastery of factual information			x
Retention, application, and transfer of factual information, concepts, and principles	x		
Mastery of concepts and principles	x		
Verbal abilities	x		
Problem-solving ability and success	x		
Cooperative skills	x		
Creative ability, divergent and risk-taking thinking, productive controversy	x		
Awareness and utilization of one's capabilities	x		
Perspective-(role-)taking abilities	x		
Speed and quantity of work on simple drill activities		x	
Competitive skills		x	
Individualistic skills			x
Simple mechanical skills			x

Source: D. W. Johnson and R. J. Johnson. 1975. *Learning Together and Alone.* Englewood Cliffs, NJ: Prentice-Hall, p. 32.

to be able to work together); individual accountability (each student is still assessed on what he or she knows); group processes (a structure exists for how students will work together); social skills (particular social skills are emphasized during the group work); and specific tasks (students work together to achieve a particular goal).

These five components clearly suggest that cooperative learning and group work are not synonymous. Teachers have used groups in classroom situations since the inception of the common school. What is different about cooperative learning is PIGSS. The teacher not only has students work together, but also has them in a structured situation working to achieve a common goal through the use of selected social skills.

For cooperative learning to work properly, the teacher needs to accomplish the following:

1. Specify appropriate instructional objectives.
2. Determine the appropriate group size.

TABLE 10-2 Appropriate Cooperative Learning

Interdependence	Positive
Type of Instructional Activity	*Any instructional activity. The more conceptual and complex the task, the greater the superiority of cooperative over competitive or individualistic learning.*
Perception of Goal Importance	*Goal is perceived to be important.*
Teacher–Student Interaction	*Teacher monitors and intervenes in learning groups to teach collaborative skills.*
Student–Materials Interaction	*Materials are arranged according to purpose of lesson.*
Student–Student Interaction	*Prolonged and intense interaction among students, helping and sharing, oral rehearsal of material being studied, peer tutoring, and general support and encouragement.*
Student Expectations	*Group to be successful. All members to contribute to success. Positive interaction among group members. All members master the assigned material.*
Room Arrangement	*Small groups.*
Evaluation Procedures	*Criteria-referenced.*

Source: D. W. Johnson and R. T. Johnson. 1987. *Learning Together and Alone* (2d ed.). Englewood Cliffs, NJ: Prentice-Hall, p. 44.

3. Assign students to groups so that groups are heterogeneously configured. Students, in time, need to be assigned specific roles within the groups so that they know how to work with their peers.

4. Arrange the room (and the groups) to facilitate group work.

Students need to work toward some defined group goal, and their success in achieving that goal must be contingent on all other group members learning the material. Cooperative learning is not one person solving the puzzle while the others watch. Cooperative learning requires that all students have input and that all students participate. As Slavin (1990) notes: "Simply putting students into mixed ability groups and encouraging them to work together are not enough to produce learning gains: students must have a reason to take one another's achievement seriously, to provide one another with elaborated explanations that are critical to the achievement effects of cooperative learning" (p. 138).

The various cooperative learning strategies outlined later in this chapter are examples of strategies that fulfill the conditions for appropriate cooperative learning. Some of the strategies are relatively simple to implement; others require more practice and time. No one strategy is the correct one, and no single strategy should be used exclusively. As teachers use the different strategies, though, the students should begin to see that the teacher is not the only intellectual resource in the classroom. Slavin (1990) reinforces this point with his observation: "Clearly, a cooperative school would have cooperative learning methods in use in most classrooms.... Students and teachers should feel that the idea that students can help one another learn is not just applied on occasion, but is a fundamental principle of classroom organization" (p. 142).

COOPERATIVE LEARNING: TEACHING PHASES

Because there are so many different types of cooperative learning strategies, it is impossible to outline precisely the specific phases for teachers to follow. In this section, therefore, we will identify some basic phases for teachers to follow in organizing a cooperative learning lesson. In the next section, we will describe different types of cooperative learning strategies that teachers can use. The format for this section is taken from the Association for Supervision and Curriculum Development (1990) Cooperative Learning Series, so readers are encouraged to access the ASCD tapes and manual activities that accompany that series if they desire more detail on the phases.

Phase I: Determine the lesson to be taught

The first phase is to identify whether the lesson to be taught matches the cooperative learning instructional model. If the teacher wants students to increase their speed in solving simple algorithms, cooperative learning would not be the best approach. If, on the other hand, the teacher is interested in enabling students to solve a puzzle or better comprehend academic content, then cooperative learning would be efficacious. In essence, the first task of teachers is to identify what they plan to teach (see Chapter 3, "Instructional Models and the Planning Process") and to determine whether students working in groups represent the best instructional approach to achieving the learning goal.

Phase II: Determine the appropriate organizational structure

As the reader will recognize in the next section of this chapter, there are a myriad of instructional variations that can be used to facilitate cooperative (positive) interactions between and among students. In essence, the major decisions relate to group size, group assignment, room arrangement, materials, and roles. Table 10.3 outlines the basic decisions associated with each of the steps. For cooperative learning to work, teachers need to identify the specific objectives they hope to achieve, and students need to know precisely what is expected of them once they start working with their peers. Students need to be in heterogeneous groups that include students of different ability levels in the content area being assigned (that is, math cooperative learning groups may be configured differently from reading cooperative learning groups). The reason for this is quite simple: Different students demonstrate different intellectual strengths depending on what topic is being investigated. The heterogeneous groups allow students to learn from peers. Altering the groups depending on the content area (math vs. reading) enables students to understand that not all students are good at all subjects.

TABLE 10-3	Decision-Making Information Sheet

Group Size	*When making decisions about group size, the teacher should consider five variables:* ■ *students' academic and social skills* ■ *amount of time students have to work* ■ *nature of the task* ■ *opportunity for each student to talk and exchange ideas* ■ *quantity of material to be covered*
Group Assignment	*When deciding how to assign students to groups, the teacher should consider these points:* ■ *Each student has different strengths and weaknesses.* ■ *Heterogeneous groups are most powerful.* ■ *Groups can be heterogeneous on several different variables: ability, sex, ethnic background, perspective, and language.* ■ *The teacher is responsible for making group assignments and so must consider all these points. Left to form their own groups, students choose to work with friends, and the resulting homogeneous groups limit students' learning experience.*
Room Arrangement	*When arranging the classroom, provide an environment that supports and encourages cooperation:* ■ *Students in groups need to be close to one another to share materials and exchange ideas quietly.* ■ *To decrease intergroup distractions, allow space between groups; you can then easily circulate among them.*
Materials	*The distribution of materials can reinforce the message of positive interdependence:* ■ *With one set of materials per group, students must share and interact frequently.* ■ *Providing each student with a different part of the materials or information ("jigsawing") requires students to learn specific portions of the lesson content and to reinforce what they have learned with their peers.* ■ *One set of materials per student allows each to have a copy to review and study.*
Roles	*Role assignments reinforce the message of positive interdependence because success depends on each group member performing his or her role. Also, role assignments can further emphasize the need to use the social skill(s) included in the lesson.* ■ *The roles must be taught and clearly understood by the students.* ■ *To give each student a chance to perform different functions, rotate the role assignments.* ■ *Examples of roles that support social skills are encourager, checker, and observer. Examples of roles that support work skills include recorder, reader, and runner.*

Source: Association for Supervision and Curriculum Development. 1990. *Cooperative Learning Series: Facilitator's Manual.* Copyright © 1990 by ASCD. Used by permission. All rights reserved.

Phase III: Define lesson objectives and "role" tasks

There is an old expression, "If you don't know where you are going, any road will get you there." That's just as true in teaching as it is in life. For teachers to reach a specific destination, they need to know what the destination is and how they will get there—they identify objectives and define and assign the various tasks to the students in the classroom. In cooperative learning lessons, the performance objectives should be both academic and social. Just as all academic skills are not emphasized in a specific lesson, so, too, not all social skills (for example, encouraging, listening) are emphasized in each assignment. Smith (1987), a high school English teacher, noted that he has "students practice only one or two...skills during any given lesson" (p. 664). For example, the teacher might have students practice the skills of listening or accepting the ideas of others. Teachers do not generate a long list of social skills for students to work on if, in fact, they want students to really practice the skills of providing feedback and monitoring the progress of others in the group. In addition, the teacher needs to articulate what roles students will play once they are in their groups. Some teachers will assign one student to be a "checker" (to make certain everyone understands the content material), another student to be a "facilitator" (to make certain everyone participates), and a third person to be a "resourcer" (to make certain all the materials are available). Role assignments are important to ensure that students know what is expected of them. It is also imperative that the roles be rotated. Teachers need to ensure that different students experience different role assignments.

Phase IV: Determine how to monitor the students' work and process the lesson

For many teachers, group work is a time for them to relax. Once the students are busy working together, the teacher has time for other endeavors (for example, grading papers, preparing the next lesson). Clearly, teachers need time to do these tasks, especially given the fact that American teachers teach longer days and have less time to plan than teachers in many other industrialized countries. Our point is that the time to "catch up" is not during a cooperative learning activity. The teacher's responsibility during this time is to monitor and facilitate how the students are working together. Teachers need to determine what student behaviors will be monitored and to specifically structure how the observations of the students' progress will be made (for example, will the teacher take notes on student interactions or use a check sheet?).

Once the lesson is completed, the students then need to take some time to discuss how the lesson progressed and how well their various groups worked together. Not all teachers complete this phase each time, especially if they are doing a lot of cooperative learning, but this phase is important. It sets a tone that suggests the importance of both the academic and the social skills. Without adequate "processing," students do not have an opportunity to reflect on their actions and their accomplishments. Some teachers have students complete a group self-assessment form. Students are asked to respond (on a 1–5 or 1–10 scale) to questions such as: How do you think your group performed? Did you participate as fully as the other group members in the learning activity?

Cooperative Learning: Instructional Variations

As indicated earlier, there are a host of cooperative learning strategies that teachers can use to enable students to effectively work together. The more options the teacher knows, the more vital cooperative learning can be as an instructional model. Some of these models are relatively simple to use; others require more practice and attention to detail. It is literally impossible to provide any comprehensive look at possible strategies in the context of a chapter such as this one. Our intention is to provide the reader with a sufficient overview so that the possibilities for classroom practice can be determined. References are made within each instructional variation description so that the reader may explore each variation in more depth.

Numbered Heads Together

This technique is the one that Ms. Bernardo used in the case study provided at the beginning of this chapter. It is a technique that fosters student mastery of content by having students consult with one another in response to a specific teacher question. Kagan (1989/1990) describes the following steps:

1. The teacher has students number themselves off within their groups, so that each student has a number: 1, 2, 3, or 4. (Groups can consist of three to five students.)

2. The teacher asks a question.

3. The teacher tells the students to "put their heads together" to make sure that everyone on the team knows the answer. (All students need to discuss the material relevant to the question and be able to respond.)

4. The teacher calls a number (1, 2, 3, or 4), and students with that number can raise their hands to respond (p. 13).

Kagan (1989/1990) notes that this cooperative learning strategy is especially helpful in enhancing academic and social skills such as checking for understanding and comprehension.

Groups of Four

This is a variation of Burns's (1981) group investigation model. Students work in small groups to solve problems that require both cognitive processing of information and social interactions that foster group interdependence. The following steps were followed by teachers in one study that sought to assess the efficacy of the Groups of Four strategy (see King, 1993).

1. Students work together in groups of four members.

2. Each group's membership composition is assigned randomly.

3. Each group member is assigned a particular role in the working of the group.

4. All groups work on the same problem or problem-solving activity....

5. Each group works toward one product for which each member receives a group reward (p. 403—direct quotation, but reformatted).

King attempted to empirically assess the thought processes of students who participated in a Groups of Four cooperative learning activity. He was especially interested in the reactions of low achievers who were participants in the Groups of Four strategy. King noted some of the problems confronted by low achievers in heterogeneous groups (for example, they were influenced by the dominant leadership style of selected high-ability students), but even more important was King's notion that for cooperative learning to accomplish its purposes, teachers need to carefully work with students on how to function within the group situation (see step III of the previous section).

Think-Pair-Share

In Think-Pair-Share, students are required to use academic skills such as hypothesizing, inductive reasoning, and application (Kagan, 1989/1990). The social skills they utilize include group participation (learning to get along with others) and listening. The technique is intended to enable students to develop concepts and critical-thinking skills. The essential steps of the model include:

1. The teacher provides the students with a topic or idea.
2. The students then reflect independently about the meaning of the topic—the teacher should give students 3–5 seconds for independent thinking.
3. The students pair up with other students to discuss the topic and to share respective thoughts. (This can be a random pairing.)
4. The students then share their thoughts with the class—the teacher needs to wait after each student shares (3–5 seconds) for all students to *think* about what has been *shared*.

The teacher might use Think-Pair-Share with students at the beginning of a unit when students are attempting to explore the meaning of a topic. This strategy is not difficult to implement and requires only limited practice before teachers and students feel comfortable and successful. It will require teacher patience, though. Most teachers are not used to waiting after the sharing. If teachers pair students to create questions, the technique is called Think-Pair-Question, and if they pair to create a "web," it is called Think-Pair-Web.

Groups of Three

The Groups of Three strategy is effective for skill building (for example, enhanced math proficiency or vocabulary development). Typically, Groups of Three can be used on an ongoing basis (that is, the group membership would remain relatively permanent for a grading period or semester). Such permanence enables students to work together over long periods of time, and to learn from one another how to develop academic and social skills. The groups are heterogeneously formed based upon academic ability. Provided below is a description of the steps and how to implement the strategy in the classroom.

1. Heterogeneous groups are formed based upon academic ability.

2. Work tasks are assigned to the group on a weekly or biweekly basis (for example, define and use vocabulary terms).

3. Opportunities are created for both group cooperation and individual accountability. (See the Jigsaw II process in the next section.)

Smith (1987) describes his use of the technique with high school English students:

> I use students' scores on a pretest to form the first-semester groups. Each group has one member from the top third of the class, one member from the middle third, and one member from the bottom third....
>
> The students look up the meanings of words independently. Early in the week, working in groups, they review the word meanings together. Since they have used a variety of dictionaries for their homework, the definitions they share with one another encompass a variety of shades of meaning.
>
> Late in the week, the students take two quizzes. They work with their groups to complete the first quiz (20 items involving sentence completion, analogies, and antonyms). The second (20 items involving synonyms) they complete individually.
>
> The group quizzes yield two obvious benefits. First, they give students a chance to review the week's words together. The more often students see, say, hear, and write the words, the more likely it is that these words will become part of their daily vocabularies. Second, the group quizzes give students another opportunity to strengthen their problem-solving skills (p. 665).

Jigsaw II

One of the more structured and more complex cooperative learning strategies is Jigsaw II. The Jigsaw II strategy, which is based on Aronson et al.'s (1978) work, requires that students learn how to work together to enhance their total understanding of a topic. Each student is given a portion of the topic to learn well (to become an expert on that part of the topic). After the students have had some period of study with other group members who have similar responsibilities, the teacher provides all students with an opportunity to share their understanding of the topic with other group members. In this way, the students develop a more comprehensive understanding of the topic.

For a more complete understanding of Jigsaw II, the essential steps include:

1. Inform students that they will be working in their Jigsaw groups to achieve the lesson goals. If students have previously used Jigsaw II, the teacher's statement will be brief. If students are using it for the first time, then students need to be oriented to: the size of the group (four members), the structure of the Jigsaw II activity (each person will be assigned a specific area to study within the broader topic), and the goal of the activity (to enable each "expert" to teach what is learned to the rest of the group members).

2. Create heterogeneous groups. There are a number of different ways to create the groups. Some teachers categorize all students in the class according to general groupings such as high ability, above-average ability, below-average ability, and low ability. They then select one person from each of these general groups to form the study groups. Other teachers literally rank students top to bottom with a number (1 through 28, for example) and then renumber the students so that seven groups of four can be formed heterogeneously (see Table 10.4).

The result would be that all the 1s form a group (that is, Fumi, Lavonne, Sarah, Tanaya). That group of students then creates a name for itself (the Fab Four, for example). At the end of this step, all students are thus assigned to a group and have a name for their group.

Bailey (1996) elaborates on the dynamics of the group assignment process:

> One technique that teachers can use to gain a picture of their classes is to develop class projects in which students serve as data collectors. Students are keen observers of the world around them. Having them keep a record of who is taking part in class can serve as a springboard for important discussions. These discussions can raise everyone's awareness of classroom dynamics, dynamics sometimes so ingrained that they have become invisible (p. 77).

3. Present rules to govern group behavior. Once the students are in their groups, the next step is to make certain that all students know what is expected of them. Gunter, Estes, and Schwab (1995) identify the following rules to govern group behavior:

   a. No student leaves the group to meet with other class members until everyone in the original group finishes the teacher-assigned task.

   b. Each student must make certain that his or her teammates become experts in the assigned group material. Each student is, thus, responsible for not only knowing the content, but making sure that group members have a thorough understanding of the same material.

   c. Each student in the group is a resource. If an individual student does not understand some of the content, that student must get help from the group members before seeking help from the teacher.

4. Present content material to the whole class. There are a number of different ways this can be done. The teacher might present a lecture on the topic and then ask the students to use supplementary texts as content resources. For example, assume a teacher is preparing to have the students read a chapter in a text on communism. The textual material examines communism in the former Soviet Union and focuses on its roots, its emergence as an ideology, and its "apparent" demise in some industrialized countries. Students are to read 17 pages of content material concerning this concept. Four topical areas of interest are identified by the teacher: 1) persons who shaped the communist movement, 2) countries that embraced the communist ideology, 3) political structures found within communist countries, and 4) the economic consequences of communist ideology.

TABLE 10-4 Group Membership Assignment: A Sample

Student Name and Rank	Group Assignment
1. Fumi	1
2. Sue	2
3. Rodrigo	3
4. Josh	4
5. Abraham	5
6. Lori	6
7. Tonya	7
8. Nikki	7
9. Jacque	6
10. Serita	5
11. Bobby	4
12. Aurora	3
13. Nicole	2
14. Lavonne	1
15. Sarah	1
16. Julianne	2
17. Lindsay	3
18. Ramone	4
19. Latoya	5
20. Zachary	6
21. Yung Chang	7
22. Sharad	7
23. Noel	6
24. Libby	5
25. Tanaya	4
26. Jerod	3
27. Shawn	2
28. Donnelle	1

Students are ranked on left column according to ability as perceived by the teacher.

The teacher at this point has identified specific academic content for the overall topic—communism—and has four specific topical areas that become the foundation for group exploration and development.

5. Develop expert groups. The heterogeneous expert groups are then asked to study the various topic areas, and each member selects one subject within the specific topic. Hence, for our Fab Four group, Fumi selects the economic consequences of communism, Tanaya selects the political figures who shaped the communist movement, and so on. Once all the students have selected one of the four topics for study, the teacher then forms the expert study teams. In essence, each person who selected a topic is going to become an expert in that area.

6. Organize expert groups. The teacher then has all the experts get together and study each topic. That is, all the students from all the groups who plan to study political figures in communism get together and investigate the topic as thoroughly as they can. They need to make certain that all group members thoroughly know the topic so that they can eventually teach this topical material to their original "home" team.

7. Return to study teams to teach expert knowledge. Once the students have had an opportunity to become experts, they then go back to their "home" study team and share their knowledge. Each individual shares with team-mates all topical material that has been acquired. The teammates ask questions, take notes, and review the content to ensure that they understand what the expert is sharing (the expert is "teaching" the other group members). Remember everyone read all the original content material, so all team members have some understanding of each topic. The experts have more knowledge because as an "expert group" they focused on the content material in different ways: they read, watched, listened, and discussed the topic in depth.

8. Evaluate student knowledge. The teacher then tests students to assess their understanding of the topic. Students are assessed in two ways and receive points based on both their contributions to the group and their own performance. Each student receives an actual score on the test. As an example, the quiz scores of the Fab Four on the communism test are: Fumi, 96; Lavonne, 86; Sarah, 81; Tanaya, 78.

The teacher then compares each student's actual quiz score with a base score. The teacher computes a base score by looking at previous quiz and test grades and averaging all available grades. The actual and base scores for the Fab Four are provided in Table 10.5 as well as the point differential between the two, which represents the improvement score, from which improvement points can be calculated using Table 10.6. (Incidentally, the improvement points scale can be adjusted based on the students' performance and the difficulty of the quiz.)

The teacher then records the actual score in the grade book. The improvement points are used for team recognition, which is described in the next step.

TABLE 10-5 Scores of Students

	Base Score	Actual Score	Improvement Score	Improvement Points
Fumi	95	96	+1	20
Lavonne	87	86	-1	10
Sarah	80	81	+1	20
Tanaya	67	78	+11	30
				Total 80
				Average 20

Source: Adapted from Cooperative Learning Series. 1990. Alexandria, VA: Association for Supervision and Curriculum Development, p. 101.

9. Provide team recognition. Prior to the team recognition step, the teacher determines what average improvement scores the teams will need for different levels of recognition. Calculate the average improvement score by having the students add their improvement scores and divide by the number of group members. For the Fab Four the total was 80 and the average was 20.

The teacher created three levels of recognition. Super teams are those with averages of 25+. Great teams are those with averages of 20+. And good teams are those with averages of 15+. The teacher then provides each team with a recognition certificate (or some other "reward") that acknowledges the team's level of performance. In the previous example, the Fab Four would be given a Great Team certificate.

Some teachers find that they do not like to use the team recognition after each testing situation. Instead of giving team certificates for super or great

TABLE 10-6 Improvement Points Scale

Quiz Score	Improvement Points
More than 10 points below base score	0
10 points below to base score	10
Base score to 10 points above base score	20
More than 10 points above base score	30
Perfect paper (regardless of base score)	30

Source: Cooperative Learning Series. 1990. Alexandria, VA: Association for Supervision and Curriculum Development, p. 101.

teams, the teacher has students accumulate team points and then exchange the points for some teacher defined "goods." For this to work, it is imperative that teams work together to decide how they will use their points. The "checker" in the group records the improvement points, then the team members can exchange their points when a certain level is achieved (for example, 50 improvement points can be exchanged for two answers on a quiz; 75 points can be exchanged for a homework assignment).

Other Structures

The five cooperative learning strategies just outlined are representative of a host of additional approaches that teachers might use. Table 10.7, which is an adaptation of Kagan's (1989/1990) analysis of how the different cooperative structures fulfill the myriad academic and social functions, provides an overview of several additional strategies. Furthermore, many teachers have found Teams-Games-Tournaments (TGT) and Student Teams Achievement Division (STAD) to be extremely useful in facilitating student learning. Both TGT and STAD (see Kagan, 1992; Devries, Edwards, and Slavin, 1978) are extremely useful when teachers are requiring students to focus on skills and content material that are clearly defined and on dealing with questions that have relatively discrete answers (for example, mathematics). The common elements to many of the cooperative learning variations are that students are heterogeneously grouped and actively engaged in conversation. Though students work together to solve problems, learn academic content, and practice social skills, they are ultimately held individually accountable for their own achievement. Teachers who want students to learn specific math skills or to learn how to define selected vocabulary may find numbered heads together useful. Teachers who are working with more conceptually abstract concepts may rely on models such as Jigsaw II.

Three Before Me   The Three Before Me concept is more philosophical than structural. American students have a tendency (indeed, a strong tendency!) to look to the teacher for answers. Three Before Me suggests that the teacher is a last resort, not a first option. Specifically, when students work in group situations, team members need to check with all other group members before they ask for the assistance of the teacher. If no team member knows the answer to a question, then the teacher goes to the cooperative learning group and explains the material. In this way, the students learn to use peers as resources, but they also have a defined process for dealing with situations when specific questions are perplexing to the whole group.

TABLE 10-7 Overview of Selected Structures

Structure	Brief Description	Functions: Academic and Social
	Teambuilding	
Round Robin	Each student in turn shares something with his or her teammates in response to teacher questions. Students take turns sharing in group by moving clockwise or counterclockwise.	Expressing ideas and opinions, creation of stories. Equal participation, getting acquainted with teammates.
	Classbuilding	
Corners	Each student moves to a corner of the room representing a teacher-determined alternative. Students discuss within corners, then listen to and paraphrase ideas from other corners.	Seeing alternative hypotheses, values, problem-solving approaches. Knowing and respecting different points of view, meeting classmates.
	Communication Building	
Match Mine	Students attempt to match the arrangement of objects on a grid of another student using oral communication only.	Vocabulary development. Communication skills, role-taking ability.
	Mastery	
Color-Coded Co-op Cards	Students memorize facts using a flash card game. The game is structured so that there is a maximum probability of success at each step, moving from short-term to long-term memory. Scoring is based on improvement.	Memorizing facts. Helping, praising.
	Concept Development	
Team Word-Webbing	Students write simultaneously on a piece of chart paper, drawing main concepts, supporting elements, and bridges representing the relation of ideas in a concept.	Analysis of concepts into components, understanding multiple relations among ideas, differentiating concepts. Role-taking.
	Multifunctional	
Partners	Students work in pairs to create or master content. They consult with partners from other teams. They then share their products or understanding with the other partner pair in their team.	Mastery and presentation of new material, concept development. Presentation and communication skills.

Source: Adapted from S. Kagan. 1989/1990. "The Structural Approach to Cooperative Learning." *Educational Leadership* 47(4), p. 14.

INSTRUCTIONAL CONNECTIONS: COMBINING TEACHING MODELS

Cooperative learning interfaces nicely with many other instructional models. Teachers would not use this model in isolation; more typically, they would use it in combination with another instructional strategy. For example, in Chapter 9 we discussed how to use direct instruction when teaching skills. The authors of this book have observed numerous lessons where direct instruction and cooperative learning are combined—teachers taught a skill using direct instruction and then used cooperative groups to check (and reinforce) student understanding of the skill. Table 10.8 provides an example of how cooperative learning is combined with concept attainment, and Table 10.9 illustrates how it is used with concept formation. The important point is that as teachers develop their mastery of the models, they can begin to combine the models in ways that enhance the overall involvement of the students so that they learn requisite material.

TABLE 10-8 Syntax for Concept Attainment and Cooperative Learning

Sequence of Phase	Teacher/Student Behavior	Cooperative Options
1. Present goals and establish set	Explains the goals of the lesson and gets students ready to learn	Think-Pair-Question
2. Present examples and nonexamples	Presents both examples and nonexamples	Think-Pair-Web
3. Compare and contrast	Emphasizes the comparison of examples and contrasting with nonexamples	Think-Pair-Share
4. Identify concept and agreement	Has students state the essential characteristics of the concept in pairs	Think-Pair-Share or Group Discussion
5. Test attainment and justify	Provides additional examples; students test the concept and justify their answers	Think-Pair-Share Group Discussion Numbered Heads Together
6. Analyze and evaluate	Helps students analyze their thinking processes and evaluate the effectiveness of their strategies	Think-Pair-Share Group Discussion Numbered Heads Together
7. Demonstrate understanding through independent practice of the concept	Has students independently create or find additional examples	Think-Pair-Share Group Discussion following the independent practice

Source: L. H. Mauro and L. J. Cohen. 1992. "Cooperating for Concept Development." P. 162 in N. Davidson and T. Worsham (eds.), *Enhancing Thinking Through Cooperative Learning*. New York: Teachers College Press.

TABLE 10-9 Syntax for Concept Formation and Cooperative Learning

Sequence of Phase	Teacher/Student Behavior	Cooperative Options
1. Listing	Asks students a question that generates a list of objects or ideas	Think-Pair-Share Round Robin Roundtable Interview
2. Grouping	Asks students to group the objects into classes	Think-Pair-Share Group Discussions Team Concept Webbing Numbered Heads Together
3. Labeling	Asks students to label the various classes of objects	Think-Pair-Share Group Discussion
4. Processing	Asks students to analyze the criteria they used for listing the items	Think-Pair-Share Interview Round Robin Group Discussion Numbered Heads Together

Source: L. H. Mauro and L. J. Cohen. 1992. "Cooperating for Concept Development." P. 162 in N. Davidson and T. Worsham (eds.), *Enhancing Thinking Through Cooperative Learning.* New York: Teachers College Press.

Ⓐpplications to Diverse Classrooms

A great deal of attention has been given recently to the restructuring of schools in order to make American education more competitive in the world market. The school restructuring, or reinvention process for most districts has focused on how to enable educators to be more accommodating to the rich human diversity found in America's schools. Reform-minded individuals, both liberals and conservatives, want schools in which all students learn, not just places that cater to the best and brightest. Of course, recommendations for how to achieve this goal vary significantly. There are, however, points of agreement, and one of those points has to do with cooperative learning.

Cooperative learning is not a fad or a fashionable idea that suits the fancy of an intellectual elite. Cooperative learning is effective because the undergirding tenets of the strategy are good for all students. Slavin (1987c) noted that "the attraction of cooperative learning for many humanistic educators probably lies not so much in accelerating student achievement as in the consistently found positive effects of cooperative learning on such variables as race relations, attitudes toward mainstream classmates, self-esteem, and other nonacademic outcomes" (p. 34). It should be of no surprise, therefore, to discover that many schools embracing the concept of character education are also espousing cooperative education (Schaps, Lewis, and Watson, 1993). The social benefits of cooperative learning represent one of its most distinguishing characteristics (Lickona, 1989).

Cooperative learning does not advantage just a few students; it advantages all students, especially if teachers recognize that cooperative learning comes in a wide variety of forms. Indeed, some critics argue that selected forms of cooperative learning (for example, those that rely on group rewards such as Jigsaw II) may be disadvantageous for some students. Kahn (1991) asserted that group rewards diminish student motivation to learn when those rewards are tangible and extrinsic. Hence, for some students, reward-based cooperative learning may be demotivating; but for the vast majority of students, regardless of cultural background, cooperative learning (even with the reward component) represents a positive step toward enhanced self-esteem and achievement.

Not all cooperative learning strategies have been used with all racial and ethnic groups. Clearly, more research is needed. However, based on the studies that have been conducted to this point, the potential impact of cooperative learning for enhancing intra- and intergroup relations is significant. Where strategies such as STAD (Student Teams Achievement Division) have been used, it appears as though intergroup cooperation is enhanced (for example, European American and Asian American students developed better attitudes toward Hispanic American students) and more "close student friendships" are created (with others from different racial groups). Slavin (1995) concluded:

> The results of the studies relating cooperative learning to intergroup relations clearly indicate that when students work in ethnically mixed cooperative learning groups, they gain in cross-ethnic friendships. This research indicates that the effects of cooperative learning on intergroup relations are strong and long-lasting, and are more likely on close, reciprocated friendship choices than on distant or unreciprocated choices. There are no clear patterns indicating more consistent results for some methods than for others. All methods have had some positive effects on intergroup relations (p. 633).

PREVALENT ISSUES IN DIVERSE CLASSROOMS

Cooperative learning is not a problem-free strategy. Like all pedagogical approaches, teachers will have to deal with all varieties of student responses to a new way of organizing the classroom environment. The first two problems highlighted below are the most common of the difficult issues teachers seem to confront as they explore the efficacy of cooperative goal structures in the classroom.

Q: *What if my students just don't work well together?*

A: One of the most difficult problems for teachers new to cooperative learning is encouraging students to communicate effectively in their assigned groups. Many teachers attempt to utilize cooperative learning groups, but never consider that students need to practice working together so that they know what is expected of them in a group situation. This is especially true if students have functioned almost exclusively within competitive or individualistic goal structures. In order for cooperative learning to work, teachers need to 1) make certain students have opportunities to practice working together, and 2) enable students to fully understand what it means to be in a group-participation situation.

One of the first steps in cooperative learning is providing students with practice opportunities to work together. The teacher needs to determine what skills students should practice and which norms must be operational. Cohen (1994) suggests that such "norms and skills are best taught through exercises and games, referred to as 'skillbuilders'" (p. 41). An example of a skillbuilder is provided at the end of this chapter; however, teachers should feel comfortable in using any activity that provides students with an opportunity to work together to solve a common problem (for example, have the students work in groups to put together picture puzzles, provide team-building experiences to help them build cohesiveness).

As students practice working together to solve problems, they will also need to work on how to communicate once they are in their assigned groups. For group participation to be effective, the teacher needs to make certain that:

1. All students in each group are talking to one another.

2. All students are making an effort to listen to the ideas of group members.

3. All students are asking questions and making contributions.

4. All students are providing reasons for their observations.

5. All students are providing constructive feedback to one another concerning participation and group cohesiveness.

Some teachers carry a clipboard around when the students are working in groups and make specific observations regarding how the students are communicating within their assigned groups. They make notes about group communication and provide feedback to members concerning social skill development. Other teachers spend a few minutes before each cooperative activity and ask the students to review how they will be expected to work with one another (for example, what words would students use to indicate they are listening to one another?). In essence, for the cooperative groups to work, students must 1) develop a sense of trust with group members, 2) work at communicating their ideas accurately, 3) support group members, and 4) work jointly to resolve academic or social conflicts within the group.

Q: *How do I deal with students who are not good at participating in group situations because they lack certain academic skills?*

A: Students in classrooms possess very different academic skills. One of the real challenges confronting teachers is to create cooperative learning situations in which all students fully and equitably participate. Recently, one of the authors of this book observed a high school science teacher teaching a lesson in which the students were expected to use cooperative learning strategies. The teacher was excellent in presenting content in a cogent fashion and in guiding the students' learning—the teacher began by using a direct instruction strategy to communicate science content knowledge. However, as the lesson progressed, the observer noticed that some students were allowing others to do all the cooperative learning. (Recall that group work and cooperative learning are not the same thing.) The groups did solve the teacher-defined problem, but there was a distinct difference in the level and quality of participation by all class members in the groups.

In many cases, the nonparticipating students are what Cohen (1994) describes as "low-status" students (that is, students who do not talk as much as their peers, and who, through their nonverbal and verbal actions, communicate a message of nonparticipation). Cohen describes two different ways to solve the low-status problem. The first is what she calls the *"multiple ability treatment."* This strategy is especially effective when the teacher assigns a task that truly demands different skills in order for students to successfully complete the task. Teachers who use this approach, according to Cohen (1994), must:

- Clearly describe the different kinds of intellectual abilities necessary for the task.
- Convince the students that the tasks they are about to do require many different intellectual abilities.
- Convince the students that no one will have all the necessary intellectual abilities, but that everyone will have some of the necessary abilities (p. 2).

A second strategy teachers can use is described by Cohen as *"assigning competence to low-status students."* In this strategy, the teacher consciously looks for those special skills that low-status students possess, and verbally communicates about these skills to the other members of the group (for example, "I think B.J.'s ability to draw will be invaluable to your group" or "Si Hong's ability to understand diagrams may be useful as you try to construct the model"). With this approach the teacher makes a "public" evaluation of a real student skill. The specific steps the teacher would follow according to Cohen include:

- Assignment of competence is specific, so the student knows exactly what he or she has done well.
- Assignment is public.
- Competence is made relevant to the task (p. 3).

With both of these strategies, the teacher's goal is to enhance the participation of all the students in the class. What better way to warrant the worth of every child (regardless of an individual's gender, racial, ethnic, or cultural background) than to find ways to ensure that each student can contribute. Catch students at what they are good at, and point out their strengths to the rest of their group members. Active students learn more than students who sit passively and allow others to do the work—teachers must find ways to make certain that all students are active learners.

Q: *How do I deal with the cooperative learning groups in Jigsaw II if I have high absenteeism rates?*

A: Student absenteeism is a major problem for many teachers, especially those in urban situations. Quite obviously, the best solution is to find a way to attract students to school—to entice them to want to be there. Still, the reality of schools is that, even with very good teachers, some students will consistently be absent. How do teachers negotiate this problem? One teacher we know uses the following strategy. On the first day (of a Jigsaw II lesson sequence) the teacher teaches the information the students need to know. Students then read the material and are responsible for knowing the answers to all the questions. When the students return the second day, the teacher forms the heterogeneous groups based on who is in attendance. Students are then assigned a number (1–4) for their expert groups, and they work in their groups to refine and extend their understandings relative to a specific question. The students return to their "home" group for that day and teach their expert material. After taking the quiz, the students calculate their team improvement points, and the teacher gives a token ("lucky bucks") to those at each level of performance (for example, three lucky bucks for super team, two for great team, and so on). The teacher distributes the lucky bucks during the team recognition time and each student must keep track of his or her own lucky bucks. Those lucky bucks can then be exchanged for "goods."

Ⓔ VALUATION CRITERIA

For cooperative learning to work effectively, the teacher must do much more than simply put students in groups and assign a project. Teachers need to think carefully about the composition of groups, the mechanism for ensuring full participation of students within groups, the roles that group members must play, and the nature of the task that students are expected to solve. The evaluation questions provided below focus on these dimensions as well as the overall structure of the cooperative learning model.

Phase I: Lesson Format

1. Is the lesson content appropriate for use with cooperative learning? ○ Yes ○ No

Phase II: Organizational Structure

1. Identify the type of cooperative learning strategy to be used. _____
   _____
   Why was this strategy chosen? _____
   _____

2. Are students placed in appropriately sized groups? ○ Yes ○ No

3. Are students placed in heterogeneous groups? (Describe how
the groups are organized.)　　○ Yes　○ No

4. Are students provided with all
the requisite materials for successfully completing the assigned
task?　　○ Yes　○ No

Phase III: Objectives and Roles

1. Does the teacher clearly define
the academic objectives students
are to achieve while in their
groups?　　○ Yes　○ No

2. Does the teacher clearly define
the social skills students are to
exhibit during the lesson?　　○ Yes　○ No

3. Does the teacher define the different roles that students are to
perform once they are in their
groups?　　○ Yes　○ No

Phase IV: Monitoring

1. Does the teacher monitor
student performance in group
situations?　　○ Yes　○ No

2. Does the teacher provide students with feedback on how they
are performing in their group?　　○ Yes　○ No

3. Is there accommodation for both
individual accountability and
group reward in the defined
cooperative learning situation?　　○ Yes　○ No

4. Do the students self-monitor
their groups?　　○ Yes　○ No

SAMPLE LESSONS

The following sample lessons illustrate alternative procedures for implementing
the cooperative learning instructional model. The first example is a case study
of a 5th grade lesson on Mexico. The second example is a high school science
lesson plan using cooperative learning.

CASE STUDY

Portia Henriques is preparing to have her 5th graders study Mexico as part of a larger unit on Latin America. The students are going to use many supplementary texts in preparation for their "excursion" into Mexico, but the one common text they will be using focuses on life in Latin America. Ms. Henriques spent the first class period using a concept formation activity. She had the students generate all that they know about Mexico. The list of terms generated by the students included almost 100 items. The students then created categories for those items (for example, foods, cities), and Ms. Henriques plans to revisit the students' work at the completion of the unit to show them how much additional information they have learned and to expand the categories they created during the concept formation lesson.

The students will be reading approximately 14 pages of material and focusing on four different aspects of Mexico, including:

1. The natural environment of Mexico: Describe the landscape and climate.

2. Land use in Mexico: Describe the crops and natural resources.

3. The people of Mexico: Describe the population growth and distribution.

4. The culture of Mexico: Describe how the people live.

She asks the students to read the material on their own for homework. The next day Ms. Henriques asks the students to get into their cooperative groups. The assigned groups have worked together on several other occasions.

Ms. Henriques asks the students to spend a few moments in their cooperative groups and to decide which question or issue each student wants to select for study. In the Barrio Brothers group, Teofilo (a high-ability student) selects issue 1, Carmelo (a middle-ability student) selects issue 2, Salvador (a middle-ability student) selects issue 3, and Ernesto (a low-ability student) selects issue 4.

Once all the students in all the groups have their assignments, Ms. Henriques asks them to get in their expert groups. All the issue 1 students get together in one corner of the room; the issue 2 students are in another corner, and so on. The students spend the rest of the class time studying together. They share information with other group members when they feel comfortable with their individual knowledge accumulation of the assigned issue. Table 10.10 is the information sheet generated by the issue 1 expert group.

The next day the students return to their cooperative groups, and each expert shares the knowledge acquired during the expert group discussion. Teofilo shares with Carmelo, Salvador, and Ernesto the information that he acquired (see Table 10.10). As he shares the information, the other students in the group take notes, ask questions, and even check the text again a couple of times to verify the accuracy of Teofilo's information. When Teofilo finishes, Carmelo begins to share his issue 2 information with his cooperative group members. The process continues until all group members have shared their ideas.

TABLE 10-10   Information Sheet

Issue 1

Describe the landscape and climate of Mexico.

1. *There are two mountain ranges that run along Mexico's coast: the Sierra Madre West and the Sierra Madre East.*

2. *The Central Plateau of Mexico begins at the border of the United States and ends where the two mountain ranges meet in the southern section of Mexico.*

3. *Mexico City, Mexico's capital, sits at the southern end of the Central Plateau, which is also the highest elevation of the plateau.*

4. *Mexico has two large peninsulas: Baja and Yucatán.*

5. *The temperatures of Mexican cities depend on their locations. Cities at high elevations have lower year-round temperatures than cities at lower elevations. Mexico City is at a high elevation.*

6. *Northern Mexico is warmer than southern Mexico. The elevation of the southern section is also higher.*

7. *Mexico has seasonal precipitation, with the heaviest precipitation in the summer months.*

At the end of the class period, Ms. Henriques spends a few minutes reviewing some of the major ideas that she wants the students to remember. One student is from Mexico and volunteers to bring in pictures of Mexico City, where one of her aunts still lives.

Ms. Henriques informs the class that tomorrow there will be a quiz that consists of 10 true/false, 10 fill-in-the-blank, and one essay question.

The next day Ms. Henriques administers the quiz. Because of the essay section, Ms. Henriques must grade all the papers herself. She records each individual student's grade and also determines, using a process similar to that described earlier in this chapter, which groups are super, great, and good teams. The next day the individual tests are returned, and the groups are given team rewards. ■

Follow-up questions

1. Identify two other cooperative learning strategies that this teacher might use.

2. What academic skills was this teacher emphasizing?

3. What social skills did this teacher emphasize?

Teachers expect students to know certain facts and to be able to memorize selected information. Assume that you are preparing to teach a high school lesson on meiosis. Meiosis, most readers will recall, occurs during all cell division and entails the process of having the nucleus divide in a way that splits the chromosomes in half.

Concepts: Meiosis I, Meiosis II, and sexual reproduction

Objectives:
1. Students will be able to define *meiosis* and state its outcome.
2. Students will be able to describe and label each phase in Meiosis I and Meiosis II.
3. Students will be able to describe why those animals that sexually reproduce have an advantage over those that reproduce exclusively by mitosis.

Definitions: Meiosis I: Occurs when the homologous chromosomes separate into separate cells.

Meiosis II: Occurs when the chromatids within the chromosomes are split into separate cells.

Synapsis: Occurs with the pairing of homologous chromosomes.

Activity: For the definition phase, identify two different strategies that could be used to teach the definitions to the students (for example, direct instruction might be used by the teacher to ensure that all students understand the process of meiosis).

For the phases of meiosis (Prophase I, Metaphase I, Anaphase I, Telophase I, Prophase II, Metaphase II, Anaphase II, Telophase II), identify two different cooperative learning strategies that could be used to ensure that all students know how to recognize each phase of meiosis and how to recognize homologues and tetrads. Also, to ensure that students can identify the phases of cell division, a mnemonic strategy could be used such as "Pitt Made A Touchdown."

Closure: Students will explore the advantages of sexual reproduction as compared with asexual reproduction.

Follow-up questions

1. What different assessment strategies could be used to assess whether students really understand sexual and asexual reproduction?
2. Is it appropriate for students to memorize the phases of meiosis? Explain. Describe other types of facts that you believe should be memorized by students in school. Is cooperative learning an effective mechanism for accomplishing the learning that you believe should occur in schools? What specific cooperative learning techniques might you use with students?
3. What other mnemonic devices could be used by the students to remember the phases of meiosis?

❶ESSON PREPARATION

Of the many instructional models discussed in this text, none has likely been researched more thoroughly than cooperative learning. Researchers have examined rather thoroughly the effects of cooperative learning strategies on the academic and social growth of students in Grades K–12. They have also explored the practical considerations that teachers have to take into account when they utilize the approach with students. The following resources should be of substantial benefit to both novice and expert teachers who are using cooperative learning.

Suggested readings

Dockerman, D. A. 1994. *Cooperative Learning and Technology.* Watertown, MA: Tom Snyder Productions (1-800-342-0236). This monograph is especially useful for teachers who have computer access and substantial personal computer expertise. Dockerman describes how different cooperative learning strategies (for example, the Jigsaw II method) can be used along with various computer software packages.

Edwards, C., and J. Stout. 1989/1990. "Cooperative Learning: The First Year." *Educational Leadership* 47(4): 38–39.

Ellis, S. 1985. "Introducing Cooperative Learning Groups: A District-Wide Effort." *Journal of Staff Development* 6: 52–59.

Johnson, D. W., and R. T. Johnson. 1989/1990. "Social Skills for Successful Group Work." *Educational Leadership* 47(4): 29–33.

———, E. J. Holubec, and P. Roy. 1984. *Circles of Learning.* Alexandria, VA: Association for Supervision and Curriculum Development.

Slavin, R. E., N. A. Madden, and R. J. Stevens. 1989/1990. "Cooperative Learning Models for the 3 R's." *Educational Leadership* 47(4): 22–28.

Suggested videotapes

"Cooperative Learning" (Tapes 1–5). Alexandria, VA: Association for Supervision and Curriculum Development. (These tapes provide an introduction to the cooperative learning concept and examples of how teachers use cooperative learning in the classroom.)

"Status Treatments for the Classroom." New York: Teachers College Press, Columbia University. (This tape is based on the work of Elizabeth G. Cohen and her text, *Designing Groupwork: Strategies for the Heterogeneous Classroom.*)

Suggested lesson development

Cooperative learning offers teachers a wide variety of options in terms of how to structure the classroom. In preparing to use the cooperative learning instructional model, the teacher should consider the following:

1. Determine what academic and social skills should be emphasized as part of the lesson.

2. Identify which cooperative learning strategy can best be used to enable students to achieve these academic and social skills.

3. Determine how to structure the heterogeneous groups. (The teams should be heterogeneously grouped by ability and by race and gender if academic and social skills are to be adequately fostered.)

4. Provide students opportunities to practice the social skills in their heterogeneous groups before having them work on specific academic skills.

5. Identify how to monitor student academic progress (that is, how will students be assessed individually and in groups?) and how to provide feedback to students about their use of selected social skills (that is, use of a social skills checklist or use of informal observations and notes using a clipboard).

ⓈUMMARY

Competition may be fundamental to American culture, but so, too, is cooperation! All those who work in business and industry know that they are individually accountable to produce quality work, but they must also be able to function effectively with peers and colleagues—to get along with others. Cooperation and competition do not represent an either-or dichotomy. Instead, the teacher must decide on the purposes of a lesson and the concomitant needs of the students involved in that lesson.

Effective teachers understand that students need to learn to work together just as much as they need to function independently. Living in a democratic society demands both types of skills. And learning both sets of skills requires teachers to carefully and intentionally arrange the classroom environment so that students have appropriate opportunities to learn requisite social and academic skills. For example, for some special projects, there is nothing wrong with intentionally arranging brighter students to work with brighter students. These "special" teams enable bright students to use their intellectual skills in a different way than is possible with heterogeneous groups.

Cooperative learning is not without problems. Teachers who are experimenting with the technique complain that some students dominate and others fail to participate. That is why the Cohen (1994) resources can be valuable. No technique is problem-free! The issue is whether teachers can persevere once they confront problems and can identify positive ways to resolve those issues that potentially threaten the success of this instructional model. Cooperative learning takes practice and instructional support: Teachers need to find ways of "playing with" the cooperative learning model, and they need to have available some support (administrative and curricular) to assist them as they confront difficulties endemic to the use of a new strategy such as cooperative learning.

ⓇEFERENCES

Aronson, E., N. Blaney, C. Stephan, J. Sikes, and M. Snapp. 1978. *The Jigsaw Classroom*. Beverly Hills, CA: Sage.

Association for Supervision and Curriculum Development. 1990. *Cooperative Learning Series: Facilitator's Manual*. Alexandria, VA: Association for Supervision and Curriculum Development.

Bailey, S. M. 1996. "Shortchanging Girls and Boys." *Educational Leadership* 53(8): 77.

Burns, M. 1981. "Groups of Four: Solving the Management Problems." *Learning* 22(2): 46–51.

Cohen, E. 1986. *Designing Groupwork: Strategies for the Heterogeneous Classroom*. New York: Teachers College Press.

———. 1994. *Status Treatment for the Classroom*. Videotape and manual. New York: Teachers College Press.

Devries, D. L., K. J. Edwards, and R. E. Slavin. 1978. "Biracial Learning Teams and Race Relations in the Classroom: Four Field Experiments on Teams-Games-Tournaments." *Journal of Educational Psychology* 70: 356–362.

Dockerman, D. A. 1994. *Cooperative Learning and Technology*. Watertown, MA: Tom Snyder Productions.

Edwards, C., and J. Stout. 1989/1990. "Cooperative Learning: The First Year." *Educational Leadership* 47(4): 38–39.

Ellis, S. 1985. "Introducing Cooperative Learning Groups: A District-Wide Effort." *Journal of Staff Development* 6: 52–59.

Gunter, M. A., T. H. Estes, and J. Schwab. 1995. *Instruction: A Models Approach* (2d ed.). Boston: Allyn & Bacon.

Johnson, D. W., and R. T. Johnson. 1975. *Learning Together and Alone*. Englewood Cliffs, NJ: Prentice-Hall.

———. 1987. *Learning Together and Alone* (2d ed.). Englewood Cliffs, NJ: Prentice-Hall.

———. 1989/1990. "Social Skills for Successful Group Work." *Educational Leadership* 47(4): 29–33.

———, E. J. Holubec, and P. Roy. 1984. *Circles of Learning*. Alexandria, VA: Association for Supervision and Curriculum Development.

Kagan, S. 1989/1990. "The Structural Approach to Cooperative Learning." *Educational Leadership* 47(4): 12–15.

———. 1992. *Cooperative Learning*. San Juan Capistrano, CA: Resources for Teachers.

Kahn, A. 1991. "Don't Spoil the Promise of Cooperative Learning." *Educational Leadership* 48(5): 93–94.

King, L. 1993. "High and Low Achievers' Perceptions and Cooperative Learning in Two Small Groups." *Elementary School Journal* 93(44): 399–416.

Lickona, T. 1989. *Educating for Character*. New York: Bantam.

Mauro, L. H., and L. J. Cohen. 1992. "Cooperating for Concept Development." Pp. 151–168 in N. Davidson and T. Worsham (eds.), *Enhancing Thinking Through Cooperative Learning*. New York: Teachers College Press.

Schaps, E., C. C. Lewis, and M. Watson. 1993. "The Child Development Project." *Educational Leadership* 51(3): 46.

Slavin, R. E. 1987c. "Cooperative Learning: Where Behavioral and Humanistic Approaches to Classroom Motivation Meet." *Elementary School Journal* 88(1): 29–38.

———. 1990. "Cooperative Learning and the Cooperative School." Pp. 137–144 in R. Brandt (ed.), *Cooperative Learning Series*. Alexandria, VA: Association for Supervision and Curriculum Development.

———. 1995. "Cooperative Learning and Intergroup Relations." Pp. 628–634 in J. A. Banks and C. A. M. Banks (eds.), *Handbook of Research on Multicultural Education*. New York: Macmillan.

———, N. A. Madden, and R. J. Stevens. 1989/1990. "Cooperative Learning Models for the 3 R's." *Educational Leadership* 47(4): 22–28.

Smith, R. 1987. "A Teacher's Views on Cooperative Learning." *Phi Delta Kappan* 68(9): 663–665.

ⓈKILLBUILDER: ALLIGATOR RIVER

Once there was a girl named Abigail who was in love with a boy named Gregory. Gregory had an unfortunate accident and broke his glasses. Abigail, being a true friend, volunteered to take them to be repaired. But the repair shop was across the river, and during a flash flood the bridge was washed away. Poor Gregory could see nothing without his glasses, so Abigail was desperate to get across the river to the repair shop. While she was standing forlornly on the bank of the river, clutching the broken glasses in her hand, a boy named Sinbad glided by in a rowboat.

She asked Sinbad if he would take her across. He agreed on the condition that while she was having the glasses repaired, she would go to a nearby store and steal a transistor radio that he had been wanting. Abigail refused to do this and went to see a friend named Ivan who had a boat.

When Abigail told Ivan her problem, he said he was too busy to help her out and didn't want to become involved. Abigail, feeling that she had no other choice, returned to Sinbad and told him she would agree to his plan.

When Abigail returned the repaired glasses to Gregory, she told him what she had had to do. Gregory was so mad at what she had done he told her that he never wanted to see her again.

Abigail, upset, turned to Slug with her tale of woe. Slug was so sorry for Abigail that he promised her he would get even with Gregory. They went to the school playground where Gregory was playing ball and Abigail watched happily while Slug beat Gregory up and broke his new glasses.

Rank these characters from "best" to "worst": Abigail, Gregory, Sinbad, Ivan, Slug. *Give reasons for your decisions.*

Source: E. Cohen. 1994. *Designing Groupwork: Strategies for the Heterogeneous Classroom.* New York: Teachers College Press: 178–179.

ELEVEN

• *Oral Discussion*

With the completion of this chapter, the reader will be able to:

1. Describe the theoretical basis for the oral discussion model.
2. Identify the basic characteristics of an effective oral discussion lesson.
3. Identify the basic strengths and weaknesses of the model.
4. Identify how the model can be beneficial with diverse student populations.
5. Create factual, interpretive, and evaluative questions for an oral discussion lesson.

❶ NTRODUCTION

Who better to quote than Socrates—the master questioner? Indeed, his questions ultimately proved to be the cause for his own demise. Socrates had an ability to ask questions that disarmed those around him. In essence, he made people think by asking them questions, not by telling them truths.

In many American classrooms, teaching consists of the teacher talking and students listening. Teachers want to tell truths (even half-truths at times) rather than ask questions that provoke thought. Indeed, many students only listen when the teacher is talking because their experience tells them that what the teacher says is important—teacher-disseminated information will be *on the test.* Excellent teachers understand, however, that meaningful ideas and the dialogue about those ideas are not the exclusive domain of one individual—those who have the capacity to think have the ability to help shape how others think. Young children sometimes have profound insights about old ideas; they see things in new or different ways. The "smartest" person is not necessarily the best thinker; the "dullest" individual is not without the capacity for great insight. Forrest Gump, though fictional, revealed the poignant truth that people of simple gifts have the capacity for extraordinary insights.

The teacher's challenge is to determine how to surface the gifts of all students in the classroom. Students who are expected to articulate and defend their ideas will more fully develop cognitively and socially than those who are not expected to publicly take a position on issues of importance. For those who doubt the importance of discussions, consider the comments of the great UCLA basketball star Bill Walton. Walton

Socrates: Every man is his own ruler, but perhaps you think that there is no necessity for him to rule himself; he is only required to rule others?

Callicles: What do you mean by his "ruling over himself"?

PLATO'S *GORGIAS*

described in a television interview his embarrassment with using language when speaking in front of others. He observed that it wasn't until he was an adult, and a "star," that a concerned friend helped him develop his verbal gifts. Prior to his friend's assistance, he felt awkward and inept at "public" speaking. Today he does public speaking (that is, motivation talks) and is an NBA broadcaster for one of the major networks.

The oral discussion model is used to help students discover their cognitive abilities through development of their own verbal gifts. It is also about trusting the educational process and allowing students to assume ownership for their learning and ideas. In a typical classroom recitation scenario, the teacher asks a question and then seeks the correct student response: *What is the name of Nathaniel Hawthorne's female protagonist in* The Scarlet Letter, *Sung Hee?" And then Sung Hee responds, "Hester Prynne."* Much of the dialogue that occurs in America's classrooms takes this shape. The teacher asks "what" questions, and the students respond with factual answers. Usually the student response mimics the specific words of a text or the specific information previously provided by the teacher. Clearly, recitations have a place in classrooms, but they must not be the dominant or exclusive form of teacher–student dialogue.

Oral discussion differs from recitation in two distinct ways. First, the students are expected to interact with others, not just with the teacher. Second, the ideas presented focus on higher cognitive outcomes, not just the recall of factual information. Oral discussion entails several student responses following an initial teacher question. The teacher sets the stage for the interactions, but students "play off" the ideas of their peers as they explore the teacher-defined topic. They listen to and contribute to the discussion, and as they do so the conceptual complexity of the ideas is enhanced. The students and teacher have what Gall and Gillett (1980) refer to as a reciprocal influence—the "students learn not only from the teacher, but from each other" (p. 99).

One other characteristic of the oral discussion model makes it particularly distinctive. Memorable discussions require that students use a variety of learning modalities in order to assimilate ideas. Students need to be able to speak, observe, and listen in an oral discussion lesson. Traditional instruction puts emphasis on student listening skills, but not upon their speaking skills. A memorable discussion is intellectually demanding for both the teacher and the student. As the following example illustrates, it forces all the participants to think more deeply about ideas and to be able to defend their thoughts.

CASE STUDY

Ms. Sargaski's 7th grade students have been studying Middle Eastern politics and the relationship of the United States to the Middle East from 1950 to the present. The students read pages 495–500 of *World Geography* (Silver Burdett Ginn, 1993) for homework. Ms. Sargaski starts the lesson by talking about some current events, such as the bombing of the World Trade Center, and then reading out loud to the class several important passages from the text. She has students read newspaper accounts of the bombing, and then she shares several ideas about the relationship between and among the Middle Eastern countries and the United States. She reviews several salient concepts related to the Islamic Revolution, the Shiites, and the theocracy that has emerged in Iran. After Ms. Sargaski is reasonably certain students understand the material well, she begins the lesson.

The students are asked to put their chairs in a large circle (whole-class roundtable) and to bring with them their books, their journals, and a copy of any notes that they have taken during their reading of the text. Once they are all situated in the group, the lesson begins.

"Class, I'm going to ask you several different types of questions. Most of these questions have several possible ways to respond, so don't look for just one correct answer. I really want to hear what you are thinking. Also, remember not to respond until I call on you.

"I'll begin with a very basic question. Why would there be such a tense relationship between the countries of Iran and the United States? Write down in your journals several explanations for the tense relationship. Don't share your ideas with anyone else at this point." The students take several minutes to jot down their ideas. The teacher then begins to ask some questions to develop the students' thinking.

Ms. Sargaski observes, "In 1979, the Islamic Revolution occurred. As you know, the Shiite revolutionaries turned Iran into a theocracy. Jamie, define *theocracy* for me."

"It's a nation that's ruled by religious laws."

"Good. And how does that differ from a democracy, Jamie?"

"Well, in a democracy, the laws are created and passed by all the people. In a theocracy, the laws are made by religious leaders."

"That's correct. Now why do leaders in any country, regardless of whether that country is a democracy like the United States or a theocracy such as Iran, believe that their form of government should be imposed on others? Lamar?"

"I guess because they want everyone to act like they do."

"Is that the only reason? Are they concerned only with actions? Marta?"

"I think it has to do with what people believe. In a democracy we believe that all people are equal and have certain rights. In a theocracy, people are told how to act. They are told what to wear and who can vote."

"Renee, are there other reasons? Or, do you think the main issues relate to actions and beliefs?"

Renee responds, "I think it's actions and beliefs. But most people want others to act like them. We're a democracy, so we want all countries to be democracies. Iran's a theocracy, so it wants other countries to be theocracies."

"Interesting. So you think that Iran would have no problem with other countries as long as those other countries are theocracies?"

"Oh. I'm not sure."

"What aren't you sure of, Renee?"

"I don't know of other theocracies in the world."

"Well, that's a good point. There are very few theocracies. Let me give you one—the Vatican."

The class responds quizzically and almost chorally, "What?"

"That's right, the Vatican is a country and it's also a theocracy. So, would

Iran and the Vatican get along well because they are both theocracies? Jeremy?"

"No. I'm Catholic and I don't think it's just the government. It is also what you believe. The leaders of the Vatican and Iran believe different stuff."

"And why is that 'different stuff' important, Jeremy?"

"Because what they believe begins to affect how they act and what is expected of them. I'm Catholic, but I'm not told what clothes to wear, or how to behave in all circumstances."

"True, but what if you went to St. Luke's [the Catholic school down the street]? Would you then be told what to wear?"

"I never thought about that. But, yeah!"

"Class, consider this for a moment: How do you think democracies and theocracies can try to get along even when they have different beliefs and rules that determine how they govern people? One thing we might want to do is to read more about the Vatican and then use some of those ideas to help us see ways of better dealing with Iran and other theocracies. Let's turn to our books and read one more time what happened prior to and after the Islamic Revolution—turn to page 498—and then let's talk more fully about the tensions described in the book." The following text material is read:

> The new revolutionary government also changed Iran's policies toward the United States. Under the Shah, Iran and the United States had been good friends. The Ayatollah and his supporters believed that the United States helped keep the Shah in power. When he was overthrown, the new government showed its hostility toward the United States by taking Americans hostage and engaging in terrorism in the Middle East.
>
> A few years later a war broke out between Iran and its neighbor, Iraq. Hundreds of thousands of Iranians and Iraqis were killed in the fighting, and Iran's economy suffered drastically. The war ended in 1988. A year later the leader of Iran's revolution, Ayatollah Khomeini, died. The new leader of Iran has made some changes in the way the country is governed.
>
> [Source: *World Geography*. 1993. Morristown, NJ: Silver Burdett Ginn, p. 498.]

After reading the material, Ms. Sargaski asked a couple of additional factual questions (for example, "Who did the Ayatollah believe helped the Shah to power?") and a series of interpretive questions (for example, "Why did Iran and Iraq go to war?" and "What types of changes might the new Iranian leader have made in how Iran is governed?"). The discussion continued for several minutes and concluded with the teacher listing some of the changes on the board. The students were then asked to read a pamphlet titled "Iran Today" and asked to compare the changes they hypothesized with what, in fact, appears to be occurring in Iran. ∎

Ms. Sargaski is using oral discussion as a means of helping students more critically examine what a theocracy is and what it means for the United States to have relations with theocracies such as Afghanistan, Sudan, Pakistan, and even the Vatican. The students are expected to know some facts, but they are also provided an opportunity to think beyond the facts that are stated in the text or by the teacher. If the teacher had asked only factual questions, she would have fostered far less cognitive processing of information (see Chapter 3 for a discussion of taxonomical levels of thought) and, most likely, far fewer forms of student participation. Oral discussions enable students to use what they *know* as support for what they *think*.

⊤HEORETICAL PERSPECTIVE

Discussions are seemingly commonplace in America's classrooms. Teachers interact with students as they attempt to explore a topic or idea. As indicated earlier, recitations and oral discussions are quite different. In recitation, the teacher is looking for a "correct" answer and the exchanges are characterized by a teacher-student-teacher-student format. In oral discussion, the teacher is working with the students to share knowledge in ways that involve more complex thinking. Gall and Gall (1976) suggest that with recitation students are recalling content, and with oral discussion the teacher is attempting to foster more critical thinking and attitude change. Given Gall and Gall's definition, it seems clear that much of what appears to be discussion in American classrooms is, in fact, recitation.

For discussions to occur, certain classroom conditions must be evidenced (Dillon, 1984). Students, for example, must feel free to express their feelings—they cannot be afraid of what others will think or how the teacher will respond—and teachers must value what students think. These conditions loom large as potential barriers to the success of a good discussion. Many students have learned to speak only when they know they are right, and to listen only when they see that the teacher is talking; students tend to ignore the contributions of their peers.

Once a teacher understands that certain preconditions must be in place in order for a discussion to occur, it then becomes possible to consider what conditions must exist in order to declare that a discussion is actually occurring. Dillon (1984), drawing on the work of a variety of other researchers, suggests three such conditions:

1. Those participating are putting forth a variety of ideas and points of view relative to a specific subject.
2. Those participating evidence a willingness to explore and examine the various ideas offered by their peers.
3. Those participating are attempting to more fully develop their understanding about the subject under discussion.

Based on these conditions, teachers, according to Gall and Gall (1976), are then in a position to achieve at least four different discussion outcomes. Understanding the outcomes is especially important for knowing when and how to use the discussion technique. Although research findings neither clearly justify nor diminish the use of discussion strategies, some evidence does suggest that if teachers want to foster enhanced subject matter mastery, attitudinal change, and problem-solving ability, then oral discussion strategies can prove to be beneficial. For instance, relative to subject matter mastery, Gall and Gall observe that it "appears that the discussion method is effective in helping students to master curriculum content, especially when cognitive outcomes beyond the level of knowledge are desired" (p. 200). In essence, discussion methods tend to foster higher cognitive achievement when the method is used in combination with other instructional models (that is, cooperative learning, synectics, inquiry). Discussion methods also tend to stimulate enhanced thinking on the part of students; students become active rather than passive participants in the learning process—they are literally constructing their own intellectual scaffolds. The consequence of this active engagement is that oral discussions can foster attitude changes in students.

For several years, researchers endeavored to determine if oral discussion strategies were more effective than other strategies such as lecture. That line of research proved to be neither especially useful nor insightful. In fact, discussion strategies have power when they are combined with other techniques, not when they are juxtaposed to them. Once again, we must emphasize that teachers really need to consider the goals of their instruction. Clearly, if the teacher is teaching a specific skill (for example, multiplying fractions), discussion may not be appropriate; the direct instruction strategy might be more useful. But, if the teacher is seeking to foster enhanced mastery of content or to engender more critical thinking on the part of students, then discussion may well be useful. As Gall and Gall (1976) note: "The nature of the intended learning outcome (for example, attitude change), rather than the curriculum content, determines the effectiveness of the discussion method" (p. 213). The academic content and process for American schools needs to focus more on awakening students' minds than in disseminating teacher-defined revelations of truth. Wiggins (1989) notes:

> What students need to experience, firsthand, is what *makes* an idea or book "great"—something hard to do well, but possible with students of all ages if teachers grasp the need for cycles of Question-Answer-Question instead of merely Question-Answer. The issue is ultimately not which great book you read but whether any book or idea is taught in a way that deadens or awakens the mind, whether the student is habituated to reading books thoughtfully, and whether the student comes to appreciate the value of warranted knowledge (as opposed to mere beliefs called "facts" by someone else).
>
> One irony in the fuss over *Cultural Literacy* is that Hirsch (1988) has written a classic liberal argument: the point of cultural literacy is to enter the Great Conversation as a coequal. But Hirsch made a fatal (and revealing) error in his prescription of a shared base of essential information. (He also erred in his portrayal of Dewey's thinking. The caricature he presents of what he calls Dewey's "formalism" overlooks a massive corpus of writings that provide substantive guidelines on how to ensure that students truly understand academic ideas of value and substance.) The capacity to understand is only partially dependent on facts; rarely do we need to know the same things that our fellow conversants know. It is far more important

for a novice to possess intellectual virtues (moral habits of mind, if you will); one must:

- know how to listen to someone who knows something one does not know,
- perceive which questions to ask for clarifying an idea's meaning or value, be open and respectful enough to imagine that a new and strange idea is worth attending to,
- be *inclined* to ask questions about pat statements hiding assumptions or confusions (p. 48).

ORAL DISCUSSION: TEACHING PHASES

Phase I: Identify the focus for discussion

One of the first steps in oral discussion requires that the teacher identify what the focus will be for the lesson. Gunter, Estes, and Schwab (1995) use the "great books" approach, which requires that the teacher begin by selecting content material for the students to read (that is, the works of Tolstoy, Bacon, Chaucer, or Virgil) and then creating different types of questions (factual, interpretive, evaluative) for students to reflect upon and respond to based on those readings. Table 11.1 includes examples of questions at each of the levels for the book *Teammates* by Peter Golenbock. *Factual questions* are essentially questions derived directly from statements connected to specific textual material. These questions elicit correct or incorrect responses. Little, if any, divergent thinking occurs at this level. *Interpretive questions* focus on meaning; the reader must move beyond facts and explore the nuances of words and/or ideas. Usually these questions ask students to take information that they understand and to apply it to a

TABLE 11-1   Types of Questions for Discussions: Three-Level Approach

Factual	1. What one fact clearly suggests that Branch Rickey was not afraid of change?
	2. What obstacles did Jackie Robinson face as a result of having made the Brooklyn Dodgers team?
Interpretive	1. What did Pee Wee Reese mean by "If he's good enough to take my job, he deserves it"?
	2. Why did Pee Wee Reese need to respond publicly to Jackie Robinson in front of the Cincinnati crowd?
Evaluative	1. In what ways does what happened to Jackie Robinson still happen to people today?
	2. Do you agree with the way in which Pee Wee Reese showed his support for Jackie Robinson?

new situation. These questions call for divergent thinking processes. *Evaluative questions* focus on the relationship between what the readers read and what they actually experience in their own lives. These questions are divergent in nature and ask students to make judgments about phenomena. They ask students to make decisions and conclusions. Some teachers reading this text will be more familiar with Bloom et al.'s (1956) taxonomy. (For a complete description, refer to Chapter 3.) Bloom orders questions hierarchically in six levels of thought processes (see Table 11.2), but like Gunter, Estes, and Schwab's question types, the lowest level focuses on factual recall of material and the highest level demands that students pull together disparate ideas and create meaningful conceptual relationships. We use the Gunter et al. approach here for the sake of simplicity—three levels rather than six. Actually, what is important is that teachers ask questions that foster different types of student thinking.

Once the teacher has the questions prepared—some prepared questions are essential for purposes of conducting a good discussion—the teacher should review the questions to make certain that they are clear and logically ordered so that students progress from convergent (factual) to divergent (evaluative) thinking processes. Convergent questions are not answerable in more than one way. Factual questions have "right" vs. "wrong" answers. Evaluative questions have responses that necessitate that students use facts to support their arguments, but the direction of the argument will vary according to the student making a particular point.

In general, teachers should ask more factual questions at the beginning of a discussion (establishing a common understanding among students regarding the contextual facts) and then proceed to the more interpretive and evaluative questions once students have established their background knowledge.

TABLE 11-2   Types of Questions for Discussion: Six-Level Approach

Knowledge	What were the baseball leagues for blacks called in the mid-1900s?
Comprehension	What does the phrase "the great experiment" mean regarding Branch Rickey and Jackie Robinson?
Application	What do you think would have happened if that great experiment had never occurred?
Analysis	How important was it that Pee Wee Reese took a public stand to support Jackie Robinson?
Synthesis	Identify other ways that Pee Wee Reese might have shown his support for Jackie Robinson.
Evaluation	What additional data about Jackie Robinson or Pee Wee Reese do you need in order to better understand what happened in Cincinnati?

Phase II: Pose the question for discussion

For oral discussions to be successful, the teacher must begin by posing a question that embraces the experiences of the students and is not cast at a level of abstraction that is inappropriate based upon the developmental level of youngsters or the development of the lesson and its content progression. The teacher, in essence, starts by creating, through the questioning process, some type of cognitive dissonance, but that dissonance should emerge from what the students already know and understand. Such dissonance can be facilitated in a couple of ways: a key question approach and playing the role of devil's advocate.

Key Question A key question is an umbrella question that supersedes all other questions. For example, for the novel *Teammates*, the teacher might begin with the key question: *"Why was it so difficult for people in the 1950s to change their beliefs about who should play baseball?"* From this question, the teacher can then lead into the various factual, interpretive, and evaluative questions that have been enumerated in Tables 11.1 or 11.2. Gunter, Estes, and Schwab (1995) label key questions as "basic." For basic questions to be workable, there can be no one correct response. Key questions foster dialogue, but they are not easily resolved or "correctly" answered. Good and Brophy (1994) also suggest the use of indirect questions. Such questions are less threatening and more inclusive in tone. For example, "Class, I wonder what would have happened if people like Pee Wee Reese were not willing to take a stand."

Devil's Advocate A second way to begin classroom discussions is by taking a position that the teacher knows will be controversial. The teacher purposefully instigates a controversial (dissonant) stand on an issue. The teacher still needs to have factual, interpretive, and evaluative questions prepared, but the oral discussion begins by the teacher's posturing of a particular position: *"Nothing good happens when those who 'have' try to help those who don't 'have.'"* This statement could be made relative to the novel *Teammates*, and discussion would center around Pee Wee Reese's decision to demonstrate his support for Jackie Robinson.

The devil's advocate approach really stirs debate; it can also create big problems if the teacher is not aware of how to handle controversy. Teachers who use this technique must be aware that some students may identify the position with the teacher and subsequently either believe that the position is one that students should accept or, worse yet, share with others their perceptions of what the teacher believes (for example, "Mom, do you know that...really believes that African Americans should never have been allowed to play baseball?"). Anyone who has ever taught knows that this latter circumstance is a real possibility. The devil's advocate approach must be used cautiously! Quite obviously, the teacher must take special care to let students "explore" the statement, but then also make them aware that the statement does not necessarily represent a personal stance.

Some teachers accomplish this by saying, "Class, some people would argue that...." By couching the statements for students in this fashion, teachers are able to personally separate themselves from owning potentially inflammatory and controversial statements.

Phase III: Foster participation

One of the most difficult aspects associated with conducting good discussions is trying to ensure broad student involvement. Some students tend to dominate; others are reticent to participate at all. Part of the difficulty with quality oral discussions relates to room arrangement. Some teachers keep students in rows (an arrangement suitable for recitation) but forget that a primary goal of oral discussion is for students to build on the remarks of their peers. Three different classroom organizational structures enable this to occur:

Whole-class Roundtable With this arrangement, all the students in the class put their chairs in one large circle and/or square. The teacher becomes one of the participants within the larger configuration (circle or square), but the structure enables everyone to hear and see what is being said to and by others. Teachers must be cautious in using this technique. Because of the large size of the group, student participation can be quite limited with a few verbal students dominating the group's deliberations. Teachers should consider using the whole-class strategy as a precursor to the myriad small-group strategies—see Chapter 10, "Cooperative Learning." Other teachers can use small-group formats to "set up" the large group design—the Touchstones Project (see Zelderman, Comber, and Maistrellis, 1992) would be an example of this approach. The Touchstones Project is based on carefully selected texts that engage students at specifically designed times to discuss these texts. The texts are short (for example, an excerpt from "About Revenge" by Francis Bacon) and are assigned to be read just prior to the discussion time. Because all students read the material at the same time, they begin the discussions on "equal footing." The teacher is not an authority on the textual material, so students are required to discern their own meanings by relying on personal interpretations and interpersonal dialogue or discussion.

Buzz Group In buzz groups the teacher divides the class into heterogeneously grouped students of four to eight. The teacher then poses a key question and asks students to identify a common response to the teacher-posed question—a response that all buzz group participants can support. One person in the group is a recorder; another serves as a reporter. The students in each group then share their ideas; the teacher has the students use factual, interpretive, and evaluative questions to refine the various concepts related to the originally posed question.

Inner Circle In an inner circle the teacher forms students into two groups—an inner small group (those engaged in the discussion) and an outer large group (those acting as observers). McKeachie (1986) and others who advocate this strategy find that the different roles enable some students to participate effectively while others try to understand the direction of the discussion and the positions of those offering different arguments. The Touchstones Project approach (described above) relies on this type of inner-circle structure. Zelderman, Comber, and Maistrellis (1992) write:

> A typical Touchstones class has a number of segments, each designed to encourage the students to take ownership of the activity and to learn to cooperate. The class generally lasts for 40 to 45 minutes. Students enter the classroom, move the chairs into a large circle, and choose where and next to whom they sit. The books are then distributed. The text to be discussed is read aloud and then silently. Students are then given time to write down a question they feel would be interesting to discuss. Next, students work in small groups of three to five members, either assisting one another in reformulating their individual questions, devising a group question, or discussing how to approach a text as if they were to lead the discussion. The small-group work is always composed of task-oriented activities requiring cooperation. When the class reconvenes, the groups report their results to the class. A Touchstones class occurring about 10 weeks into the year raises the cooperative task to a different level. In this meeting, the students are divided into two groups. For the first 10 to 12 minutes one of the groups will discuss a text while the other group sits in an outside circle and uses a student observation sheet. The observers keep track of the speech incidents, determine the reason for silences if these occur, and evaluate the discussion itself—giving a grade and justifying it. In the second segment of the class, the groups switch roles and go through the same process. In the last 12 minutes of the class, the entire class is reunited. The students in the outer circle present their reports, propose recommendations for class improvements, and discuss these. At this stage the students begin to cooperate, not only on specific tasks, but also on the issue of how to deal with those areas where the group is failing to cooperate (pp. 145–146).

Before initiating any discussion, it is imperative to establish certain ground rules with the students. Discussions are intended to help students better understand their own ideas—to explore what they believe and why they believe it. For that reason, discussions require that students:

1. Have a reasonable knowledge base before dialogue begins.

2. Listen to the contributions of their peers. No two people should speak at the same time. Discussions are not the functional equivalent of *Crossfire* (the CNN talk show) simulations; they are an opportunity for students to critically examine ideas in ways that enable them to synthesize reasonable conclusions.

3. "Play off" the ideas of other students, not just the statements or questions asked by the teacher.

4. Defend their assertions. Teachers need to ask a lot of "why" questions when students suggest ideas. Teachers should also seek out how other students feel—"*Esteban, do you agree with Tameka's observation?*" When students offer

an idea that appears to lack support, the teacher should not hesitate to critically explore the idea.

Phase IV: Summarize the students' positions

All too often teachers conduct discussions but fail to bring closure in ways that really help students clarify their thinking. As one of our colleagues suggests, discussions can become nothing more than a sharing of collective ignorance. To avoid this, it is absolutely imperative that students start with a knowledge base and then have an opportunity to synthesize their understandings. This synthesis can occur by using one of three techniques:

Whole-Group Synthesis   The teacher writes the students' ideas on the board as they are shared and then asks the students to write in paragraph form a summary of what has been shared.

Small-Group Synthesis   The teacher asks students to work in small groups (4–8) and identify salient ideas that they all can support. They then share those ideas with the class by putting the information down on poster paper. For example, recently we observed a 6th grade lesson on owl pellets. At the completion of the lesson, the students were required to work in groups to discuss the dietary habits of owls and then write down their conclusions on poster paper. Each group then stood up and shared its conclusions with the rest of the class.

Personal Synthesis   Based on all that has been discussed concerning the concept or idea, the teacher asks each student to write a brief statement of personal belief. The writing of personal belief statements enables students to more pointedly comprehend what they understand and do not understand relative to a given situation. (Refer to Chapter 3, "Affective Domain" discussion.)

❶NSTRUCTIONAL VARIATIONS

The preceding discussion presumes that the teacher has established a content topic and identified questions that need to be explored related to that topic. Quite obviously, such a strategy is not always necessary or desirable. Three instructional variations—tutorial, inquiry group, and Socratic seminar—are described in this section. Once again, before deciding upon an instructional strategy, it is absolutely essential to determine the objective of the interactions the teacher desires among the students. The first strategy listed below is intended to enhance academic and social skills, and the second focuses more on problem-solving abilities. The first might be a complement to a direct instruction lesson; the second would be more efficacious with the inquiry model.

Tutorial

One of the most powerful instructional strategies known in education is the tutorial. Walberg (1995) observed that the tutorial achievement effects were substantial for both tutors and tutees, and especially evident in content areas such as mathematics, where skill definition is more clearly articulated. Students who work in tutoring situations get direct and immediate feedback and they experience enhanced achievement. With the tutorial discussion, the emphasis is on ensuring that specific students exhibit task mastery. According to Orlich et al. (1985), the teacher first identifies specific students with high levels of expertise and then groups them with students who lack those same skills. The teacher then has the tutors:

1. Pinpoint the learning problems of the tutored students—what don't they understand?

2. Provide the requisite knowledge that the "tutee" student lacks—the tutor teaches the information and/or helps in practicing the skills needed by the tutee.

3. Encourage the tutee students to ask their own questions and direct their own learning.

Group sizes in tutorials should be kept small—no more than four students and preferably smaller. The learning tasks must be relatively specific (for example, the tutor helps students memorize math facts or understand the steps in long division), and the tutors must truly have enhanced skill competency.

Inquiry Group

The inquiry group focuses on student problem-solving. The desired group size for inquiry is 6 to 10 students. Teachers who use this strategy should have students who have familiarity with inquiry as an instructional model (see Chapter 5). According to Orlich et al. (1985) this oral discussion strategy fosters scientific thinking and the enhancement of student problem-solving skills. Either teachers or students can lead inquiry groups. Before implementing this strategy, teachers need to make certain that students know how to make thoughtful observations and how to ask questions to solve a problem.

The teacher starts by presenting a problem. The problem should be one for which there is not a readily apparent answer (a discrepant event). Once students recognize the problem, they then break into their inquiry groups and create questions for which they need a solution relative to the problem. The students should generate as many questions as they can think of. Once all the questions are listed, the students then must work together to answer those questions. Rather than relying on the teacher for the answer to a "yes" or "no" question (as occurred with inquiry—see Chapter 5), the students must rely on themselves for the information. For example, the teacher might start by stating, *"How is it possible to remove an eggshell without using your fingers?" The teacher then provides the students with the following: a 1-pint jar with a lid, 1 raw egg, 1 pint of water, 1 pint of vinegar, and 1 pint of clear pop. She tells the students that by using these materials they can remove the eggshell. The students then move into their groups and begin asking questions and forming hypotheses. They should record all of their questions and answer those to which they know the answers. Based on what they know, they then test each hypothesis.* (Incidentally, the correct solution is: vinegar in a closed jar with the egg submerged—vinegar is acetic acid; egg shells are calcium carbonate. The reaction between the acid and the calcium carbonate causes the eggshell to disappear.)

Socratic Seminar

The Socratic seminar is an outgrowth of Tredway's (1995) work to engage students in critical-thinking activities. The process for discussing a Socratic seminar are relatively simple and straightforward, but quite intellectually demanding for all involved. Tredway writes:

They [Socratic seminars] typically consist of a 50–80 minute period once a week. Students, usually in groups of 25 or fewer, read a common text prior to or during the seminar—a novel, poem, essay, or document. Or, they may study an art reproduction. They then respond to questions the teacher (or other facilitator) asks about concerning what they've read or seen.

At Paul Junior High School in Washington, D.C., for example, a group of 7th graders were engaged recently in a series of seminars on "How to Be Kind and Forgiving in a World That Is Often Not," a compelling issue in the lives of many young people. They read excerpts from two works— "About Revenge," an essay by Francis Bacon, and *Middle Passage*, a novel by Charles Johnson in which the main character (Ngonyama) leads an uprising on a slave ship, but insists there be no revenge against his captors.

The teacher then posed this question:

To what extent would Francis Bacon agree with the ideas and actions of Ngonyama—totally, mostly, some, not at all?

The students voted on the answer, and their votes ran the gamut. To support their positions, they cited evidence from the text, disagreeing with one another's reasoning, asking one another questions, and, in a few cases, changing their minds based on classmates' ideas. Several times during the seminars, students set up comparable situations from their own experiences with friends or in the community to determine whether they agreed with the advice of Bacon or Johnson.

The question the teacher posed required students to evaluate options and make decisions. They then participated in a conversation about it. All subsequent questions in the seminar were based on the students' ideas and contributions in response to this initial question. Thus, the term *Socratic* seminar. The technique is derived from an ancient form of discourse— Socratic dialogue: Through doubt and systematic questioning of another person, one gets to ultimate truth (p. 26).

ⒶPPLICATIONS TO DIVERSE CLASSROOMS

One of the recurring themes of this book is that teachers should vary their instructional models (or teaching strategies) so that they can better accommodate the learning needs of all students. Because so many students from so many of America's diverse racial and ethnic groups tend to be field-sensitive learners, it becomes absolutely essential that teachers move beyond teacher-dominated forms of instruction and allow students to express their own ideas. Gollnick and Chinn (1994) describe this as "dialogue inquiry." In essence, with dialogue inquiry the teacher intentionally focuses on what the students know and how they are able to express it. Gollnick and Chinn write: "Too often teachers ignore students' attempts to engage in dialogue and, as a result, halt further learning by many students" (p. 302).

Part of what happens when students are encouraged to express their ideas is that they learn more about themselves and others. The wife of one of the authors of this book is an inner-city junior high school teacher. Her observation about urban youngsters is that many of them have verbal skills that are more refined than are their abilities in written expression. Life on the streets requires some measure of advanced verbal acumen. These same "verbal" students, however, are evaluated at school more exclusively through traditional written assessments—tests, portfolios, and so on. Teachers cannot and should not disdain traditional assessments, but instead they need to operate more bicognitively. Bicognitive teaching enables teachers to structure lessons so that students have opportunities to play to their strengths as well as to deal with their weaknesses. The concept of bicognitive development is not new. Ramirez and Castaneda (1974) described its efficacy for schools over 20 years ago. What is needed now are teachers who act on what researchers and educators now know. Teachers tend to "force" students to learn in certain ways. As we will argue in Chapter 12, *subversive teachers* operate in ways that enable students to define and refine their own abilities, not just conform to extant school structures. Subversive teachers find ways to build on students' strengths.

Teachers who use the oral discussion model effectively will find that the model accommodates both relational and analytical styles of learning (see Table 11.3). In that regard, it is an especially important instructional model for teachers to use. It allows students to be creative and expressive, but it also demands that students be able to logically present ideas and use factual knowledge to ground personal argument.

As readers will recall, in the previous chapters, the instructional models have distinctly favored particular cognitive approaches: Cooperative learning favors relational; direct instruction favors analytical. The oral discussion model represents, perhaps, a balance of the two and may, therefore, be an especially important bicognitive strategy for teachers to use, especially if they can deal with the types of issues described in the next section.

TABLE 11-3 Relationship of Oral Discussion Model to Cognitive Styles

Model	Relational	Analytical
■ Oral Discussion	■ Creativity	■ Memory for specific facts
	■ Global views	■ Linear
	■ Divergent thinking*	■ Convergent thinking*
	■ Expressive	■ Task specific
	■ People-oriented	■ Individually oriented

*Depends on the type of discussion

PREVALENT ISSUES IN DIVERSE CLASSROOMS

Any teacher who has ever conducted a classroom discussion understands quite well some of the inherent problems associated with utilizing the oral discussion model with students. Two major questions appear particularly troublesome for teachers.

Q: *How do I deal with the differential participation of students? Some dominate; others have no desire to become involved!!*

A: There are several strategies that teachers can use to involve students in discussions. Each has power when used appropriately to foster student engagement.

Use of Nonparticipants

Some students will not participate unless the teacher intentionally calls on them. Teachers often call on nonparticipants who look distracted or who appear to be off-task—the question becomes a classroom management strategy. The effect of calling on such off-task students is to cause embarrassment. To avoid this situation, teachers should randomly call on students. Simply take a stack of 3 × 5 cards and place each student's name on a different card. When preparing to have an oral discussion with the class, shuffle the cards and select cards at random. Many teachers use this type of strategy to ensure that every student has an equitable opportunity to participate. (Incidentally, once a student's card is used, place it back in the stack so that he or she is "eligible" to be called upon again—once called upon, a student is not "free.") The side benefit of this strategy is that it also keeps some students from "stealing" all the time.

Of course, when teachers call on nonparticipants they also get more off-the-wall responses. Teachers have three choices in such instances. When a student appears unresponsive or responds inappropriately:

Teacher Choice One

If the student is nonresponsive: Reword the question (do not repeat it!) to ensure that it is clear. Assume "the best" of each student at first. That is, assume that the student did not understand the question. Reword the question and then wait for a student response. Do not move to another student until the momentum of the lesson is jeopardized—this is typically 3–5 seconds, which in some classrooms can be an eternity.

Teacher Choice Two

If the student provides a thoughtful but illogical response: Call on other students to see if they agree—*"Claude, do you agree with Peg that baseball is just for boys because it requires physical strength?"* Teachers have a great deal of power in the classroom. They can accept or dismiss an idea with a nonverbal gesture or verbal utterance. Indeed, teachers may have too much power in some respects over the ideational content of a lesson. One way to limit the teachers' power is to involve students in evaluating the ideas of their peers.

Teacher Choice Three

If the student provides an illogical and unthoughtful remark: Ignore the student and move on to another student. One of the main reasons students misbehave is to get attention. Often when students participate in discussions they offer "cute" remarks in order to elicit a reaction from the class and the teacher. That teacher reaction is what the student wants! If a teacher is going to react, react privately, after the class period is over and the student no longer has an audience.

Q: *What types of questions should be avoided when conducting a discussion?*

A: All teachers fall into certain patterns when conducting discussions. Asking good questions requires thought and preparation—few teachers have the ability to spontaneously create plenty of good questions. We suggest that before a discussion begins, the teacher develop sample questions that are factual, interpretive, and evaluative. As teachers use these different types of questions, they will find that they are better able to think of questions on the spur of the moment. Researchers have found that teachers have acquired several bad habits when it comes to leading oral discussions. Good and Brophy (1994) describe a couple of these—"tugging" and "leading." "Tugging" occurs when the teacher responds to a student's statement with "What else?" Such responses seem innocuous, but they lack a clear focus for the additional thought the teacher desires. Provided below is an example of a negative "tugging" sequence; it is followed by a positive dialogue interaction:

> *Negative Sequence*
> Teacher: Why did South Carolina secede from the Union?
> Student: Because they were mad at Abraham Lincoln.
> Teacher: Say more!

Positive Sequence
Teacher: Why did South Carolina secede from the Union?
Student: Because they were mad at Abraham Lincoln.
Teacher: And what specifically caused them to be angry?

"Leading" occurs when the teacher makes a statement and then asks the class whether they agree, or subtly tries to co-opt them into concurring with a teacher's observation. An example follows.

Negative Example
Teacher: Class, don't you believe that Abraham Lincoln had no choice regarding his treatment of the South? Lincoln was correct in dealing harshly with the southern states, don't you agree?

Positive Example
Teacher: What choices did Lincoln have once the states in the South decided to secede from the Union?

Dillon (1984) once observed that "discussions are hard to conduct and they are hard to learn how to conduct. Contrary to common sense, questioning is a complex skill" (p. 53). Questioning *is* a complex skill, and for that reason teachers need to really practice developing and using different types of questions. Without such practice, teachers foster too much "tugging" and "leading" and not enough critical thinking.

❸VALUATION CRITERIA

Because oral discussion takes so many different forms, the assessment of classroom interaction patterns and processes is quite difficult. Like all of the instructional models, however, good discussions require that teachers do some preplanning of what questions they want to ask and what overall learning objectives they seek to achieve.

Phase I: Identify the focus for discussion

1. Identify the focus for the discussion. What major ideas are the students exploring?

_____
_____
_____
_____

2. Identify at least two questions at each of the following levels that are asked during the lesson.

Factual:
1. _____
2. _____
Interpretive:
1. _____
2. _____
Evaluative:
1. _____
2. _____

Phase II: Pose the question for discussion

1. What is the first question that is asked of the students?

_____
_____
_____

2. Is the initial teacher-initiated question structured to foster cognitive dissonance in the students?

◯ Yes ◯ No

3. What kind of questioning process does the teacher use to create the cognitive dissonance?

_____ Key question
_____ Devil's advocate

Phase III: Foster participation

1. What type of classroom organizational structure does the teacher use to enable oral discussion?

_____ Whole-class roundtable
_____ Buzz group
_____ Inner circle

2. As the discussion progresses, does one student speak at a time?

◯ Yes ◯ No

3. As the discussion progresses, do students "play off" (utilize) comments of their peers as well as respond to the questions of the teacher?

◯ Yes ◯ No

4. Does the teacher ask a lot of "why" questions in order to force students to defend their answers?

◯ Yes ◯ No

Phase IV: Summarize the students' positions

1. Does the teacher require students to synthesize the ideas suggested during the discussion?

◯ Yes ◯ No

2. What synthesis organizational strategy does the teacher use?

_____ Whole-group synthesis
_____ Small-group synthesis
_____ Personal synthesis

SAMPLE LESSON

The following lesson illustrates a teacher using the *devil's advocate* strategy. The case study presented at the beginning of this chapter is illustrative of the *key question* approach.

CASE STUDY

Ms. Gwendolyn Walker has been teaching a unit on homelessness to a group of high school youngsters in Chicago. The students have read articles and books about homelessness, had guest speakers (that is, sociologists, psychologists, and justice personnel) discuss the implications of homelessness on families and society, and interviewed the homeless and those social service workers who provide services to the homeless.

The class is now ready to begin synthesizing all of these experiences through discussion and problem-solving activities. Ms. Walker begins this segment of the unit by saying: "Class, during the past couple of weeks, we have been reading books that deal with homelessness. Let's review for a couple of minutes some of the reasons why there are homeless people here in Chicago. Luis, identify some of the reasons for homelessness in our society."

"Well, some people are mentally ill. They just can't take care of themselves. Others are drug addicts. If you go down to where my mother works, you can see them on the corner, just sitting around."

"Are there any other reasons that you can think of, Julianna?"

"Well, a lot of the homeless are children."

"That's correct. Remember the one article we read estimated that between 250,000 to 750,000 school-age children are homeless. I think the stories we've read and the experiences we have encountered provide us with a good sense of what it must be like to be homeless. But I would like for us to consider what some reformers are proposing to alleviate the plight of the homeless. Specifically, they suggest people are homeless by choice, and that if we try to take care of them we only make the situation worse. We are going to use a buzz group approach today, so you'll need to get into your cooperative groups."

The students get into their assigned groups, and Ms. Walker asks for their attention. She identifies a recorder, leader, and facilitator in each group. The recorder lists the students' ideas, the leader makes certain the group stays on topic, and the facilitator makes certain everyone participates. Ms. Walker assigns several more readings to the students. Most are quite short and can be analyzed quickly.

Ms. Walker initiates the buzz group activity with, "I want you to use the material I've provided to either support or reject my statement that the homeless chose their condition, and that helping them will only make matters worse. Try to first see if your group members can agree on a response, and then look for evidence that you can use to support your ideas. Also, I would like for you to prepare some questions that you think need to be addressed."

The class begins its group work; the students discuss their ideas and prepare position statements based on the readings. The students work for almost 20 minutes before Ms. Walker tells them to wrap up their group assignment.

After the students have completed their readings and discussed their perceptions and findings from the articles, Ms. Walker begins the oral discussion phase of this lesson by asking various levels of questions. She begins by calling on Mark. "Mark, did your group decide to accept or reject my statement?"

"We rejected it."

"Why?"

"Well, first of all, kids can't help it if they're homeless, and the one article said that children are the fastest growing group of homeless people in the United States."

Most of the groups in the class reject the statement originally presented by Ms. Walker. The students offer explanations similar to that provided by Mark and his group. The teacher then asks the students for their questions. Most of the questions the students ask are factual:

- "Are more girls than boys homeless?"
- "Are more blacks than whites homeless?"

The teacher, though, adds a couple of questions of her own:

- "What does it mean in the article that new medicines will allow mentally ill people to live near-normal lives?" (interpretive)
- "In what ways might the conditions of homelessness that we've read about become worse during the next few years?" (evaluative)

Ms. Walker then lists all the questions on the board (some the students generated, while others are teacher developed) and then assigns the questions as homework for the students. She tells them to answer all the questions (she suggests some resources) and to be prepared to work in their groups the next day to see how their peers responded to the questions. ■

Follow-up questions

1. Identify other ways in which Ms. Walker could have initiated the discussion. This teacher chose the devil's advocate strategy. What other strategies might have proven useful?

2. What other follow-up strategies might be used by the teacher to extend the students' thinking?

❶ESSON PREPARATION

The oral discussion instructional model is one of the most commonly used and least understood techniques. Part of the problem is that teachers inadequately prepare to implement the oral discussion model in the classroom. For success, teachers need to have a number of questions ready (and these questions should be framed around a taxonomical hierarchy of thinking) before oral discussions are initiated. If prior lesson preparation does not occur, the classroom discussions will lack focus and direction.

Suggested readings

Dillon, J. T. 1984. "Research on Questioning and Discussion." *Educational Leadership* 42(3): 50–56.

Gall, M. D., and J. P. Gall. 1976. "The Discussion Method." Pp. 116–216 in N. L. Gage (ed.), *Psychology of Teaching Methods.* NSSE 75th Yearbook, Part 1. Chicago: University of Chicago Press.

Gall, M. D., and M. Gillett. 1980. "The Discussion Method in Classroom Teaching." *Theory Into Practice* 19(2): 95–103.

Suggested videotapes

There are no videotapes that we are aware of that specifically deal with oral discussion strategies. However, the ASCD Episode #10 videotape ("12th Grade History") demonstrates how a teacher utilizes a panel discussion in a Malthusian economics lesson. The reader may find this videotape useful in observing how a teacher prepares students to discuss Malthus's economic theory.

Suggested lesson development

Oral discussion is an important strategy for teachers to help reinforce the learning of students. In order for oral discussion to "work," teachers need to:

1. Determine the specific focus for the discussion. What is it that the teacher wants to accomplish?
2. Identify factual, interpretive, and evaluative questions that need to be asked.
3. Identify the strategy (key question or devil's advocate) that will be used to initiate the discussion. What specific question will then be used?
4. Identify what methods will be utilized to enhance student participation (whole-class roundtable, buzz group, or inner circle).
5. Identify how the students will be required to summarize their positions.

We did not provide a lesson plan for this model (following the second case study) as we have for all the other models (Chapters 4–10). Using the same format as we use in the earlier chapters and using the above questions as prompts, develop a lesson plan that utilizes the oral discussion model.

ⓈUMMARY

One of the greatest barriers for most teachers in terms of creating effective discussions is a lack of preplanning regarding questions for focus during the lesson. Teachers are accustomed to planning lessons that have innovative components or hands-on experiences, but they are less inclined to spend a great deal of time preparing lessons involving discussions. Because of the lack of planning, many oral discussions quickly lose focus—the comments of students seem to drift among lots of different ideas, many of which are not apparently relevant to the defined topic. Teachers can mitigate the "drifting" effect by clearly understanding what questions need to be addressed and by periodically providing an internal summary of what has transpired. The teacher, in providing a summary, need not suggest conclusions, but rather can use the opportunity to make certain that all students clearly understand the major points that have been made.

Many students feel that they are not learning when they are discussing ideas. Furthermore, many teachers perceive that they are not teaching when the students are sharing their thoughts. Actually, oral discussion may be one of the most demanding of all pedagogical strategies. If the teacher just allows the students to move aimlessly around a topic, it is not a demanding instructional lesson. But if the teacher expects students to focus on a certain set of questions and to critically think through the nuances of an idea, then the intellectual demands on a teacher are substantial. Some teachers reduce the intellectual risk by asking only questions that they already have answers for—factual questions. Teachers who use interpretive and evaluative questions ensure that students involve themselves in higher-order thought processes. There are no "right" answers for interpretive and evaluative questions. Instead, what teachers must do is help students examine the efficacy of their ideas and the merits of their arguments—such exploration is not easy and requires practice and coaching, even for veteran teachers.

One additional note. The movie *Dangerous Minds* provides insights into how Louann Johnson sought to reach a group of urban high school students. The students, especially as portrayed in the movie, are racially and ethnically diverse and academically deficient. Ms. Johnson does two things to reach the students. First, she uses culturally congruent ideas (that is, the poetry of the streets). Second, she uses oral discussion as a way of involving the students in their own learning. The students discuss (and research) which Dylan Thomas poems and Bob Dylan song lyrics are similar and the meaning of their respective ideas. She especially focuses on interpretive questions—"Who is the tambourine man?"—as a way of moving the students toward an appreciation of literature. Even assuming some romanticization of Ms. Johnson's teaching, it is clear that what she did is part of what authors like Amy Tan (author of *The Joy Luck Club* and *The Hundred Secret Senses*) might call the secret senses—moving beyond direct experience and what common sense dictates. Good teachers know how to "read" students, and good teachers know that teaching is not just telling, it is also listening. No strategy demands this skill more than oral discussion.

❶ EFERENCES

Bloom, B., M. Englehart, E. Furst, W. Hill, and D. Krathwohl. 1956. *Taxonomy of Educational Objectives: The Classification of Educational Goals Handbook I: Cognitive Domain.* New York: David McKay.

Dillon, J. T. 1984. "Research on Questioning and Discussion." *Educational Leadership* 42(3): 50–56.

Gall, M. D., and J. P. Gall. 1976. "The Discussion Method." Pp. 116–216 in N. L. Gage (ed.), *Psychology of Teaching Methods.* NSSE 75th Yearbook, Part 1. Chicago: University of Chicago Press.

Gall, M. D., and M. Gillett. 1980. "The Discussion Method in Classroom Teaching." *Theory Into Practice* 19(2): 95–103.

Golenbock, P. 1990. *Teammates.* San Diego, CA: Gulliver Books, Harcourt Brace Jovanovich.

Gollnick, D. M., and P. C. Chinn. 1994. *Multicultural Education in a Pluralistic Society* (4th ed.). New York: Macmillan.

Good, T., and J. E. Brophy. 1994. *Looking in Classrooms* (6th ed.). New York: HarperCollins.

Gunter, M. A., T. H. Estes, and J. H. Schwab. 1995. *Instruction: A Models Approach* (2d ed.). Boston: Allyn & Bacon.

Hirsch, E. D. 1988. *Cultural Literacy.* New York: Vintage Books.

McKeachie, W. 1986. *Teaching Tips* (8th ed.). Lexington, MA: D. C. Heath.

Orlich, D. C., R. J. Harder, R. C. Callahan, C. H. Kravas, D. P. Kauchak, R. A. Pendergrass, and A. J. Keogh. 1985. *Teaching Strategies: A Guide to Better Instruction* (2d ed.). Lexington, MA: D. C. Heath.

Ramirez, M., III, and A. Castaneda. 1974. *Cultural Democracy, Bicognitive Development, and Education.* New York: Academic Press.

Tredway, L. 1995. "Socratic Seminars: Engaging Students in Intellectual Discourse." *Educational Leadership* 53(1): 26–29.

Walberg, H. 1995. "Productive Teaching." Pp. 41–55 in A. C. Ornstein (ed.), *Teaching: Theory into Practice.* Boston: Allyn & Bacon.

Wiggins, G. 1989. "The Futility of Trying to Teach Everything of Importance." *Educational Leadership* 47(3): 44–59.

World Geography. 1993. Morristown, NJ: Silver Burdett Ginn.

Zelderman, H., G. Comber, and N. Maistrellis. 1992. "The Touchstones Project: Learning to Think Cooperatively." Pp. 138–150 in N. Davidson and T. Worsham (eds.), *Enhancing Thinking Through Cooperative Learning.* New York: Teachers College Press.

C

• *Reflecting on Instructional Model Usage*

Developing Teachers for the Culturally Diverse

In previous chapters of *Strategies for Teaching in a Diverse Society: Instructional Models*, we emphasized the need for current and prospective teachers to be cognizant of the different ways in which students learn. These learning preferences, as we found from the literature (Cabezas, 1981; Cooper, 1987; Damico, 1983; Garcia, 1991; Hale-Benson, 1986; More, 1990; Pang, 1990, 1995; Ramirez and Castaneda, 1974; Shade and Edwards, 1987; Soldier, 1989; and Vasquez, 1991), vary from student to student primarily because of family child-rearing practices and the cultural characteristics that are a very real part of the nurturing process. In addition, we provided the reader with eight alternative instructional models that can be matched with the specific learning strengths of students; the models also enhance a teacher's instructional repertoire in order to help all students learn based upon their learning preferences. The rationale for the latter is important in order to help students acquire and apply learning skills that they have not been previously disposed to use in the classroom setting. Only by developing and using different cognitive skills, both relational and analytical, can students understand and solve the array of complex problems that will confront them in American society.

Children from different cultures process information and perceive phenomena differently. The cultural background of youngsters plays an important role in determining how students receive and communicate information. All youngsters, male and female, no matter what their cultural background, grow up in a cultural and family context that molds their preferences for how they learn. Vygotsky (1978) describes how any new learnings are built upon prior knowledge and skills—what is about to be learned is based upon what has been

Coming to school every day becomes a hopeless task for some of our children unless they succeed at what they do. We teachers are the sentries against that hopelessness.

UNKNOWN

learned. Thus, the teacher needs to consider and determine both the prior learnings of each student and how to relate new learnings in culturally congruent contexts. Because cultural dynamics influence learning, some youngsters learn best by taking the whole of phenomena and dividing it into its component parts; other youngsters learn best by taking the various components and creating new wholes. Some youngsters work best in a highly structured and teacher-directed classroom environment; other youngsters learn best in a more informal, student-initiated environment (for example, one youngster may develop cognitively through frequent and direct contact with a teacher, while another youngster may grow in a relatively independent manner). Some youngsters learn best through deductive thinking processes (reasoning from the general to the specific); other youngsters must use inductive thinking processes (reasoning from specifics to the general). In other cases, youngsters learn best in a classroom environment that helps students relate academic information to familiar (concrete) world experiences, whereas in other situations students enjoy playing with abstractions as they contemplate concrete possibilities. Some youngsters learn best visually, others learn through auditory modes, and still others learn through the use of kinesthetic/tactile activities. Finally, some youngsters learn best by working with peers in a collaborative manner (field dependent); other youngsters prefer to learn in an isolated manner (field independent).

As described in the cognitive style discussion of this text (Chapter 2), there are students in our nation's schools who have been taught at home to be involved in the issues of the family (discussions at the family meal), while in other families students have been taught to be "seen and not heard." In each case, the student will behave quite differently when interacting with teachers and fellow students, and through the choice of alternative instructional models and strategies. In essence, to be effective, a teacher must:

1. Recognize that some students, based upon gender and cultural group affiliation, learn in quite unique and idiosyncratic ways.

2. Recognize that students in America's classrooms vary from one another according to their cognitive style of learning.

3. Recognize that there is a positive correlation between specific student cognitive styles and the need for teachers to expand upon their instructional model repertoire.

4. Recognize the usefulness of acquiring alternative instructional models as part of a teaching repertoire.

Thus, students and even their teachers are not the same in terms of how they perceive and process phenomena; react to different situations; instruct in terms of teaching style; and communicate their thoughts, desires, and understandings. This may pose a real dilemma for schools, but to ignore its importance and use only one kind of instructional delivery system would be a disservice to those youngsters teachers are expected to serve. McDiarmid (1990) speaks against exclusive use of traditional forms of instruction when he says: "While 'all children can learn' has become the latest mantra of teacher education, the evidence is that many teachers and prospective teachers continue to believe that not all children can learn the same things" (p. 19). Only those teachers who believe in the inherent abilities of all youngsters to learn, and who utilize a variety of instructional models, will be successful in maximizing the achievement of all students. Recall (Chapter 1) that we asserted that teachers, in their pursuit of instructional change, should begin basing their instructional decisions upon three new fundamental assumptions:

New Belief 1. All youngsters can learn at significantly higher levels if teacher instructional practice changes to accommodate the diverse learning styles of students.

New Belief 2. Teachers can learn how to teach more successfully if they are provided with the proper preparation experiences.

New Belief 3. Teachers must reflect considerably higher expectations for students. If students are to achieve their full academic potential, teachers must believe students can achieve more.

The previous chapters in this text have been grounded upon these "new beliefs," and the case studies, narratives, and activities presented focused on developing the teaching behaviors, values, and attitudes needed for working with youngsters in a culturally diverse society. Through the acquisition and application of a repertoire of alternative instructional models, our nation's youngsters will be able to acquire the variety of cognitive skills necessary to both strengthen and transcend their natural learning inclinations—in essence, to reach their full potential. Teachers need to utilize their students' cognitive strengths and develop in them the cognitive and affective skills necessary to maximize their learning opportunities. Why?—because students in today's schools must be prepared for a world that demands that they be able to change and to solve problems in a myriad of ways.

The ideas, research findings, and instructional models presented provide a rich set of data concerning the possible classroom environment of the future. We would now like to focus more specifically on the teacher and the aspects of the teacher's role in a culturally diverse society:

1. Teacher Leadership
2. Teacher Career Stages
3. Teacher Inclusiveness
4. Teachers for Tomorrow's World

The fourth aspect, Teachers for Tomorrow's World, suggests that the next generation of teachers will have to evidence skills that have not previously been emphasized. Specifically, the "new" teacher will need to:

• Foster inclusiveness in the classroom context.
• Create action plans to foster personal growth.
• Identify a professional coach to enhance personal growth.

The emphasis of this chapter will be upon teacher self-renewal and the processes and procedures that individuals can use in liberating themselves as professionals in maximizing student growth and development.

❶EACHER LEADERSHIP

The teacher's work in the American classroom is more complex than ever. Teachers must respond to the needs of a diverse and changing student clientele; an increasingly changing technology; a new set of demands for both excellence and equity from all segments of society; a clamor to shrink the gap between the haves and have-nots; and an array of requests to meet the social, economic, health, and educational needs of students. The global economic marketplace raises the stakes even higher in its performance demands upon schools. The role of teacher-leader is a natural and necessary outgrowth of the increased demands for excellence being placed on schools. Addressing and overcoming the problems plaguing schools require a new and dynamic form of leadership—a leadership that can come only from this nation's teachers. Teachers of the future must assume leadership positions not only in the classroom but also within the school community. Such leadership will enable teachers to utilize a repertoire of instructional models, to coach and mentor professional colleagues, to inquire about and reflect upon the various aspects of the classroom culture, to develop curricular and instructional resources for youngsters, and to strengthen the relationship between the school and home.

Max DePree (1989), the former CEO of Herman Miller (one of the country's largest producers of office furniture), described the art of leadership as "liberating people to do what is required of them in the most effective and humane way possible" (p. xx). Thus, the leader is the "servant" of the followers (students and other teachers); the leader (in this instance, the teacher) removes those obstacles that prevent others (students) from doing their work. The true teacher (leader) enables students to realize their full potential.

Much of the current literature on leadership utilizes ecclesiastical terms to delineate the qualities and characteristics of effective leaders. The notion of liberating followers and becoming a "servant" of the followers has fascinating connotations. The meaning of "liberating followers" relates to the transition from a bureaucratic, authoritarian style of leadership found in most schools today, to a postindustrial model (collaboration, team-building, problem-solving, technology-orienting, and change-producing), with the goal of educating all youngsters no matter what their cultural affiliation or gender. "Servant-leaders" learn to lead by empowering others rather than by controlling others through their line authority. They do this by building a covenant, by basing what they do on cooperation and democratic leadership, and by ministering to the needs of others rather than exerting power over their followers (Bolin, 1989; Sergiovanni, 1989, 1991). A perfect case in point that exemplifies this concept of leadership has been ably demonstrated by the South African President, Nelson Mandela. In his party's presidential and parliamentary victory rally, he addressed those in attendance not as his followers but as fellow leaders to whom he listened and from whom he learned. Mandela asserted:

> I am your servant. I don't come to you as a leader, as one above others. We are a great team. Leaders come and go, but the organization and the collective leadership that has looked after the fortunes and reversals of this

organization will always be there. And the ideas I express are not ideas invented in my own mind.

Mandela exemplifies key principles of leadership: trustworthiness, respect for the dignity of all human beings, service, faithfulness, consistency, and keeping promises—all qualities that teachers as leaders will need to practice in the twenty-first century if schools are to be the vital force that Americans want for transmitting necessary cultural knowledge to students.

Given this role description of "servant-leader," writers have begun describing the need for value-based leadership (O'Toole, 1995), moral leadership (Sergiovanni, 1992), the moral purpose of schooling (Fullan, 1993), and the moral imperatives of schools (Goodlad, 1990a; Goodlad, Soder, and Sirotnik, 1990b). Moral leadership connotes the use of values and value judgments in the selection, extension, and day-to-day practices of educational leaders. A moral leader is consistently cognizant of the central purpose of schooling. All curricular programs, instructional delivery systems, interactions with students and colleagues, and assessment policies and procedures are intricately related to the moral purpose of schools. Such educators view their task more as a mission than a job (Murphy, 1991), and "as a meaningful calling of the highest order" (Roberts, 1990, p. 134). Moral educators are grounded in a sensitivity "to racial issues and to the goal of equal educational opportunity" (Culbertson, 1988, p. 28), responsive to the disenfranchised and undereducated youngsters rather than molding them to the outdated goals of schools (Astuto, 1990; Clark, 1990; Greenfield, 1990); and these practices call for examining current organizational structures (tracking, Carnegie units, grade levels, and so on) in order to educate all children to guarantee their future success.

The major premise used by Fullan (1993) to explain the rationale for educational change and the critical role teachers must play revolves around the idea that "the moral purpose [of teachers] is to make a difference in the lives of students regardless of background, and to help produce citizens who can live and work productively in increasingly dynamic complex societies" (p. 4). What is new about this definition, besides the use of the term *moral purpose*, is that it places teachers precisely at the center of continuous school improvement and change. Teachers are charged with educating critical thinkers and problem-solvers, and in making a difference in the lives of students regardless of their students' cultural backgrounds. It is a "mission" and a "calling" that teachers must embark upon in order to help youngsters reach their full potential.

To embark upon such a mission, educators (as leaders) in this nation's classrooms must be clear about their own beliefs. They must think through their assumptions about human nature and how youngsters learn, about the potential of all youngsters to learn and grow in today's society, about the role of the school and its place in the development of society, and about the measures of performance needed by their students and by themselves as teachers.

The basic requirement for change is *hope*. Teachers must consistently encourage students to believe that it is possible to create a better society. When this occurs, schools will be in a better position to mobilize large numbers of previously passive and hopeless youngsters and to enable them to believe in themselves and to achieve their potential. Classroom cultures need to be designed so that positive, optimistic opportunities are discovered, explored, and created. Thomas Jefferson spoke eloquently about the value of equality of opportunity—the realization that all individuals have the right to achieve their personal potential; all people should have the opportunity to exercise some considerable control over their own destiny. The classroom culture must present youngsters with these same opportunities of choice; those choices are essential for a fulfilled life. Aristotle asserted long ago that all people could achieve happiness only if they fully explored *all* their abilities. To fully develop their abilities, our nation's students need to believe that better living conditions can be created, and that there is a role for all citizens to play in the process of fostering equitable social participation. Teachers in classrooms across this country should begin a process of pedagogical entrepreneurship—choosing from alternative value positions, seeking alternative solutions, valuing and taking risks, being advocates for their students, and acting as the best hope for the children they serve.

TEACHER CAREER STAGES

From sunup to sundown, the schoolteacher works harder than you do—no matter what you do. No calling in our society is more demanding than teaching, more selfless than teaching, and more central to the vitality of a democracy.

ROGER MUDD

The concept of teacher leadership, which was discussed in the previous section, has implications for an analysis of teacher career stages. A number of researchers (Adams, 1982; Ball and Goodson, 1985; H. Becker, 1977; Newman, 1979; Peterson, 1964; and Super, 1957) have delineated the stages individuals in most professions experience as they progress in their careers. One model we have found useful in understanding the professional careers of educators, and in helping school systems design staff-development programs, was created by Fuller (1969) and Fuller and Bown (1975). Fuller's development of teacher career stages was motivated by her observation that many teachers experience similar patterns of change in the concerns they have relative to teaching.

The Fuller model consists of four developmental stages (though only three of these stages will be discussed here). Actually, Fuller noted that at the first (preteaching) stage, the individual would evidence few concerns. Once the individual began to experience some pedagogical responsibilities, this nonconcern quickly evaporated. Fuller's stages are not based on an educator's chronological age or the number of career years in the profession. In fact, there are, unfortunately, a number of educators who never advance from one career stage to another during their professional lives. Most educators, we contend, travel almost nondevelopmentally within and among the career stages, and this is due to 1) changes in leadership either in the building or school district, 2) changes in one's personal life (for example, death of a child, divorce) and its effect upon one's professional life, and 3) changes in teaching specific curricular areas and/or grade levels from one year to the next. With any of the changes just listed, measures of security and insecurity begin to play a part in how teachers approach both new and known experiences. Career changes should provide the opportunities to learn and grow professionally. However, the process of career development is fraught with many pitfalls.

Stage 1: Self/Survival

Teachers in this stage are concerned with their survival and sense of personal adequacy. They consistently ask questions such as "Will I make it?" and "Am I up to this kind of work for the rest of my life?" During this beginning stage, the teacher is concerned with classroom management and discipline, with "making it" from day-to-day and week-to-week during the first years of teaching. Dominant issues such as establishing a classroom routine, learning about district and school procedures, acquainting oneself with the organization's rules and regulations, and fitting into the school culture occupy most of a survival teacher's time. Teachers during the survival stage seldom see beyond the immediate demands of each teaching episode; they are oriented to the practical (what works!); thus, most philosophical directions learned from the literature and discussions in courses and seminars are rarely put to use in the everyday work of the teacher. Because "survivors" are so concerned with classroom control, they have a strong need for an orderly classroom—one that makes them feel secure that they will succeed and that students will comply with their requests. Finally, teachers functioning within this stage, especially teachers who have remained or returned to this stage, have the attitude that they know what works for them and their students; they are very skeptical about using new instructional ideas. Many new teachers and a small number of veteran teachers can be found functioning within this stage.

Stage 2: Task

Task teachers know that they can cope with the multiple demands of teaching. They have learned how to create a classroom that functions in an orderly fashion, and they know how to get students to do what must be done. They understand that because of their past experiences as teachers, they will survive! However, task teachers are not especially concerned with how students structure and organize the knowledge they are acquiring. Instead, their orientation is toward keeping students busy, even if the students' academic tasks lack intellectual meaning. Teachers at this stage tend to limit the number of ways in which they approach the delivery of content to their students. They expect students to adjust to their teaching style rather than to modify their instruction to fit student learning needs. Task teachers have not really clarified their philosophical views about instruction nor have they operationalized alternative instructional systems as a part of their pedagogical behavior. Educators at this stage need specific reasons for utilizing alternative instructional procedures. We contend, and this is a nonempirical assertion, that the vast majority of experienced educators across this nation are task teachers. They have adjusted their teaching to meet the demands of classroom life and have learned a set of coping strategies for negotiating the increasingly complex nature of the teaching–learning process.

Stage 3: Impact

Teachers at this stage are self-directed! Impact teachers emphasize the mastery of the central core of their work, the identification of areas of strength, the negotiation of a satisfying work environment, and the specific instructional skills needed to make an impact upon individual student lives. Impact teachers are very aware of the many demands of the teaching role, but they also expect excellence from themselves and their students. Because of this drive for excellence, such educators are frequently very critical of themselves when students do not achieve what is expected. The response by these teachers is more "What didn't I do appropriately?" or "What can I do more effectively to help my youngsters?" Impact teachers examine classroom phenomena from multiple perspectives and recognize how the decisions they make influence the learning that occurs. Teachers who are found within this stage value both the practical and theoretical (frequently they "play" with theoretical constructs and manipulate them in such a way as to use them in a pragmatic manner); they manage ambiguity very well and are relatively secure in their abilities and skills. A limited number of educators are found within this stage. Finally, impact teachers challenge the status quo by looking at new ways to approach the study of phenomena, and by challenging the basis for established teaching practices. They are comfortable in doing this and have little need for defensiveness when challenges and alternatives are presented to them.

Implications

The use of teacher career stages is offered here as a way to think about the need to design and implement meaningful professional development programs in a complex and diverse society. Our conceptualization of the Fuller model is useful for four reasons. First, in today's world, numerous groups actively seek to influence the policies and procedures of schools. These groups—religious, cultural, political action, handicapped rights, the gifted, and so on—represent views ranging from the far right to the ultraliberal. Each has its own agenda on how to reform and remake educational institutions, and each creates its own agenda using whatever means are available to influence school boards, legislative committees, and state policy agencies.

Second, schools mirror the problems and perspectives of the communities they serve. The school does not exist in an atmosphere of social and political isolation. The issues and problems discussed in the early chapters of this text—single-parent families, poverty and welfare, dropout rates, drug and alcohol abuse, economic aspiration no matter what the social consequences, and cultural pluralism—are all an integral part of what influences the school both positively and negatively. Additionally, all of these issues are reflected in the values and attitudes people hold about the successes and failures of schools and teachers.

Third, compounding the complexity of calls for educational reform and the influence of cultural diversity is the fact that the population of the United States is aging because of lower birth rates and lower mortality rates (Pifer and Bronte, 1986). The critical issue here is a public policy and resource allocation dilemma not previously felt in this country's history (U.S. Select Committee on Aging and American Association of Retired Persons, 1984). Additionally, most of the teachers in this country have entered their middle-age years. The data suggest that at least one-half of the current teacher workforce will retire in the next 10 years (*Job Search Handbook for Educators*, 1996 ASCUS Annual). In some school districts, teachers who are retiring are being replaced by individuals who are hired precisely because they have broader cultural understandings. Rochester, New York, for example, fostered a recent buyout of experienced teachers with new teachers who could more readily and effectively negotiate the cultural realities of urban life. These new teachers were identified through the use of special interview processes that identify the ability of new teachers to try new techniques with students.

The typical classroom teacher has taught for approximately 20 years—most of which has been in the same district. While it would seem that this typical teacher is at a career peak, opportunities for advancement, salary increases, and/or career development have been severely hampered because of the lack of resources and the lack of personal will to continue career growth. Many teachers report the lack of opportunity for growth or reward to be their major disappointment and source of dissatisfaction. Add to this dissatisfaction the changing student body—with its cultural diversity, complex family structures, pluralistic value systems, endemic social and economic ills, and lack of resources for real educational reform—and the result is disenfranchisement and professional alienation.

Finally, Fuller's career stages have much relevance for staff-development efforts because of the current nature of the student body and teacher workforce in schools. Most teachers who teach in America's schools are European American; unfortunately, it is likely that even more of the teachers in the future will be so! Yet the students in our schools, and especially in our urban schools, are increasingly racially and ethnically diverse (Graham, 1987). Demographic projections indicate that by the end of this century, over one-third of all students attending schools across this country will be students of color (Baratz-Snowden, 1986; McNett, 1983; U.S. Bureau of the Census, 1991). Despite increased diversity among America's students, the workforce in America's schools is becoming less diverse—the typical teacher is European American, middle class, and female, and has approximately 20 years of experience (Balch, 1991). The demographic figures on teachers of color make it clear that the education profession, which presently evidences an underrepresentation of persons of color, will confront an even more serious shortage of such individuals in the future (Bell and Morsink, 1986; Cheatham, 1982; Graham, 1987; Hilliard, 1984; Matczynski and Shugarman, 1989; Reed, 1986). In short, as the number of students of color is increasing in the schools, the number of teachers of color is decreasing (Haberman, 1989); by the year 2000, that percentage is projected to be about 3 percent of the total teacher workforce (*Digest of Education Statistics*, 1986). Educational policymakers must be mindful of the importance for youngsters to observe in the classroom context teachers of color who serve as role models— role models to European American youngsters in promoting multicultural understanding, and role models to students of color in promoting achievement and social justice concerns.

The disparity of large numbers of students of color in relationship to small numbers of teachers of color is cause for concern because of the tacit messages being sent to young people: "[T]he race and background of (children's) teachers tells them something about authority and power in contemporary America and influence(s) children's attitudes toward school, their academic accomplishments, and their views of their own and others' intrinsic worth" (Carnegie Forum on Education and the Economy, 1986, p. 79).

Additionally, research has pointed out how cultural differences can affect communication and create misunderstandings, misperceptions, and miscommunication (Heath, 1983). Feldman (1980), for example, found that within classrooms different communication patterns exist between teachers and students from mixed racial groups. The communication patterns result in subtle nonverbal messages, and those messages have potentially real consequences for student performance. Feldman writes:

> First, both white and black teachers appear to behave more positively toward members of their own race than toward members of other racial groups. Second, the nonverbal behavior of teachers seems to be related to their racial attitudes. The mere presence of a white or black student may be sufficient to evoke the nonverbal behaviors associated with particular attitudes (pp. 47–48).

The cultural dissonance that Feldman argues exists between culturally diverse students and their teachers inadvertently fosters lowered student expectations on the part of teachers. Why?—because teachers who are unaware of the cultural heritage and cognitive styles of culturally diverse youngsters underestimate and "misread" the experiential background, knowledge base, and skills of students because they have not learned to understand the manner in which these students learn, perceive, and think about phenomena (Haberman, 1989; Hull et al., 1991).

The traditional experience called "schooling" de-emphasizes the worth of culturally diverse students. Schools, for the most part, are not able to accept the diversity found in this country—a diversity that inherently emphasizes different needs, abilities, and aspirations; it is the teacher who is unprepared and unaware of how to instruct youngsters from culturally diverse environments. The remainder of this text is devoted to a discussion of *teacher behaviors* (Chapters 4–11 focus on instructional practices) that prevent or promote the inclusiveness of culturally diverse students in the school. Because schools will not receive a great flux of teachers of color in the near future, it is incumbent upon all those who plan to work with diverse populations to know how to adjust their instruction to better meet the students' needs. Schools have not accommodated such cultural diversity in the past; the school as an institution has expected individual students to accommodate to its structure, operation, and goals rather than for the school to accept, accommodate, and adjust to the student.

With this in mind, we move toward the essence of the message of this text: a discussion of teacher inclusionary and noninclusionary behaviors that have the potential to promote or prevent student learning. Identification and discussion of these behaviors are critical in helping fashion new teacher education and staff-development programs. The following discussion is important in helping change the very perceptions of current and prospective teachers in terms of their expectations, teaching behaviors, communication strategies, and values and attitudes about culturally diverse students.

Ⓣeacher Behaviors That Foster Noninclusiveness or Inclusiveness

You cannot teach a child you do not love. You cannot teach a child you do not respect. You cannot teach a child you do not understand.

Jawanza Kunjufu

Because the teacher-leader is the key player in determining the success or failure of students in the classroom, what teachers do or intend to do is of primary importance to students. As soon as students enter the classroom, they are learning from the teacher's verbal and nonverbal behaviors (that is, what the teacher does, what the teacher says, how the teacher decorates the room, and so on). The culture of the classroom—the climate the teacher creates, the language that is used, how the teacher dresses and treats the students—all serve as strong indicators for what the teacher *expects* from the students. How teachers interact with their students, evaluate students' progress, communicate what they expect from them, recognize their individual needs, and demonstrate how, positively or negatively, they feel about them as individuals provide a very clear signal about what they value in them as students and the attitudes they wish to instill.

The authors once met a teacher of urban youngsters who always dressed, day in and day out, as if she were going out to a fancy restaurant. After a few weeks of observing this 5th grade teacher, we asked her why she always dressed so well. She looked at us in astonishment and said, "Why, I'm doing the most important work of humankind. I'm teaching! And, I'm working with the most important group of people in the world. My students! They are our future! Wouldn't you communicate their importance by the way you dress for them?"

Teachers who hold youngsters dear to their hearts demonstrate their respect for their students by dressing up for them; recognizing their needs and desires in life; selecting from alternative instructional strategies; and expecting only the best from and for them in their academic pursuits. The teacher of the twenty-first century never thinks in unidimensional terms in a multidimensional world. Teaching is not easy work! It requires much time, commitment, understanding, and knowledge in order to function effectively for the welfare of youngsters. Zeichner (in press) indicates that those individuals who wish to teach in the twenty-first century need to acquire the following qualities:

1. A clear sense of their own cultural identity.
2. High expectations for student success.

3. The expectation that all students can succeed and that they will be successful if teachers help them succeed.

4. A commitment to achieve equity for all students.

5. The ability to accommodate different learning styles and abilities.

6. The ability to bond with students as a result of genuinely caring about young people and their welfare.

7. A strong multicultural knowledge base that encompasses ethnic studies, gender concerns, and sensitivity to persons with special needs.

The teacher of the future has a very tough road to travel! The road is winding and hilly, narrow and wide, with sharp curves and sheer cliffs, but the rewards of "holding the road" are necessary to sustain the human spirit—of the teacher and the students. In their pedagogical travels, teachers need to be aware of their own inclusive and noninclusive behaviors and how these behaviors are perceived/received by those they serve. Let us first look at those pernicious teacher behaviors that exclude youngsters and have such a devastatingly negative effect upon them.

Noninclusive Beliefs and Behavior Dispositions

1. *Belief in the hierarchies of power, authority, and control.*

   Teachers who act upon this belief communicate that they are the source of learning, the source for what students must do, and the source of all permissible behavior for students. Teachers who are consumed by control and authority function as if they are "the sage on the stage"; they perceive themselves in the role of taking charge, they issue nonnegotiable directives to students, and they control by overmonitoring student behavior. Teachers in such a setting view their role as that of the "authority"—one who exclusively controls and leads the teaching–learning process. Students have few decision-making rights to determine their learning regimens in such teachers' classrooms. The student role in this type of classroom is to comply with the teacher's instructions and to behave in compliant ways. Students have little opportunity to think, make decisions, experiment through trial and error, or practice responsible behavior or democratic principles. As noted earlier from the research of Philips (1972, 1983, 1993), Ramirez and Castaneda (1974), and Soldier (1989), this type of power relationship is very contradictory to the personal and social needs of culturally diverse youngsters. There is an absence of culturally congruent instruction (Ladson-Billings, 1994) operating within power-dominated classroom environments. Marginal student empowerment occurs in such classrooms, and few opportunities to practice democratic ideals occur. In culturally congruent classrooms, teachers and students work together on tasks; teachers win over student followership by "proving" that they are worth following; and teachers and students explore phenomena through questioning procedures, trial and error activities, and the testing of numerous alternatives.

Some of the most innovative schools in the country are working to restructure themselves to avoid artificial hierarchies. The Hyde School (a private high school in Bath, Maine) accomplishes this by placing more responsibility on students for their own learning and on parents for supporting student learning. Such a perspective is not good just for students of color; it is good for all students regardless of their color.

2. *Belief that culturally diverse students are incapable of learning academically rigorous subjects.*

Teachers who operationalize this belief do so from two different perspectives, both of which are equally damaging to culturally diverse students. In the first perspective, some teachers truly believe that students from culturally diverse backgrounds do not have the intellectual background, mental acuity, and academic discipline to maintain a highly rigorous schedule of courses such as algebra, geometry, chemistry, physics, and trigonometry. As a consequence, without the opportunities or encouragement to enroll in these courses, students are not adequately prepared for college or for successful participation in a global economy. With appropriate encouragement, even students from at-risk backgrounds can begin to excel. No circumstance more clearly illustrates this than does Bob Moses's work with the Algebra Project (Cambridge, Massachusetts). Jetter (1993) writes that Moses's idea was both simple and problematic:

> Without algebra, the door to college and most skilled professions is locked. But many black and Hispanic students, if they take algebra at all, learn it too late to get on the college-prep mathematics track. So why not expose every child to algebra in middle school?
>
> Moses has just begun to assess his project's long-term impact; as yet, there is insufficient data to judge its success. But anecdotal information and standardized tests from several schools appear to confirm what Algebra Project teachers have long suspected: "When these kids get the privilege of creating their own mathematics, they become independent learners," says Dorothy Strong, director of mathematics for the Chicago public schools. "And that works on the whole child" (pp. 18, 35).

Some teachers view their students as victims who are incapable of escaping the environmental conditions that prevent academic achievement; other teachers never provide students with intellectual opportunities because the students are viewed as intellectually incapable of learning. Both perspectives are racist and help maintain the negative attitude toward culturally diverse learners. Too often such teachers delude themselves as "helping culturally diverse students" by counseling them into "softer" subject areas in the scheduling process, or by telling students that they are either incapable of learning such subjects or will never have the opportunity to use such academically rigorous subjects anyway. The advice and behavior emanating from this belief drastically limit students in their pursuit of personal dreams.

3. *Belief that cultural and linguistic diversity presents serious barriers to learning.*

Instead of believing that culturally and linguistically diverse students bring a rich background of knowledge, experience, and language proficiency to America's schools, many teachers blame poor school performance on the very diversity of students. Educators, through verbal and nonverbal behaviors, cast aspersions either by indicating that "they [the students] lack the ability, character, or motivation" (Cuban, 1989, p. 781) or by blaming the "perceived" poor home life and cultural background of the students. Students quite easily "pick up" on these negative attitudes—attitudes that subsequently have a profoundly negative impact upon them. It is interesting and at the same time discouraging to hear some educators speak so negatively about culturally diverse students. Rarely if ever do these same educators suggest that student failure may be caused by educators' own beliefs and behaviors or by the school's structural or curricular inadequacies in serving diverse populations. The very structure of the school and/or the lack of accommodation to the concept of diversity cause students to feel denigrated in terms of their needs, abilities, and experiences.

The movie *Renaissance Man* provides an excellent illustration of the last two noninclusive teacher behaviors. In the movie, Bill Rago, an unemployed advertising salesman, gets a job teaching a group of new army recruits. Rago has accepted a teaching position to help a "special" group of new recruits "get ready" (that is, learn reading, writing, and the thinking skills) to become regular army. The class is composed of all males except for one female, and all students are either African American, Hispanic American, or Appalachian. This group of students has been classified by their fellow recruits on the base as "Double D's" ("Dumb as Dogshit") similar to the group "Sweat Hogs" in the television show *Welcome Back, Kotter.*

After Rago requires some initial tasks to determine the students' needs and abilities—writing a short theme and discussing a piece of writing purchased at the PX—the students ask Rago to tell them what he is reading. He responds, *"Hamlet!"* Two of the students ask him what it is about, and he responds, "It's a story about sex, murder, insanity, and incest." This piques their interest, but it is Leroy who asks Rago to tell them about the story. Rago responds, "You guys don't want to hear about *Hamlet.*" Roosevelt Hobbs then responds, "I guess you don't think we're smart enough." Rago says, "It's not that. It's very...complicated." To that the group moans and groans, and one hears in the background, "Here we go again"; "Oh, man"; and finally, "We're here. We're listening!" To that Rago responds by beginning to explain what the play is about. In subsequent lessons through the movie, Rago takes the students back to the historical period of the play, helps them understand figures of speech (that is, similes, metaphors, oxymorons), draws relationships to present-day figures in government and the community, and actively engages the students in the purpose and meaning of *Hamlet.* Initially, however, Rago never expected this group of students to be interested in or motivated by *Hamlet* given their backgrounds, past performances, and perceptions by others on the army base. Once he engaged the students in the subject matter and related it to real-life situations that the students could understand, their enthusiasm and interest carried them to new levels of learning and comprehension.

4. *Unawareness of unique cultural characteristics of students and how these characteristics play a critical role in learning.*

    Teachers described by this statement are not aware of the multicultural literature that identifies and describes some of the unique characteristics of diverse students. Unfortunately, because teacher education institutions are rarely composed of diverse faculty and rarely emphasize multicultural education, most teachers in our nation's schools are unaware of the multiplicity of cultural characteristics and dynamics. The development of multicultural concepts has major implications for how the teacher delivers instruction; how the teacher uses the curriculum to develop knowledge, skills, and attitudes in students; and what culturally relevant curricular concepts should be used in fostering the interest and motivation of students. The literature is rich with research findings as well as practical guides for working with culturally diverse student populations. That literature is not prescriptive; it is suggestive. That means that teachers cannot look for easy solutions ("OK, he's African American, so he needs concrete experiences first in order to understand abstractions"); but, rather, teachers must look at how they structure classrooms so that varied student needs are met through a variety of alternative learning experiences. The use of varied instructional strategies does not serve the interests of just African American or Hispanic American students; it enhances the quality of all students' educational experiences.

5. *Unawareness that public criticism of students by teachers is culturally incongruent and psychologically damaging.*

    One example of the lack of knowledge of unique cultural characteristics of diverse students relates to the use of public criticism. Many teachers regularly use public criticism and critiques to either provide feedback or "make an example" of students who exhibit unacceptable behavior. When this occurs, the child may view this as a "put-down" and either withdraw or react violently. As an example, the cultural reaction to public criticism for many Native American and African American youngsters is to put one's head down (or to lower one's eyes) as a sign of respect to the individual who is doing the criticizing (Byers and Byers, 1972). This nonverbal behavior is learned in the home and is quite common among members of both cultural groups. However, if a teacher is not knowledgeable about this natural reaction, the teacher may interpret the lowered head as disrespectful, impolite, and/or rebellious. The common response sought by most teachers would be that the youngster look at the face of the individual speaking (for example, "Marcus, look me in the eye when I'm talking to you!"). The natural, culturally learned response by youngsters in selected ethnic and racial groups, however, is just the opposite. Only through a knowledge of and appreciation for student behaviors in different cultural contexts can teachers more adequately respond to and interact positively with their students.

6. *Belief that learning is an individual responsibility.*

In many cultures, cooperation and collaboration are highly valued processes—valued much more than individualized accomplishments. Research by Philips (1972, 1993) and Soldier (1989) with Native Americans, Au and Kawakami (1985) with Asian Americans, and Shade (1994) with African Americans has found that children from these cultural groups come to school with a disposition to value group-oriented activities. The values of cooperation and collaboration are held dearly in Native American, African American, and Hispanic American communities and are taught to youngsters through specific child-rearing practices.

The school, however, teaches personal property rights, individual responsibility and freedom, and pits children against one another through various competitive situations. The diverse cultural groups described in this text tend to emphasize the importance of large extended families whose members share property with one another and who place more value on family and how the family perceives the individual rather than on the individual desires and needs of each person within the family unit (Ramirez, 1982, 1989). Schools, however, tend to design and implement instruction through individualized processes (that is, learning alone, winning a spelling bee, having individual seating assignments by row) that are contrary to the natural learning styles of many diverse students.

Other noninclusive teacher beliefs exist that mitigate the learning of culturally diverse youngsters. The above descriptions are intended to be illustrative, not exhaustive. We will now identify and describe selected inclusive behaviors that teachers need to focus upon in working with diverse student populations. These behaviors also emerge out of beliefs, but in this case they have a beneficial rather than a poisoning effect on the students' actions.

Inclusive Beliefs and Behavior Dispositions

The following discussion provides a description of the inclusive behaviors that teachers should utilize in working with diverse students. The list is not comprehensive. There are other behaviors that teachers should exhibit, some of which have been discussed in the previous chapters of this text. Whatever the source for inclusive behaviors, teachers of culturally diverse students need to be well versed in multicultural concepts because such a knowledge base (coupled with expanding research) will help them to become more knowledgeable and sensitive in promoting the growth and development of all of America's children.

1. *Ability to match the culture of the school with the culture of the home.*

For many children in our nation's schools, the classroom environment is a mysterious and foreign place. The classroom does not look or feel like the environment or community within which children live. The pictures, bulletin boards, resource materials, structure of the desks, and teacher behaviors not only are unfamiliar to many culturally diverse youngsters, but often are in stark contrast to the messages that are communicated at home. In classrooms that seek to match the culture of the home, purposeful classroom linkages are created and sustained by both the curricular content and instructional delivery of the teacher. Students in these classrooms find it acceptable to use their past and present experiences as resources for learning (Foster, 1994; Henry, 1990; Ladson-Billings, 1990, 1991). The classroom experience builds upon acquired student experiences, which are legitimized because they become part of the formal curriculum (Ladson-Billings, 1994). In addition, students of color learn within an academic community (where cooperative learning strategies are valued) rather than in an isolated, linear-sequential manner in which one set of skills or academic content is difficult to relate to another set of skills or academic content (Ladson-Billings, 1994).

Effective teachers are those individuals who utilize community resources, topics, issues, events, and experiences in designing curriculum and delivering instruction. These teachers construct curriculum by designing community activities as examples to demonstrate the relationship between "what is worth knowing"—the curriculum—to the child's real world—the community and home life, which is familiar and knowable. Such teaching links community and home experiences... "and incorporates familiar cultural and communicative patterns into the classroom practices, routines, and activities" (Foster, 1994, p. 237).

2. *Ability to utilize all types of culturally relevant materials in the instructional process.*

Teachers who are interested in including culturally diverse students in the instructional process make use of instructional materials, bulletin boards, classroom decorations, and audiovisual aids that are grounded in the culture of the students. Such teachers make a commitment to link culturally familiar experiences with the abstract concepts of learning. Part of the reason for doing this is to bridge the gap between the community and the school. A number of research studies shed light upon the use of culturally relevant materials and their effect upon students.

Heath (1983), who conducted research with African American youngsters, found that using culturally related materials (that is, advertisements, street signs, food labels) had a positive effect upon student interest and motivation. Teachers could describe and demonstrate how students used the skills of reading, writing, and mathematics. Students could recognize the relationship of these skills, follow instructions on using a game or toy, price store objects and make change, and read labels and food ingredients.

Bradley (1984) found similar data in mathematics instruction conducted with Native American youngsters. Various types of geometric patterns found in Navajo Indian blankets were used to teach Euclidean geometry, number theory, coordinate geometry, and measurement processes. Such culturally familiar patterns helped students understand the study of geometry—a very complex subject area—by linking their familiarity with geometric shapes and physical objects to a very abstract academic content area.

Teachers of K–12 mathematics can use "street" math—blackjack, craps, penny pitching, and/or the trading of sports cards or other items—to link the world of mathematics with the real world. Many streetwise youngsters are very skilled at mathematical processes. It is up to the teacher to bring these "street experiences" into the classroom and use this knowledge and concomitant skills in formal ways. The various instructional models presented in Chapters 4 through 11 provide opportunities for students to connect their personal worlds with the instructional world created by the teacher. The concept formation model uses the schema of the students, while the mnemonics model can build upon the spatial intelligence of children to enable them to create visual techniques that help them remember ideas and facts.

Teachers who use culturally relevant materials in the classroom—whether these are origami paper, the celebration of Kwanzaa, or culturally linguistic newspapers—are bringing the familiar environment of the child into the classroom. When teachers do this, they are communicating to students that they value the youngster's cultural environment (and the youngster!), and this helps develop a culturally affirming atmosphere within the classroom.

3. *Belief that learning can take many forms through many modalities.*

   Strategies for Teaching in a Diverse Society: Instructional Models has been presented to affirm the inclusive behaviors of teachers. Most of the research findings in Chapter 2 describe cultural learning dispositions. By affirming students' prior experiences and the richness of the culture that they bring to the classroom, educators are able to "capture" youngsters for the learning process. Various learning modalities (that is, kinesthetic, observation of phenomena, verbal descriptions, visual-spatial relationships, auditory processes, and linear-sequential skills) are but a few ways in which youngsters process information. Jaime Escalante, the famed *Stand and Deliver* teacher, reflects this perhaps better than any other teacher. Escalante used what was familiar to the students within their homes to teach them concepts that were unfamiliar to them at school—see, once again, our illustration of this in Chapter 9.

4. *Ability to utilize cooperative and collaborative instructional activities.*

   One of the instructional models presented in this text is cooperative learning. Cooperative and collaborative instructional activities are another example of a culturally congruent model that teachers should use with diverse youngsters (Bradley, 1984; Gilbert and Gay, 1985). The use of cooperative activities builds upon the natural learning dispositions of a wide variety of cultural groups; educators stress group or team achievement rather than individual accomplishments. Student achievement increases for culturally diverse youngsters when learning occurs as a social activity—in a collaborative environment—rather than as an independent, competitive activity (Bishop, 1986; Philips, 1983; Ramirez, 1982, 1989; Treisman, 1985). To permit youngsters to learn in cooperative groups is a natural use of their cultural experience.

   Previously, we learned that culturally diverse students favor group work over individual activities (Osborne and Bamford, 1987; Philips, 1972, 1983; Shade, 1994; Soldier, 1989). These students do not focus their attention on personal ownership, though they do value personal accomplishments. Many culturally diverse group members have highly developed social skills (that is, group activities, sharing material possessions, taking turns on tasks) because of the child-rearing practices that foster community harmony rather than individual competition. This factor may explain why Slavin and Oickle (1981) and Slavin (1987b, 1987c) found that Hispanic Americans, Native Americans, and African Americans achieve much more effectively than European Americans when cooperative learning is a major instructional strategy in classrooms.

Educators must be vigilant and cognizant of the social makeup, the political composition, and class and gender differences that children bring to the classroom. Sensitivity to these differences, and a cautious view to cultural history and variances, are necessary. However, through the process of group interaction and cooperative learning strategies, differences in class, race, and gender can be minimized over time (Cooper et al., 1980; Hansell and Slavin, 1981; Johnson and Johnson, 1981; Kagan et al., 1985; Oishi et al., 1983; Slavin, 1977, 1979, 1987b, 1987c, 1995; and Weigel et al., 1975).

Finally, teachers can vary the cooperative experiences of youngsters by periodically grouping youngsters according to similar learning styles, interests and/or needs dispositions, cultural/political groupings, homogeneous and heterogeneous groupings, role designations, and so on. Such groupings should be designed based upon specific instructional objectives. Use of cooperative learning communicates that the school values the natural cultural and learning dispositions of students as well as the use of their social and cultural patterns of communication.

5. *Ability to teach youngsters how to function in different cultural and learning-style contexts.*

One of the responsibilities of educators is to extend the learning-style preferences of youngsters. As described in the research of Ramirez and Castaneda (1974), most youngsters learn how to learn through the cultural context in which they were reared. The more exposures to varying cultural child-rearing practices that a child has, the more that child can draw upon learning-style alternatives in order to understand, use, and apply phenomena.

In most classrooms across America, teachers tend to introduce new academic information and concepts through verbal instructions and directions (Appleton, 1983; Rohner, 1965). Such teacher-centered instructional styles, as examined previously, are, in many instances, in conflict with the traditional cultural patterns developed in many Native American, African American, and Hispanic American homes. As described earlier in this section, not only should educators try to connect the culture of the school and the culture of the home, but they should also help students extend their learning preferences in order to maximize their learning opportunities. Teachers need to be cognizant of which instructional behavior is appropriate for what situation, when such situations should occur, and how these situations should be assessed.

It is possible for students, given the appropriate classroom climate and skills of teachers, to alter learning-style behaviors. However, this should be conducted in a conscious, deliberate, and intentional manner by the teacher. We recommend that teachers spend classroom time discussing different learning-style preferences with students, and providing learning-style assessments (Dunn and Griggs, 1988; Myers and McCaulley, 1985; Oxford, 1990; Weinstein et al., 1983) for students to determine their dominant and supporting learning styles. Although this may seem difficult to do, it is possible. We know of one teacher in an urban context who spends the first part of each semester helping students recognize their learning-style preferences and then showing them how to use those preferences as they learn the content in her class. Suggestions concerning learning-style development are provided by O'Malley and Chamot (1990), Oxford (1990), and Wenden and Rubin (1987). Oxford's text lists and describes many learning activities and teaching strategies that can be used by educators to expand student learning styles. Her descriptions are valuable, not only because they utilize many learning domains (that is, creating mental linkages, structuring and reviewing, organizing and arranging learning, and learning study skills), but also because they provide thorough descriptions of sample lessons that teachers can use in developing learning-style skills in youngsters.

6. *Ability to engage students in problem-solving strategies to be used in real-life situations.*

In order for teachers to be effective, they must not only have a thorough knowledge of their subject matter, but also know their students. This knowledge is critical in designing an instructional process that teaches youngsters problem-solving strategies that can be used in challenging the status quo. Through the use of the instructional models such as concept formation, inquiry, and synectics, student thinking is extended and problem-solving skills are introduced, practiced, and applied. By using real-life issues through case studies and by posing questions and/or problems not immediately solvable, students will be engaged in critical thinking by relating academic content, community issues, and problem-solving strategies in a meaningful manner. Instead of solely using a routinized pedagogical cycle, as is found in many school classrooms (see Figure 12.1), students should be engaged in the process of learning as a contextualized experience that relates subject matter, problem-solving skills, personal and community issues, and a challenge to the status quo of most culturally diverse families (Ladson-Billings, 1994).

In her study of teachers of culturally diverse students, Ladson-Billings (1994) describes how some teachers challenge the pedagogical cycle, including the assumptions undergirding the structure of the schools.

> The teachers I studied work in opposition to the school system that employs them. They are critical of the way that the school system treats employees, students, parents, and activists in the community. However, they cannot let their critique reside solely in words. They must turn it into action by challenging the system. What they do is both their lives and livelihoods. In their classrooms, they practice a subversive pedagogy (p. 128).

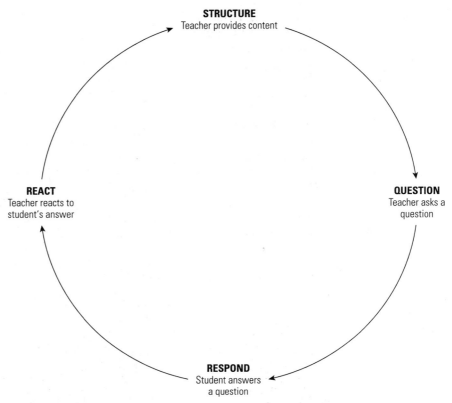

STRUCTURE
Teacher provides content

QUESTION
Teacher asks a
question

RESPOND
Student answers
a question

REACT
Teacher reacts to
student's answer

FIGURE 12-1 The Pedagogical Cycle Common to American Classrooms

Adapted from M. P. Sadker and D. M. Sadker. 1994. *Teachers, Schools and Society.* New York: McGraw-Hill, p. 43.

Teachers who practice subversive pedagogy (see Table 12.1) question the policies, procedures, and practices of those who employ them and of those institutions that prevent individual opportunity and growth. Such challenges utilize the knowledge and problem-solving skills learned through the instructional models described in this text, which can help play a large part in challenging the status quo and the low expectations ascribed to culturally diverse populations.

Though the term *subversive pedagogy* is a relatively recent educational term, the concept emanates from the works of Freire (1970), Giroux (1983), Herndon (1968), Holt (1967), Kohl (1967), Kozol (1967), and Postman and Weingartner (1969). Ideally, through the use of questions, posed by either the teacher or the students, a culturally congruent curriculum is constructed that engages all participants in examining the real-world problems of the community. The teacher's role in this process is not to dictate what students

TABLE 12-1   Subversive Pedagogy

....

Subversive pedagogy is the process by which teachers and students raise questions concerning human behavior within society, the school community, and the classroom community. These questions are not addressed directly but, instead, pose a tacit threat to the established order of society.

Perspectives and Emerging Questions

Society

- *Democratic beliefs are based upon equality of opportunity, and the dignity of humans, yet individuals and institutions are allowed and even encouraged to practice racism and sexism. Why? What are the alternatives?*

- *Census figures demonstrate a growing cultural diversity, while pressure is applied to keep the American citizenry within the narrow boundaries of Western culture, language, and tradition. Why? What are the alternatives?*

- *Demands are made to ensure that critical thinking and individual freedoms are developed and practiced while censorship of materials and practices occurs. Why? What are the alternatives?*

- *Public schools are called upon to educate all youngsters, yet they are blamed for the social and economic disparities that severely detract from their chances of successfully accomplishing specific goals. Why? What are the alternatives?*

Local and School Community

- *Relationships between academic phenomena and the curriculum are disconnected and fragmented. Why? What are the alternatives?*

- *Legislators and police officers are charged with protecting the public, yet these same groups often cause great harm to those whom they serve. Why? What are the alternatives?*

- *Good, quality housing is protected for all Americans through laws and regulations, while at the same time slum landowners are allowed to operate substandard apartments and rentals. Why? What are the alternatives?*

- *Various forms of substance abuse are outlawed in our society, while at the same time drugs of various forms are permitted to enter the country and infest our neighborhoods. Why? What are the alternatives?*

School Classroom

- *Educators talk about the importance of cooperation and collaboration, yet competition dominates. Why? What are the alternatives?*

- *Instructional materials and the curriculum speak little to the contributions of Native Americans, African Americans, and other groups. Why? What are the alternatives?*

- *Athletics are more important than academics. Why? What are the alternatives?*

- *Classroom cultures require more passive learning than active involvement. Why? What are the alternatives?*

- *Students have little involvement in setting learning objectives, choosing learning activities, or evaluating their performance. Why? What are the alternatives?*

- *Educators speak about an inclusive society, yet they have limited interactions with special-needs student. Why? What are the alternatives?*

....

Developed with the assistance of Joseph F. Rogus, University of Dayton.

are to learn, but rather to facilitate and collaborate with students as mutual learners. Together teachers and students plan and design curriculum, determine how best to examine agreed-upon community issues, determine from whom to seek data and alternative solutions, and determine how to proceed in this journey of exploration and possible solution to community issues.

7. *Belief that one of their roles as educators is to challenge the societal status quo with students.*

One way that students and teachers can practice their problem-solving skills is to utilize these skills in real-life situations in the community (for example, neighborhood voter registration and turnout, community environmental issues, or the elimination of drug and prostitution houses). Besides being a culturally congruent instructional behavior, challenges to the status quo are especially consistent with educators' roles as agents of societal change.

Teachers also have an important responsibility in helping students understand that society tacitly communicates low expectations regarding culturally diverse students (Ladson-Billings, 1994). Teachers must join with students to prove that these low expectations are unacceptable! Culturally diverse students must have teachers who have exceedingly high expectations for them and who consistently communicate these expectations whenever possible.

Educators who challenge the status quo also question the social and political realities that culturally diverse students face. Utilizing the problem-solving skills learned through the instructional strategies described in this text, students will develop the skills needed to better embrace the educational opportunities available to them. Educators need to become critics of society and to engage students in a transformative process. Preparing students to pursue individual opportunities for growth and development must be a major goal for teachers of diverse student populations. Teachers who engender this are individuals who are naturally curious. More importantly, they design plans to alleviate the conditions that prevent student growth.

8. *Belief that community volunteers/aides are an integral part of the teaching–learning process.*

Because most of America's teachers are European American, the use of community volunteers/aides has a number of purposes:

a. To serve as cultural role models, especially if the teacher does not share the cultural background of students.

b. To serve as teacher aides of ESL teachers who speak primarily English.

c. To help students make curricular connections between the academic subject matter and the local community setting.

d. To help identify culturally familiar materials to be used in the instructional process.

Paraprofessionals, parents, community residents, and workers within the community can serve as strong role models in achieving the four purposes listed above. Heath (1983) found that parents who helped teachers link abstract curricular concepts with culturally familiar personnel and/or materials from the community served to reinforce what students were expected to learn. When parents participated, student achievement rose and student satisfaction toward school was positive even though the coordination of these community resources put an added burden upon teachers.

Ⓐ ction Plan Schema

Throughout this text, we have provided the reader with a number of advance organizers to understand and use the various concepts and teaching strategies. As we conclude, we would like you to consider one final organizer in developing the instructional models and teacher-inclusive behaviors in your repertoire as an effective educator. This organizer, Figure 12.2, and the steps that follow have been found to be of value to the teachers who have worked with us on these instructional concepts, skills, and attitudes.

In order to utilize this action plan schema, we suggest that you identify a coach (for example, a teaching colleague, your supervisor, or a university faculty member) so that this individual can observe your teaching performances, make notes of your behaviors, and provide feedback concerning your teaching behaviors. We suggest a coach or mentor because we believe most great teachers learn from others as well as from their own experiences. Indeed, for the ideas within this text to take life, a coach is almost essential. Let us examine what we mean by the term *coach*.

Every athlete, from the peewee to the professional leagues, has a coach. Even professional track and field athletes have personal coaches. The purposes of the coach are to observe; to note actual behaviors as they relate to optimal skill; and to provide feedback in order to teach the athlete how to improve, grow, and develop in terms of desired performance. In some cases, coaches may specialize (for example, line vs. quarterback coaches, pitching vs. hitting coaches). The inherent idea is that a coach has specialties that are used to help strengthen, support, and make the athlete more sophisticated in the performance desired.

The same is true of professionals in medicine, law, architecture, and so on. The professional draws upon the expertise of colleagues (often a mentor with more experience) through vehicles such as staff meetings (watch the beginning

Instructional Model to Emphasize _____

Career Stage _____

Improvement Goal(s) _____

OBJECTIVES	STRATEGIES TO ACCOMPLISH OBJECTIVES	ASSESSMENT PROCEDURES

FIGURE 12-2 Teacher Behavior Action Plan

of each *L.A. Law* television show), formalized mentoring programs, and career stages (for example, intern, resident, law clerk, associate, and so on). In fact, even the skilled trades (that is, carpenters, electricians, and plumbers) utilize coaches to help nurture new members and teach the knowledge, skills, and attitudes necessary for becoming an effective artisan. The skilled trades use what is called an *apprenticeship* in order to intern their members to proficiency and success in the chosen field of work.

Curiously, education does very little to encourage coaching within its membership. For the most part, individual teachers work alone or in isolation; little interaction is required or facilitated in terms of curricular or instructional articulation; and each individual is left alone in terms of professional growth and development (Jackson, 1968; Lortie, 1975; Sarason, 1982, 1983). The coaching of teaching first suggested by Joyce and Showers (1980) is an exception rather than the rule in most schools across the nation. The Joyce and Showers staff-development model is a five-step process that begins with providing new information or skills to the teacher; it culminates with the coaching step. Coaching, according to Joyce and Showers, is the act of matching an experienced colleague with a fellow teacher in order for the coach to help the teacher with the following: analyzing that teacher's instructional lesson; observing the teacher teach the lesson; collecting data during the observation; providing feedback to the teacher; asking clarifying questions of the teacher concerning the lesson observed; suggesting alternative lesson procedures; and helping the teacher design a new instructional lesson plan in order to continue the improvement cycle. One of the first studies to assess the usefulness of the Joyce and Showers model was conducted by Bush in the early 1980s and is reported by Hord (1994). In an analysis of staff-development activities and their effects upon individual teacher growth, Bush found that when staff developers:

1. Provided new information by lecturing to teachers, 10 percent of the teachers used the new skill in the classroom.

2. Demonstrated and modeled a new strategy for teachers, 2–3 percent more teachers performed the new skill in the classroom.

3. Practiced the new skill in simulated settings, 2–3 percent more teachers transferred the new skill to the classroom.

4. Provided a structure for and honest feedback to the teacher, another 2–3 percent more teachers added the skill to their repertoire.

Thus, only 16–19 teachers out of 100 were able to transfer the new skill to and perform the new skill in the classroom. However, when a fifth component was added—*coaching*—up to 95 percent of all teachers transferred their new learnings/skills into the classroom.

Recall that earlier we described Fuller and Bown's (1975) three teacher career stages. Teachers at all three stages need a coach. A coach can provide valuable support, though this support will vary from stage to stage, for teachers interested in improving their instructional repertoire and positively impacting children's learning. As an example, for the *survival teacher* instructional improvement goals should be practical and related to the concerns unique to "surviving." Table 12.2 provides examples of instructional improvement goals that a survival

TABLE 12-2 Stage 1: Self/Survival
Sample Instructional Improvement Goals

1. *To reduce overall misbehavior by enforcing my classroom assertive discipline plan.*

2. *To increase the "time-on-task" ratio within my classroom.*

3. *To reduce the number of office referrals for students by better enforcing my classroom rules. (I need to catch misbehavior before it becomes severe.)*

4. *To increase the use of learning centers by developing two learning/interest centers— one on a Mexican culture unit and one on an electricity unit. (The units will combine hands-on activities with alternative learning experiences.)*

teacher and coach (peer or supervisor) could emphasize and work toward. Developmental tasks should focus upon: what to do, how to do it, and the circumstances under which the goal is to be accomplished. Specific, clear expectations—procedures, duties, outcomes, and assessment procedures—need to be identified so that when improvement goals and objectives are not attained, further development, experimentation, and assessment procedures can be used to help the survival teacher acquire the knowledge and skills necessary to perform effectively. Notice that the teacher tends to use verbs such as "to increase" and "to reduce," which provide a clearer measure of the intended objective for teacher and student behavior.

Self-improvement goals for *task teachers* extend the instructional repertoire of most educators. Table 12.3 provides examples of such goals. Notice that the conceptual complexity of these goals is somewhat greater than the conceptual complexity of goals evidenced for survival teachers. The teacher is focusing less on the management of behavior and more on the type of thinking he or she is seeking to develop in the students. Task objectives still focus on a teacher's classroom behavior but focus more on enhancing alternatives and less on a specific behavior. Providing alternatives to the teacher in terms of professional goals and

TABLE 12-3 Stage 2: Task
Sample Instructional Improvement Goals

1. *To develop more interpretative and evaluative questions (higher-order thinking questions) that I can use in my oral discussion sessions with students.*

2. *To develop alternative learning strategies using at least three modalities for a three-week unit on mixed numbers.*

3. *To videotape a series of concept formation instructional model lessons, and have a peer coach collect data on and assess my performance regarding: implementation of model phases, types and uses of questioning, and involvement of the student group.*

4. *To assess over a 2-week period (during my fractions unit) the effects of increased monitoring of independent seatwork on homework completed and on the students' acquisition of desired skills.*

how to achieve these instructional goals (that is, seminars, books and articles, demonstrations, videotapes, observations) is a starting point. Goal-setting is crucial at this stage because the role of the coach is to provide support for teacher exploration of ideas, and to grant permission to take risks even though failure may be a real possibility. The coach should consistently provide alternatives in the form of alternative instructional models in order to utilize and/or strengthen the cognitive styles of youngsters. This process can occur only if the coach helps create a culture that is nonthreatening in nature. Such a culture hinges upon the valuing of exploration and experimentation, and building a supportive relationship through the use of modeling processes, demonstrations, readings from the literature, and positive reinforcement. In working with the teacher, the coach should demonstrate and practice all of the instructional strategies that are expected of the teacher in working with students.

Finally, Table 12.4 presents examples of possible goals that an *impact teacher* would seek to develop. The impact teacher moves beyond a consideration of alternatives and attempts to holistically assess the philosophical basis for teaching practice. A peer and/or supervisor coach working with an impact teacher should never function in a directive, authoritarian manner (Glickman, Gordon, and Ross-Gordon, 1995). The impact teacher who seeks a sense of freedom to inquire will surely suffer professionally if a culture of command and control is practiced within the school setting. Coaches should ask clarifying and extension questions, and create environmental conditions for impact teachers to reach decisions based upon their own forms of reflection and practice.

One additional point must be made concerning the affective dimension of impact teachers. Based on our experience, impact teachers seem to be very hard on themselves. It may be necessary, therefore, for coaches to provide affective support and encouragement so that discouragement and depression do not occur. Kind words, a focus upon the positive, the use of clarifying questions to

TABLE 12-4   Stage 3: Impact
Sample Instructional Improvement Goals

1. *To organize my history course using a conceptual as opposed to a chronological approach to teaching and learning.*

2. *To foster creativity by using the synectics instructional model and to have a peer coach and my students assess the implementation based upon specific criteria.*

3. *To assume a mentoring role of new teachers in my department, and to help them address problems and assess the effects of my efforts.*

4. *To administer a sociogram, identify the isolates in the group, develop and implement a plan to involve them in class activities, and assess the effects of my efforts.*

5. *To participate effectively on the district and curriculum committee as evidenced by:*

   a. *making a specific contribution as noted by the chair; and*

   b. *seeking leadership on a subcommittee dealing with interdisciplinary concepts and producing an identifiable product.*

draw out teacher alternatives, and the presentation of alternative instructional strategies by the coach can provide the support needed for the impact teacher to enhance and refine instructional skills and make a positive impact upon children's lives.

Ⓢ TRATEGIES FOR IDENTIFYING A COACH

The greatest coaches are those who know how to motivate others to succeed, stay focused, believe in themselves, and overcome disappointments. Coaches inspire others to aim higher, work harder, and to enjoy doing it! Coaches are expected to motivate, inspire, instruct, lead, and correct those whom they coach.

There are two vehicles to provide professional development experiences for educators; these can be either external and internal strategies. The external coach takes the form of a colleague or superior who will help and support a teacher over time in increasing professional skills. The internal coach takes the form of self-analysis by the teacher for purposes of professional improvement. Let us take a closer look at what we mean by external and internal coaching strategies.

External Coaching Strategies

Choosing a coach is more difficult than it seems. In the first place, your choice must be someone you trust and someone with whom you can build a positive relationship. After all, you will be exposing all of your human and professional frailties; the coach, therefore, should be both a helpful and a trustworthy individual. In the second place, choosing a coach is difficult because you need to find an individual who is knowledgeable and experienced in the instructional process and in the background and development of culturally diverse youngsters. Be very deliberate in how you make your choice, observe various individuals over time, and ask them plenty of questions concerning what and how they teach and the reactions of and results with their youngsters. Once you are fairly satisfied with your observations and the responses to your questions, try the individual (coach) out. Make them a "trial coach" until you feel very comfortable and satisfied with the relationship and advice.

In choosing your coach, there are a number of alternatives to consider. Your coach can be either a colleague, your immediate supervisor, another superior within the organization, or even a faculty member at a local college. Coaches are chosen one of three ways:

1. The teacher makes a conscious choice based upon a sense of respect for the instructional skills this individual possesses.

2. The teacher and coach strike up a friendship, and this friendship unconsciously evolves into a protégé–coach relationship.

3. The coach consciously chooses the individual to coach based upon the perceived potential qualities and skills of the teacher.

Each of the above has potential to develop positive effects upon the instructional development of teachers. The only barrier preventing this relationship from occurring is personal insecurity. Someone needs to take a chance, and because the educational institution has not formalized such relationships as other professionals have, each of us individually needs to take responsibility for our own professional growth. Recall from earlier in this section that the research is quite clear concerning the positive results of coaching (Hord, 1994).

Finally, if your coach does the type of work expected from this collegial relationship, the outcomes that follow can be expected. Coaching will vary according to the career stage of each teacher. Thus, the outcomes that follow may differ depending upon the needs disposition of each individual teacher.

1. *Awareness of organizational politics and culture.*

   The coach can teach and expose the protégé to "accepted" activities, policies, and procedures of the organization. This means that the coach helps to initiate the teacher into the organization: whom to approach with certain issues or questions and whom not to; where and when certain activities may or may not be "the norm"; and where the varied services, internal and external to the organization, can be found. Nothing works better in learning an organization's culture than a guided tour by a "native." Once this takes place, the individual teacher can make choices concerning how and when to engage in the organizational culture.

2. *Appreciation of networking.*

   Coaching means helping the teacher see the value of *networking*. Networking means helping the teacher recognize and learn from the other educators in the organization who will most likely help this teacher grow professionally. This may mean scheduling time for the teacher to observe other exemplary teachers and to meet other professionals in the district, introducing the teacher to administrative personnel in the district, and exposing the teacher to various professional associations.

3. *Eagerness to learn.*

   Through the coaching process, it becomes more possible for protégé teachers to become avid and ongoing learners. They are taught to value and seek additional training and education which can take the form of encouraging further reading, enrolling in workshops, attending regional and national conferences, or enrolling in college courses. Any of these alternatives can help provide the additional instructional skills that may be needed.

4. *Movement toward "mastery" status.*

   Effective coaching results in the teacher moving toward mastery status. As teachers learn and practice, they will start to become specialists. Through the coaching of teaching, individuals not only learn how to know, but also learn how to do. One way of accomplishing this may be the use of the "mechanical ear" approach. The mechanical ear (referred to as "bug in the ear," or BIE) is nothing more than a small, wireless one-way communication instrument. The protégé would use the mechanical ear to receive precise cues or prompts from the coach. Giebelhaus (1994) found that "students" (practicing teachers) who used the devices could effect immediate change in their teaching behaviors. Instead of waiting for a postobservation conference and then having the coach say, "You need to ask more factual questions to establish a common base of student understanding," the coach can use the BIE to say "Ask additional factual questions" or "Give an example."

Internal Coaching Strategies

Internal coaching strategies are not as threatening to individual teachers because these strategies take the form of self-analysis. Teachers who utilize self-analysis procedures are secure in themselves, have many years of experience, are usually highly trained in instructional delivery systems, and can be classified as impact or master teachers.

One form of self-analysis is the use of videotapes to analyze instructional behavior. This internal strategy is very similar to micro-teaching strategies developed by Bush and Allen (1964) and Allen and Fortune (1967). Though it was originally designed to help new or prospective teachers develop specific instructional skills with the help of expert teachers and colleagues, videotaping can be a viable vehicle for teacher self-analysis. The internal coaching strategy uses the following steps:

1. *Planning*

   During this step the teacher reflects upon instructional practice by identifying an instructional skill (that is, evaluative or interpretative questioning, establishing the focus for instruction) or an instructional model (that is, concept attainment, mnemonics, oral discussion) that is in need of development or refinement. Once the instructional practice is delimited, the teacher begins planning a process of improvement by acquiring information through reading, observing other teachers, and/or taking a workshop or seminar. The teacher will receive instruction on how to perform either an instructional skill or the steps in implementing one of the instructional models. Also occurring during the planning step is the development of a mini-lesson (usually no more than 15–30 minutes in length) complete with performance objectives, teaching strategies, and so on. (For a more thorough description of such plans, refer to the discussion of action planning later in this chapter.)

2. *Teaching*

   During this step the teacher implements the planned mini-lesson with students. While the lesson is being taught, a video camera is taping the teacher and students engaged in the lesson. The videotape will be used in the next step of the process—to assess and plan for further instructional refinement.

3. *Playback*

   Following lesson implementation, the teacher plays back the video and self-critiques the instructional delivery in terms of how the skill and/or model was implemented. An excellent source of criteria to assess the implementation of one of the instructional models would be the evaluation criteria found toward the end of each instructional model chapter. These criteria are enumerated for each model phase and can be a starter in evaluating instructional performance.

4. *Redesign*

Once teachers have observed and critiqued themselves using videotapes, they can then begin to identify skill areas or instructional model phases that may be in need of refinement. The action planning process begins anew, and the micro-teaching process described above continues.

This internal strategy is an attempt to focus the teacher's attention on the implementation of specific instructional skills or on specific phases of the instructional models. Because the teacher is interested in conducting a self-analysis into instructional behavior, the use of videotaping is critical for teachers to observe and assess what they see and hear. One could also use audiotape recordings of lessons; however, nonverbal behaviors by both teachers and students are lost in using audiotape recorders.

What we are suggesting by the previous discussion is a promotion, either formal or informal, of coaching strategies to help implement the concepts and strategies presented in this text. If you will seek out just one of your colleagues to initiate an improvement effort for yourself, you will see an amazingly positive result in your teaching behaviors. By working with this colleague, the two of you can: observe one another; collect data concerning the implementation of an instructional model and its phases; share the data collected and possible alternative strategies to practice; and develop a new action plan in order to refine and enhance the implementation of one of the instructional models. Each time we have used this format, teachers have been pleased with their instructional improvement, and students have been pleased and satisfied with instructional variation and the improvement of their own learning skills.

In order to utilize the teacher behavior action plan (Figure 12.2), the following format is presented in order to help in the creation of an action plan with your coaching partner. A sample action plan is provided in Figure 12.3. The following tasks need to be addressed in refining your instructional repertoire.

1. *What is the instructional model that you would like to implement or refine? Choose just one model each time you use the action plan organizer.*

From our experience working with teachers, we recommend that you choose just one instructional model at a time to emphasize. Your refinement of the instructional model can be implemented for three to nine months depending upon the level of sophistication you are seeking. By working with your coach and focusing first upon the major components of the instructional model and then upon its nuances, you will use the following cycle of the action planning process—develop plan, implement plan, receive feedback, redevelop plan, reimplement plan, and so on. You can use this cycle for as long as you and your coach seek to develop and refine the implementation of an instructional model. If you wish to focus upon one of the inclusive behaviors discussed previously in this chapter, just substitute this behavioral indicator for the instructional model designator. The action plan format can work just as effectively with either emphasis.

Instructional Model to Emphasize ___Inquiry___

Career Stage ___Task Stage___

Improvement Goal(s)
1. To understand how case study problems are created. (Task)
2. To understand how to promote divergent thinking skills in students. (Task)
3. To reorganize course content so that case studies complement the conceptual focus of the unit. (Impact)

OBJECTIVES	STRATEGIES TO ACCOMPLISH OBJECTIVES	ASSESSMENT PROCEDURES
A. To design a case study problem concerning low voter turnout (see goal 1).	1. Read texts on how to write a case study that focuses upon a problem that is not immediately solvable. 2. Acquire real community data concerning voter turnout in selected city precincts. 3. Find sample case studies and study them for ideas on how to write a case study. 4. Write sample case study drafts for my coach to assess and identify three different ways to teach the "cases."	1. Coach to provide assessment of written case study. 2. Coach and self-assessment of student verbal and nonverbal reactions to the case study. 3. Coach and I determine lesson effectiveness based upon identified student campaign ideas from their assigned projects. 4. Student attitude survey to assess lesson effectiveness.
B. To identify the different types of higher-order questions that will be used with the completed case study (see goal 2).	1. Read Sanders's *Classroom Questions: What Kinds?* for knowledge and ideas on factual, interpretative, and evaluative questioning levels (use the cognitive taxonomy). 2. View videotape of teacher using factual, interpretative, and evaluative questioning procedures in a lesson. 3. Given the case study for the lesson, write out all questions to be used on the following thinking levels: application, analysis, synthesis, and evaluation. 4. Videotape my lesson for the coach and me to observe and assess.	1. Coach to observe lesson and tally number of questions which are convergent v. divergent and determine percentage. 2. Coach to observe and videotape lesson and tally number of questions based upon levels of thinking. 3. Self-assess lesson based upon observation of videotape. 4. Administration of student attitude survey. 5. Coach and myself determine lesson effectiveness based upon identified student campaign ideas from their assigned projects.
C. To reorganize the unit to include case studies (see goal 3).	1. Examine how other teachers use cases within units. 2. Create a concept map unit.	1. Coach to discuss how cases complement unit instruction. 2. Coach to respond to concept and map.

FIGURE 12-3 Teacher Behavior Action Plan

Next, you need to identify:

2. *What career stage best describes your current professional practice?*

   If you have addressed this question honestly, based upon our previous discussion in this chapter, this will be very important to your coach. The importance lies in how you will encourage the coach to approach and work with you in the development, implementation, and assessment of the action plan. Each individual teacher at a career stage has different instructional needs, motivations, and aspirations. Likewise, each career stage utilizes different coaching approaches and techniques in helping teachers refine their skills. In the plan, the teacher should identify some objectives that move beyond the current level. For example, task teachers should develop some task-type objectives and at least one impact-type objective. Figure 12.3 illustrates that the teacher has created two task goals and one impact goal.

   The next step asks you to:

3. *List the instructional goals that are important to you for your personal and professional growth.*

   The following examples are provided to help guide you with this task:

   a. To create mnemonics for my unit on cells for my low-ability students to better motivate them to remember important terms. (Survival)

   b. To understand how to use different teaching strategies to promote higher-order thinking levels in my students. (Task)

   c. To identify and use culturally relevant instructional materials that can be used in teaching a unit on low voter turnout. (Impact)

   With the listing of these goals, a delimitation is initiated for the possible goals of the action plan. This is most important in refining the instructional focus that you and your coach will emphasize.

   The next step in the plan is to:

4. *Rank these instructional goals (needs statements) on the basis of most to least importance.*

   This ranking is done purposefully in order to force you to emphasize only the most important instructional goal(s). Too often educators try to be all things to all people; they fail miserably because they diffuse their efforts and have scattered results. This step asks you to rank order your needs, and in the next step to choose no more than two of these needs in order to refine and enhance your knowledge and skills.

5. *Select the top two instructional goals (needs statements).*

   Based upon your selection, transpose these selections to the action plan (see Figure 12.3). These become your self-development targets you will work toward with the help of your coach for the next number of months.

   Next, you need to:

6. *Convert each instructional goal into at least one performance objective.*

The following examples are provided to help in accomplishing this task:

a. Learn how to use games in reinforcing basic skills and memory work.

b. Identify and read a book on questioning techniques to elicit student higher-order thinking levels.

c. View a videotape and practice problem-solving activities using cooperative learning strategies.

d. Identify resource people who can assist me in designing culturally relevant materials for a mathematics unit on fractions.

The performance objectives you choose need to be written in the space provided in the sample action plan (see Figure 12.3). These become your focal points in terms of instructional strategies and assessment procedures to determine the achievement of each performance objective. These objectives are what you will seek to achieve, and your coach will steer you in the months ahead toward the accomplishment of these performance objectives.

The next task is in the form of a question:

7. *How will you accomplish the self-improvement objectives that you have identified for yourself? What will be your strategies?*

With this step, your task is to design strategies (see Figure 12.3) you can use with your coach in achieving the performance objectives you have identified. The following are examples that could be used to achieve performance objectives listed above:

a. Identify by November 1 different age-appropriate, skill-based reading games for use with my class.

b. Determine how to modify these reading games to ensure maximal participation of all my students.

Under the watchful and thoughtful eye of your coach, these strategies and their variations may be implemented many times over many weeks. Refinement will occur after much practice and care in how you implement these strategies. Your coach will be very helpful to you by providing feedback related to how you are performing the instructional behaviors to be emphasized, the reactions of the youngsters during implementation, possible instructional alternatives or refinements that could be practiced, and how you seem to react during different phases of the lesson implementation.

The final step in designing an action plan is:

8. *How will you know if you have achieved the instructional objectives you have identified for yourself? What assessment procedures will you use?*

The purpose of this final step is to identify assessment procedures in order to determine if and when your instructional objective has been achieved. You should identify at least one assessment procedure for each objective listed (see Figure 12.3), but you certainly are not limited to just one! In fact, there are times when you will want more than one assessment procedure to verify that a performance objective has been achieved. Assessment data can be gathered by your coach. This is the time in the process when the coach is really valuable to your professional growth! Assessment procedures that you identify can come from many sources: student attitude instruments, student achievement results, student test results from a teacher-made test, data-gathering procedures conducted by your coach (that is, time-on-task devices, questioning-type inventories, classroom traffic-flow processes), and self-assessment procedures (for example, completion of seminar or workshop, attitude inventory, completion of book or periodical related to the teaching profession). If you are using a coach in the implementation of an action plan, the coach is especially valuable to you at this step because this individual will provide you with the following valuable information: possible assessment strategies, objective data from the observations made, and possible instructional strategies that can be used for further instructional refinement. As indicated at the beginning of this section, the action plan format has been used many times by us in our consulting practice with all types of educators. These educators have found *action planning for instructional improvement* to be an important and valuable tool, along with a colleague-coach, in implementing the instructional models described in this text, practicing the various instructional skills presented within each model, and helping to have an instructional impact upon the students they serve.

❶EACHERS FOR TOMORROW'S WORLD

The mediocre teacher tells. The good teacher explains. The superior teacher demonstrates. The great teacher inspires.

WILLIAM ARTHUR WARD

This chapter has attempted to focus upon the role of the teacher in an increasingly diverse society: teacher as leader, teacher career stages, teacher noninclusive and inclusive behaviors, and teacher action planning for continuing growth and improvement. In this analysis of teacher role, we have emphasized the need to develop teachers who are knowledgeable about the cultural backgrounds of their students, sensitive to the uniqueness that each student brings to the classroom, knowledgeable about how students receive and process information, committed to seek only the best from their students, and instructionally responsive to the educational needs of youngsters. One of the more sound ways to accomplish these ideals is through the use of the instructional models presented in this text. Each model has a different instructional purpose (that is, helping youngsters interact effectively, taking various informational items to create a new idea, or practicing problem-solving strategies using culturally relevant organizers); focuses upon specific learning skills for youngsters (that is, questioning/thinking levels, evaluating, retaining factual information, or working cooperatively with others); and plays to the natural learning dispositions of youngsters (that is, is relationship-oriented, uses oral discussion, emphasizes the tactile or auditory, or is interested in the tangible and concrete).

One of the more important aspects of acquiring a repertoire of instructional models discussed in this text deals with the appropriateness of their use. Put another way, to identify a specific instructional model to teach a lesson (that is, synectics vs. mnemonics vs. concept formation) is of little value unless the model chosen is appropriate in teaching the lesson objectives (the purposes of the lesson and what students are expected to achieve). Further, the instructional model chosen for the lesson must also correspond to the cognitive styles and developmental levels of the youngsters who will be taught that same lesson. The basic premise of this text has been that teachers must be able to draw from a number of instructional alternatives in order to facilitate a congruency relationship between the teaching approach, student cultural background, and student learning disposition. The teacher for tomorrow's world must be a highly skilled practitioner able to make a myriad of instructional decisions each day in order to meet the needs of students.

Our responsibilities as educators are not only to help youngsters learn new wonders of the world, but to help students develop the learning skills and intellectual abilities needed for this new society. We believe that Goodlad et al. (1990a) put it so well when they identified what they label as the *four moral imperatives of schooling for the future*. The following imperatives are Goodlad's, but the descriptions represent our analysis of the implications of these imperatives for teachers working with diverse student populations.

1. *Teachers need to be able to facilitate critical enculturation.*

   The role of schools is to help youngsters understand and take part in this nation's system of government—a democracy. The school's role is to help students acquire the knowledge and skills associated with this country's history and government. This is important so that students can make informed decisions concerning this nation's initiatives and future direction. The simple explanation of this imperative boils down to cultural literacy. The school has an obligation to develop in all students an understanding of our cultural heritage from a multicultural perspective; an understanding of how this nation was formed and structured—its political system and processes; an understanding of the major political, social, technological, and scientific issues that we face; and an understanding of our individual responsibilities in participating in this democracy—keeping informed, communicating with others on the issues, and the ultimate participatory act in a democracy—voting.

2. *Teachers need to provide students with access to knowledge.*

   The school is the only societal institution charged with providing all youngsters with access to the basic structure of each academic discipline and the concomitant skills associated with each discipline. The teacher's role is a social justice responsibility: to ensure that all youngsters have equal access to this knowledge. All students have a right to be exposed to the structure of each academic discipline (Bruner, 1960) so that they understand the concepts, generalizations, and methodological processes of inquiry unique to that discipline. The school should expect that all students are well versed in these subject areas, whether they be algebra, biology, American government, or a foreign language. The responsibility of educators is to provide every opportunity and experience to all students no matter what their cultural, ethnic, or gender characteristics. These educational opportunities are a basic Jeffersonian right of all youngsters in this nation.

3. *Teachers need to create an effective teacher–student connection.*

The responsibility of all teachers is to ensure that pedagogy goes beyond the *mechanics* of teaching to a process that transcends the mere recitation of dates, details, and descriptions. Teachers must combine the principles of growth and development, alternative instructional models, disciplinary knowledge, and a sensitivity to the social and political barriers that prevent learning. The teacher of the twenty-first century will need to develop partnerships with parents and community agencies in order to address the needs of students. Because many of the students in our schools today suffer a myriad of "diseases" (for example, physical and sexual abuse, neglect, substance abuse, inconsistent value structures, and unstable home environments), the teacher and school need to take to heart the old African proverb, "It takes a whole village to raise a child." Every effort needs to be expended in developing collaborative cultures within the school and within the community.

4. *Teachers need to practice good stewardship.*

If schools are to become learning organizations—institutions striving to grow and develop, seeking to help youngsters solve their dilemmas, and designing programs that better serve their communities—then they must be in the business of continual staff renewal. The responsibility of teachers is to continually seek the path of self- and organizational development during their careers. Career renewal must be of paramount concern for individual teachers and the educational organization. As teachers remain in the profession, they move through career stages. These stages serve as developmental passages because they have implications for addressing individual teacher needs and objectives. The responsibility for schools is to develop a learning environment that accommodates individual teacher renewal and in the process renews its own organizational culture.

The teacher for tomorrow's world will need to embody and exemplify the qualities and characteristics inherent in these moral imperatives. Each of these moral imperatives has clear implications concerning the responsibilities of teachers as educators and members of the educational profession. The question left for us is how we plan to implement these goals in a consistent fashion for all youngsters.

If schools continue to disregard the gifts, talents, and presence of culturally diverse youngsters, schools will be dangerously close to jeopardizing America's future and tomorrow's world. That future will belong to only those individuals who can function in an increasingly high-tech, internationally competitive world. The youngsters of today will be successful in tomorrow's world only if they acquire the necessary knowledge and skills from the different disciplines, exhibit and practice a willingness to continue to learn, practice problem-solving/critical-thinking skills, are willing to innovate and look for new ways of doing business, participate in cooperative, team-oriented activities, utilize various forms of technology, and respond quickly to the needs and desires of customers.

Society in general and schools in particular must create a dialogue and a sense of urgency in addressing the following questions concerning youngsters—our national treasures:

What are the dreams of this nation with regard to its children?

How will this nation prepare all of its youth to be full partners in these dreams?

Only those individuals who either cling to the past or have not had the opportunity to realize the possibility of their "futures" will be left behind. Those educators who cling to the "old ways" of teaching will doom generations of "young folk" to menial work or the nonproductive and violent ways of this nation. Educators have a moral calling and responsibility—a mission and sense of purpose—to preserve this nation's treasures—its children—in a safe, opportunity-enhancing, and productive educational environment. This environment must be a place where all youngsters have the opportunity to realize their dreams for tomorrow's world.

ⓡ EFERENCES

Adams, R. 1982. "Teacher Development: A Look at Changes in Teachers' Perceptions Across Time." *Journal of Teacher Education* 33(4): 40–43.

Allen, D., and J. Fortune. 1967. "An Analysis of Micro-Teaching: New Procedures in Teacher Education." Pp. 1–11 in D. Allen et al., *Micro-Teaching: A Description.* Stanford, CA: Stanford University Press.

Appleton, N. 1983. *Cultural Pluralism in Education: Theoretical Foundations.* New York: Longman.

Astuto, T. 1990. *Reinventing School Leadership.* Working memo prepared for the Reinventing School Leadership Conference. Cambridge, MA: National Center for Educational Leadership.

Au, K., and A. Kawakami. 1985. "Research Currents: Talk Story and Learning to Read." *Language Arts* 62(4): 406–411.

Balch, P. 1991. "California's Future Teacher-Student Mismatch: Recruiting Successful Minority Teacher Education Candidates." *Teacher Education Quarterly* 18: 19–22.

Ball, S., and I. Goodson. 1985. *Teachers' Lives and Careers.* Sussex: Falmer Press.

Baratz-Snowden, J. 1986. "Black Participation in the Teacher Pool." Prepared for the task force on Teaching as a Profession, Carnegie Forum on Education and the Economy.

Becker, H. 1977. *Sociological Work: Method and Substance.* Brunswick, NJ: Transaction Books.

Bell, M. L., and C. V. Morsink. 1986. "Quality and Equity in the Preparation of Black Teachers." *Journal of Teacher Education* 37(2): 16–20.

Bishop, M. 1986. "Update." *Sports Illustrated* 10(February): 204–206.

Bolin, F. S. 1989. "Empowering Leadership." *Teachers College Record* 91(1): 81–96.

Bradley, C. 1984. "Issues in Mathematics Education for Native Americans and Directions for Research." *Journal for Research in Mathematics Education* 15(2): 96–106.

Bruner, J. S. 1960. *The Process of Education.* Cambridge, MA: Harvard University Press.

Bush, R., and D. Allen. 1964. "Micro-Teaching: Controlled Practice in the Training of Teachers." Paper presented at the Santa Barbara Conference on Teacher Education, Ford Foundation, Santa Barbara, CA.

Byers, P., and H. Byers. 1972. "Nonverbal Communication and the Education of Children." Pp. 3–31 in C. B. Cazden, V. P. John, and D. Hymes (eds.), *Functions of Language in the Classroom.* New York: Teacher's College Press.

Cabezas, A. 1981. *Early Childhood Development in Asian and Pacific American Families: Families in Transition.* San Francisco: Asian.

Carnegie Forum on Education and the Economy. 1986. *A Nation Prepared: Teachers for the 21st Century.* Report of the task force on Teaching as a Profession. Washington, DC: Carnegie Forum on Education and the Economy.

Cheatham, H. 1982. "Recruiting Minority Students: An Evaluation." *Journal of College Student Personnel* 23(1): 29–32.

Clark, D. 1990. *Reinventing School Leadership.* Working memo prepared for the Reinventing School Leadership Conference. Cambridge, MA: National Center for Educational Leadership.

Cooper, G. C. 1987. "Right Hemispheric Dominance, Holistic Cognitive Style, and Black Language." Pp. 61–86 in J. A. Anderson (ed.), *Benjamin E. Mays Monograph Series* 1(1).

Cooper, L., D. Johnson, R. Johnson, and F. Wilderson. 1980. "Effects of Cooperative, Competitive, and Individualistic Experiences of Interpersonal Attraction Among Heterogeneous Peers." *Journal of Social Psychology* 111(2): 243–252.

Cuban, L. 1989. "The 'At-Risk' Label and the Problem of Urban School Reform." *Phi Delta Kappan* 70(10): 784–785.

Culbertson, J. 1988. *Tomorrow's Challenges to Today's Professors of Educational Administration.* 1988 Walter Hoching lecture presented to the National Council of Professors of Educational Administration, Kalamazoo, MI.

Damico, S. B. 1983. "The Two Worlds of School: Differences in the Photographs of Black and White Adolescents." Paper presented at

annual meeting of American Educational Research Association, Montreal.

DePree, M. 1989. *Leadership Is an Art.* New York: Doubleday.

Digest of Education Statistics. 1986. Washington, DC: U.S. Government Printing Office.

Dunn, R., and S. A. Griggs. 1988. *Learning Styles: Quiet Revolution in American Schools.* Reston, VA: National Association of Secondary School Principals.

Feldman, R. S. 1980. "Nonverbal Behavior, Race, and the Classroom Teacher." *Theory Into Practice* 24(1): 45–49.

Foster, M. 1994. "Effective Black Teachers: A Literature Review." Pp. 225–242 in E. R. Hollins, J. E. King, and W. C. Hayman (eds.), *Teaching Diverse Populations: Formulating a Knowledge Base.* Albany, NY: State University of New York Press.

Freire, P. 1970. *Pedagogy of the Oppressed.* New York: Continuum.

Fullan, M. 1993. *Change Forces: Probing the Depth of Educational Reform.* London, NY: Falmer Press.

Fuller, F. 1969. "Concerns of Teachers: A Developmental Perspective." *American Educational Research Journal* 6: 207–226.

————, **and O. H. Bown.** 1975. "Becoming a Teacher." Pp. 25–52 in K. Ryan (ed.), *Teacher Education.* 74th Yearbook of the National Society for the Study of Education. Chicago: University of Chicago Press.

Garcia, E. 1991. "Effective Instruction for Language Minority Students: The Teacher." *Journal of Education* 173(2): 130–141.

Giebelhaus, C. 1994. "The Mechanical Third Ear Device: A Student Teaching Supervision Alternative." *Journal of Teacher Education* 45(5): 365–373.

Gilbert, S., and G. Gay. 1985. "Improving the Success in School of Poor Black Children." *Phi Delta Kappan* 67(2): 133–137.

Giroux, H. A. 1983. *Theory and Resistance in Education: A Pedagogy for the Opposition.* South Hadley: Bergin and Garvey.

Glickman, C., S. Gordon, and J. Ross-Gordon. 1995. *Supervision of Instruction: A Developmental Approach* (3d ed.). Boston: Allyn & Bacon.

Goodlad, J. 1990. "Studying the Education of Educators: From Conception to Findings." *Phi Delta Kappan* 71(9): 698–701.

————, R. Soder, and K. A. Sirotnik (eds.). 1990. *The Moral Dimensions of Teaching.* San Francisco: Jossey-Bass.

Graham, P. 1987. "Black Teachers: A Drastically Scarce Resource." *Phi Delta Kappan* 68(8): 598–605.

Greenfield, W. 1990. *Reinventing School Leadership.* Working memo prepared for the Reinventing School Leadership Conference. Cambridge, MA: National Center for Educational Leadership.

Haberman, M. 1989. "More Minority Teachers." *Phi Delta Kappan* 70(10): 771–776.

Hale-Benson, J. 1986. *Black Children: Their Roots, Culture, and Learning Styles* (rev. ed.). Baltimore, MD: Johns Hopkins University Press.

Hansell, S., and R. E. Slavin. 1981. "Cooperative Learning and the Structure of Interracial Friendships." *Sociology of Education* 54: 98–106.

Heath, S. B. 1983. *Ways with Words: Language, Life, and Work in Communities and Classrooms.* Cambridge, NY: Cambridge University Press.

Henry, A. 1990. "Black Women, Black Pedagogies: An African-Canadian Context." Paper presented at the American Educational Research Association, Boston.

Herndon, J. 1968. *The Way It Spozed to Be.* New York: Simon and Schuster.

Hilliard, A. G., III. 1984. *Saving the African-American Child.* Report of the National Alliance of Black School Educators, 14(11): 1–54.

Holt, J. 1967. *How Children Fail.* New York: Pitman.

Hord, S. 1994. "Change Process Strategies: Field Test Data and Practices." Paper presented at the annual meeting of the American Educational Research Association, New Orleans, LA.

Hull, G. A., M. Rose, K. Fraser, and M. Castellano. 1991. "Remediation as Social Construct: Perspective from an Analysis of Classroom Discourse." *College Composition and Communication* 42(3): 299–329.

Jackson, P. 1968. *Life in Classrooms.* New York: Holt, Rinehart and Winston.

Jetter, A. 1993. "Mississippi Learning." *New York Times Magazine* 6(February 21): 28–72.

Job Search Handbook for Educators, 1996 ASCUS Annual. Evanston, IL: Association for School, College and University Staffing.

Johnson, D. W., and R. T. Johnson. 1981. "Effects of Cooperative and Individualistic Learning Experiences on Interethnic Interaction." *Journal of Educational Psychology* 73(3): 444–449.

Joyce, B., and B. Showers. 1980. "Improving Inservice Training: The Messages of Research." *Educational Leadership* 37(5): 379–385.

Kagan, S., G. L. Zahn, K. F. Widaman, J. Schwarzwald, and G. Tyrell. 1985. "Classroom Structural Bias: Impact of Cooperative and Competitive Classroom Structures on Cooperative and Competitive Individuals and Groups." Pp. 277–312 in R. E. Slavin, S. Sharan, S. Kagan, R. Hertz-Lazarowitz, C. Webb, and R. Schmuck (eds.), *Learning to Cooperate, Cooperating to Learn.* New York: Plenum.

Kohl, H. 1967. *36 Children.* New York: New American Library.

Kozol, J. 1967. *Death at an Early Age: The Destruction of the Hearts and Minds of Negro Children in the Boston Public Schools.* Boston: Houghton Mifflin.

Ladson-Billings, G. 1990. "Like 'Lightning' in a Bottle: Attempting to Capture the Pedagogical Excellence of Successful Teachers of Black Students." *International Journal of Qualitative Studies in Education* 3(4): 335–344.

————. 1991. "Returning to the Source: Implications for Educating Teachers of Black Students." Pp. 227–244 in M. Foster (ed.), *Readings on Equal Education. Volume II: Qualitative Investigations into Schools and Schooling.* New York: AMS Press.

————. 1994. *The Dreamkeepers.* San Francisco: Jossey-Bass.

Lortie, D. 1975. *School Teacher: A Sociological Study.* Chicago: University of Chicago Press.

Matczynski, T., and S. Shugarman. 1989. "Minority Recruitment: Backgrounds and Promising Practices." Pp. 83–91 in D. G. Carter (ed.), *Equity in Excellence in Education.* Bloomington, IN: Indiana University's Center for Urban and Multicultural Education.

McDiarmid, G. 1990. *What to Do About Differences? A Study of Multicultural Education for*

Teacher Trainees in the Los Angeles Unified School District. Research Report 90-11. East Lansing, MI: National Center for Research on Teacher Education, Michigan State University.

McNett, I. 1983. *Demographic Imperatives: Implications for Educational Policy.* Washington, DC: Institute for Educational Leadership.

More, A. J. 1990. "Learning Styles of Native Americans and Asians." Paper presented at the annual meeting of the American Psychological Association, Boston. ERIC Document Reproduction Service No. ED 330 535.

Murphy, J. 1991. *Restructuring Schools: Capturing and Assessing the Phenomena.* New York: Teachers College Press.

Myers, I. B., and M. McCaulley. 1985. *Manual: A Guide to the Development and Use of the Myers-Briggs Type Indicator.* Palo Alto, CA: Consulting Psychologists Press.

Newman, K. 1979. "Middle-Aged Experienced Teachers' Perceptions of Their Career Development." Paper presented at the annual meeting of the American Educational Research Association, San Francisco.

Oishi, S., R. E. Slavin, and N. A. Madden. 1983. "Effects of Student Teams and Individualized Instruction on Cross-Race and Cross-Sex Friendships." Paper presented at the annual meeting of the American Educational Research Association, Montreal (April).

O'Malley, J., and A. Chamot. 1990. *Learning Strategies in Second Language Acquisition.* Cambridge, NY: Cambridge University Press.

Osborne, B., and B. Bamford. 1987. "Torres Strait Islanders Teaching Torres Strait Islanders I." North Queensland, Townsville: Department of Pedagogics and Scientific Studies in Education, James Cook University.

O'Toole, J. 1995. *Leading Change: Overcoming the Ideology of Comfort and the Tyranny of Custom.* San Francisco: Jossey-Bass.

Oxford, R. 1990. "The Strategy Inventory for Language Learning (SILL)." *Appendix to Language Learning Strategies: What Every Teacher Should Know.* New York: Newbury House/Harper & Row.

Pang, V. 1990. "Asian-American Children: A Diverse Population." *Educational Forum* 55(1): 49–66.

———. 1995. "Asian Pacific American Students: A Diverse and Complex Population."

Pp. 412–424 in J. Banks and C. Banks (eds.), *Handbook of Research on Multicultural Education.* New York: Macmillan.

Peterson, W. 1964. "Age, Teachers Role and the Institutional Setting." Pp. 268–315 in B. Biddle and W. Ellena (eds.), *Contemporary Research on Teacher Effectiveness.* New York: Holt Rinehart.

Philips, S. 1972. "Participant Structures and Communicative Competence: Warm Springs Children in Community and Classroom." Pp. 370–394 in C. Cazden, V. John, and D. Hymes (eds.), *Functions of Language in the Classroom.* New York: Teachers College Press.

———. 1983. *The Invisible Culture: Communication in Classroom and Community on the Warm Springs Indian Reservation.* New York: Longman.

———. 1993. *The Invisible Culture: Communication in Classroom and Community on the Warm Springs Indian Reservation.* Prospect Heights, IL: Waveland Press.

Pifer, A., and L. Bronte. 1986. *Our Aging Society.* New York: Norton.

Postman, N., and C. Weingartner. 1969. *Teaching as a Subversive Activity.* New York: Delacorte.

Ramirez, M., III. 1982. "Cognitive Styles and Cultural Diversity." Paper presented at the annual meeting of the American Educational Research Association, New York City.

———. 1989a. "A Bicognitive-Multicultural Model for a Pluralistic Education." *Early Child Development and Care* 51: 129–136.

———, and A. Castaneda. 1974. *Cultural Democracy, Bicognitive Development, and Education.* New York: Academic Press.

Reed, D. F. 1986. "Wanted: More Black Teacher Education Students." *Action in Teacher Education* 8(1): 31–36.

Roberts, L. 1990. *Reinventing School Leadership.* Working memo prepared for the Reinventing School Leadership Conference. Cambridge, MA: National Center for Educational Leadership.

Rohner, R. 1965. "Factors Influencing the Academic Performance of Kwakiutl Children in Canada." *Comparative Education Review* 9: 331–340.

Sadker, M. and D. Sadker. 1994b. *Teachers, Schools and Society.* New York: McGraw-Hill.

Sanders, N. M. 1966. *Classroom Questions: What Kinds?* New York: Harper & Row.

Sarason, S. 1982. *The Culture of the School and the Problem of Change* (rev. ed.). Boston: Allyn & Bacon.

————. 1983. *Schooling in America: Scapegoat and Salvation.* New York: Free Press.

Sergiovanni, T. J. 1989. *Schooling for Tomorrow: Directing Reforms to Issues that Count.* Boston: Allyn & Bacon.

————. 1991. *The Principalship: A Reflective Practice Perspective.* Boston: Allyn & Bacon.

————. 1992. *Moral Leadership: Getting to the Heart of School Improvement.* San Francisco: Jossey-Bass.

Shade, B. J. 1994. "Understanding the African American Learner." Pp. 175–189 in E. Hollins, J. King, and W. Hayman (eds.), *Teaching Diverse Populations: Formulating a Knowledge Base.* Albany, NY: State University of New York Press.

————, and **P. A. Edwards.** 1987. "Ecological Correlates of the Educative Style of Afro-American Children." *Journal of Negro Education* 86: 88–99.

Slavin, R. E. 1977. *Student Team Learning Techniques: Narrowing the Achievement Gap Between the Races.* Report No. 228. Baltimore, MD: Johns Hopkins University, Center for the Study of Social Organization of Schools.

————. 1979. "Effects of Biracial Learning Teams on Cross-Racial Friendships." *Journal of Educational Psychology* 71(3): 381–387.

————. 1987b. *Cooperative Learning: Student Teams* (2d ed.). Washington, DC: National Education Association.

————. 1987c. "Cooperative Learning: Where Behavioral and Humanistic Approaches to Classroom Motivation Meet." *Elementary School Journal* 88(1): 29–38.

————. 1995. "Cooperative Learning and Intergroup Relations." Pp. 628–634 in J. A. Banks and C. A. M. Banks (eds.), *Handbook of Research on Multicultural Education.* New York: Macmillan.

————, and **E. Oickle.** 1981. "Effects of Cooperative Learning Teams on Student Achievement and Race Relations: Treatment by Race Interactions." *Sociology of Education* 54: 174–180.

Soldier, L. 1989. "Cooperative Learning and the Native American Student." *Phi Delta Kappan* 71(2): 161–163.

Super, D. 1957. *The Psychology of Careers: An Introduction to Vocational Development.* New York: Harper & Row.

Treisman, V. 1985. "A Study of the Mathematics Performance of Black Students at the University of California at Berkeley." Unpublished doctoral dissertation, University of California, Berkeley.

U.S. Bureau of the Census, Economic and Statistics Administration. 1991. *1990 Census Profile: Race and Hispanic Origin.* Report No. 2.

U.S. Select Committee on Aging and American Association of Retired Persons. 1984. *Aging in America: Trends and Projections.* Washington, DC: American Association of Retired Persons.

Vasquez, J. A. 1991. "Cognitive Styles and Academic Attainment." Pp. 163–179 in J. Lynch, C. Modgil, and S. Modgil (eds.), *Cultural Diversity and the Schools: Consensus and Controversy.* London: Falconer Press.

Vygotsky, L. S. 1978. *Mind in Society: The Development of Higher Psychological Expectations.* Cambridge, MA: Harvard University Press.

Weigel, R. H., P. L. Wiser, and **S. W. Cook.** 1975. "Impact of Cooperative Learning Experiences on Cross-Ethnic Relations and Attitudes." *Journal of Social Issues* 31(1): 219–245.

Weinstein, C. E., A. C. Schulte, and **E. C. Cascallar.** 1983. *The Learning and Study Strategies Inventory (LASSI): Initial Design and Development.* Manuscript, University of Texas, Austin.

Wenden, A., and **J. Rubin.** 1987. *Learner Strategies in Language Learning.* Englewood Cliffs, NJ: Prentice-Hall.

Zeichner, K. (In press.) "Educating Teachers for Cultural Diversity." In K. Zeichner, S. Melnick, and M. L. Gomez (eds.), *Currents of Reform in Preservice Teacher Education.* New York: Teachers College Press.

APPENDIX

Learning Style Annotated Bibliography

GENERAL

Learning Style Inventory by Rita Dunn, Kenneth Dunn, and Gary Price, Price Systems, Box 3271, Lawrence, KS 66044, 1978, 1981.

> A self-report 100-item questionnaire designed to assess how Grades 3–12 students prefer to learn. The variables that are covered are: immediate environment, emotionality, sociological needs, and physical needs.

Learning Style Inventory: Primary Version by Janet Perrin, St. John's University, Jamaica, NY 11439, 1981.

> Based upon the Dunn, Dunn, and Price instrument, this version can be used with K–2 youngsters. The questionnaire consists of pictures and questions that determine style in four areas: environment, emotional tendencies, sociological needs, and physical requirements. The questionnaire is administered individually and takes approximately 20 minutes.

COGNITIVE

Gregoric Style Delineator by Anthony Gregoric, Doubleday Road, Columbia, CT 06237, 1979.

> A self-report instrument that analyzes an individual's concrete vs. abstract and random vs. sequential styles. It takes approximately 5 minutes to administer and consists of 40 words in 10 sets of 4 each. The student rank orders each set through forced-choice options.

"Cognitive Profiles" by Charles A. Letteri in C. A. Letteri, *Cognitive Profile: Basic Determinant of Academic Achievement.* Burlington, VT: Center for Cognitive Studies, 1980.

> This instrument takes seven tests of cognitive style—field independence/dependence, scanning/focusing, breadth of categorization, cognitive complexity/simplicity, reflectiveness/impulsiveness, leveling/sharpening, and tolerant/intolerant—that in combination predict student achievement level.

Ⓐ FFECTIVE

"Paragraph Completion Method" by David E. Hunt in *Assessing Conceptual Level by the Paragraph Method* by D. E. Hunt et al., Toronto: Ontario Institute for Studies in Education, 1978.

> Used to assess learning styles as Conceptual Level—describes students in terms of their requirements for structure in an educational environment. It describes students in terms of their stage of development from unsocialized to dependent to independent. Grades 6–12.

SRI Student Perceiver Interview by Donald Clifton, Selection Research, Inc., 2546 South 48th Street, Lincoln, NE 68506.

> Used to assess affective styles from age 8 through adulthood. The process uses an 80-question, structured, low-stress interview as a way to identify unique characteristics of individual students. Can be administered in 30 minutes and offers information concerning the talents and interests of students.

Ⓒ OGNITIVE/ⒶFFECTIVE

Myers-Briggs Type Indicator by Isabel Briggs Myers and Katherine Briggs, Consulting Psychologists Press Inc., 577 College Avenue, Palo Alto, CA 94306, 1980.

> Instrument that measures personality dispositions based upon Jung's personality types. Used for individuals from adolescence through adulthood. Categorizes individuals into 16 personality types. It provides information about the ways students prefer to perceive meaning, to express values, and to interact with the world.

"Multiple Intelligences Checklist" by Thomas Armstrong in T. Armstrong, *Multiple Intelligences in the Classroom.* Alexandria, VA: Association for Supervision and Curriculum Development, 1994.

> Provides a checklist around Gardner's seven intelligences—linguistic, logical-mathematical, spatial, bodily-kinesthetic, musical, interpersonal, and intrapersonal—that teachers can use in conjunction with other assessment information. Each intelligence area on the checklist has a list of statements by which a teacher can assess students on their abilities based upon observations and interactions.

Bibliography

Adams, R. 1982. "Teacher Development: A Look at Changes in Teachers' Perceptions Across Time." *Journal of Teacher Education* 33(4): 40–43.

Albas, D. D., K. W. McCluskey, and C. A. Albas. 1976. "Perception of the Emotional Content of Speech." *Journal of Cross-Cultural Psychology* 7: 481–490.

Aldrich, H. E. 1979. *Organizations and Environment.* Englewood Cliffs, NJ: Prentice-Hall.

Allen, D., and J. Fortune. 1967. "An Analysis of Micro-Teaching: New Procedures in Teacher Education." Pp. 1–11 in D. Allen et al., *Micro-Teaching: A Description.* Stanford, CA: Stanford University Press.

"American Demographics." 1989. *All Our Children* (May).

Anderson, J. A. 1988. "Cognitive Styles and Multicultural Populations." *Journal of Teacher Education* 39: 2–9.

Anderson, L. M., C. M. Evertson, and J. E. Brophy. 1979. "An Experimental Study of Effective Teaching in First Grade Reading Groups." *Elementary School Journal* 79: 193–223.

Annie E. Casey Foundation. *Kids Count Data Book 1994: State Profiles of Child Well-Being.* 1994. Greenwich, CT: Annie E. Casey Foundation.

Appleton, N. 1983. *Cultural Pluralism in Education: Theoretical Foundations.* New York: Longman.

Aronson, E., N. Blaney, C. Stephan, J. Sikes, and M. Snapp. 1978. *The Jigsaw Classroom.* Beverly Hills, CA: Sage.

Ascher, C. 1993. *The Changing Face of Racial Isolation and Desegregation in Urban Schools.* Report No. 91. ERIC/CUE Document Reproduction Service No. ED 358 199.

Association for Supervision and Curriculum Development. 1990. *Cooperative Learning Series: Facilitator's Manual.* Alexandria, VA: Association for Supervision and Curriculum Development.

Astuto, T. 1990. *Reinventing School Leadership.* Working memo prepared for Reinventing School Leadership Conference. Cambridge, MA: National Center for Educational Leadership.

Au, K., and A. Kawakami. 1985. "Research Currents: Talk Story and Learning to Read." *Language Arts* 62(4): 406–411.

Ausubel, D. P. 1960. "The Use of Advance Organizers in the Learning and Retention of Meaningful Verbal Material." *Journal of Educational Psychology* 17(3): 400–404.

Bailey, S. M. 1996. "Shortchanging Girls and Boys." *Educational Leadership* 53(8): 75–79.

Baker Miller, J. 1986. *Toward a New Psychology of Women* (2d ed.). Boston: Beacon.

Balch, P. 1991. "California's Future Teacher-Student Mismatch: Recruiting Successful Minority Teacher Education Candidates." *Teacher Education Quarterly* 18: 19–22.

Ball, S., and I. Goodson. 1985. *Teachers' Lives and Careers.* Sussex: Falmer Press.

Baratz-Snowden, J. 1986. "Black Participation in the Teacher Pool." Prepared for task force on Teaching as a Profession, Carnegie Forum on Education and the Economy.

Barker, J. A. 1992. *Future Edge: Discovering the New Paradigms of Success.* New York: William Morrow.

Baxter Magolda, M. B. 1989. "Gender Differences in Cognitive Development: An Analysis of Cognitive Complexity and Learning Styles." *Journal of College Student Development* 30(3): 213–220.

———. 1990. "Gender Differences in Epistemological Development." *Journal of College Student Development* 31(4): 555–561.

Becker, H. 1977. *Sociological Work: Method and Substance.* Brunswick, NJ: Transaction Books.

Becker, W. C. 1977. "Teaching Reading and Language to the Disadvantaged— What We Have Learned from Field Research." *Harvard Educational Review* 47: 518–543.

Belenky, M. F., B. M. Clinchy, M. R. Goldberger, and J. M. Tarule. 1986. *Women's Ways of Knowing: The Development of Self, Voice, and Mind.* New York: Basic Books.

Bell, M. L., and C. V. Morsink. 1986. "Quality and Equity in the Preparation of Black Teachers." *Journal of Teacher Education* 37(2): 16–20.

Benjamin, D. P., S. Chambers, and G. Reiterman. 1993. "A Focus on American Indian College Persistence." *Journal of American Indian Education* 32(2): 24–40.

Bennett, C. I. 1986. *Comprehensive Multicultural Education: Theory and Practice.* Boston: Allyn & Bacon.

———. 1995. *Comprehensive Multicultural Education: Theory and Practice* (3d ed.). Boston: Allyn & Bacon.

Bereiter, C., and S. Engelmann. 1966. *Teaching Disadvantaged Children in the Preschool.* Englewood Cliffs, NJ: Prentice-Hall.

Bert, C. R. G., and M. Bert. 1992. *The Native American: An Exceptionality in Education and Counseling.* ERIC Document Reproduction Service No. ED 351 168.

Bibens, R. F. 1980. "Using Inquiry Effectively." *Theory Into Practice* 19(2): 87–92.

Bishop, M. 1986. "Update." *Sports Illustrated* 10(February): 204–206.

Bloom, B., M. Englehart, E. Furst, W. Hill, and D. Krathwohl. 1956. *Taxonomy of Educational Objectives: The Classification of Educational Goals, Handbook I: Cognitive Domain.* New York: David McKay.

Bolin, F. S. 1989. "Empowering Leadership." *Teachers College Record* 91(1): 81–96.

Borich, G. 1988. *Effective Teaching Methods.* Columbus, OH: Merrill.

Borko, H., C. Brown, R. Underhill, M. Eisenhart, P. Jones, and P. Agard. 1990. *Learning to Teach Mathematics for Understanding.* College Park, MD: University of Maryland.

Bornstein, A. 1983. *Bornstein School of Memory Training.* Los Angeles: Bornstein School of Memory Training.

Bowsher, J. E. 1993. "Why and How to Restructure Education Systems." Paper presented at meeting of Association for Supervision and Curriculum Development, Washington, DC (March).

Boyer, E. L. 1983. *High School: A Report on Secondary Education in America.* New York: Harper & Row.

Boykin, A. W. 1994. "Harvesting Culture and Talent: African-American Children." Pp. 324–371 in J. Spencer (ed.), *Achievement and Achievement Motives.* Boston: W. H. Freeman.

Bradley, C. 1984. "Issues in Mathematics Education for Native Americans and Directions for Research." *Journal for Research in Mathematics Education* 15(2): 96–106.

Branson, R. K. 1988. "Why Schools Can't Improve: The Upper Limit Hypothesis." *Journal of Instructional Development* 10(4): 15–26.

Brewer, A. 1977. "An Indian Education." *Integrated Education* 15: 21–23.

Brooks, J. G., and M. G. Brooks. 1993. *The Case for Constructivist Classrooms.* Washington, DC: Association for Supervision and Curriculum Development.

Brophy, J. 1982. "Successful Teaching Strategies for the Inner-City Child." *Phi Delta Kappan* 63: 527–530.

———. 1983. "Research on the Self-Fulfilling Prophecy and Teacher Expectation." *Journal of Educational Psychology* 75: 631–661.

Brown, R. 1973. "Taba Rediscovered." *Science Teacher* 40(8): 30–33.

Bruner, J. S. 1960. The Process of Education. Cambridge, MA: Harvard University Press.

———, **J. J. Goodnow, and G. A. Austin.** 1956. *A Study of Thinking.* New York: John Wiley.

———. 1959. *A Study of Thinking.* New York: John Wiley and Sons: 56, 67.

———. 1990. *A Study of Thinking.* New Brunswick, NJ: Transaction.

Bryant, H. W. 1986. "An Investigation into the Effectiveness of Two Strategy Training Approaches on the Reading Achievement of Grade One Native Indian Children." Unpublished doctoral dissertation. Vancouver: University of British Columbia.

Burns, M. 1981. "Groups of Four: Solving the Management Problems." *Learning* 22(2): 46–51.

Bush, R., and D. Allen. 1964. "Micro-Teaching: Controlled Practice in the Training of Teachers." Paper presented at Santa Barbara Conference on Teacher Education, Ford Foundation, Santa Barbara, CA.

Byers, P., and H. Byers. 1972. "Nonverbal Communication and the Education of Children." Pp. 3–31 in C. B. Cazden, V. P. John, and D. Hymes (eds.), *Functions of Language in the Classroom.* New York: Teachers College Press.

Cabezas, A. 1981. *Early Childhood Development in Asian and Pacific American Families: Families in Transition.* San Francisco: Asian.

Cajete, G. 1994. *Look to the Mountain: An Ecology of Indigenous Education.* Durango, CO: Kivaki Press.

Canady, R. L., and M. D. Rettig. 1995. "The Power of Innovative Scheduling." *Educational Leadership* 54(3): 4–10.

Carnegie Forum on Education and the Economy. 1986. *A Nation Prepared: Teachers for the 21st Century.* Report of task force on Teaching as a Profession. Washington, DC: Carnegie Forum on Education and the Economy.

Carnegie Foundation for Advancement in Teaching. 1990. *The Condition of Teaching: A State-by-State Analysis.* Lawrenceville, NJ: Princeton University Press: 12, 34, 37–44.

Carney, R. N., M. E. Levin, and J. R. Levin. 1993. "Mnemonic Strategies: Instructional Techniques Worth Remembering." *Teaching Exceptional Children* 25(4): 24–30.

Carter, K. 1990. "Teachers' Knowledge and Learning to Teach." Pp. 291–310 in W. R. Houston (ed.), *Handbook of Research on Teacher Education.* New York: Macmillan.

Carter, T. P., and M. L. Chatfield. 1986. "Effective Bilingual Schools: Implications for Policy and Practice." *American Journal of Education* 95(1): 200–232.

Casserly, M. 1992. *National Urban Education Goals: Baseline Indicators* 1990–91. Washington, DC: Council of Great City Schools. ERIC Document Reproduction Service No. ED 351 422.

Cheatham, H. 1982. "Recruiting Minority Students: An Evaluation." *Journal of College Student Personnel* 23(1): 29–32.

Clark, D. 1990. *Reinventing School Leadership.* Working memo prepared for Reinventing School Leadership Conference. Cambridge, MA: National Center for Educational Leadership.

Clayton, J. B. 1996. *Your Land, My Land: Children in the Process of Acculturation.* Portsmouth, NH: Heinemann.

Cohen, E. 1986. *Designing Groupwork: Strategies for the Heterogeneous Classroom.* New York: Teachers College Press.

————. 1994. *Status Treatment for the Classroom.* Videotape and manual. New York: Teachers College Press.

Cohen, R. A. 1969. "Conceptual Styles, Culture Conflict, and Nonverbal Tests of Intelligence." *American Anthropologist* 71: 838–856.

Cooper, G. C. 1987. "Right Hemispheric Dominance, Holistic Cognitive Style, and Black Language." Pp. 61–86 in J. A. Anderson (ed.), *Benjamin E. Mays Monograph Series* 1(1).

Cooper, H., and T. Good. 1983. *Pygmalion Grows Up: Studies in Expectation Communication Process.* New York: Longman.

Cooper, L., D. Johnson, R. Johnson, and F. Wilderson. 1980. "Effects of Cooperative, Competitive, and Individualistic Experiences of Interpersonal Attraction Among Heterogeneous Peers." *Journal of Social Psychology* 111(2): 243–252.

Cordova, F. 1983. *Filipinos: Forgotten Asian Americans.* Dubuque, IA: Kendell and Hunt.

Cox, B., and M. Ramirez III. 1981. "Cognitive Styles: Implications for Multiethnic Education." Pp. 61–71 in J. Banks et al. (eds.), *Education in the 80s: Multiethnic Education.* Washington, DC: National Education Association.

Cuban, L. 1988. "Constancy and Change in Schools." Pp. 85–103 in P. W. Jackson (ed.), *Contributing to Educational Change: Perspectives on Research and Practice.* Berkeley: McCutchan.

————. 1989. "The 'At-Risk' Label and the Problem of Urban School Reform." *Phi Delta Kappan* 70(10): 784–785.

Culbertson, J. 1988. *Tomorrow's Challenges to Today's Professors of Educational Administration.* 1988 Walter Hoching lecture presented to National Council of Professors of Educational Administration, Kalamazoo, MI.

Damico, S. B. 1983. "The Two Worlds of School: Differences in the Photographs of Black and White Adolescents." Paper presented at annual meeting of American Educational Research Association, Montreal.

Darling-Hammond, L. 1995. "Restructuring Schools for Student Success." *Daedalus* 124(4): 153–162.

Davis, J. K., and B. M. Frank. 1979. "Learning and Memory of Field Independent-Dependent Individuals." *Journal of Research in Personality* 13: 469–479.

Deal, T. E., and L. D. Celotti. 1980. "How Much Influence Do (and Can) Educational Administrators Have on Classrooms?" *Phi Delta Kappan* 61: 471–473.

De La Rosa, D., and C. E. Maw. 1990. *Hispanic Education: A Statistical Portrait 1990.* Washington, DC: National Council of La Rosa.

Delgado-Gaitan, C. 1992. "School Matters in the Mexican-American Home: Socializing Children to Education." *American Educational Research Journal* 29(3): 495–513.

DePree, M. 1989. *Leadership Is an Art.* New York: Doubleday.

Devries, D. L., K. J. Edwards, and R. E. Slavin. 1978. "Biracial Learning Teams and Race Relations in the Classroom: Four Field Experiments on Teams-Games-Tournaments." *Journal of Educational Psychology* 70: 356–362.

Dillon, J. T. 1984. "Research on Questioning and Discussion." *Educational Leadership* 42(3): 50–56.

Dinges, N. C., and A. R. Hollenbeck. 1978. "Field-Dependence-Independence in Navajo Children." *International Journal of Psychology* 13: 215–220.

Dockerman, D. A. 1994. *Cooperative Learning and Technology.* Watertown, MA: Tom Snyder Productions.

Donmoyer, R. 1996. "The Concept of a Knowledge Base." Pp. 92–115 in F. B. Murray (ed.), *The Teacher Educator's Handbook.* San Francisco: Jossey-Bass.

Donnelly Marketing Information Services. *D and B: Donnelly Demographics.* 1988. Stamford, CT: Donnelly Marketing Information Services.

Drucker, P. F. 1993. *Post-Capitalist Society.* New York: HarperCollins.

Duckett, W. 1988. "Using Demographic Data for Long Range Planning." *Phi Delta Kappan* 70(2)(October): 166–170.

Dunn, R. 1993. "Learning Styles of the Multiculturally Diverse." *Emergency Librarian* 20(4): 24–30.

———, **and K. Dunn.** 1979. "Using Learning Style Data to Develop Student Prescriptions." Pp. 109–122 in National Association of Secondary School Principals, *Student Learning Styles: Diagnosing and Prescribing Programs.* Reston, VA: NASSP.

Dunn, R., J. Gemake, F. Jalali, R. Zenhausern, P. Quinn, and J. Spiridakis. 1990. "Cross-Cultural Differences in Learning Styles of Elementary-Age Students from Four Ethnic Backgrounds." *Journal of Multicultural Counseling and Development* 18(2): 68–93.

Dunn, R., and S. A. Griggs. 1988. *Learning Styles: Quiet Revolution in American Schools.* Reston, VA: National Association of Secondary School Principals.

Dunn, W. 1993. "Educating Diversity." *American Demographics* (April): 40.

Dusek, J. (ed.). 1985. *Teacher Expectations.* Hillsdale, NJ: Erlbaum.

Edwards, C., and J. Stout. 1989/1990. "Cooperative Learning: The First Year." *Educational Leadership* 47(4): 38–39.

Eggen, P. D., and D. P. Kauchak. 1988. *Strategies for Teachers* (2d ed.). Englewood Cliffs, NJ: Prentice-Hall.

Ellis, S. 1985. "Introducing Cooperative Learning Groups: A District-Wide Effort." *Journal of Staff Development* 6: 52–59.

England, D. A., and J. K. Flatley. 1985. *Homework—and Why*. Bloomington, IN: Phi Delta Kappa.

Enright, D. S. 1987. "Cognitive Style and First Language Background in Second Language Test Performance." *TESOL Quarterly* 21: 565–569.

Exter, T. G. 1993. "The Declining Majority." *American Demographics* (January): 59.

Feldman, R. S. 1980. "Nonverbal Behavior, Race, and the Classroom Teacher." *Theory Into Practice* 24(1): 45–49.

Finkelstein, B. 1989. *Governing the Young*. New York: Falmer Press.

Flaugher, R. L., and D. A. Roch. 1977. "Patterns of Ability Factors Among Four Ethnic Groups." Research Memorandum No. 7. Princeton, NJ: Educational Testing Service.

Foster, M. 1993. "Constancy, Change, and Constraints in the Lives of Black Women Teachers: Some Things Change, Most Stay the Same." *NWSA Journal* 3(2): 233–261.

———. 1994. "Effective Black Teachers: A Literature Review." Pp. 225–242 in E. R. Hollins, J. E. King, and W. C. Hayman (eds.), *Teaching Diverse Populations: Formulating a Knowledge Base*. Albany, NY: State University of New York Press.

Freire, P. 1970. *Pedagogy of the Oppressed*. New York: Continuum.

Fullan, M. 1993. *Change Forces: Probing the Depth of Educational Reform*. London, NY: Falmer Press.

Fuller, F. 1969. "Concerns of Teachers: A Developmental Perspective." *American Educational Research Journal* 6: 207–226.

———, **and O. H. Bown.** 1975. "Becoming a Teacher." Pp. 25–52 in K. Ryan (ed.), *Teacher Education*. 74th Yearbook of National Society for the Study of Education. Chicago: University of Chicago Press.

Gage, N. L., and M. C. Needels. 1989. "Process-Product Research on Teaching: A Review of Criticisms." *Elementary School Journal* 89(3): 253–300.

Gagne, R. M. 1977. *The Conditions of Learning* (3d ed.). New York: Holt, Rinehart and Winston.

Gall, M. D., and J. P. Gall. 1976. "The Discussion Method." Pp. 116–216 in N. L. Gage (ed.), *Psychology of Teaching Methods*. NSSE 75th Yearbook, Part 1. Chicago: University of Chicago Press.

Gall, M. D., and M. Gillett. 1980. "The Discussion Method in Classroom Teaching." *Theory Into Practice* 19(2): 95–103.

Garcia, E. 1991. "Effective Instruction for Language Minority Students: The Teacher." *Journal of Education* 173(2): 130–141.

Gardner, H. 1985. *Frames of Mind* (rev. ed.). New York: Basic Books.

———. 1991. *The Unschooled Mind: How Children Think and How Schools Should Teach*. New York: Basic Books.

———. 1995. "Reflections on Multiple Intelligences: Myths and Messages." *Phi Delta Kappan* 77(3): 200–209.

Gardner, J. 1996. *Sophie's World*. New York: Berkley.

Gibson, M. A. 1987. "The School Performance of Immigrant Minorities: A Comparative View." *Anthropology and Education Quarterly* 18(4): 262–275.

Giebelhaus, C. 1994. "The Mechanical Third Ear Device: A Student Teaching Supervision Alternative." *Journal of Teacher Education* 45(5): 365–373.

Gilbert, S., and G. Gay. 1985. "Improving the Success in School of Poor Black Children." *Phi Delta Kappan* 67(2): 133–137.

Gilligan, C. 1982. *In a Different Voice: Psychological Theory and Women's Development*. Cambridge, MA: Harvard University Press.

Giroux, H. A. 1983. *Theory and Resistance in Education: A Pedagogy for the Opposition.* South Hadley: Bergin and Garvey.

————. 1992. "Educational Leadership and the Crisis of Democratic Government." *Educational Researcher* 21(4): 4–11.

Glickman, C., S. Gordon, and J. Ross-Gordon. 1995. *Supervision of Instruction: A Developmental Approach* (3d ed.). Boston: Allyn & Bacon.

Goldstein, R. 1971. *Black Life and Culture in the United States.* New York: Thomas Crowell.

Golenbock, P. 1990. *Teammates.* San Diego, CA: Gulliver Books, Harcourt Brace Jovanovich.

Gollnick, D. M., and P. C. Chinn. 1994. *Multicultural Education in a Pluralistic Society* (4th ed.). New York: Macmillan.

Good, T., and J. E. Brophy. 1991. *Looking in Classrooms* (5th ed.). New York: HarperCollins.

————. 1994. *Looking in Classrooms* (6th ed.). New York: HarperCollins.

Good, T., and D. Grouws. 1979. "The Missouri Mathematics Effectiveness Project: An Experimental Study in Fourth-Grade Classrooms." *Journal of Educational Psychology* 71: 355–362.

Goodlad, J. 1990a. "Studying the Education of Educators: From Conception to Findings." *Phi Delta Kappan* 71(9): 698–701.

————. 1990b. *Teachers for Our Nation's Schools.* San Francisco: Jossey-Bass.

————, **R. Soder, and K. A. Sirotnik** (eds.). 1990a. *The Moral Dimensions of Teaching.* San Francisco: Jossey-Bass.

————. 1990b. Places Where Teachers Are Taught. San Francisco: Jossey-Bass.

Gordon, W. 1961. *Synectics: The Development of Creative Capacity.* New York: Harper & Row.

Gore, A. 1994. *National Telecommunications Reform: Bring the Information Revolution to Every Classroom, Hospital, and Library in the Nation by End of the Century.* Speech given by Vice President Al Gore at University of California, Los Angeles.

Graham, P. 1987. "Black Teachers: A Drastically Scarce Resource." *Phi Delta Kappan* 68(8): 598–605.

Grantham-Campbell, M. 1992. "Successful Alaska Native Students: Implications 500 Years After Columbus." Paper presented at meeting of American Anthropological Association, San Francisco (December).

Greenfield, W. 1990. *Reinventing School Leadership.* Working memo prepared for Reinventing School Leadership Conference. Cambridge, MA: National Center for Educational Leadership.

Guild, P., and S. Garger. 1985. *Marching to Different Drummers.* Alexandria, VA: Association for Supervision and Curriculum Development.

Gunter, M. A., T. H. Estes, and J. H. Schwab. 1990. *Instruction: A Models Approach.* Boston: Allyn & Bacon.

————. 1995. *Instruction: A Models Approach* (2d ed.). Boston: Allyn & Bacon.

Guttentag, M. 1972. "Negro-White Differences in Children's Movement." *Perceptual and Motor Skills* 35: 435–436.

Haberman, M. 1989. "More Minority Teachers." *Phi Delta Kappan* 70(10): 771–776.

————, **and L. Post.** 1995. "Multicultural Teaching in the Real World." Pp. 337–353 in A. C. Ornstein (ed.), *Teaching: Theory and Practice.* Boston: Allyn & Bacon.

Hale-Benson, J. 1982. *Black Children: Their Roots, Culture, and Learning Styles.* Baltimore, MD: Johns Hopkins University Press.

———. 1986. *Black Children: Their Roots, Culture, and Learning Styles* (rev. ed.). Baltimore, MD: Johns Hopkins University Press.

Hall, E. 1989. "Unstated Features of the Cultural Context of Learning." *Educational Forum* 54(1): 21–34.

Halverson, B. 1976. "Cognitive Style of Preschool Seminole Indian Children." Unpublished doctoral dissertation. Florida State University, Tallahassee.

Hansell, S., and R. E. Slavin. 1981. "Cooperative Learning and the Structure of Interracial Friendships." *Sociology of Education* 54: 98–106.

Hansen, L. 1984. "Field Dependence-Independence and Language Testing: Evidence from Six Pacific Island Cultures." *TESOL Quarterly* 18: 311–324.

Hansen-Strain, L. 1987. "Cognitive Style and First Language Background in Second Language Test Performance." *TESOL Quarterly* 21: 565–569.

Hanson, H., H. Silver, and R. Strong. 1986. *Teaching Styles and Strategies*. Moorestown, NJ: Hanson, Silver, Strong, and Associates.

Harrow, A. J. 1972. *A Taxonomy of the Psychomotor Domain*. New York: David McKay.

Harry, B. 1992. *Cultural Diversity, Families, and the Special Education System*. New York: Teachers College Press.

Heath, S. B. 1983. *Ways with Words: Language, Life, and Work in Communities and Classrooms*. Cambridge, NY: Cambridge University Press.

Henry, A. 1990. "Black Women, Black Pedagogies: An African-Canadian Context." Paper presented at American Educational Research Association, Boston.

Henry, J. 1955. "Docility, or Giving Teacher What She Wants." *Journal of Social Issues* 11(1): 33–41.

Henson, K. T. 1986. "Inquiry Learning: A New Look." *Contemporary Education* 57(4): 181–183.

Herndon, J. 1968. *The Way It Spozed to Be*. New York: Simon and Schuster.

Herring, R. D. 1989. "Counseling Native American Children." *Implications for Elementary School Guidance and Counseling* 23(April): 272–281.

Higbee, K. L. 1996. *Your Memory* (2d ed.). New York: Marlowe.

Hilliard, A. G., III. 1976. *Alternatives to IQ Testing: An Approach to the Identification of Gifted Minority Children*. Final report to California State Department of Education.

———. 1984. *Saving the African-American Child*. Report of National Alliance of Black School Educators, 14(11): 1–54.

———. 1989. "Teachers and Cultural Styles in a Pluralistic Society." *NEA Today* 1: 65–69.

———. 1992. "Behavioral Style, Culture, and Teaching and Learning." *Journal of Negro Education* 61(3): 370–373.

Hirsch, E. D. 1988. *Cultural Literacy*. New York: Vintage Books.

Hodges, L. 1996. "Blood Ties." *New York Times* (July 19): A15.

Hodgkinson, H. L. 1989. *The Same Client: The Demographics of Education and Service Delivery Systems*. Washington, DC: Institute for Educational Leadership/Center for Demographic Policy.

———, **and J. Outtz.** 1992. *The Nation and the State: A Profile and Data Book of America's Diversity*. Washington, DC: Institute for Educational Leadership/Center for Demographic Policy.

Holt, J. 1967. *How Children Fail*. New York: Pitman.

Hord, S. 1994. "Change Process Strategies: Field Test Data and Practices." Paper presented at annual meeting of American Educational Research Association, New Orleans, LA.

Howard, B. C. 1987. *Learning to Persist/Persisting to Learn.* Washington, DC: Mid-Atlantic Center for Race Equity, American University.

Howe, C. 1994. "Improving the Achievement of Hispanic Students." *Educational Leadership* 51(8): 42–44.

Hull, G. A., M. Rose, K. Fraser, and M. Castellano. 1991. "Remediation as Social Construct: Perspective from an Analysis of Classroom Discourse." *College Composition and Communication* 42(3): 299–329.

Hunkins, F. P. 1972. *Questioning Strategies and Techniques.* Boston: Allyn & Bacon.

Hunter, M. 1976. *Prescription for Improved Instruction.* El Segundo, CA: TIP.

————. 1984. "Knowing, Teaching, and Supervising." Pp. 169–192 in P. L. Hosford (ed.), *Using What We Know About Teaching.* Alexandria, VA: Association for Supervision and Curriculum Development.

————. 1985. "What's Wrong with Madeline Hunter?" *Educational Leadership* 42(5): 57–60.

————. 1986. "Comments on the Napa County, California, Follow Through Project." *Elementary School Journal* 87(2): 173–179.

Hyerle, D. 1996. *Visual Tools.* Washington, DC: Association for Supervision and Curriculum Development.

Hyman, R. T. 1980. "Fielding Student Questions." *Theory Into Practice* 19(1): 38–44.

Jackson, P. 1968. *Life in Classrooms.* New York: Holt, Rinehart and Winston.

Jarolimek, J. 1990. *Social Studies in Elementary Education.* New York: Macmillan.

Jetter, A. 1993. "Mississippi Learning." *New York Times Magazine* 6(February 21): 28–72.

Job Search Handbook for Educators, 1996 ASCUS Annual. Evanston, IL: Association for School, College and University Staffing.

Johnson, D. W., and R. T. Johnson. 1975. *Learning Together and Alone.* Englewood Cliffs, NJ: Prentice-Hall.

————. 1981. "Effects of Cooperative and Individualistic Learning Experiences on Interethnic Interaction." *Journal of Educational Psychology* 73(3): 444–449.

————. 1987. *Learning Together and Alone* (2d ed.). Englewood Cliffs, NJ: Prentice-Hall.

————. 1989/1990. "Social Skills for Successful Group Work." *Educational Leadership* 47(4): 29–33.

————, E. J. Holubec, and P. Roy. 1984. *Circles of Learning.* Alexandria, VA: Association for Supervision and Curriculum Development.

Johnston, W. B., and A. E. Packer. 1987. *Workforce 2000: Work and Workers for the Twenty-First Century.* Indianapolis, IN: Hudson Institute.

Joyce, B., and B. Showers. 1980. "Improving Inservice Training: The Messages of Research." *Educational Leadership* 37(5): 379–385.

Joyce, B., and M. Weil. 1972. *Models of Teaching.* Boston: Allyn & Bacon.

————. 1986. *Models of Teaching* (3d ed.). Englewood Cliffs, NJ: Prentice-Hall.

————. 1992. *Models of Teaching* (4th ed.). Boston: Allyn & Bacon.

————. 1996. *Models of Teaching* (5th ed.). Boston: Allyn & Bacon.

Jung, C. G. 1971. *Psychological Types.* Bollinger Series, Vol. 6. Princeton, NJ: Princeton Press.

Kagan, J. 1966. "Reflection-Impulsivity: The Generality and Dynamics of Conceptual Tempo." *Journal of Abnormal Psychology* 71: 17–24.

Kagan, S. 1989/1990. "The Structural Approach to Cooperative Learning." *Educational Leadership* 47(4): 12–15.

———. 1992. *Cooperative Learning*. San Juan Capistrano, CA: Resources for Teachers.

———, and R. Buriel. 1977. "Field Dependence-Independence and Mexican-American Culture and Education." Pp. 279–328 in J. L. Martinez, Jr. (ed.), *Chicano Psychology*. Orlando, FL: Academic Press.

Kagan, S., and G. P. Knight. 1981. "Social Motives Among Anglo American and Mexican American Children: Experimental and Projective Measures." *Journal of Research in Personality* 15(1): 93–106.

Kagan, S., and M. C. Madsen. 1971. "Cooperation and Competition of Mexican, Mexican-American, and Anglo-American Children of Two Ages Under Four Instruction Sets." *Developmental Psychology* 5: 32–39.

Kagan, S., and G. L. Zahn. 1976. "Field Dependence and the School Achievement Gap Between Anglo-American and Mexican-American Children." *Journal of Educational Psychology* 67: 643–650.

———, K. F. Widaman, J. Schwarzwald, and G. Tyrell. 1985. "Classroom Structural Bias: Impact of Cooperative and Competitive Classroom Structures on Cooperative and Competitive Individuals and Groups." Pp. 277–312 in R. E. Slavin, S. Sharan, S. Kagan, R. Hertz-Lazarowitz, C. Webb, and R. Schmuck (eds.), *Learning to Cooperate, Cooperating to Learn*. New York: Plenum.

Kahn, A. 1991. "Don't Spoil the Promise of Cooperative Learning." *Educational Leadership* 48(5): 93–94.

Kanter, R. M. 1989. *When Giants Learn to Dance*. New York: Simon and Schuster.

Keefe, J. W. 1979. "Learning Styles: An Overview." Pp. 1–17 in *Student Learning Styles: Diagnosing and Prescribing Programs*. Reston, VA: National Association of Secondary School Principals.

Keefe, S. E., and A. M. Padilla. 1987. *Chicano Ethnicity*. Albuquerque, NM: University of New Mexico Press.

Kellogg, J. B. 1988. "Forces of Change." *Phi Delta Kappan* 70(3) (November): 199–204.

Kelly, J. A. 1984. "Influence of Culture, Gender and Academic Experience on Cognitive Style." Unpublished dissertation. Vanderbilt University, Memphis, TN.

Keogh, B. K., M. F. Welles, and A. Weiss. 1972. "Field Dependence-Independence and Problem-Solving Styles of Preschool Children." Technical Report. Los Angeles: University of California.

King, L. 1993. "High and Low Achievers' Perceptions and Cooperative Learning in Two Small Groups." *Elementary School Journal* 93(44): 399–416.

Knight, G. P., and S. Kagan. 1977. "Development of Prosocial and Competitive Behaviors in Anglo-American and Mexican-American Children." *Child Development* 48(4): 1385–1394.

Kochman, T. 1972. *Rappin' and Stylin' Out: Communication in Urban Black America*. Urbana, IL: University of Illinois Press.

Kohl, H. 1967. 36 *Children*. New York: New American Library.

Kolb, D. 1984. *Experiential Learning*. Englewood Cliffs, NJ: Prentice-Hall.

Kozol, J. 1967. *Death at an Early Age: The Destruction of the Hearts and Minds of Negro Children in the Boston Public Schools*. Boston: Houghton-Mifflin.

Krathwohl, D., B. Bloom, and B. Masis. 1964. *Taxonomy of Educational Objectives, Handbook II: Affective Domain*. New York: David McKay.

Ladson-Billings, G. 1990. "Like Lightning in a Bottle: Attempting to Capture the Pedagogical Excellence of Successful Teachers of Black Students." *International Journal of Qualitative Studies in Education* 3(4): 335–344.

——. 1991. "Returning to the Source: Implications for Educating Teachers of Black Students." Pp. 227–244 in M. Foster (ed.), *Readings on Equal Education. Volume II: Qualitative Investigations into Schools and Schooling.* New York: AMS Press.

——. 1992. "Liberatory Consequences of Literacy: A Case of Culturally Relevant Instruction for African American Students." *Journal of Negro Education* 61(3): 378–391.

——. 1994. *The Dreamkeepers.* San Francisco: Jossey-Bass.

LaFrance, M., and C. Mayo. 1976. "Racial Differences in Gaze Behavior During Conversation." *Journal of Personality and Social Psychology* 33: 258–285.

LaFromboise, T., P. Dauphinais, and P. Lujan. 1981. "Verbal Indicators of Insincerity as Perceived by American Indians." *Journal of Nonwhite Concerns in Personnel and Guidance* 9: 87–94.

Laosa, L. M. 1982. "School, Occupation, Culture, and Family: The Impact of Parental Schooling on the Parent-Child Relationship." *Journal of Educational Psychology* 74(6): 791–827.

Lasley, T. J., S. J. Williams, and P. M. Hart. 1991. "Nonexamples: Why Teachers Don't Use Them and Why Teacher Educators Should." *Mid-Western Educational Researcher* 4(3): 2–6.

Levin, J. R. 1993. "Mnemonic Strategies and Classroom Learning: A Twenty Year Report Card." *Elementary School Journal* 94(2): 235–244.

Levin, M. E., and J. R. Levin. 1990. "Scientific Mnemonomies: Methods for Maximizing More than Memory." *American Educational Research Journal* 27(2): 301–321.

Lickona, T. 1989. *Educating for Character.* New York: Bantam.

Loftin, J. D. 1989. "Anglo American Jurisprudence and the Native American Tribal Quest for Religious Freedom." *American Indian Culture and Research Journal* 13(1): 1–52.

Longstreet, W. S. 1978. *Aspects of Ethnicity.* New York: Teachers College Press.

Lorayne, H., and J. Lucas. 1966. *The Memory Book.* New York: Briercliff Manor.

——. 1974. *The Memory Book.* New York: Ballantine.

Lortie, D. 1975. *School Teacher: A Sociological Study.* Chicago: University of Chicago Press.

Losey, K. M. 1995. "Mexican American Students and Classroom Interaction: An Overview and Critique." *American Educational Research Journal* 65(3): 283–318.

Lucas, T., R. Henze, and R. Donato. 1990. "Promoting the Success of Latino Language-Minority Students: An Exploratory Study of Six High Schools." *Harvard Educational Review* 60(3): 315–340.

Luria, A. R. 1968. *The Mind of a Mnemonist.* Chicago: Henry Regnery.

Macias, C. J. 1989. "American Indian Academic Success: The Role of Indigenous Learning Strategies." *Journal of American Indian Education* (August, special issue): 43–52.

Mager, R. 1984. *Preparing Instructional Objectives* (3d ed.). Palo Alto, CA: Fearon.

Marshall, H., and R. Weinstein. 1984. "Classrooms Where Students Perceive High and Low Amounts of Differential Teacher Treatment." Paper presented at annual meeting of American Educational Research Association, New Orleans, LA.

Mastropieri, M. A., T. E. Scruggs, and J. R. Levin. 1987. "Learning Disabled Students' Memory for Expository Prose: Mnemonic Versus Nonmnemonic Pictures." *American Educational Research Journal* 24(4): 505–519.

Matczynski, T., and S. Shugarman. 1989. "Minority Recruitment: Backgrounds and Promising Practices." Pp. 83–91 in D. G. Carter (ed.), *Equity in Excellence in Education.* Bloomington, IN: Indiana University's Center for Urban and Multicultural Education.

Mathematics Plus. 1992. Orlando, FL: Harcourt Brace Jovanovich.

Mathews, J. 1988. *Escalante.* New York: Holt.

Maton, A. 1993. *Cells: Building Blocks of Life.* Chapter 1, "Chemistry of Living Things." Englewood Cliffs, NJ: Prentice-Hall: 35–37.

Matthews, W. 1981. "Race- and Sex-Related Differences in High School Mathematics Enrollment." Doctoral dissertation, University of Chicago, 1980. *Dissertation Abstracts International* 41: 3934A.

Mauro, L. H., and L. J. Cohen. 1992. "Cooperating for Concept Development." Pp. 151–168 in N. Davidson and T. Worsham (eds.), *Enhancing Thinking Through Cooperative Learning.* New York: Teachers College Press.

McCaulley, M. H., G. P. MacDaid, and R. E. Kainz. 1985. "Estimated Frequencies of the MBTI Types." *Journal of Psychological Type* 9: 3–8.

McDiarmid, G. 1990. *What to Do About Differences? A Study of Multicultural Education for Teacher Trainees in the Los Angeles Unified School District.* Research Report 90-11. East Lansing, MI: National Center for Research on Teacher Education, Michigan State University.

McKeachie, W. 1986. *Teaching Tips* (8th ed.). Lexington, MA: D. C. Heath.

McKinney, C. W. 1985. "A Comparison of the Effects of a Definition, Examples, and Nonexamples on Student Acquisition of the Concept of 'Teacher Propaganda.'" *Social Education* 49: 66–70.

McNett, I. 1983. *Demographic Imperatives: Implications for Educational Policy.* Washington, DC: Institute for Educational Leadership.

———. 1984. *Demographic Imperatives: Implications for Educational Policy.* Washington, DC: American Council on Education.

McShane, D. 1980. "A Review of Scores of American Indian Children on the Weschler Intelligence Scales." *White Cloud Journal* 1: 3–10.

Messick, S. 1970. "The Criterion Problem in the Evaluation of Instruction: Assessing Possible, Not Just Intended, Outcomes." Pp. 183–202 in M. C. Wittrock and G. D. E. Wiley (eds.), *The Evaluation of Instruction: Issues and Problems.* New York: Holt.

Meyer, J. W., and B. Rowan. 1983. "The Structure of Educational Organizations." Pp. 283–296 in J. W. Meyer and R. Scott, *Organizational Environments: Ritual and Rationality.* Beverly Hills, CA: Sage.

Meyer, J. W., and R. Scott. 1983. *Organizational Environments: Ritual and Rationality.* Beverly Hills, CA: Sage.

Moll, L. C. 1988. "Some Key Issues in Teaching Latino Students." *Language Arts* 65(5): 465–472.

Moore, M. R. 1972. "Consideration of the Perceptual Process in the Evaluation of Musical Performance." *Journal of Research on Music Education* 20: 273–279.

More, A. J. 1990. "Learning Styles of Native Americans and Asians." Paper presented at annual meeting of American Psychological Association, Boston. ERIC Document Reproduction Service No. ED 330 535.

Morgan, H. 1981. "Factors Concerning Cognitive Development and Learning Differentiation Among Black Children." Pp. 14–22 in A. E. Harrison (ed.), *Conference on Empirical Research in Black Psychology* 6.

Murphy, J. 1991. *Restructuring Schools: Capturing and Assessing the Phenomena.* New York: Teachers College Press.

Myers, I. B. 1962. *The Myers-Briggs Type Indicator Manual.* Palo Alto, CA: Consulting Psychologists Press.

———, and M. McCaulley. 1985. *Manual: A Guide to the Development and Use of the Myers-Briggs Type Indicator.* Palo Alto, CA: Consulting Psychologists Press.

National Commission on Excellence in Education. 1983. *A Nation at Risk: The Imperative for Educational Reform.* Washington, DC: U.S. Department of Education.

National Education Association. 1987. *Status of the American Public School Teacher, 1985–86.* National Education Association Response. Washington, DC: National Education Association: 70.

National Endowment for the Humanities. 1987. *American Memory: A Report on the Humanities in the Nation's Public Schools.* Washington, DC: U.S. Government Printing Office.

National Foundation for Women Business Owners. 1994. *Styles of Success: The Thinking and Management Styles of Women and Men Entrepreneurs.* Washington, DC: National Foundation for Women Business Owners (July).

National Science Foundation. 1983. *Educating Americans for the 21st Century: A Plan of Action for Improving Mathematics, Science and Technology Education for All American Elementary and Secondary Students So That Their Achievement Is the Best in the World by 1995.* Report to the American People and the National Science Board. Washington, DC: National Science Foundation.

Neubert, G., and J. Binko. 1992. *Inductive Reasoning in the Secondary Classroom.* Washington, DC: National Education Association.

Newman, K. 1979. "Middle-Aged Experienced Teachers' Perceptions of Their Career Development." Paper presented at annual meeting of American Educational Research Association, San Francisco.

Newmann, F. M., and G. G. Wehlage. 1993. "Five Standards of Authentic Instruction." *Educational Leadership* 50(7): 8–12.

Obiakor, F. E. 1992. "A Cultural Ecology of Competence Among Inner-City Blacks." Pp. 45–60 in M. Spencer, G. Brookins, and W. Allen (eds.), *Beginnings: The Social and Affective Development of Black Children.* Hillsdale, NJ: Lawrence Erlbaum Associates.

Ogbu, J. U. 1978. *Minority Education and Caste: The American System in Cross-Cultural Perspective.* New York: Academic Press.

———. 1983. "Cultural Discontinuities and Schooling." *Anthropology and Education Quarterly* 13: 290–307.

———. 1987. "Variability in Minority School Performance: A Problem in Search of an Explanation." *Anthropology and Education Quarterly* 18(4): 312–334.

———. 1989. "The Individual in Collective Adaptation: A Framework for Focusing on Academic Underperformance and Dropping Out Among Involuntary Minorities." Pp. 181–204 in L. Weis, E. Farran, and H. Petrie (eds.), *Dropouts from School: Issues, Dilemmas, and Solutions.* Albany, NY: State University of New York Press.

Ogle, L. T., N. Alaalam, and G. T. Rogers. 1991. *The Condition of Education: Vol. 1. Elementary and Secondary Education.* Washington, DC: U.S. Department of Education, Office of Educational Research and Improvement, National Center for Educational Statistics. ERIC Document Reproduction Service No. ED 330 121.

Ohio Department of Natural Resources. *Investigating Solid Waste Issues.* 1994. Columbus, OH: Ohio Department of Natural Resources.

Oishi, S., R. E. Slavin, and N. A. Madden. 1983. "Effects of Student Teams and Individualized Instruction on Cross-Race and Cross-Sex Friendships." Paper presented at annual meeting of American Educational Research Association, Montreal (April).

Olstad, R., J. Juarez, L. Davenport, and D. Haury. 1981. *Inhibitors to Achievement in Science and Mathematics by Ethnic Minorities.* Bethesda, MD: ERIC Document Reproduction Service No. ED 223 404.

O'Malley, J., and A. Chamot. 1990. *Learning Strategies in Second Language Acquisition.* Cambridge, NY: Cambridge University Press.

O'Neil, J. 1995. "Finding Time to Learn." *Educational Leadership* 53(3): 11–15.

Orlich, D. C., R. J. Harder, R. C. Callahan, C. H. Kravas, D. P. Kauchak, R. A. Pendergrass, and A. J. Keogh. 1985. *Teaching Strategies: A Guide to Better Instruction* (2d ed.). Toronto, Canada: D. C. Heath.

Ornstein, A. C. 1995. *Strategies for Effective Teaching.* Madison, WI: Brown and Benchmark.

Osborne, B., and B. Bamford. 1987. "Torres Strait Islanders Teaching Torres Strait Islanders I." North Queensland, Townsville: Department of Pedagogics and Scientific Studies in Education, James Cook University.

Osborne, D., and T. Gaebler. 1992. *Reinventing Government.* Reading, MA: Addison-Wesley.

O'Toole, J. 1995. *Leading Change: Overcoming the Ideology of Comfort and the Tyranny of Custom.* San Francisco: Jossey-Bass.

Oxford, R. 1990. "The Strategy Inventory for Language Learning (SILL)." Appendix to *Language Learning Strategies: What Every Teacher Should Know.* New York: Newbury House/Harper & Row.

Pang, V. 1990. "Asian-American Children: A Diverse Population." *Educational Forum* 55(1): 49–66.

———. 1995. "Asian Pacific American Students: A Diverse and Complex Population." Pp. 412–424 in J. Banks and C. Banks (eds.), *Handbook of Research on Multicultural Education.* New York: Macmillan.

Parker, W. C. 1987. "Teaching Thinking: The Pervasive Approach." *Journal of Teacher Education* 38(3): 50–56.

Pease-Alvarez, L., E. Garcia, and P. Espinoza. 1991. "Effective Instruction for Language Minority Students: An Early Childhood Case Study." *Early Childhood Research Quarterly* 6(3): 347–363.

Peters, E., and R. Dixon. 1987. "Special Focus: Effective Instruction in Reading." *Teaching Exceptional Children* 19(2): 61–63.

Peterson, W. 1964. "Age, Teachers Role and the Institutional Setting." Pp. 268–315 in B. Biddle and W. Ellena (eds.), *Contemporary Research on Teacher Effectiveness.* New York: Holt Rinehart.

Philips, S. 1972. "Participant Structures and Communicative Competence: Warm Springs Children in Community and Classroom." Pp. 370–394 in C. Cazden, V. John, and D. Hymes (eds.), *Functions of Language in the Classroom.* New York: Teachers College Press.

———. 1983. *The Invisible Culture: Communication in Classroom and Community on the Warm Springs Indian Reservation.* New York: Longman.

———. 1993. *The Invisible Culture: Communication in Classroom and Community on the Warm Springs Indian Reservation.* Prospect Heights, IL: Waveland Press.

Pifer, A., and L. Bronte. 1986. *Our Aging Society.* New York: Norton.

Polling, A. 1995. "Gender Balance: Lessons from Girls in Science and Mathematics." *Educational Leadership* 53(1): 30–33.

Porter, A. C. 1986. "From Research on Teaching to Staff Development: A Difficult Step." *Elementary School Journal* 87(2): 159–164.

Postman, N., and C. Weingartner. 1969. *Teaching as a Subversive Activity.* New York: Delacorte.

Pressley, M., J. R. Levin, and H. D. Delaney. 1982. "The Mnemonic Keyword Method." *Review of Educational Research* 52: 61–91.

Pressley, M., J. R. Levin, and G. E. Miller. 1981. "How Does the Keyword Method Affect Vocabulary Comprehension and Usage?" *Reading Research Quarterly* 16: 213–226.

Prom, S. E. 1982. "Salient Content and Cognitive Performance of Person- and Thing-Oriented Low Income Afro-American Children in Kindergarten and Second Grade." Doctoral dissertation. Howard University, Washington, DC.

Rachal, J. R. 1989. "The Social Context of Adult and Continuing Education." Pp. 3–14 in S. Merrian and P. Cunningham (eds.), *Handbook of Adult and Continuing Education*. San Francisco: Jossey-Bass.

Ramirez, M., III. 1973. "Cognitive Styles and Cultural Democracy in Education." *Social Science Quarterly* 53: 895–904.

———. 1982. "Cognitive Styles and Cultural Diversity." Paper presented at annual meeting of American Educational Research Association, New York City (May).

———. 1989a. "A Bicognitive-Multicultural Model for a Pluralistic Education." *Early Child Development and Care* 51: 129–136.

———. 1989b. "Pluralistic Education: A Bicognitive-Multicultural Model." *Clearinghouse Bulletin* 3: 4–5.

———, **and A. Castaneda.** 1974. *Cultural Democracy, Bicognitive Development, and Education*. New York: Academic Press.

———, **and D. R. Price-Williams.** 1974. "Cognitive Style of Three Ethnic Groups in the U.S." *Journal of Cross-Cultural Psychology* 5(2): 212–219.

Randle, W. 1990. "Some Firms Facing Facts on Workforce Diversity Dictates Major Changes." *Chicago Tribune* (January 2): C-1.

Ravitch, D., and C. E. Finn, Jr. 1987. *What Do Our 17-Year Olds Know?* New York: Harper & Row.

Reed, D. F. 1986. "Wanted: More Black Teacher Education Students." *Action in Teacher Education* 8(1): 31–36.

Reed, I. 1988. "America: The Multinational Society." *Multi-Cultural Literacy*. St. Paul, MN: Graywolf Press.

Ribadeneira, D. 1990. "Educators Say School Reform Is Not Enough." *Boston Globe* (1)(November 13): 1.

Riche, M. F. 1991. "We're All Minorities Now." *American Demographics* (October): 26–34.

Robbins, P. 1986. "The Napa-Vacaville Follow-Through Project: Qualitative Outcomes, Related Procedures, and Implications for Practice." *Elementary School Journal* 87(2): 139–158.

Roberts, L. 1990. *Reinventing School Leadership*. Working memo prepared for Reinventing School Leadership Conference. Cambridge, MA: National Center for Educational Leadership.

Roberts, S. 1993. *Who We Are*. New York: Times Books.

Rodriguez, D., and J. Rodriguez. 1994. *Times Tables the Fun Way*. Sandy, UT: Key.

Rohner, R. 1965. "Factors Influencing the Academic Performance of Kwakiutl Children in Canada." *Comparative Education Review* 9: 331–340.

Rollman, S. A. 1978. "The Sensitivity of Black and White Americans to Nonverbal Cues of Prejudice." *Journal of Social Psychology* 105: 73–77.

Rose, C. 1985. *Accelerated Learning*. New York: Dell.

Rose, M. 1995. *Possible Lives: The Promise of Public Education in America*. New York: Houghton-Mifflin.

Rosenshine, B. 1983. "Teaching Functions in Instructional Programs." *Elementary School Journal* 83(4): 335–352.

———. 1986. "Unsolved Issues in Teaching Content: A Critique of a Lesson on Federalist Paper No. 10." *Teaching and Teacher Education* 2(4): 301–308.

————. 1987. "Explicit Teaching." Pp. 75–92 in D. C. Berliner and B. Rosenshine (eds.), *Talks to Teachers*. New York: Random House.

Rosenthal, R., and L. Jacobson. 1968. *Pygmalion in the Classroom: Teacher Expectation and Pupils Intellectual Development*. New York: Holt, Rinehart and Winston.

Rothman, R. 1995. *Measuring Up*. San Francisco: Jossey-Bass.

Rumbaut, R., and K. Ima. 1988. "The Adaptation of Southeast Asian Refugee Youth: A Comparative Study." Report prepared for U.S. Department of Health and Human Services, Family Support Administration, Office of Refugee Resettlement, Washington, DC.

Sadker, M., and D. Sadker. 1994a. *Failing at Fairness*. New York: Charles Scribner's Sons.

————. 1994b. *Teachers, Schools and Society*. New York: McGraw-Hill.

Sanders, N. M. 1966. *Classroom Questions: What Kinds?* New York: Harper & Row.

Saracho, O. N., and B. Spodek. 1984. *Cognitive Style and Children's Learning: Individual Variation in Cognitive Processes*. ERIC Document Reproduction Service No. ED 247 037.

Sarason, S. 1982. *The Culture of the School and the Problem of Change* (rev. ed.). Boston: Allyn & Bacon.

————. 1983. *Schooling in America: Scapegoat and Salvation*. New York: Free Press.

Sautter, R. C. 1994. "Who Are Today's City Kids?" *City Schools* (Fall–Winter): 6–10.

Schaps, E., C. C. Lewis, and M. Watson. 1993. "The Child Development Project." *Educational Leadership* 51(3): 46.

Schimizzi, N. V. 1985. *Mathematics Achievement Scores in High School: Are They Related to the Way We Teach in the Earlier Grades?* ERIC Document Reproduction Service No. ED 265 012.

Schnailberg, L. 1993. "Immigration's Final Frontier." *Education Week* (February): 31.

Select Committee on Children, Youth, and Families. 1988. *Children and Families: Key Trends in the 1980's*. Washington, DC: Select Committee on Children, Youth, and Families.

Sergiovanni, T. J. 1989. *Schooling for Tomorrow: Directing Reforms to Issues that Count*. Boston: Allyn & Bacon.

————. 1991. *The Principalship: A Reflective Practice Perspective*. Boston: Allyn & Bacon.

————. 1992. *Moral Leadership: Getting to the Heart of School Improvement*. San Francisco: Jossey-Bass.

Shade, B. J. 1981. "Racial Variation in Perceptual Differentiation." *Perceptual and Motor Skills* 52: 243–248.

————. 1984. "Afro-American Patterns of Cognition: A Review of the Research." Paper presented at annual meeting of American Educational Research Association, New Orleans, LA.

————. 1989. "The Influence of Perceptual Development on Cognitive Style: Cross Ethnic Comparisons." *Early Child Development and Care* 51: 137–155.

————. 1994. "Understanding the African American Learner." Pp. 175–189 in E. Hollins, J. King, and W. Hayman (eds.), *Teaching Diverse Populations: Formulating a Knowledge Base*. Albany, NY: State University of New York Press.

————, **and P. A. Edwards.** 1987. "Ecological Correlates of the Educative Style of Afro-American Children." *Journal of Negro Education* 86: 88–99.

Shanker, A. 1996. "Succeeding in School." *New Republic* (July 1): 17.

Shulman, L., and P. Tamir. 1973. "Research on Teaching in the Natural Sciences." Pp. 1098–1148 in R. M. W. Travers (ed.), *Second Handbook of Research on Teaching.* Chicago: Rand McNally.

Shutiva, C. 1991. "Creativity Difference Between Reservation and Urban American Indians." *Journal of American Indian Education* 31(1): 33–52.

Sizer, T. R. 1984. *Horace's Compromise: The Dilemma of the American High School: The First Report from a Study of High Schools.* Report co-sponsored by National Association of Secondary School Principals and Commission on Educational Issues of the National Association of Independent Schools. Boston: Houghton-Mifflin.

———. 1992. *Horace's School: Redesigning the American High School.* Boston: Houghton-Mifflin.

Slaughter-DeFoe, D. T., K. Nakagawa, R. Takanishi, and D. J. Johnson. 1990. "Toward Cultural/Ecological Perspectives on Schooling and Achievement in African- and Asian-American Children." *Child Development* 61: 363–383.

Slavin, R. E. 1977. *Student Team Learning Techniques: Narrowing the Achievement Gap Between the Races.* Report No. 228. Baltimore, MD: Johns Hopkins University, Center for the Study of Social Organization of Schools.

———. 1979. "Effects of Biracial Learning Teams on Cross-Racial Friendships." *Journal of Educational Psychology* 71(3): 381–387.

———. 1980. *Using Student Team Learning* (rev. ed.). Baltimore, MD: Johns Hopkins University, Center for Social Organization of Schools.

———. 1987a. "Cooperative Learning and Cooperative School." *Educational Leadership* 45(3): 7–13.

———. 1987b. *Cooperative Learning: Student Teams* (2d ed.). Washington, DC: National Education Association.

———. 1987c. "Cooperative Learning: Where Behavioral and Humanistic Approaches to Classroom Motivation Meet." *Elementary School Journal* 88(1): 29–38.

———. 1990. "Cooperative Learning and the Cooperative School." Pp. 137–144 in R. Brandt (ed.), *Cooperative Learning Series.* Alexandria, VA: Association for Supervision and Curriculum Development.

———. 1995. "Cooperative Learning and Intergroup Relations." Pp. 628–634 in J. A. Banks and C. A. M. Banks (eds.), *Handbook of Research on Multicultural Education.* New York: Macmillan.

———, **N. A. Madden, and R. J. Stevens.** 1989/1990. "Cooperative Learning Models for the 3 R's." *Educational Leadership* 47(4): 22–28.

Slavin, R. E., and E. Oickle. 1981. "Effects of Cooperative Learning Teams on Student Achievement and Race Relations: Treatment by Race Interactions." *Sociology of Education* 54: 174–180.

Smith, D. M., and D. Kolb. 1986. *Users Guide for the Learning Style Inventory: A Manual for Teachers and Trainers.* Boston: McBer.

Smith, R. 1987. "A Teacher's Views on Cooperative Learning." *Phi Delta Kappan* 68(9): 663–665.

Soldier, L. 1985. "To Soar with Eagles: Enculturation and Acculturation of Indian Children." *Childhood Education* 61: 185–191.

———. 1989. "Cooperative Learning and the Native American Student." *Phi Delta Kappan* 71(2): 161–163.

Stallings, J., and P. Kaskowitz. 1974. *Follow Through Classroom Observation Evaluation, 1972–73.* Menlo Park, CA: Stanford Research Institute.

Stallings, J., and E. M. Krasavage. 1986. "Program Implementation and Student Achievement in a Four-Year Madeline Hunter Follow-Through Project." *Elementary School Journal* 87(2): 117–138.

Steinberg, L. D. 1996. *Beyond the Classroom: Why School Reform Has Failed and What Parents Need to Do.* New York: Simon and Schuster.

Sternberg, R. J. 1994. "Commentary: Reforming School Reform: Comments on Multiple Intelligences: The Theory in Practice." *Teachers College Record* 95(4): 561–568.

Stevenson, H. W., C. Chen, and S. Lee. 1993. "Mathematics Achievement of Chinese, Japanese, and American Children: Ten Years Later." *Science* 259: 53–58.

Stevenson, H. W., and J. W. Stigler. 1992. *The Learning Gap.* New York: Summit.

Suarez, Z. E. 1993. "Cuban Americans: From Golden Exiles to Social Undesirables." Pp. 164–176 in H. P. McAdoo (ed.), *Family Ethnicity: Strength in Diversity.* Newbury Park, CA: Sage.

Suchman, R. J. 1962. *The Elementary School Training Program in Scientific Inquiry.* Report to U.S. Office of Education, Project Title VII. Project No. 216. Project of Illinois Studies of Inquiry. Urbana, IL: University of Illinois Press.

Super, D. 1957. *The Psychology of Careers: An Introduction to Vocational Development.* New York: Harper & Row.

Suzuki, B. H. 1983. "The Education of Asian and Pacific Americans: An Introductory Overview." P. 23 in D. T. Nakanishi and M. Hirano-Nakanishi (eds.), *Education of Asian and Pacific Americans: Historical Perspectives and Prescriptions for the Future.* Phoenix, AZ: Oryx Press.

Swisher, K., and D. Deyhle. 1987. "Styles of Learning and Learning Styles: Educational Conflicts for American Indian/Alaskan Native Youth." *Journal of Multilingual and Multicultural Development* 8(4): 350.

———. 1989. "The Styles of Learning Are Different, But the Teaching Is Just the Same: Suggestions for Teachers of American Indian Youth." *Journal of American Indian Education* (August, special issue): 1–14.

Taba, H. 1966. *Teaching Strategies and Cognitive Functioning in Elementary School Children.* Cooperative Research Project 2404. San Francisco: San Francisco State College.

———. 1971. *Hilda Taba Teaching Strategies Program.* Miami, FL: Institute for Staff Development.

Tafoya, T. 1982. "Coyote Eyes: Native Cognition Styles." *Journal of American Indian Education* 21(2): 21–33.

Tennyson, R. D., and M. Cocchiarella. 1986. "An Empirically Based Instructional Design Theory for Teaching Concepts." *Review of Educational Research* 56: 40–71.

Tennyson, R. D., and O. Park. 1980. "The Teaching of Concepts: A Review of Instructional Design Research Literature." *Review of Educational Research* 50(1): 55–70.

Toffler, Alvin. 1990. *Powershift.* New York: Bantam Books.

Tooker, E. 1983. *The Development of Political Organization in Native North America.* Washington, DC: American Ethnological Society.

Torrance, E. P. 1986. "Teaching Creative and Gifted Learners." Pp. 630–647 in M. C. Wittrock (ed.), *Handbook of Research on Teaching.* New York: Macmillan.

Tredway, L. 1995. "Socratic Seminars: Engaging Students in Intellectual Discourse." *Educational Leadership* 53(1): 26–29.

Treisman, V. 1985. "A Study of the Mathematics Performance of Black Students at the University of California at Berkeley." Unpublished doctoral dissertation. University of California, Berkeley.

Trueba, H. J., L. Jacobs, and E. Kirton. 1990. *Cultural Conflict and Adaptation: The Case of Hmong Children in American Society.* New York: Falmer Press.

Tuck, K., and A. Boykin. 1989. "Verve Effects: The Relationship of Task Performance to Stimulus Preference and Variability in Low-Income Black and White

Children." Pp. 84–85 in A. Harrison (ed.), *The Eleventh Conference on Empirical Research in Black Psychology*. Washington, DC: NIMH Publications.

Tyson, H. 1994. *Who Will Teach the Children?: Progress and Resistance in Teacher Education*. San Francisco: Jossey-Bass.

U.S. Bureau of the Census, Economics and Statistics Administration. 1991. *1990 Census Profile: Race and Hispanic Origin*. Report No. 2.

U.S. Department of Commerce, Economics and Statistics Administration, Bureau of the Census. 1993a. *We, the American Asians*.

———. 1993b. *We, the American Blacks*.

———. 1993c. *We, the American Foreign Born*.

———. 1993d. *We, the American Hispanics*.

———. 1993e. *We, the American Pacific Islanders*.

———. 1993f. *We, the First Americans*.

U.S. Department of Education, National Center for Education Statistics. 1986. *Digest of Education Statistics. 1986*. Washington, DC: U.S. Government Printing Office.

———. 1991a. *Digest of Education Statistics*. Washington, DC: U.S. Government Printing Office: 234, 276.

———. 1991b. *Trends in Academic Progress*. Washington, DC: U.S. Government Printing Office: 1–10.

———. 1992. *The Condition of Education*. Washington, DC: U.S. Government Printing Office: 144–145.

U.S. Department of Education, National Education Goals Report. 1994. *Building a Nation of Learners*. Washington, DC: U.S. Government Printing Office: 8–11.

———. Executive Summary. 1995. *Improving Education Through Family-School-Community Partnerships*. Washington, DC: U.S. Government Printing Office: 6–9.

U.S. Department of Labor. 1991. *The Secretary's Commission of Achiever Necessary Skills*. Washington, DC: U.S. Government Printing Office.

U.S. Select Committee on Aging and American Association of Retired Persons. 1984. *Aging in America: Trends and Projections*. Washington, DC: American Association of Retired Persons.

"U.S. Youth at Risk." 1994. *Futurist* 28(6)(November–December): 60.

Utley, C. A. 1983. "A Cross-Cultural Investigation of Field-Independent/Field-Dependent as a Psychological Variable in Menominees Native American and Euro-American Grade School Children." Madison, WI: Wisconsin Center for Education and Research.

Vasquez, J. A. 1991. "Cognitive Style and Academic Attainment." Pp. 163–179 in J. Lynch, C. Modgil, and S. Modgil (eds.), *Cultural Diversity and the Schools: Consensus and Controversy*. London: Falconer Press.

Vernon, P. A., D. N. Jackson, and S. Messick. 1988. "Cultural Influences on Patterns of Abilities in North America." Pp. 208–231 in S. H. Irvine and J. W. Berry (eds.), *Human Abilities in Cultural Context*. Cambridge, MA: Cambridge University Press.

Vernon, P. E. 1984. "Abilities and Achievements of Ethnic Groups in Canada with Special Reference to Canadian Natives and Orientals." Pp. 382–395 in R. Samuda, J. Berry, and M. Laferriere (eds.), *Multiculturalism in Canada: Social and Educational Perspectives*. Toronto: Allyn & Bacon.

Vye, N. J., and J. D. Bransford. 1981. "Programs for Teaching Thinking." *Educational Leadership* 26: 26–28.

Vygotsky, L. S. 1978. *Mind in Society: The Development of Higher Psychological Expectations.* Cambridge, MA: Harvard University Press.

Walberg, H. 1995. "Productive Teaching." Pp. 41–55 in A. C. Ornstein (ed.), *Teaching: Theory Into Practice.* Boston: Allyn & Bacon.

Weaver, W. T., and G. M. Prince. 1990. "Synectics: Its Potential for Education." *Phi Delta Kappan* 71(5): 378–388.

Weick, K. E. 1976. "Educational Organizations as Loosely Coupled Systems." *Administrative Science Quarterly* 21: 1.

Weigel, R. H., P. L. Wiser, and S. W. Cook. 1975. "Impact of Cooperative Learning Experiences on Cross-Ethnic Relations and Attitudes." *Journal of Social Issues* 31(1): 219–245.

Weinstein, C. E., A. C. Schulte, and E. C. Cascallar. 1983. *The Learning and Study Strategies Inventory (LASSI): Initial Design and Development.* Manuscript. University of Texas, Austin.

Wenden, A., and J. Rubin. 1987. *Learner Strategies in Language Learning.* Englewood Cliffs, NJ: Prentice-Hall.

West, C. 1994. *Race Matters.* New York: Vintage Books.

Whimbey, A. 1977. "Teaching Sequential Thought: The Cognitive Skills Approach." *Phi Delta Kappan* 58: 255–259.

Whittington, D. 1991. "What Have 17-Year-Olds Known in the Past?" *American Educational Research Journal* 28(4): 759–780.

Wiederhold, C., and S. Kagan. 1992. "Cooperative Questioning and Critical Thinking." P. 203 in N. Davidson and T. Worsham (eds.), *Enhancing Thinking Through Cooperative Learning.* New York: Teacher's College Press.

Wiggins, G. 1989. "The Futility of Trying to Teach Everything of Importance." *Educational Leadership* 47(3): 44–59.

Witkin, H. A., R. B. Dyk, H. F. Faterson, D. R. Goodenough, and S. A. Karp. 1962. *Psychological Differentiation.* New York: Wiley.

Witkin, H. A., C. A. Moore, D. R. Goodenough, and P. W. Cox. 1977. "Field-Dependent and Field-Independent Cognitive Style and Their Educational Implications." *Review of Educational Research* 47: 1–64.

Wlodkowski, R. J., and M. B. Ginsberg. 1995. "A Framework for Culturally Responsive Teaching." *Educational Leadership* 53(1): 17–21.

Wlodkowski, R. J., and J. H. Jaynes. 1990. *Eager to Learn.* San Francisco: Jossey-Bass.

World Geography. 1993. Morristown, NJ: Silver Burdett Ginn.

Worthley, K. M. 1987. "Learning Style Factor of Field Dependence/Independence and Refugee Students." Master's Thesis. University of Wisconsin, Stout (July).

Wright, E. L. 1981. "Fifteen Simple Discrepant Events that Teach Science Principles and Concepts." *School Science and Mathematics* 81: 575–580.

———, **and G. Govindarajan.** 1992. "Stirring the Biology Teaching Pot with Discrepant Events." *American Biology Teacher* 54(4) (April): 205–210.

Yoshiwara, F. M. 1983. "Shattering Myths: Japanese American Educational Issues." P. 23 in D. T. Nakanishi and M. Hirano-Nakanishi (eds.), *Education of Asian and Pacific Americans: Historical Perspectives and Prescriptions for the Future.* Phoenix, AZ: Oryx Press.

Young, V. H. 1970. "Family and Childhood in a Southern Negro Community." *American Anthropologist* 72: 269–288.

———. 1974. "A Black American Socialization Pattern." *American Ethnologist* 1: 405–413.

Yu, A., and B. Bain. 1985. *Language, Social Class and Cognitive Style: A Comparative Study of Unilingual and Bilingual Education in Hong Kong and Alberta.* Hong Kong: Hong Kong Teachers' Association.

Zeichner, K. (In press.) "Educating Teachers for Cultural Diversity." In K. Zeichner, S. Melnick, and M. L. Gomez (eds.), *Currents of Reform in Preservice Teacher Education.* New York: Teachers College Press.

Zelderman, H., G. Comber, and N. Maistrellis. 1992. "The Touchstones Project: Learning to Think Cooperatively." Pp. 138–150 in N. Davidson and T. Worsham (eds.), *Enhancing Thinking Through Cooperative Learning.* New York: Teachers College Press.

Zevin, J. 1969. "Mystery Island: A Lesson in Inquiry." *Today's Education* 58: 42–43.

• *Index*